Bizet's *Carmen* Uncovered

Bizet's *Carmen* Uncovered

Richard Langham Smith

THE BOYDELL PRESS

First published 2021
The Boydell Press, Woodbridge

ISBN 978-1-78327-525-0

The Boydell Press is an imprint of Boydell & Brewer Ltd
PO Box 9, Woodbridge, Suffolk IP12 3DF, UK
and of Boydell & Brewer Inc.
668 Mt Hope Avenue, Rochester, NY 14620–2731, USA
website: www.boydellandbrewer.com

A catalogue record of this publication is available
from the British Library

This publication is printed on acid-free paper

Typeset in Adobe Arno Pro by
Sparks Publishing Services Ltd—www.sparkspublishing.com

To the memory of my mentors,
Wilfrid Mellers & Edward Lockspeiser

Contents

List of Illustrations ix
Preface xv
Acknowledgements xxiii
Note on the Text xxvii

PART I PREPARING THE GROUND

1 Vitoria and Waterloo: French Music and the Peninsular Wars 3
2 Pictures and Jottings: *Carmen* and the Rise of Andalusian Tourism 36
3 Spain on the Paris Stage 64

PART II FICTIONS, REALITIES, STRUCTURES

4 From Novella to Libretto 91
5 Libretto into Opera 124
6 The Forgotten Englishman 161

PART III CHARACTERISATION, MUSIC AND THE STAGING OF PLACE

7 Carmen's Places 193
8 Carmen the Gypsy 219
9 In the Pit, On the Stage 245

Select Bibliography 275
Index 289

Illustrations

COLOUR PLATES

I Manuel Cabral Aguado Bejarano (1827–1891), *The Death of Carmen* (1890). Oil on canvas, 37.5 cm × 56.5 cm. Private collection. © Sotheby's / akg-images.

II Eugenio Lucas Velázquez (1817–1870), *Majas al balcón* [Ladies on a Balcony] (1862). Oil on canvas, 108 cm × 81 cm. Prado, Madrid / Bridgeman Images.

III Manuel Cabral Aguado Bejarano, *Un borracho en un mesón* [A Drunkard in an Inn] (1850). Oil on canvas, 60 cm × 74.5 cm. © Colección Carmen Thyssen-Bornemisza, Malaga, CTB. 1998.3.

IV Alfred Dehodencq (1822–1882), *Un baile de gitanos en los jardines del Alcázar* [Gypsies Dancing in the Gardens of the Alcázar in Seville] (1851). Oil on canvas, 111.5 cm × 161.5 cm. © Colección Carmen Thyssen-Bornemisza, Malaga, CTB. 1996.30.

V Illustration of an Opéra ball with Spanish dancers. From *Universal und Europaisade Modenzeitung*, 'Le Progrès: Modes de Paris pour l'Académie européenne des modes' (January 1866).

VI A lady's entry ticket for a masked ball (*en travesti*) at the Paris Opéra (1854). Author's collection.

VII Life-size model of a *banda taurina*, the signalling band employed at the *Plaza de toros* in Seville. Courtesy of Colección Real Maestranza de Caballería de Sevilla.

VIII Juan Mata Aguilera, model of the bullring in Alcalá (1843–1846), detail. Museo de historia de Madrid.

IX Entry of the *cuadrilla* (procession into the bullring). From *Tauromachia; or, The Bullfights of Spain* [...] drawn and lithographed by Lake Price; with preliminary explanations by Richard Ford (London, 1852). © The British Library Board, General Reference Collection C.52.i.2.

x The Austrian dancer Fanny Elssler as Florinda in *Le Diable boiteux*. 19th-century engraving. Historisches Museum der Stadt Wien / © A Dagli Orti / De Agostini Picture Library / Bridgeman Images.

xi Rouargue brothers, illustration of gypsies dancing in Triana. From Émile Bégin, *Voyage pittoresque en Espagne et en Portugal* (Paris, 1852). Courtesy Bibliothèque nationale de France, FRBNF30077184.

xii Gustave Fraipont, 'En Espagne "aux taureaux" on fume à tous les étages' ('In Spain at the bullfight one smokes at all levels'). From Spire Blondel, *Le tabac* (Paris, 1891). © The British Library Board, General Reference Collection 12330.k.49.

xiii Gustave Fraipont, 'Sortie des "cigarellas" à la manufacture de Seville ('Exit of the *cigarellas* from the factory in Seville']. From Spire Blondel, *Le tabac* (Paris, 1891). © The British Library Board, General Reference Collection 12330.k.49.

xiv D. Antonio Chaman, 'Cigarreras'. Lithograph from his *Costumbres andaluzas* (Seville, [1850]). Classic Image / Alamy Stock Photo.

xv Carlos Vazquez, '… y así granizaron sobre ella cuartos, que la vieja no se daba manos á cogerlos' ('… and so many *cuartos* were thrown down for her, that the old *gitana* had not enough hands to pick them up'). From *Ilustración Artistica* 1902, vol. 1357, Barcelona, 1908. Biblioteca Nacional de España.

xvi Carlos Vazquez, 'La gitanilla, por otro nombre La Preciosa' ('The gypsy girl, otherwise known as La Preciosa'). From *Ilustración Artistica* 1902, vol. 1357, Barcelona, 1908. Biblioteca Nacional de España.

xvii Front cover of Catulle Mendès and Rodolphe Darzens, *Les Belles du monde : Égyptiennes*, illustrated by Lucien Métivet (Paris, [1890]). Author's collection.

xviii Charles Auguste Steuben, *La Esméralda* (1839). Oil on canvas, 195.3 cm × 145 cm. Musée des Beaux-Arts, Nantes, France. Photo © RMN (Réunion des Musées Nationaux), Paris, 99-014937.

xix Édouard Manet, *Portrait of Émilie Ambre as Carmen* (1880). Oil on canvas, 92.4 cm × 73.5 cm. Philadelphia Museum of Art. Pennsylvania, PA, USA, Gift of Edgar Scott / Bridgeman Images.

BLACK AND WHITE PLATES

1.1 Cover page of a piano arrangement of Beethoven's *Wellingtons Sieg; oder, Die Schlacht bei Vittoria* [Wellington's Victory; or, The Battle of Vitoria] (Wien: Steiner, c.1815). Beethoven-haus, Bonn / akg-images. 5

1.2 Title page of Don Preciso's *Colección de las majores coplas, seguidillas, tiranas y polos*, vol. 1 (Madrid, 1816). British Library: General Reference Collection 1464.a. (16). 10

1.3 Title page of Fernando Sor's *Three Favorite Spanish Boleros*, arranged with accompaniment for the Spanish guitar or pianoforte (London, [c.1815]). British Library: Music Collections G.425.tt. (26). 20

1.4 Example 6 from Fernando Sor's article 'Séguedille-Boléro' in Ledhuy and Bertini's *Encyclopédie pittoresque de la musique* (Paris, 1835). Courtesy Brian Jeffrey. 23

1.5 Cover of the sheet music for Soriano Fuertes's 'L'Éventail' [El Abanico; The Fan] (Paris, [c. 1870]). British Library: Music Collections H.2004.c.(4). 27

1.6 Ornate title page of *Échos d'Espagne : Chansons et danses populaires*, ed. P. Lacome and J. Puig y Alsubide (Paris, [1872]). Author's collection. 30

2.1 Francisco Lameyer's frontispiece to the first edition of Serafín Estébanez Calderón's *Escenas andaluzas* (Madrid, 1847). Author's collection. 43

2.2 Plate by Hyacinthe Royet for the illustrated edition of the *Carmen* vocal score (Paris: Choudens, c.1890), showing the scene outside the bullring for Act IV. Courtesy Bruno Forment. 47

2.3 The set for Act IV of *Carmen* in the 1898 revival by Albert Carré. The set is by Lucien Jusseaume and is modelled on the Seville bullring as it was rebuilt in the 1880s, after the 1875 run of *Carmen* at the Opéra-Comique. Photograph from *Le Théâtre*, January 1898. Author's collection. 48

2.4 Francisco Lameyer's second illustration for Serafín Estébanez Calderón's *Escenas andaluzas* (Madrid, 1847). Author's collection. 52

2.5 Gustave Doré, *La navaja*, illustration for Baron Davillier's *L'Espagne* (Paris, 1862, rpt. 1874). Author's collection. 53

2.6 Gustave Doré, *L'escrime au couteau – lanzar la navaja*, illustration for Baron Davillier's *L'Espagne* (Paris: 1862, rpt. 1874). Author's collection. 54

3.1 Elaborate cover of the sheet music for Zacharie Astruc's *Sérénade* for Lola de Valence, with an illustration by Édouard Manet. Courtesy Chicago Institute of Art. 87

5.1 Anon., illustration of a mutiny in the tobacco factory in Seville (19th century). Courtesy Altadis. 140

5.2 Anon., 'Jealousy in the Factory', a further image of female disputes. Courtesy Altadis. 141

5.3 Plate by Hyacinthe Royet for the illustrated edition of the *Carmen* vocal score (Paris: Choudens, c.1890), showing José watching Carmen dance the *romalis*. Courtesy Bruno Forment. 151

6.1 *Plantation* for the opening scene in Act I, including directions for the staging of the 'Scène de l'Anglais'. Typescript from a folder in the collection of the Association de la Régie théâtrale. Courtesy Bibliothèque historique de la ville de Paris. 167

6.2 Page from the *livret de mise en scène* indicating the 'Scène de l'Anglais' and the children knocking him over on the steps, marked 'Ancienne mise en scène' ('old production') in red ink. Collection of the Association de la Régie théâtrale. Courtesy Bibliothèque historique de la ville de Paris. 170

6.3 Page from the *livret de mise en scène* showing the exit of an Englishman, marked 'Ancienne mise en scène' ('old production') in red ink. Collection of the Association de la Régie théâtrale. Courtesy Bibliothèque historique de la ville de Paris. 171

6.4 Gustave Doré, *Despoilers of the Azulejos of the Alhambra*, illustration for Baron Davillier's *Spain* (English edition). Author's collection. 181

6.5 Gustave Doré, *Mi Lord Anglais at Mabille*, illustration for Blanchard Jerrold's *The Cockaynes in Paris; or, Gone Abroad* (London, 1871). Author's collection. 182

6.6 Gustave Doré, *A Dancing Academy, Seville*, illustration for Baron Davillier's *Spain* (English edition). Author's collection. 183

6.7 Cham [Amédée Charles Henry Noé], cartoon depicting an Englishman observing the aftermath of the Paris Commune. Author's collection. 185

6.8 Gustave Doré, *On the Boulevards*, sketch of English couple wandering around Paris, for Blanchard Jerrold's *The Cockaynes in Paris; or, Gone Abroad* (London, 1871). Author's collection. 186

7.1 Gustave Doré, *Cigarreras au travail* [*Cigarreras* at Work], illustration for Baron Davillier's *L'Espagne* (Paris, 1874). Author's collection. 207

7.2 E. Beauchy, photograph of *cigarreras* working in the Seville tobacco factory (late 19th century). Courtesy Altadis. 208

7.3 Anon., photograph of a *cigarrera* in traditional costume. Courtesy Altadis. 209

8.1 Gustave Doré, *El ole gaditano* [*Ole* from Cadiz], illustration for Baron Davillier's *L'Espagne* (Paris, 1874). Author's collection. 234

8.2 Gustave Doré, *Toilette d'une gitana* [Gypsy Girl at Her Toilette], illustration for Baron Davillier's *L'Espagne* (Paris, 1874). Author's collection. 236

9.1 Ornate cover of Choudens's *mise en scène* for *Carmen*. Courtesy Bibliothèque historique de la ville de Paris. 254

9.2 First page of Choudens's *mise en scène* for the first staging of *Carmen.* Courtesy Bibliothèque historique de la ville de Paris. 255
9.3 Drawing by Léon Sault of the opening scene from the first staging of *Carmen,* published in *La Comédie illustré* shortly after the premiere. Author's collection. 258
9.4 Cover for the sheet music of the Habanera (Choudens), with a portrait of the first Carmen: Célestine Galli-Marié. Courtesy Hugh MacDonald. 268
9.5 Cover for the sheet music of the Toréador song (Choudens), with a portrait of the first Escamillo: Jacques Bouhy. Courtesy Hugh MacDonald. 269
9.6 Plate by Hyacinthe Royet for the illustrated edition of the *Carmen* vocal score (Paris: Choudens, c.1890), showing Carmen at her toilette and José entering. Courtesy Bruno Forment. 271
9.7 Auguste Lamy, the scene for Act II of *Carmen* as printed in *L'Illustration,* surrounded by vignettes of other moments in the opera (1875). Author's collection. 272

MUSIC EXAMPLES

1.1 First page of *España de la guerra* or *The Spanish Patriot's War-Song,* allegedly Lord Wellington's favourite song. Courtesy Brian Jeffrey. 6
1.2 Manuel Garcia, 'Tirana', from *Caprichos líricos españoles* (Paris, 1830), bars 61–73. 15
1.3 Manuel Garcia, 'Cuerpo bueno, alma divina', cadenza. 17
1.4 The opening of the first *bolero* from Fernando Sor's *Three Favourite Spanish Boleros.* (London, [c. 1815]) British Library: Music collections G. 425.tt. 21
1.5 Vocal part of Soriano Fuertes's 'El Abanico', with indications for the movements of the fan. (Paris, [c. 1870]) British Library: Music Collections H. 2004. c. (4). 28
1.6 Opening of 'Cuerpo bueno' ('Tu dors, la belle amoureuse') as arranged in *Échos d'Espagne.* RLS collection. 31
2.1 Smugglers' chorus, *Carmen,* Act III, bar 47 et seq. 'Take care not to make a false step!' 59
4.1 *Carmen,* Act I, No. 6 (Duo: José and Micaëla), bars 36–41, modified 'Palestrina-style' accompaniment for the reference to José's mother attending church with Micaëla. 121
5.1 'Le mode mineur tsigane' ('the minor gypsy scale') and Carmen's motive. 129

5.2 Franz Liszt, Sonata in B minor for piano, opening, making use of the gypsy scale. 129
5.3 Extract from the middle-section of the abandoned version of Carmen's entry, 'L'amour, l'amour !'. 135
5.4 Opening of Sebastian Yradier, 'El arreglito' [The Betrothal], the model for the Habanera in *Carmen.* RLS collection. 136
5.5 *Carmen,* Act I, the opening of the Habanera. 137
5.6a *Carmen,* Act I 'Scène et Pantomime' from the first Choudens vocal score, bars 1–11. 144
5.6b *Carmen,* Act I 'Scène et Pantomime' from the first Choudens vocal score, bars 77–93, the so-called *Séguedille.* 145
5.7 Casimir Gide, *bolero* for *Le Diable boiteux* [The Devil on Two Sticks], whose *cachucha* achieved worldwide fame. 147
5.8 Three sections of Escamillo's Toréador song, his middle section a *pasodoble taurino* characterising the different aspects of the *torero*'s art. 148
5.9 *Carmen,* Act II, No. 16 (Duo: José and Carmen), bars 7–12, Carmen's humorous operatic *récit.* 151
5.10 'Canción de cuna', from Felipe Pedrell's *Cancionero musical popular español* (Valls, 1918–1922), vol. 1. RLS collection. 153
5.11 Theme of final entr'acte in *Carmen,* woven around Carmen's motive. 156
5.12 *Fioriture* in Casimir Gide's *bolero* for *Le Diable boiteux,* resembling similar passage in Bizet's final entr'acte for *Carmen.* 157
5.13 Bizet, woodwind motive in Entr'acte to final act of *Carmen.* 159
6.1 Opening bars of the 'Scène de l'Anglais', *Carmen,* first vocal score (1875). 163
6.2 *Carmen,* Act I 'Scène et Pantomime', bars 77–93. From Peters Edition (2013), ed. Richard Langham Smith, trans. David Parry. 165
8.1 Georges Bizet, 'La Bohémienne' (*Chants du Rhin,* No. 4), opening. 243

The author and publisher are grateful to all the institutions and individuals listed for permission to reproduce the materials in which they hold copyright. Every effort has been made to trace the copyright holders; apologies are offered for any omission, and the publisher will be pleased to add any necessary acknowledgement in subsequent editions.

Preface

I think we must face the fact
That the *Carmen* by Bizet
Is no more Spanish
Than the Champs Élysées.[1]

So went Noel Coward's nice little song. But (to add another line):

He was wrong, wrong, wrong!

This book sets out to counter the attitude that *Carmen* has nothing really Spanish about it. It explores the Spanishness behind the opera in some depth: how that Spanishness infused the opera in several ways; and how Spanish customs, costumes and personalities penetrated both libretto and music. It opposes the view that *Carmen* is merely a French *espagnolade* or, in the more elevated words of modern theoretical studies, an example of 'auto-exoticism'. The book does not concur with the many literary scholars and critics who have seen the opera as a dilution of Prosper Mérimée's original novella.[2] Indeed, it presents arguments against this common view.

Certainly, *Carmen*'s librettists researched the exoticism of this 'other' place – in this case the opera's authentic Spanish elements – much more than did the librettists of the many oriental (and exotic) operas that surrounded it in the last third of the nineteenth century, many of which employed all-purpose orientalist musical languages, and texts based on shallow stereotypical characters and concepts. *Carmen* – I hope to persuade – certainly does not do that. Quite the reverse.

In his exhaustive study of musical exoticism Ralph P. Locke has placed *Carmen* within the context of Western classical music's canon of exotic works,

1 Noel Coward, 'Opera Notes', in *Collected Verse* (London, 2014).

2 See the seminal collection of reviews in Lesley Wright, *'Carmen': Dossier de presse Parisienne* (Weinsberg, 2001).

and has stressed its particular complexity by unearthing and discussing some of the Spanish musical sources that Bizet skilfully transformed for the rich resources of a fully fledged French nineteenth-century operatic orchestra. Locke's own studies of Bizet's models have deepened our understanding of how this *opéra à numéros* was put together. Locke counters Noel Coward's view succinctly:

> One still sometimes reads today that Bizet's *Carmen* makes no use of Spanish music. Scholars have established, though, that some of the most Hispanic-sounding numbers in the opera are indeed modelled on specific Spanish performance traditions and on folk-style pieces by professionally trained Spanish composers.[3]

The present volume suggests a few further Spanish models that Bizet may have used, in addition to those identified by Locke.

In terms of discussion of the 'exotic' Locke observes a complex layering; there is not only a 'Spanish exotic' in *Carmen*, but also a 'gypsy exotic', which he calls an 'internal other'. Gypsy customs, moralities, lifestyle and particular gifts (divination, skills with animals etc.) are all stressed in both the Mérimée sources and the libretto. Bizet takes this further by distinguishing gypsy music from music based more on the Spanish music of the *Escuela bolera* (Bolero School). To the displaced characters from the north, who include the soldiers posted south to Andalusia, gypsy ways are exotic in themselves – as is their music. This binary opposition between gypsy and non-gypsy is stressed throughout both novella and libretto.

Particularly focussed upon as characters who have moved south from the northern provinces are Don José Lizzarabengoa (almost a parody of a Basque name); Zuniga (Zúniga is a Basque name and Zúñiga a town in Navarre); Micaëla (with her blue dress and blonde tresses) and possibly Carmen herself, if we are to believe her claim to come from Etchalar (in the Basque country).[4] Chapter Six, based on a close reading of what we would now call the 'production books', uncovers yet another layer of even more northern exoticism in the 'forgotten Englishman' – a figure who, by the time of the

3 Ralph P. Locke, 'Spanish Local Color in Bizet's *Carmen*: Unexplored Borrowings and Transformations', in Annegret Fauser and Mark Everist (eds), *Music, Theater and Cultural Transfer: Paris, 1830–1914* (Chicago, 2009), pp. 316–360; Ralph P. Locke, *Musical Exoticism: Images and Refections* (Cambridge, 2009), particularly the section 'Gypsy Characters and Poor Andalusians'. The quotation is from p. 161.

4 See Lola San Martín Arbide, '*Carmen* at Home: Between Andalusia and the Basque Provinces (1875–1936)', in Langham Smith and Rowden, *'Carmen' Abroad: Bizet's Opera on the Global Stage* (Cambridge, 2020) chapter twenty.

opera, had become ubiquitous in the principal tourist streets of old Seville, *Sierpes*, translated by Mérimée as the 'rue de la Serpent'.[5]

The first section of the book – Preparing the Ground – deliberately delays in discussing the opera itself, which is too readily seen as the root of a line of Spanish-inspired French music stretching through Lalo, Massenet, and Chabrier (his *España* and Habanera), to Debussy and Ravel. *Carmen* was, on the contrary, a mid-point, the result of various movements inciting Hispanomania in France and creating an environment – clearly recognised by Bizet and his librettists – in which a skilfully texted and composed opera based on one (or two) minor literary masterpieces by Mérimée might be turned into a successful Opéra-Comique.[6] *Carmen* had many musical predecessors, in dance and in opera, as well as in *zarzuelas, canciones* and guitar music.

Primarily predicated on Mérimée's novella *Carmen,* many among the opera's French audiences would have been familiar with this principal literary source. They would ask questions and read the critics. How would it work as an opera? What were the processes of transformation: first from novella to libretto, and second from libretto into opera? Many writings on Bizet's opera have rather sidestepped its Spanish *topos,* concentrating more on the relationship between Carmen and José, and to a lesser extent on Escamillo's and Micaëla's interventions into this relationship. Productions have often taken a similar approach, divorcing the opera from its Spanish context in order to focus on the central relationship. That relationship has been imaginatively read in many ways: like many operas, commentators have speculated that perhaps its title is wrong. Maybe it should have been called 'José' – just as Debussy's *Pelléas et Mélisande* should perhaps have been called *Golaud* – because it is in those two male characters that the incurable jealousy lies, essentially causing the 'love and death' trajectory that forms the basis of their stories.

Among writers who have taken this line – which is a fertile one – are Dominique Maingeneau, Susan McClary, Nelly Furman and Christine Rodriguez – to make a selection.[7] Their analysis of the dynamics between these characters, including the differences of their occupations, motivations and, above all, race and gender, have without doubt affected subsequent productions. This book attempts to persuade its readers that despite the fascination

5 Exoticism is often confused with orientalism or assigned mainly to places further south. This is wrong: we should remember the work of Pierre Jourda, *L'exotisme dans la littérature française depuis Chateaubriand,* whose first chapter is 'Les Anglais'.

6 Opéra-Comique has nothing to do with 'Comic opera', but rather derives from the traditions of the institution of the Opéra-Comique, which demanded works to alternate spoken sections with musical numbers. Its name derives from the words *comédien* and *comédienne,* meaning actor and actress.

7 See the Bibliography for details of these writings.

of these relationships – and the fun of recasting and resituating them – the opera was first regarded as closely linked to a Spanish *topos*, whether through Mérimée himself, by French travellers who had succumbed to the rife Spanish fever, or through productions whose scenography went to great pains to set the work in its Spanish context.

What I have written is probably a deeply unfashionable book, in a climate where directors look primarily for new concepts of characters and relationships, for changes of place and time and thus costume and scenery. Never mind! By contrast, we might remind ourselves of some classic *Carmens* that have gone to some lengths to place the opera in a vividly Spanish context and retained its original setting. At the Opéra-Comique its Spanish setting was prescribed from the outset, as Choudens – in common with other French publishers – operated in an entirely different way from today's operatic infrastructure. They were responsible not only for the performing materials but also for the staging, distributing a *mise en scène* detailing the sets and movements of the characters along with the hired *matériel* for performance – the scores and parts.

From the outset, one of the principal attractions of the opera was the gypsy tavern scene (the Act II *Chanson bohème*), which clicked with castanets, was a feast of colour and in which the trio of Carmen, Frasquita and Mercédès was augmented by imported Spanish-style dancers. This Spanish aspect was further intensified in Albert Carré's revival of the opera in 1898, which continued to run as a sort of benchmark performance at the Opéra-Comique while other completely different interpretations flourished throughout the world alongside.[8] Carré himself was unquestionably a victim of the Hispanomania, and although his first Carmen, Georgette Leblanc, was not a success, he travelled with her to Spain to research details, breathe the Spanish air and live its life, so as to infuse his new production with still more realism than the first staging.

This study of the Spanish elements, it is suggested, was also fuelled by the extensive Spanish community of painters, artists, writers and musicians who were deeply embedded in Paris, partly as exiles who had collaborated with the French during the Napoleonic occupation. Parallel to these migrants – though moving in the opposite direction – was the flourishing tourism trade: travellers going to Spain, which was becoming increasingly easy to reach, and bringing back Spanish accoutrements of all kinds (not forgetting sheet music). Shops opened in Paris selling a variety of Spanish goods and aids to getting around Spain.

8 See Michela Niccolai, '*Carmen* dusted down', in Langham Smith and Rowden, Carmen *Abroad*, chapter four.

'Exoticism' may be one approach, but another is to consider the opera with the umbrella-term 'realism' in mind. Is that equally problematic? Probably, yes. Of course opera cannot be realistic, but it can attempt to portray slices of reality and many have cited *Carmen* as one of the first operas to do this. Mérimée's experiences, expressed in minute detail in the opera's two literary sources (the *Lettres d'Espagne* and *Carmen*), provided an inescapable vein of observed realism and a disdain for both narrative embroidery and dilution. For the experienced librettists – although they never visited Spain – there was a similar motivation to incorporate genuine experiences into the libretto, largely derived from a detailed reading of the Mérimée sources alongside the countless other travelogues by established literary figures from France and elsewhere.

Bizet's music may suggest that theories of 'exoticism' and notions of 'realism' need nuancing. The Spanish numbers in *Carmen* are neither realistic nor are they exactly exotic. The *polo* (examined in Chapter Five) is a prime example. Bizet counters the sources from which he may have taken it, by, to put it crudely, giving it back its balls, even though the final (brilliant) entr'acte into which he embeds its theme is 'full-orchestral French'. Perhaps an approach better than nuancing either 'exoticist' theories or searching for 'realism' is to consider the opera in terms of its 'hybridisation': this was surely the overall challenge for both Bizet and his librettists. Their challenge was to steer a distinctly original path between gritty Spanish sources and the sugar-craving expectancy of Opéra-Comique audiences. Chapter Four aims to convince that the librettists attempted to incorporate many of the visceral details of Bizet's sources into the libretto, and that the compilers of the staging manual were also harnessed to the Mérimée original. After all, the over-arching aim for everyone was financial success, as Halévy's detailed accounts of daily receipts indicate.

The Spanish music was largely gleaned from sources the composer had found in Paris libraries, but also perhaps from performances by the extensive Spanish community of musicians in Paris, which Bizet witnessed not too far from his *quartier*. As for writing for the traditions of the Opéra-Comique, Gounod-esque though they might be, the Toréador song, Micaëla's duet with José, José's flower song and Micaëla's aria when she finds José in the mountains – all these have become pinnacles in the repertoire of that house.

This book attempts to show that an avid quest for the real Spain of sometime after 1813 (when the country regained independence) permeated the opera at all levels, even if 'dating' *Carmen* proves to be somewhat difficult. The libretto dates the action to 'around 1820'. Mérimée went to Spain – and only once to Andalusia – in 1830, by which time the region was already considerably more developed than it would have been a decade earlier. It was then ten years (though he did visit Spain again) before he wrote his novella from his memories of Andalusia, sometimes getting his details a little wrong.[9] And it was thirty years later still that the opera would be created.

In the 1830s, when he went to the south, Mérimée self-confessedly wanted to experience the 'real' Spain – and its Black Legend. His chance meeting with the author Estéban Calderón, who guided him on his first visit, proved crucial. He maintained a copious and continuous correspondence with Spanish friends, and his novella *Carmen* was infused with realist – not exoticist – detail; in this way Mérimée was unlike many of his contemporary travellers, who idealised Andalusia. His way of writing up his travelogue contrasted with theirs, too, as it was constructed around what he saw as significant events – executions, meetings with gypsies, available women (nothing unusual for him), bullfights, gypsy dancing (and drinking) in a tavern. His experiences of his first visit were captured in his *Lettres d'Espagne*, some details of which are retained in the libretto (though this is often forgotten).

Although the librettists themselves never went to Spain, they were a highly professional and experienced team, having learned their trade through their many collaborations with Offenbach and others. Their transformation of Mérimée's novella has been much maligned, especially by literary scholars and those who take delight in the old game of making derogatory comparisons between literary sources and opera librettos, forgetting that transformation into opera was an art in itself. Chapter Four, on the way Henri Meilhac and Ludovic Halévy adapted Mérimée's novella, aims to reassess this process, suggesting that their adaptation transformed and transferred Mérimée's 'significant events' into their narrative rather skilfully, realising the potential for his emphasis on the 'moment' to be converted into texts suitable for musical and performative numbers.

When the all-important moment came for the opera to take its final leap onto the stage, more input was also committed to retention – if not augmentation – of its Spanish elements. The original staging was Spanish enough, as can be seen from illustrations of its sets. But for Albert Carré's revival – beyond the scope of the current book – *Carmen*'s authenticity needed to be still further enhanced. The important theatre critic Gustave Larroumet remarked on Carré's determined quest for still more authenticity, to the extent of commissioning new military costumes from exactly the right region and all kinds of other details gleaned from his visit to Spain.[10]

9 For example, he remembered *gazpacho* as a salad rather than a cold soup.

10 See Michela Niccolai, '*Carmen* Dusted Down', in Langham Smith and Rowden, Carmen *Abroad*.

Carré's staging of *Carmen* ran until the 1960s and could be considered an old-school, 'authentic', version of the opera. Alongside it have been many productions that downplayed the work's original grounding in Spanish soil in favour of a focus on Carmen herself, on the turbulent (or dominating, if one sees it that way) relationship between her and José, or on Escamillo and the bull. Many others, however, have gone to some lengths to re-inject the opera with Andalusian elements – directors, scenographers and singers among them – and their input in 're-Spanishising' *Carmen* should not be underestimated. Unforgettable in this respect is Francesco Rosi's 1984 film of the opera, which has become a benchmark in itself. Set in Ronda, which has a perfectly preserved operant bullring, it resituated the opera within a thoroughly Spanish context without losing any of the tense relationships between all the characters: José and Carmen, José and Micaëla, José and Escamillo, and – of course – Escamillo and Carmen. The tobacco factory was not the real one, but it was presented most evocatively by adapting a block of flats.[11]

Why yet another book on *Carmen*? This is certainly not an 'opera guide' and it does take its time in getting to discussion of the opera itself – quite deliberately. The book is more about what lay behind *Carmen* and its tremendous success subsequent to its initial failure. What brought it to the stage? What was its relationship with the novella of Mérimée which – even on the posters – was mentioned as its major source? To what extent was it a betrayal of Mérimée's deep research – and experiences – of Spain? Did it perhaps attempt to retain the 'salt and spice' of his experiences, even through the music? Those are a few of the questions this book attempts to answer. It is not in any way concerned with *Carmen*'s afterlife – what Jonathan Miller called its 'subsequent performances'. That would be another – very interesting – very voluminous book.

This volume is addressed to those who think the Spanish context of the story may still be of interest in putting *Carmen* on stage. Some have passionately believed that story works best if set in its original context, others don't. My over-arching mission in this book is to question the wisdom of wrenching the story out of its Spanish context when interpreting the opera and to suggest that restoring *Carmen* to Spain might not be a bad idea. Read on.

11 See Daniel Snowman, *The World of Placido Domingo* (London, 1985), pp. 217–218.

Acknowledgements

PEOPLE and institutions who have helped with this book go back much further than its relatively recent commissioning, for which thanks, above all, must go to Michael Middeke of Boydell & Brewer for his early conversations and immediate support for the venture. Before this there is a history in which many have been involved. Edition Peters, who initially commissioned me to undertake a feasibility study on whether a new edition of *Carmen* might be viable, were the first step in my becoming professionally involved in an opera which – of course – I had seen a few times, without knowing much about its complex web of sources. Behind this were the Peter Moores Foundation, who were planning a *Carmen* for their Opera in English series for Chandos Records. This commission may well have been based on my success in 'taming' another celebrated Spanish woman: Chimène, wife of *El Cid* and the heroine of Debussy's 'other' opera, *Rodrigue et Chimène,* which had reached the stage of the new *Opéra de Lyon* in 1993 and has subsequently been published in the Debussy *Œuvres complètes.*[1]

Nicolas Riddle and Peter Owens at Peters must be thanked for this introduction, the latter for being particularly insistent about the *espaces sécables* of the French language: the convention of putting spaces before certain punctuation marks in the French language. This was a process meticulously carried over into both the vocal and orchestral scores of *Carmen,* which have undergone a revision and re-edition with additional materials on the Peters

1 Debussy, *Rodrigue et Chimène,* ed. Richard Langham Smith, Œuvres Complètes de Claude Debussy, ser. 6, vol. 1 (Paris, 2003). See also Richard Langham Smith, 'Taming Two Spanish Women: Reflections on Editing Opera', in Barbara L. Kelly and Kerry Murphy (eds), *Berlioz and Debussy: Sources, Contexts and Legacies; Essays in Honour of François Lesure,* (London, 2007), pp. 83–102.

website.[2] Subsequent personnel at Peters who also contributed to the progress of the edition include John Snelson (who continues as a lively correspondent on the opera), Cathy Hill, Andrew Hanley, David Lewiston Sharpe and, most recently, Daniel Lewis, whose input into the transformation of the scores from the old Acorn platform to the more modern PC and Mac platform has been invaluable. Also important has been the input of Katie Tearle into the dissemination of the edition.

The conclusion of the viability study was that a new approach to the opera was needed, not a score based on Bizet's sketchy manuscript score (or what's left of it). Rejecting the confused term 'Urtext', the decision was taken to call the new edition a 'Performance Urtext', that is, a score based on what was done at the Opéra-Comique in the first run, for part of which Bizet was still alive and 'around'. The unique point of this score was that it included material about the staging as well as presenting a text based on a careful consideration of the various sources.

My colleague Clair Rowden (as I write a Reader in Music at Cardiff University), who was resident in the outskirts of Paris in the early stages of preparing the edition, assisted in this, continuing what I had begun in combing the one source which was to be the basis of the edition: the *Partition ayant servi à la première representation à l'Opéra-Comique le 3 mars 1875* (the score used for the premiere at the Opéra-Comique on 3 March 1875). These were compared with the other sources – both of the music and of the staging (all of which are detailed here in Chapter Nine).

So much for the musicological process. Through the detailed reading of every word and every note I succumbed to more than a slight bout of the Hispanomania of those travellers described in Chapter Two. By way of a Debussy colleague, Denis Herlin, I got in touch with Jean-Paul Goujon (who has written on Debussy and Paul Louÿs in Seville), and via him reached José Rodriguez Gordillo, director of the archives of the Fábrica Real de Tabacos de Sevilla (the Royal Tobacco Factory in Seville) and author of several seminal studies of it and its personnel. His work has been invaluable to Chapter Seven, 'Carmen's Places'. Visits to the museum of the Real Maestranza de Caballería de Sevilla led me to its academic publications, including studies of the place of music in *tauromachie* (bullfighting).

Continuing musicological work in Paris, the staff at the Bibliothèques de la musique et de l'Opéra have always been of great assistance. Mme Odile Gigou at the Bibliothèque historique de la ville de Paris helped specifically

2 See <www.editionpeters.com/product/carmen/ep7548a?TRE00000/>. The tab 'Links' leads to a more up-to-date bibliography than in the printed edition, and a comparative list of tempo markings from the various sources.

in sharing her particular views on the staging materials for *Carmen*, which at that time were under her curation. Her insights into the *mises en scène* there proved invaluable, especially for the material in Chapter Six. All this work could not have been achieved without the support of Gresham College, who awarded the University of Exeter a grant to support my *Carmen* project, appointing me as a Professor of the college.

Subsequent to this my position at the Open University was tied to the production of a third-level unit and supporting materials on *Carmen* for a 'Music and Words' module.[3] Particular thanks go to Fiona Richards for facilitating this, and also to other colleagues there for our rich group discussions – particularly with Martin Clayton, Robert Phillip, Robert Fraser, Byron Dueck and Delia da Sousa Correa. The staff of the Bibliothèque historique de la ville de Paris have helped considerably over the years: first Odile Gigou and subsequently Pauline Girard and Bérengère de l'Épine.

Following this Gary Kahn commissioned some materials for a new Overture Opera Guide on *Carmen*, designed to supersede the already valuable English National Opera (ENO) opera guide by Nicholas John. My contributions to this new resource included a wide-ranging essay, 'Carmen: From Mérimée to Bizet', and a full dual-language translation of the libretto including both the spoken passages and the texts of Guiraud's *récits*. This was a considerably modified version of a translation previously written for the Open University.[4] Many French friends and colleagues helped me with this and other translations connected with this project: Christine Menguy, Sue Taylor-Horrex and Pierre-Maurice Barlier all deserve thanks for this aid. Contacts with Dramaturges and others involved in the production of opera programmes have also helped me in many ways: above all Alison Latham at the Royal Opera House in London, Agnès Terrier at the Opéra-Comique and Christopher Cook at ENO. Thanks also to Shay Loya for help with the gypsy scale.

Hugh MacDonald, already a researcher deeply interested in Bizet and more recently his major Anglophone biographer, has been a continual correspondent and advisor. Other Bizet scholars have been quick respondents to questions that baffled me: Lesley Wright, Hervé Lacombe, Rémy Stricker, Michael Christoforidis, Liz Kertesz, Ralph P. Locke, Kerry Murphy. Others who have helped include Roger Parker, Brian Jeffrey, David Charlton,

3 Richard Langham Smith, 'Bizet's *Carmen* in Context', in Martin Clayton (ed.), *Words and Song* (Milton Keynes, 2007), pp. 191–263.

4 Richard Langham Smith, '*Carmen*: From Mérimée to Bizet', in Gary Kahn (ed.), *Georges Bizet: Carmen*, Overture Opera Guide (in association with ENO), pp. 9–34; dual-language translation, pp. 98–335.

Marie Rolf and Chris Collins *entre autres.* Reconnecting with Clair Rowden, through a transnational project called *Carmen* Abroad an international team of contributors was recruited; the project has subsequently hosted a conference and a website (Carmenabroad.org) and has a book in press.[5] Collaboration with all these contributors (over twenty of them) has been enlightening but I would like to single out Bruno Forment, David Cranmer, Lola San Martin Arbide and Michela Niccolai in particular for ideas that have gone into the current volume.

I have also been helped immeasurably by my colleagues at the Royal College of Music: Colin Lawson for his constant support, and more recently Richard Wistreich, whose initiatives in inaugurating the Musicology Forum have boosted the discipline considerably and enhanced the level of collegiality among staff. Of particular assistance have been Carola Darwin, who read Chapter Six; Trevor Herbert for input into the social history side; and Natasha Loges and Wiebke Thormählen, who have been a constant stimulus to the Musicology Forum. It has been a privilege to talk to singers in the common room: Nick Sears for his constant support for French music, and Sally Burgess, who was herself a celebrated Carmen.

It remains for me to thank those who have helped with the production of this book: Joe Duddell for setting the examples, Tim Jones for advice on these, Elizabeth Etheridge for sourcing the illustrations and my two anonymous readers of the original proposal.

Finally thanks are due to my family, Sue and Lily, for putting up with being dragged around museums in Ronda, Madrid and Seville in search of titbits for the book, and in Sue's case for endless proofreading and suggestions, not to mention providing me with first-class sustenance, better than if I had dining rights in the best of Oxbridge colleges.

5 Richard Langham Smith and Clair Rowden (eds), Carmen *Abroad: Bizet's Opera on the Global Stage* (Cambridge, 2020).

Note on the Text

Page references to Mérimée's *Carmen* and the *Lettres d'Espagne* refer to the edition by Maurice Parturier: Prosper Mérimée: *Romans et Nouvelles* (2 vols), Paris, Garnier, 1967.

References to the score of Bizet's *Carmen* are to my edition of the opera published in Vocal Score by Peters Edition (Leipzig, London, New York: EP7548a). The website for this edition contains a longer preface than the printed score, a further bibliography and a comparison of tempos markings between various sources. An orchestral score, currently on hire, is in production for purchase. See:

https://www.editionpeters.com/product/carmen/ep7548a
Click 'links' for additional resources.

A dual-language version of the original *mise en scène* (with English translation) is available on the Carmen *Abroad* website (Carmenabroad.org).

PART I

PREPARING THE GROUND

CHAPTER ONE

Vitoria and Waterloo: French Music and the Peninsular Wars

HOWEVER perverse it might seem to begin the story of *Carmen* with discussion of a ruddy-faced British battle-commander, the Duke of Wellington was a key figure in the chain of events preparing the ground for Bizet's celebrated opera long before it was first staged in 1875. The influence on the course of European history of the Irish-born Arthur Wellesley was tremendous. Most celebrated for his victory over Napoleon at Waterloo in 1815, for the Spanish – and for an important Spanish strand in the development of French music – his earlier victory over Joseph Napoleon (Bonaparte's brother) in 1813 at the battle of Vitoria in northern Spain was crucially important. It was decisive in Spanish history, effectively ending Napoleonic rule and the Peninsular Wars in which Spain, England and Portugal had allied to oppose the invading French armies. In that battle, on 21 June 1813, Wellington finally vanquished the Napoleonic forces, and restored the Spanish crown to Fernando VII. The musician Narciso Paz dedicated his *Troisième collection d'airs espagnols* to Wellington in recognition of his liberation of Spain, though the collection was published in France.[1]

By the time Wellesley entered the fray in the Iberian peninsula the British armies there had recruited and trained a substantial number of Portuguese troops and several Spanish generals commanded trustworthy battalions, most notably General Álava. One of Wellington's strengths was in his meticulous organisation of a supply chain, which was vital if an army was to survive the harsh extremes of weather in the north of Spain. By contrast, the French armies had less back-up: writers on the period often quote a saying that 'In Spain, large armies starve, and small ones get beaten.' Thus, although the majority of paintings of the decisive battle of Vitoria were by

1 Narcisse Paz, *Troisième collection d'airs Espagnols avec acct. de piano et guitare* (Paris, n.d.).

British artists, it is a mistake to assume that the outcome was a triumphalist victory for the British. Nevertheless, on his return to England Wellesley was hailed as a hero, and it was his victories in the peninsula which earned him his dukedom, after already having been honoured by the Spanish. For Spain, the battle of Vitoria was a decisive event, resulting in the end of the *era Josefina* (1808–1813).[2]

As can be seen from the extensive collection of weapons and other artefacts in the Museo de Armeria (Museum of Armoury) in Vitoria, where Wellington's elegant sword is enshrined, his *equipage* also included a tea-set; perhaps the successful military strategies leading to his victory were conceived over an English- (or Irish-) style cup of tea.

It should not be forgotten that the paintings of the battle were complemented by its Europe-wide musical celebration by Beethoven in a piece which had great success: *Wellingtons Sieg; oder, Die Schlacht bei Vittoria* – sometimes known as the 'Battle Symphony' or 'Wellington's Victory' (often thought, erroneously, to celebrate the battle of Waterloo). It was reprinted for domestic use with an illustrated cover depicting the battle (Plate 1.1).

Music played a considerable role in Wellington's campaigns, and several songs have texts that mention his name. A particular song, which had both English and Spanish words, became a favourite: *España de la guerra,* whose title in English was given as *The Spanish Patriot's War-Song* in an edition published in London in 1811. Its words were advertised as 'as sung at the Theatre of Cadiz' and it was 'arranged by a British Officer.' Anticipating later English and French publications of Spanish music, there was no hint of a Spanish style: a symmetrically phrased melody is supported by a one-line Alberti bass. The song is in the sunny key of A major except for a middle-section in the tonic minor: an effect strikingly similar to the same section in the Marseillaise, with which it also shares the rising fourth of the opening and the sung arpeggio, in this case at the words 'la traición, la traición' (in the Marseillaise at the words 'l'étandard sanglant est levé'). The two phrases rising to a high D seem especially suited to the male tessitura, achievable by basses at the top of their voices: a rousing gesture that the soldiers no doubt delighted in singing together, competing with each other for that top D. No surprise that Wellington admired it.

2 See Ian Robertson, *An Atlas of the Peninsular War, 1807–1814* (New Haven and London, 2010).

Plate 1.1 Cover page of a piano arrangement of Beethoven's *Wellingtons Sieg; oder, Die Schlacht bei Vittoria* [Wellington's Victory; or, The Battle of Vitoria] (Wien: Steiner, c.1815).

Although there are many variants of the text, the London printing gives the following:

España de la Guerra	Spain is hoisting
Tremola su pendón	The flag of war
Contra el poder infame	Against the infamous power
Del vil Napoleón.	Of the vile Napoleon.
Sus crímenes oíd,	Hear of his crimes!
Escuchad la traición	Listen to the treachery
Con que a la faz del mundo	He has spread
Se ha cubierto de horror.	Over the face of the world.[3]

The occupation had begun in 1808, and by the following year the French had imposed an organised system of regional rule, which provided literate, liberal-minded Spaniards with relatively well-paid employment. There was also the opportunity for them to join the military forces, though that involved the serious risk that those who signed up would be forced to fight their own

3 This material is taken from Brian Jeffrey, *España de la guerra: The Spanish Political and Military Songs of the War in Spain, 1808–1814* (London, 2017).

countrymen. Despite this, the regime was cautiously welcomed by liberals who were in favour of desperately needed social reform. The implementation of the French regime became largely upheld by Spanish intellectuals working alongside Napoleon's agents, later to become known as *afrancesados* – liter-

Example 1.1 First page of *España de la guerra*, or *The Spanish Patriot's War-Song*, allegedly Lord Wellington's favourite song.

ally meaning 'those who had turned French'.[4] The term acquired a pejorative meaning – that of betrayal – even though the so-called traitors had tried to act as a pressure-group on the regime to admit a non-hereditary Spanish monarch and not impose direct rule. But Joseph had ignored this, proclaiming himself monarch.

Most importantly for the beginning of our story – which traces the genesis and growth of Hispanomania in France – Wellington's victory at Vitoria resulted in Spanish musicians moving north, whether because of fear for their lives or simply to seek a better fortune. They fled to two countries above all – France and England – both of which were connected by an infrastructure of concerts and music publishers.

Among those forced to emigrate were a few musicians who helped to prepare the way for *Carmen*, both by their legacy of music, and by helping to foster the French taste – and later mania – for Spanish culture. Some had left before the crucial year of 1808, when Napoleon's brother had taken the throne, and before the celebrated bloody uprising on 2 May (the *Dos de mayo*), when the Madrileños rose against the French but were quashed.

THE *AFRANCESADOS* AND MUSIC IN FRANCE

Those who supported Joseph – the *afrancesados* – were in several ways distinct from the already established Spanish liberals, though both factions shared a desire for social change. Bifurcated Spanish politics now trifurcated: the fundamental axes – of opposition between absolutists who supported the hereditary monarchy established by the Bourbon lineage, and liberals who did not – was now compounded by the new group of those who, in a limited way, were drawn to Napoleon's ideas of regenerating Spanish fortunes through a unified, revolutionary Europe, though without the bloodshed of the French Revolution.

As far as music was concerned, the instability of Spanish politics and economics, over the turn of the eighteenth century and into the nineteenth, was a negative force, each new crisis resulting in fewer opportunities for its many talented musicians, both as players and students. For jobbing musicians – whatever their political allegiances – the livelier artistic scene of the north-

4 See Juan López Tabar, *Los famosos traidores* [The Famous Traitors] (Madrid, 2001) p. 50, for a detailed diagram of the *administración Josefina* employing 2,416 people in high positions in the Napoleonic regime in Spain.

ern countries offered attractive possibilities. And there was always South America.

The peninsular wars had been triggered by Portugal refusing to ban trade-relations with Napoleon's supreme enemy: the English. The French invasion of Portugal had been a walkover, with the Portuguese royal family capitulating and fleeing to Brazil. It was also a pretext for the French forces to move into Spain. Spanish supporters of the regime could join up and sign an oath of allegiance. Those who complied had the opportunity to be promoted to positions within the administration – such as the composer, guitarist and experienced military man Fernando Sor (1778–1839), who was promoted to the position of Commissioner of Police (*commissaire principal*) in the province of Jerez.

The Napoleonic hold over Spain was, however, patchy, and fiercely opposed by regional *juntas* who began to decree reprisals against the *afrancesados,* whom they saw as traitors and collaborators. In some provinces these 'traitors' risked the confiscation of their property and possessions, and their wives were liable to be incarcerated in convents unless bails were paid. The decrees stressed that such reprisals were to be taken regardless of rank: nobility who were involved were in no way exempt. Eventually tribunals were set up to judge the level of involvement, which was officially divided into degrees of collaboration punishable by three different penalties.

After the defeat of Napoleon's brother at Vitoria in 1813, the witch-hunt for *afrancesados* intensified, particularly for those who had – like Sor – been high-ranking functionaries under Joseph. There followed the exodus of the first *afrancesados* northwards into France, perhaps encouraged by news that the French government had promised to look after those who had worked for it in Spain. A detailed *Instruction relative à la distribution des secours accordés par S. M. l'Empereur aux espagnols refugiés en France* promised material help to those who had supported the regime during the occupation, while a contrary decree from Spain instructed border controls not to allow any such collaborators to cross back into the country.[5] Such strictures had been increasing in severity for some years, and had been catalysed by the arrival of Wellington and the British forces in the crucial year of 1808. The *afrancesados* were pursued not only by Spanish loyalists, but also by the British military.

The first exodus, in the immediate wake of Wellington's victory, was relatively small, but further rounds of reprisals against reformists took place in the 1820s, first in the period of the *trienio liberal,* an unstable period of three years when liberals were in power in a constitutional monarchy, and more acutely

5 See 'Apéndice Documental' to Miguel Artola, *Los afrancesados* (Madrid, 1998, rpt. 2008), pp. 285–290.

from 1823, when Ferdinand's absolutism was restored. No one from either side spoke up for these *traidores* (traitors). This was the period when the greatest number of French supporters were forced to flee the country. Only after 1833, after the death of Ferdinand and when Isabelle II (aged three) was proclaimed queen, were amnesties granted under the initial interim regency.[6]

DON PRECISO

Musicians fleeing the country would have had the *discurso* to one rather important publication – several times republished – ringing in their ears as they moved north: the preface to a *Colección de las mejores coplas de seguidillas, tiranas y polos*, originally published in Madrid in 1799, under the pseudonym Don Preciso. Already aware of the threat to national Spanish music posed by the influx of French dance and Italian aria, this little book is a well-argued plea for Spanish musicians to remain true to their rich heritage. It contains poems but no music, though it discusses music considerably in its introduction. At the foot of the ornate first title page is a tiny poem summing up its message:

Vivan nuestras seguidillas	Long live our seguidillas
Fandango, polo y tiranas	Fandangos, polos and tiranas
Que á pesar de necios, son	Which despite what fools think,
El chiste y la sal de España.	Are Spain's spice of life.

On the second title page the work's argument is made more precise: it is 'on the causes of the corruption and disgrace of Spanish music'.[7] The book is in fact a collection of *seguidillas* (just the poems), arranged by theme and by whether or not they had *estrivillos* (refrains). Notably, the subsequent editions were published in 1805 and 1815, either side of the Napoleonic occupation: no doubt the book's fanning of the flames of Spanish nationalism and criticisms of French music and dance would not have been tolerated during the *era Josefina*. By its third edition the book might well have been seen as propaganda against the *afrancesados*.

6 See Rafael Sanchez Mantero, 'L'émigration politique sous le règne de Ferdinand VII', in *Exil politique et migration économique : Espagnols et Français aux XIXe–XXe siècles* (Paris, 1991), pp. 17–29.

7 Don Preciso [pseudonym for Juan Antonio de Iza Zamácola], *Colección de las mejores coplas de seguidillas, tiranas y polos que se han compuesto para cantar a la guitarra … Con un discurso sobre las causas de la corrupción y abatimiento de la música española* (Madrid, 1799), with subsequent editions in 1815 and 1816 (these were not mere reprints but were newly edited and printed).

COLECCION
de las mejores coplas
DE
SEGUIDILLAS
TIRANAS Y
POLOS
que ſe han compueſto
para cantar á la
Guitarra:
TOMO I.
POR D. PRECISO.

Vivan nueſtras seguidillas,
Fandango, polo, y tiranas,
Que á pesar de necios, son
El chiste y la sal de Eſpaña.

Plate 1.2 Title page of Don Preciso's *Colección de las mejores coplas de seguidillas, tiranas y polos* (Madrid, 1816).

THE GARCIA DYNASTY

In the European context it was particularly in Paris and London that the Spanish immigrants formed communities, which flourished though the rest of the nineteenth century, their roots rapidly growing into fusion cultures. Undoubtedly the most important Spanish family to settle in Paris in the first decade of the nineteenth century was the Garcia household: Manuel Garcia *père* (1775–1832) and his celebrated offspring.[8] They had in 1808 established themselves in lodgings close to the Salle Favart (the Opéra-Comique), and their residence became a magnet and first port-of-call for many immigrant Spanish musicians. Other areas of Paris also became enclaves for Spanish immigrants, for example the Marais and the rue Saint-Honoré. Functionaries of all levels formed this community, including the ex-minister Gonzalo O'Farrill and the poet and dramatist Leandro Fernández de Moratín. The cemetery at Père Lachaise is testimony to the number of Spanish who moved to Paris and stayed there for the rest of their lives after the turbulence of the peninsular wars.[9]

Manuel Garcia *père*, the Andalusian tenor, actor and composer, was welcoming to many, helping them to find their feet in Paris, having arrived without either a *sous* or a word of French. His extrovert way of singing had captivated the French on his arrival in 1808 and he and his family were to play a considerable part in the promotion of Spanish music in France, even though their fame largely rested on their talents in the field of Italian opera. He had left his first wife, Manuela Morales, like him a celebrated dancer of *boleros*, with a child of whose fortune we know nothing. With his second wife, an established singer named Joaquina Briones (married bigamously), he was sire to a famous dynasty who not only made their mark on French musical culture, but also became known internationally as far afield as both North and South America, as well as in Russia.

Manuel was the father – in order – of the singing teacher and inventor of the laryngoscope, Manuel García II (Manuel Patricio García, 1805–1906); of the singer Maria García, who through an unsuccessful marriage became Maria Malibran and was celebrated under the name 'La Malibran' (1808–1836), and was later the lover of the Belgian violinist Charles de Bériot;[10] and

8 García dropped the accent on his name in France.

9 For a more extensive list see *Homenaje a Alberto Gil Novales: Sociabilidad y liberalismo en la España del siglo XIX* (Milan, 2001), p. 21.

10 Mérimée was an opera-goer but he sided with La Malibran's great rival Giuditta Pastia, delighting in anti-Malibran invective – sometimes in obscene terms. He vented his spleen on her with his fellow correspondent Stendhal, who shared his taste for scatological writing. In a letter to Henry Beyle of 1 December 1831 he accused her of losing pitch when she farted, which according to him she did a lot: 'Chaque coup de cul qu'elle donne lui ôte une note et elle en donne beaucoup' ('At every fart she does she misses the note, and she does them a lot'). See Prosper Mérimée, *Correspondance générale,* supplément, pp. 25–26. On this rivalry see Susan Rutherford, '"La cantante delle passion": Giuditta Pasta and the Idea of Operatic Performance', *Cambridge Opera Journal* (2007), pp. 107–138.

of Pauline (1821–1910), a talented singer who became a *compositrice* of considerable standing under the name of her husband, Louis Viardot (1800–1883).[11]

Viardot was himself an influential figure, not only as director of the Théâtre Italien in Paris for a short period (November 1838–February 1840) but also as a translator of Cervantes and a Hispanicist who took a keen interest in the relationship between France and Spain in the wake of the Napoleonic Wars.[12] Among his many activities he later became an important commentator on gypsies. All of Garcia's family were important in keeping their father's Spanish heritage alive in France, through their publications, their teaching, their performances in salons and, in Pauline's case, her own compositions.

The Garcias had left Spain in 1807 and by 30 May of that year Manuel was in Bayonne, *en route* for Paris, asking for money from his wealthy patrons.[13] By the following month he was established there. Although he must have been aware of the proximity of the Napoleonic forces, he had left a year before the Napoleonic occupation of Spain, probably more out of a wish for professional advancement than political necessity.[14]

Quite apart from the growing military strife, his musical activities pinpoint the two opposing musical forces that acted upon Spanish musicians in the first years of the nineteenth century. A glance at some of the *tonadillas* and *sainetes* he had composed in his last years in Spain reveal that, although he wrote in the fashionable Italian style, he infused his music with Spanish elements: its idiosyncratic harmonic twists; its elaborate, often improvised, ornamentation; and, above all, its passion. He had lived through a period when Italian fever, and to a lesser extent a fashion for French pieces, had reached such a point that a decree was passed in 1801 requiring all staged music in the theatres of Madrid to be sung in Spanish. The decree in no way caused a revival of Spanish-style music, quite the reverse: it merely meant more translations of Italian music – above all Rossini – had to be done. But

11 On the courtship between Louis Viardot and Pauline a most extraordinary document survives in the form of a rather cruel series of cartoons by no lesser figure than Alfred de Musset, largely centred on the size of Louis Viardot's nose. It is reproduced in full in April Fitzlyon, *The Price of Genius: A Life of Pauline Viardot* (London, 1964). See also Michael Steen, *Enchantress of Nations* (London, 2007).

12 His *Lettres d'un Espagnol* (Paris, 1826) were particularly influential in securing better conditions for captured Spanish soldiers imprisoned in France. Viardot worked to improve relations between the two countries. See Jean-Réné Aymes, *La Déportation sous le Premier Empire : Les Espagnols en France* (Paris, 1983), pp. 30–32.

13 See James Radomsky, *Manuel García* (Oxford, 2000), p. 85 et seq.

14 His letter to a minister, Don Pedro Ceballos, dated 29 March 1807, survives. Garcia suggests that he would be of 'more useful and worthy to his country' if he were allowed to travel to France and Italy, where he could 'acquire […] new knowledge'.

for many émigrés, allegiances to their native music could not be permanently extinguished. The important commentaries of the aforementioned Don Preciso, who was violently opposed to the new fashion for Italian music at the turn of the eighteenth century, and a defender of the Spanish style, must have weighed heavily on Spanish musicians defecting to the Italian style in music, and – even worse – to the French politic of governing their peninsula. Already in 1799, Don Preciso had noted the superior grace and beauty of Spanish dances when compared with French ones –'the languid and tedious minuets and passepieds composed by the stupid and quixotic French of the last century'.[15]

Following commonplace stereotyping of anyone from the Midi or further south, Garcia was regarded as having national 'passion' in his blood. Brought up in a deprived *barrio* outside the city walls of Seville, he was adept at the *boleros* and songs of the people, including the gypsies (to whose race several commentators wrongly assigned him). Like every Spanish musician, the art of accompanying himself on the guitar had become second nature – an activity in which he was still engaging in his final years in Paris. The skill displayed in his compositions was in part due to his time as a chorister in the fashionable church of San Salvador in Seville, which performed elaborate music including the rich repertoire of Spanish Renaissance counterpoint. A little later he was much in demand as a singer in the theatres of Cadiz. Many accounts, and the anecdotes that surrounded him, confirm that he never lost what northern Europeans saw as the character of Andalusians. It was perhaps deliberately cultivated and went down well in the burgeoning climate of Romanticism when he relocated to Paris. This fiery temperament was anecdotally stressed – and no doubt exaggerated – by Arthur Pougin in his turn-of-the-century biography:

> This much is certain – and all the evidence corroborates it absolutely – that he brought up his daughter with excessive sternness, was a severe father, often a hard master, exacting and impatient, not content to chide merely, when the child could not at once perfectly overcome the tasks he set her, and beating her pitilessly, in order to correct an involuntary slip, or to get the effect he wanted. They say that one day Paër with a friend was passing by beneath the windows of Garcia's house just when agonizing screams became audible; and in reply

15 '... el lánguido y fastidioso del minué y paspié, obra de aquellos franceses estúpidos y aquixotados del siglo pasado'. Don Preciso, *Colección de las mejores coplas de seguidillas, tiranas y polos*, 1816 edition, section XIII.

> to the friend's questions, Paër said with a smile: 'It's only Garcia beating his daughter to teach her to get her beats and trills right!'[16]

François-Joseph Fétis, in his *Biographie universelle des musiciens*, quotes the esteemed tenor Dominique Garat, who sang beside Garcia, admiring 'the Andalusian fury of the man which brings everything to life', adding that Garat was a 'good judge of both the faults and good qualities of singers'.[17]

From the imaginative perspective of Romantic Paris, Garcia was frequently identified with the text of one of his most famous songs, 'Yo que soy contrabandista' ('I am a smuggler'). When George Sand commented that 'like Chopin, the life of the smuggler, beyond the rules of society, he was a model for the life of the Romantic artist', she no doubt had in mind the extraordinarily long-lived popularity of this number. It is singled out by Rafael Mitjana in his seminal 1914 encyclopedia article on Spanish music of the nineteenth century, suggesting that it somehow embodied the authentic spirit of Andalusia and its people: 'because its lively, virile rhythm recalls the constant anxiety of a man who lives without respect for law, and the strange, wild melody evokes the heady perfumes of rosemary and lentisk.'[18] Pure *andalucismo*!

Certain musical characteristics branded Garcia as an Andalusian who brought to the classical repertoire some of the idiosyncrasies of Spanish singing: his sometimes harsh top register, his tendency to add extra ornamentation (second nature to Spanish singers) and, above all, his total identification with the characters he was projecting on the stage – a passionate way of performing that was perhaps more captivating than that of his northern counterparts. The real exotic.

CANCIONES ESPAÑOLAS

In 1819 Garcia had published the *Chansons espagnoles à une et plusieurs voix avec accompagnement de guitare*, their popularity ensuring several reprints and providing models for any French composer – including Bizet – who wanted to add more than a dash of *españolismo* to his music. In 1830 Garcia brought out an extensive collection of his songs solely under the Spanish title *Caprichos líricos españoles*, even though they were published in Paris; their sale was

16 Arthur Pougin, *Marie Malibran: The Story of a Great Singer* (London, 1911), p. 12.

17 François-Joseph Fétis, *Biographie universelle des musiciens*, 1st ed., entry on Garcia (Brussels, 1835), and repeated in many subsequent editions.

18 Rafael Mitjana, 'XIXe siècle, Espagne', in *Encyclopédie de la musique et dictionnaire du Conservatoire*, 1re partie, 'Espagne, Portugal' (Paris, 1920), p. 2296.

Example 1.2 Manuel Garcia, 'Tirana', from *Caprichos líricos españoles* (Paris, 1830), bars 61–73.

no doubt partly aimed at the ever-increasing Spanish community now establishing itself in the French capital, for more and more *afrancesados* were arriving in the oppressive period of the Carlist wars.

Almost all the pieces in the *Caprichos líricos* are in triple time, in the style of the *tirana, polo* or *vals* (waltz). Some are more classical and strophic, but with Spanish ornaments here and there and with hesitations, little cadenzas and, above all, ejaculations: 'Ay-ay-ay' and the characteristic quick triplet before cadences. One *tirana,* simply entitled 'Tirana' and with a text in praise of singing *tiranas,* has the distinctly Spanish harmonic hallmark of using the flattened Phrygian second degree of the scale, and also the characteristic of the Spanish dances to change time-signature without warning, in this case from 3/8 to 2/4 (See Example 1.2). Note that the Tirana is in the same 3/8 rhythm as the wrongly titled *Séguedille* from Act I of *Carmen,* a question which will be returned to.

Following the successful publication of the *Caprichos*, the prolific publisher Pacini (Antonio-Francesco-Saverio Pacini, 1778–1866) – and later, others – began to exploit the market for Spanish salon songs with volumes containing works by several composers. With a similar ring to its title, *Regalo lírico*, Pacini brought out a collection of 'Boleras, Seguidillas, Tiranas and other pieces, Songs, Spanish pieces, by the most important Spanish composers'. Its price was offered – no doubt to the Spanish community – in *duros*, and its Spanish title was untranslated.[19] In fact these 'most important Spanish composers' were all exiles living in Paris: Garcia, José Melchior Gomis (1791–1836) and Fernando Sor. Pacini's business, in the rue Favart, was a few paces from Garcia's home until 1819, when he moved (not very far) to the Boulevard des Italiens, just opposite the Théâtre Italien.

One of the most celebrated of Garcia's songs – and the most extrovertly Spanish – was a *polo* known as 'Cuerpo bueno, alma divina'. This was a number from his opera *El criado fingido* [The Man Masquerading as a Servant], composed while he still lived in Spain. Although it dated from Garcia's years in Madrid, where it had been previously published, it was included in the *Regalo lírico* collection, as were several others, and was later reprinted in two separate editions in 1874 and 1875, along with his even more celebrated *El contrabandista*.[20] 'Cuerpo bueno' was the *polo* used by Bizet as a model for the final entr'acte in *Carmen*. It had been in the public eye through the century, mostly without its remarkable ornaments, no doubt performed by Garcia himself and probably by his daughters.[21]

In 1831 he gave a dinner in honour of Rossini where reports referred to him as a 'famous Spanish singer'. The celebrated singer who had gone to Paris to study in her teens, and former wife of Rossini, Isabella Colbran, sang, and she insisted Garcia perform some of his *seguidillas*.

Garcia was active in performing Spanish music to the last: the father-figure of French musical *hispanomanie* in the first half of the nineteenth century. His enthusiasm for his native Spanish music outlived him, not least through his three illustrious offspring.

19 *Regalo lírico, colección de boleras, seguidillas, tiranas y demás: Canciones españolas, por los mejores autores de está nación* (Paris: Pacini, 1831).

20 *Cantos españoles* (Málaga, 1874) and *El cancionero popular* (Madrid, 1875). See Manuel García, *Canciones y caprichos líricos*, ed. Celsa Alonso, Musica Hispana 1 (Madrid, 2003), introduction, for a list of variants and a vocal score.

21 The similarity was first observed by Mitjana, in 'XIX siècle, Espagne', p. 2299, and its variants have been exhaustively studied by Ralph P. Locke, see 'Spanish Local Color in Bizet's *Carmen*: Unexplored Borrowings and Transformations', in Annegret Fauser and Mark Everist (eds), *Music, Theater and Cultural Transfer: Paris, 1830–1914* (Chicago, 2009), pp. 316–360.

Example 1.3 Manuel Garcia, 'Cuerpo bueno, alma divina', cadenza; note the proliferation of highly virtuosic melismas.

FERNANDO SOR(S)

Another important and complementary figure must be looked at a little more closely: the guitarist, composer and dancer Fernando Sor, who performed at the aforementioned dinner given to Rossini by Garcia, along with another celebrated Spanish guitarist, Dionisio Aguado (1784–1849). Sor was certainly of equal importance to Garcia in promoting the French fashion for Spanish music, and with his fellow guitarists he created a craze for the guitar, not least among society females. Although he came from the other end of the Spanish peninsula, Catalonia (hence the original 's' on the end of his name), Sor also shared Garcia's ability in two musical languages. He is known better for his classical output of pieces influenced by Haydn and Rossini than for his Spanish pieces, but although his published guitar music is mostly in this former vein he had a Spanish side.

His early musical activities confirm this, and the events of his life show him as a highly adaptable, enterprising man of considerable initiative. When his father died Sor entered the celebrated Escalonia de Montserrat, which is still active in singing Renaissance church music to this day. The substantial posthumous article on him in Ledhuy and Bertini's *Encyclopédie de la musique* of

1835 contains extensive passages written eloquently by Sor himself, telling in great detail of his musical experiences there.[22] He was enthralled by the music of the Barcelona composer Joan Cererols (1618–1676), but, as in Cadiz, a great deal of Haydn's music was played and sung: symphonies and masses were regularly performed in the chapel. Later, Sor tells us that he studied Haydn's string quartets in some detail.

His twenties were spent in the Spanish army: he joined a corps in Villa Franca, not far from Barcelona, and rose quickly in the ranks. Already proficient on both the piano and the guitar he impressed his colleagues there, composing patriotic songs. One memoir of him at a grand party in Barcelona remarks that he came across as having the character of a French dandy (*un currataco*).[23] Later, in Madrid, we know that he associated with French musicians, but immediately after the Napoleonic invasion he joined the anti-French Cordoban Volunteers.[24] In 1809 these volunteers fought against the French at La Mancha and in Aranjuez; Sor may well have been with them.

SOR THE TURNCOAT

Then Sor changed sides. After signing the oath of fidelity to the Napoleonic regime, he secured a highly responsible position as Commissioner of Police in Jerez de la Frontera. His acceptance of this prestigious post was a first step that would ultimately lead to his expulsion from Spain and change his fortunes irrevocably. Sor stayed in Jerez until about 1812, by which time Wellington had arrived in Spain and occupied Madrid, and the French had left Andalusia. Invited to Valencia by a general in Napoleon's service, Mazzuchelli, who

22 The article on Sor in Ledhuy and Bertini, *Encyclopédie pittoresque de la musique* (Paris, 1835), probably written by Sor himself, is an important source of biographical information. The definitive biography on Sor is Brian Jeffrey, *Fernando Sor, Composer and Guitarist* (London, 1977). Considerable detail on his defection to the Napoleonic regime may be found in Josep Mangado Artigas, 'Fernando Sor: Aportaciones biográficas', in Luis Gásser (ed.), *Estudios sobre Fernando Sor* (Madrid, 2010), p. 45 et seq.

23 'En sos trajes i caps hi havia molt que reperar – segons la moda curratac a –, i en la joventud militar, i de nostres paisans no menos Fernando Sors, lo cap de la dansa per lo que sembla en això més prest gavatx que catalá i fill de Barcelona.' ('As for their clothes and their hair there was not much they could be reproached for – as in the usual *currataca* way – and among the young military and our own countrymen not the least was Fernando Sors, the chief of the dance, so much so that in it he seemed more like a Frenchy than a Catalan and a son of Barcelona'). From a diary reporting a ball held in Barcelona in 1799. Quoted Brian Jeffrey, introduction to Fernando Sor, *Seguidillas*, book 2 (London, 1999).

24 Jeffrey, *Fernando Sor*, recounts how these volunteers also gave concerts and encouraged music and composed patriotic songs. See also Jeffrey, *España de la guerra.*

was also a musical enthusiast, Sor was presented to the Duchess of Albufera, an accomplished singer. He obliged her by writing a cantata for her, all this reinforcing his status as a confirmed *afrancesado*. There was no return.

In 1813, when Sor was 35, Wellington's victory at Vitoria put him in considerable danger due to his former high-ranking position in the police. Had anyone looked into his life, they would without doubt have regarded him as a traitor. He and many others fled to Paris in protected convoys with the defeated Josephinist soldiers, and he was the most-mentioned *afrancesado* musician in all histories of the period. But, as is clear from even the skimpiest accounts of his youth, he was a man of many talents: an administrator, an experienced soldier, a fine composer and guitarist and a budding musicologist. It was to these musical talents that he was forced to turn on his arrival in France. He wasted no time.

Soon after his arrival there he returned to the Spanish style of composition in which he had been particularly active around 1806, just before the French invasion.[25] He found publishers in both London and Paris and brought out three of his *seguidillas* under the title 'Three favorite [*sic*] Spanish Boleros: as sung by Made Vaccari, with accompaniments for voice and piano' (London: Monzani & Hill). The layout of these finely printed scores, whose date is estimated as 1815, is of particular interest and became a common format: the four-stave score has the voice part (which is in Spanish only) between the two instrumental staves, the piano part beneath and the guitar part above. The two accompaniments are completely different. As one would expect, the guitar part is totally idiomatic, adhering to the conventional *seguidilla-bolero* rhythm with the second quaver of the 3/4 bar often divided into a triplet of semiquavers and the last three quavers of each bar given emphasis. The piano part, by contrast, is more like an accompaniment to a salon song, supported by an Alberti bass. To perform it with piano transforms the song completely, and the piece loses its Spanish libido.

The *bolero* rhythm is not lost entirely, but it is obscured, even emasculated. This was probably a deliberate decision by the publishers – in this case the London firm Monzani & Hill, who held a royal charter – with commercial gain in mind. A guitar accompaniment on the piano, after all, does not lie well under the fingers and denies the pianist the chance to use the instrument's lower register: far better to write a new, idiomatic part. Furthermore, some of the intricacies of the guitar part are less effective on the piano, especially on instruments with sluggish actions before advances in escapements. A similar strategy was adopted by some other publishers right up to the turn of the

25 See Artigas, 'Fernando Sor', p. 43; and Brian Jeffrey, 'Sor and the *Seguidillas Boleras* Form', in Gásser, *Estudios sobre Fernando Sor*, pp. 341–357.

Three Favorite
SPANISH BOLEROS,
Composed by F. Sor,
As Sung by
Mad.e Vaccari,
Arranged with an Accompaniment for the
SPANISH GUITAR,
OR Piano Forte, BY
F. Vaccari
Ent. at Sta. Hall Price 5s/
LONDON,
Published by Monzani & Hill, Music Sellers to H.R.H. the Prince Regent.
24, Dover St. Piccadilly.
Where may be had the 1st Set of Spanish Boleros & 3 Italian Arietts by the above Author.
F. Vaccari

Plate 1.3 Title-page of Fernando Sor's *Three Favorite Spanish Boleros* (London [c. 1815]), published soon after Sor fled Spain.

century (for example in the songs presented by Lacome). Others, however, either reproduced guitar parts for the piano, or, in the case of the *Regalo lírico*, simplified versions of music that was previously orchestral. The idea of the dual-purpose, dual-expression song with two totally different accompaniments in opposing styles was a novel one, arising from the cultural migration of Spanish music. It was certainly more appealing than the all-purpose transcriptions of the *Regalo lírico* and its offspring. This was transnationalism operating in the lucrative world of music publishing, its axes being the production of sheet music in London and Paris, with commercial links between the two capitals.

Example 1.4 The opening of the first *bolero* from Fernando Sor's *Three Favorite Spanish Boleros*, showing totally different styles of accompaniment above and below the vocal line. The upper guitar accompaniment is idiomatically Spanish while the lower part accompanies on the piano in the style of a salon song.

Before he emigrated Sor had written songs for his colleagues, and he was an accomplished dancer in his twenties, when he first began to write his *seguidillas*. The music historian Antonio Peña y Goni heard a celebrated Catalan singer, Lorenzo Pagans, sing some of them and considered their liveliness of rhythm 'much superior to those of Manuel Garcia and Yradier. Above all we owe to Sor some *boleros* which are real jewels.'[26]

Publishing Spanish music in France was hardly going make Sor a fortune. But he tried. The addition of two or three other voices made 'Boléros de société' – exactly what the *Chanson bohème* is in *Carmen*. On the one hand he turned to compositions in more fashionable classical style, and on the other to catalysing French interest in guitar playing. As a virtuoso he was increasingly in demand, as he was as a teacher, eventually publishing his seminal *Méthode pour la guitare* in 1830, a work that to this day is held as one of the foundations of modern guitar technique.

There was another important way in which Sor informed the French about Spanish culture: in his erudite entry on the *bolero* in Ledhuy and Bertini's illustrated *Encylopédie* (1835). Essentially the article is about the *seguidilla*, and he explains how this essentially poetic form was transformed into the *bolero*. After outlining the metrical structure of *seguidilla* poetry, he provides details of the steps and how they fit the music, and writes about its various accretions and variants – including some of which he disapproves, claiming they came from gypsy culture. Several musical examples show how the poetry fits the music, and how the castanets can superimpose cross-rhythms. It remains the most detailed study of the dance to this day.

THE SPANISH GUITAR IN PARIS

In 1826 – another period of intense emigration – Sor had been joined by another Spanish virtuoso guitarist, Dionisio Aguado, who was perhaps not forced to flee Spain for political reasons, but rather realised that a guitarist could profit from the burgeoning enthusiasm for the instrument in France, without doubt fostered by Sor's presence there. Their techniques differed completely – Sor advocated plucking with the nails, Aguado recommended the flesh of the fingers – but they existed in mutual respect, and both wrote treatises in which there is absolutely no mention of the Spanish roots of guitar playing. Quite the reverse: Sor's treatise seems deliberately to marginalise his own encounter with the Spanish guitar and instead relates the origin

26 '... la viveza del ritmo aventajan con mucho á las de Manuel García é Yradier. Débense sobre todo á Sors algunos boleros que son verdaderas joyas.' Quoted Brian Jeffrey, introduction to Fernando Sor, *Seguidillas* (London, 1976) p. 9.

Plate 1.4 Example 6 from Fernando Sor's article 'Séguedille-Boléro' in Ledhuy and Bertini's *Encyclopédie pittoresque de la musique* (Paris, 1835). This was the most detailed article ever written on the Seguidilla-Bolero. Extending to 12 densely printed pages with diagrams, it details the origins of the dance and literary forms, the music, the text, and the dance steps and choreography.

of guitar playing to the seventeenth-century French guitar composer Robert de Visée. Like Sor's, most of Aguado's compositions are in a classical style – an exception is his *Fandango*; he largely kept Spanish music as an exotic sideline, only occasionally to be brought out for inspection.

Another regular guitar player in Paris was Trinidad Huerta, who according to several commentators combined the sublime with the vulgar. He had arrived in Paris with the second crucial wave of émigrés – liberals who were forced to flee after the re-establishment of the monarchy – in 1823. Mitjana recounts how he would pepper his playing with *rasgueadas* (strumming), regarded in more sophisticated circles as rather bad taste, but delighting those thirsty for a romantic-exotic *frisson*.[27]

JOSÉ MELCHIOR GOMIS

Another important *afrancesado* forced to flee north was the composer José Melchior Gomis, who came from yet another region of Spain: the town of Ontinyent, inland from Valencia. After enjoying the brief period during which liberalism flourished in Madrid (1820–1823, the so-called 'liberal triennium'), he was caught up in the violent and bloody reaction against it which followed the fall of Trocadero – a fort near Cadiz, the last bastion of the *liberales*. He escaped to Paris in July 1823. This second wave of emigrations was a result of the restoration of the absolutism in the person of Fernando VII, after which, once again, liberal sympathizers were rounded up and executed.

Once in Paris, Gomis quickly joined the Spaniards already established there. There were many: intellectuals, poets, artists, bankers and even clergy, kept under strict surveillance by the French police. One centre in Paris particularly favoured by musicians was the area around the Hotel Favart, where salons were regularly held, not least due to the proprietress Madame Mestrallet, who had developed a passion for Spanish music. Among them were the Madrileño composer and pianist Santiago de Marsanau, who had also fled north and had gained a reputation in London, and Ramón Carnicer, who achieved fame as composer of the Chilean national anthem.[28] The rue de Marivaux, where Gomis lived, was just a step away from the Théâtre Italien, now the site of the Opéra-Comique, the second Salle Favart. The area also drew other Spaniards – bankers and other artists among them. Most famously, for two months from June 1824 the painter Goya also sojourned

27 'Huerta était un virtuose étrange, plein tout à la fois d'extravagance et de génie. Peu musicien, il accompagnait ses mélodies par des harmonies souvent fort peu correctes. Il avait des procédés d'un goût douteux, comme celui qu'il appelait *tutti* et qui était une sorte de *rasgueado* dont l'effet gâtait parfois les plus délicats passages.' Rafael Mitjana, 'Histoire de la musique : Espagne', in *Encylopédie de la musique et dictionnaire du Conservatoire*, 1ère partie (Paris, 1920), p. 2349.

28 Gomis's biographer, Rafael Gisbert, cites an informative document from the Archives nationales dating from September 1825 concerning Marsanau, who mixed with other Spanish musicians living, like him, in the rue de Marivaux: 'quelques espagnols qui se livrent comme lui à l'étude de la musique et qui logent également rue Marivaux'. Rafael Gisbert, *José Melchior Gomis: Un músico romántico y su tiempo* (Ointinyent, 1988), p. 79n.

in the area, travelling north not for political reasons but, frail and old, to take medicinal waters.[29]

The émigrés supported one another, and Gomis needed it. Garcia knew all the major figures of the Paris musical establishment – especially Rossini – but also Cherubini, the Italian Ferdinando Paër, and later Liszt, who taught the piano to his daughter Pauline. Her husband, Louis Viardot (1800–1883), nine years younger than Gomis, has already been mentioned as a Hispanophile but he also became a friend and collaborator of Gomis, writing the libretto for his first opera, *La favori*. Like Sor, Gomis published a steady stream of what might be called pseudo-Spanish compositions: essentially Spanish-language songs with a few Spanish inflections – mostly rhythmic – but essentially in the Italian style and with harmonies more Rossinian than Andalusian.

Gomis's Spanish songs are appealing and skilful, and steer a course midway between the Italian fever and Romantic Spanishness. Although published in Paris, they were often promoted in several languages – French, Spanish and English. Like several other Spanish musicians and composers Gomis also enjoyed much success in London, not least because his Spanish-style music found favour with the increasing number of *afrancesados* who had settled there (where they congregated in Somerstown, a little north of King's Cross). His *canción* 'El Corazón en venta' [The Heart for Sale] became particularly popular, and it should be remembered that popular songs inevitably found their way into *zarzuelas*, widely performed among the Spanish communities in Paris. Although Rossinian, its *estribillo* (refrain) consists mostly of ululation – '¡Ays!' – embellished with Spanish ornaments, even though its harmonic underlay, and its indulgence in Italian idiosyncrasies and modulations, brands it as a hybrid.

Meanwhile, Romanticism had taken its hold on France, and the Spanish influx proved to be something of a catalyst to the movement. Instead of Spain being regarded as an undeveloped place, inhabited by the uncultured, the violent and the half-Arab primitives, it began to appear as an exotic place whose culture had appeal. Its 'wildness' was suddenly attractive, as was its position as halfway to Africa: a melting pot of the Muslim and the Christian. The legacy of the first *afrancesados* was prolonged. Others entered the field and printed music in the Spanish vein proliferated. Parisian publishing houses had become the main disseminators of émigré Spanish music from the 1830s, and Spanish-style music went into many reprints. By the time Bizet's research for *Carmen* began, the Bibliothèque nationale had amassed a vast corpus for him to consult in modelling his opera, and we know that he frequented this

29 A full account of Spanish musician-émigrés to Paris will be found in Montserrat Bergadà, 'Musiciens espagnols à Paris entre 1820 et 1868', in Louis Jambou (ed.), *La Musique entre France et Espagne* (Paris, 2003), pp. 17–38.

library and asked to access this repertoire, quite apart from the Spanish music in his own carefully documented collection.[30]

SPANISH MUSIC AT THE TIME OF *CARMEN*

Towards the time when Bizet embarked upon *Carmen,* there was a notable change in the way in which Spanish music was presented: it could be said that it became less 'authentic' and more romanticised. This chapter has deliberately excluded discussion of the new fashion for Latin-American music, which will be discussed in relation to *Carmen*'s celebrated Habanera, but two examples of the way in which Spanish pieces were presented serve well as a conclusion to this discussion of *hispanomanie,* first a curious version of a song, 'L'Éventail', by the celebrated Mariano Soriano Fuertes, published in France around 1870. The piece, presented in a piano score, also includes two separate vocal parts – in Spanish and French respectively – both with notated parts for the fan, with detailed indications of how the fan should be rhythmically agitated.

Soriano Fuertes was not only a composer important for the development of the *zarzuela* but was also a scholar and prolific writer on music, including a ground-breaking study of the cross-cultural relations between Spanish and Arabic music.[31] It is hardly surprising that his songs reflect his studies. His output as a writer far exceeded his compositional production, but the songs he produced and published in Paris are not without interest. His musicological erudition had clearly caused him to analyse the scalic and harmonic features of Andalusian music, which were also known to Bizet. Those features have been described in many ways, and will be returned to later, but essentially involve prominent use of the flattened scale steps above both the tonic and dominant. The essence of the music is ambiguity as to its tonic, which often seems to be the dominant – a process that has been referred to as 'dual tonicity' and which is evident at several numbers in *Carmen.*[32]

30 See Winton Dean, *Georges Bizet: His Life and Work,* rev. ed. (London, 1965), p. 229. Dean claims that a member of staff of the Conservatoire library in Paris found an application slip bearing the words 'I request a list of the Spanish songs in the possession of the library' – BIZET. No original source is given. The inventory of his own collection of scores still exists in the Bibliothèque nationale de France. It contained the anthology of Spanish music by Paul Lacome and several songs by Sebastian Yradier.

31 Mariano Soriano Fuertes, *Música árabe española y conexión de la música con la astronomía, medicina y arquitectura* (Barcelona, 1853).

32 See Peter Manuel, 'From Scarlatti to "Guantanamera": Dual tonicity in Spanish and Latin-American Musics', *Journal of the American Musicological Society,* 55 (2002), pp. 311–336.

Plate 1.5 Cover of the sheet music for Soriano Fuertes's 'L'Éventail' [El Abanico; The Fan] (Paris, c.1870).

Faut-il croire aux assurances des galants ?
Oh ! Non, señor, non, señor !
Ils nous leurrent d'espérances ;
Ce sont tous les bouches d'or !
Qui ce sont des bouches d'or Ah !------
Ma souveraine, L'amour m'enchaîne,
D'amour, ma reine,
Je meurs pour toi !
Et pour qu'il vive, Elle craintive,
Réponds naïve : Oui, sois mon roi !
Mais ... brise folle Que sa parole !
Dans sa parole, D'amour fait peu !

Coups d'éventail
Ah que ce temps m'agite ! Du vent ! bien vite !
L'air est de feu ! En mes mains d'espagnole
Éventail, vole ! L'air est en feu. Quel ciel de feu !

Must one believe the assurances of gallants?
Oh no, señor, oh no!
They deceive our hopes
With their golden words
Which say: 'Ah!------
My sovereign, Love has ensnared me
with love, my Queen!
I am dying for you!'
And to keep him alive, she, fearfully
replies, naively: 'Yes be my King!'
But foolish breeze, how his words
say nothing of love!

Waving the fan
Ah how this weather troubles me. Air please, and quickly!
The air is on fire. But fly, fan, in my Spanish hands.
The air is on fire, the sky is on fire.

Example 1.5 Vocal part of Soriano Fuertes's 'El Abanico', with indications for the movements of the fan.

While Soriano's notation of a part for a fan is unusual, the fan was nonetheless one of the most popular artefacts associated with Spain, ubiquitous in paintings of *majas*.

A version of Garcia's 'Cuerpo bueno, alma divina' presented in the dual-language French and Spanish collection *Échos d'Espagne*, dating from 1872, is also of particular interest since it forms the basis for the final entr'acte in *Carmen*. Although the French translations are very free and the *polo* is turned into a salon song with piano accompaniment ('Tu dors, la belle amoureuse'), the arranger, Lacome, gives it a quiet rippling piano part transposed down into C minor, which is not at all a Spanish key (most of Garcia's *boleros* were in the guitar keys of E or A minor). His arrangement is interesting. The song would at first seem to have been so 'Frenchified', made to suit a salon without guitars or castanets in sight, that its Spanishness has been entirely tamed, if not almost obliterated. The spiky octave accompaniment of the original is replaced with a piano part based on an Alberti bass, thus diluting the *polo* rhythm. Yet Lacome puts a curious but illuminating instruction at the head of the score:

> This beautiful serenade is very popular in the whole of the southern Spain where the clement weather and the gentle nights are well suited to this pleasant amorous pastime. It must be sung in a half-tint, and in a tremulous voice.[33]

Talk about Romanticism! What was an energetic *polo* has been turned into a *rêverie*, and Lacome's claim that it was a popular twilight song in Andalusia is highly suspect in terms of authenticity but interesting in terms of marketing. Bizet's adaptation of the *polo* for the final entr'acte of *Carmen* reverts to a less abstruse key, and has nothing of the twilight love-song prescribed by this edition; his adaptation is considerably more muscular, and he may well have got it from an earlier, more virile, source. The description of the half-light singing does ring true with the tentative opening Bizet uses for the Gypsy 'carousel' – the *Chanson bohème* – at the beginning of Act II of *Carmen*, which uses the traditional guitar key of E minor and begins the gypsy scene very quietly with fluttering flutes.

33 'Cette belle sérénade est très populaire dans tout le sud de l'Espagne où la clémence du ciel et des nuits discrètes permettent encore cet amoureux passe-temps. Elle doit se chanter en demi-teinte, et d'une voix tremblotante.' The editors wrongly attribute the number to 'El poeta calculista'. P. Lacome and J. Puig y Alsubide, *Échos d'Espagne : Chansons & danses populaires* (Paris, 1872). Lacome, who spent many months of each year in his home village Le Houga, in the Pyrenees, close to Spain, was a friend of Chabrier.

Plate 1.6 Ornate title page of *Échos d'Espagne : Chansons et danses populaires*, ed. P. Lacome and J. Puig y Alsubide (1872). These are dual-language versions of popular songs. Note the stereotypical images of the woman on the first floor looking down at a street scene with dancers. The tower of La Giralda is superimposed on the background.

Échos d'Espagne was the sequel to another collection, the undated *Fleurs d'Espagne*, and Lacome's preface to the volume stresses the anonymity of all the songs, apart from Garcia's *polo.* Lacome, who originated from near to the Spanish border, was important in the dissemination of Spanish music in the second half of the century and his mission – rather similar to that of Canteloube later on – was 'to guard against the surprises of novelty' by preserving the heritage of the old world, in his case of Spain.[34] This one-page preface was important in that for the first time it pointed out the wide variety of the

34 'Le monde est si vieux, et nous en savons si peu l'histoire, qu'il est bon de se tenir en garde contre les surprises de la nouveauté, car l'invention n'est souvent que de la transformation, et le neuf le renouvelé.' *Le Ménestrel*, 18 June 1886.

Example 1.6 Opening of 'Cuerpo bueno' ('Tu dors, la belle amoureuse'), as arranged in *Échos d'Espagne*.

POLO[1]

SÉRÉNADE.

Transcrite par **J. PUIG Y ALSUBIDE.** Traduite par **P. LACOME.**

Cette belle sérénade est très populaire dans tout le sud de l'Espagne où la clémence du ciel et les nuits discrètes permettent encore cet amoureux passe-temps. Elle doit se chanter en demi-teinte, et d'une voix tremblotante.

(1) Ce POLO est tiré d'un opéra de Manuel Garcia.(*) Les éditeurs ont reçu de Madame Pauline Viardot-Garcia et de Monsieur Manuel Garcia (fils) la gracieuse autorisation de le publier dans ce recueil.
(*) EL POETA CALCULISTA.

D. S.

music of Spain. While claiming that Spanish music was 'the least European of our continent', he stresses that 'Spain is a political mosaic of diverse provinces quite indifferent to each other and will never be the victim of centralization. It follows that Spain has as many genres of music as it does provinces.' Distinguishing two basic traditions, between the north and south with a dividing-line at the 'Caliphate of Cordoba', he observes that the former is mainly monorhythmic, while the latter is polyrhythmic, delighting in 'the superimposition of different rhythms in the melody and accompaniment'. Emmanuel Chabrier's notation of these superimposed rhythms rings true with Lacome's remark – he had noted superimposed rhythms from the streets of Seville and Granada, and incorporated them into his *España*. Although that piece postdates *Carmen*, Bizet clearly observed similar features that emerge in the Spanish numbers in *Carmen*, albeit to a lesser degree.

While many of Garcia's published songs have few Spanish characteristics except for the words, his *canciones* were many times selected and printed in other collections, keeping them in the public eye throughout the nineteenth century. Naturally many of these capitalized on the reputation of his daughters, whose names appear on many sheet-music editions from 1830 onwards, when Malibran was at the height of her fame. An edition of the famous *caballo* known as *El contrabandista*, published by Pacini, indicates that she sang it in Rossini's *Barber of Seville*, while a German edition published in 1838 – two years after her untimely death in Manchester – advertises the piece as a 'Tirana sung in every concert by Mme. Malibran'. Malibran and her sister sang together in salons.

Later in the century Pauline Viardot and Manuel Garcia Jr were active in promoting their father's works. In the case of Pauline it cannot be claimed that her Spanish heritage was of major importance in the development of her career, though it might have played a more prominent role had she not fallen under the spell of the literary figure Ivan Turgenev. Rather than adding a musical dimension to her husband Louis's Spanish connections, she spent a lot of time singing and composing in Russian. However, there was a Spanish side: even early in her career she was well known for her singing of Chopin mazurkas to whose melodies she added Spanish words, though these were published only later with words in French and German.[35] Bursts of nostalgia perhaps, or her well-known eye for a market, also resulted in some Spanish songs mainly brought out in the 1840s and 1850s, which she frequently per-

35 See Patrick Waddington, *The Musical Works of Pauline Viardot-Garcia (1821–1910)* (Upper Hutt, New Zealand, 2004).

formed in concerts.[36] In 1875, the same year as the premiere of *Carmen*, she brought out an album of her father's songs, provided 'with new accompaniments by Mme Viardot' and with their Spanish texts translated into French. Her contribution to the development of 'Spanish fever' was perhaps modest, but it should not be forgotten.

THE 'BASQUE DANDY' AND THE EMPRESS

The last figure who must be introduced into this tableaux of Spanish Francophiles was perhaps the most important because Bizet openly modelled what is arguably the most important moment in *Carmen* – and the most celebrated – on one of his songs, or at least on one he presented. This is Sebastian Yradier (or Iradier, 1809–1865), a Basque composer – one commentator has called him the 'Basque Dandy' – who arrived in Paris in the 1850s. One of his pieces, an *habanera* called *El arreglito* [The Betrothal], would eventually be Bizet's model for Carmen's introductory dance-song in the opera. (The full story – as much as we know it – will be recounted in a later chapter.)[37]

Yradier came from Lanciego, near Ávala in the Alta Rioja, and studied and worked as an organist in Vitoria, the very place where the celebrated battle had resulted in the Napoleonic defeat. There is no evidence that he was forced to flee, since he came of age long after that battle, but he was known as a liberal, and his charmed life – where luck seemed always to be on his side – led him to follow the paths of the earlier *afrancesados*. His teenage skills were as a *tiple* (treble) and organist, and his native town was a magnet for musicians since it housed a very fine organ – the oldest in the province. His liberalism might have been a factor, even if not the deciding one, in his move to Madrid in 1833. His skills in ecclesiastical music supported him there at first, but he also infiltrated society salons, where he taught the guitar and singing. Gradually he veered away from the church and towards secular music, and in particular the heritage of Spanish song.

In 1840 he brought out the important and beautifully produced *Album filarmónico*, which presented some Spanish songs with accompaniments, interspersed with finely detailed engravings of scenes of Spanish life; by this time there was clearly a market for printed music with such illustrations, particularly those depicting Andalusian life. The print run, according Yradier's biographer, Val, ran only to 100. The Bibliothèque nationale did not (and

36 Waddington, *The Musical Works*, lists 'Los oficialitos' and 'La jota de los estudiantes' as her best-known Spanish pieces.

37 See Venancio del Val, *Sebastián Yradier*, Los Alaveses 10 (Álava, 1994).

does not) hold a copy, though it is inconceivable that Yradier would not have brought examples of this elegant publication to Paris where he was to move ten years later, joining the community of musicians already established there.

Undoubtedly the most important introduction of Yradier's life after his move to Madrid was his entrance into the Montijo household. María Manuela Montijo was a society figure married to a military *afrancesado* (who was partly Scottish) and a close friend of Mérimée; she was even perhaps – as will be explored – an influence on his composition of the *Carmen* novella. She engaged Yradier to teach her two daughters, Eugenia and Maria Francisca. Yradier encountered Eugenia (the younger daughter) during her teens, and from this felicitous meeting grew a lasting relationship with her and her family that essentially launched his career. In 1844 he accompanied *sevillanas* at a fiftieth-birthday celebration for Madame de Montijo.

Yradier's activities blossomed in Madrid, not least because song-composers, if they had a 'hit', would have their songs incorporated into *zarzuelas*, which were then performed in the various theatres of Madrid and the Spanish provinces. Famous singers took up Yradier's songs: Francisco Salas was one, and there were Italian singers who also performed them, not least in the late 1840s when the 'Zarzuela nueva' was born. Yradier's 'El Charrán' [The Salamancan] was incorporated into stage shows alongside Garcia's now ubiquitous 'Yo que soy contrabandista'.

In 1850, Mme de Montijo (now Countess of Montijo) was 41 and her daughter the Condesa de Teba (Eugenia, now going by the French version of her name, Eugénie) was 24. They moved to Paris and Yradier followed them, not for political reasons, although he was a confirmed *afrancesado* if ever there was one. He soon made important contacts and friends there, among them the dancers Maria Taglioni, Fanny Elssler and Carlota Grisi, as well as Louis Viardot. Yradier's songs became known in all the fashionable places, and though he had none of the effeminacy suggested by his appellation 'The Basque Dandy', the name was not far off the mark: he was certainly attractive, good at making friends and always 'rodeado de damas' ('surrounded by women'). He brought out albums of his more popular songs in French editions, and the *Fleurs d'Espagne* subsequently published by Schott in Mainz. More common was the 1865 edition, several times reprinted with French words. A far cry from the earlier editions with engravings, this was a workaday, budget-price collection of Yradier's greatest hits without any visual embellishment.[38]

Meanwhile, the Montijos had quickly established themselves in Paris society and their circle included events at the Elysée Palace. Eugénie, in her

38 *Chansons espagnoles del Maestro Yradier*, ed. Paul Bernard and D. Tagliafico (Paris, 1865).

twenties, was renowned for her ease and charm in salon life in the higher echelons of society, and it was at the Elysée Palace that she encountered her future husband – none other than Napoleon III, the nephew of Napoleon I. Yradier's pupil and friend had reached the pinnacle of French society and was even its regent when her husband was away. Yradier was thus a central member of the royal court.

He lived two lives according to his biographer, Venancio del Val: on the one hand he was a bohemian who frequented the low-life taverns of Paris, and on the other he dressed up to attend society events held by the aristocracy, where he was equally at ease. Musically his most important contributions to French music were his importations from Latin America, notably of the *habanera,* a new form that became all the rage in both France and Spain during the 1860s. Yradier published many of these in Paris, and it is well known that Bizet adapted one of them – some might say diluted it – for Carmen's entry. Yradier's song *El arreglito,* on which his *habanera* is based, has been many times reprinted and discussed. Suffice to say that its innovation lay in not modulating. It veers from tonic major to tonic minor, as did its models. Its characterization of Carmen is superb, offering an essentially performative dance-song to show off her assets: physical, vocal and choreographic.

This chapter has dealt with some repercussions of a few key events in European history, and with a few important immigrants out of many more. A wider context now needs to be sketched in: first, that of French travellers and tourists (including artists) who propagated the mania for *andalucismo* in their native country; and second, the question of how the stage for *Carmen* was prepared in the theatres of Paris – theatres that were multiplying because of post-Revolutionary legislation allowing their unlicensed establishment. These stages hosted a wealth of both home-grown and imported performances, heightening the Spanish fever already contracted in the salons. Added to this will be the contribution made by the visual arts and literature.

CHAPTER TWO

Pictures and Jottings: *Carmen* and the Rise of Andalusian Tourism

THE scenic aspect of the first productions of *Carmen* sprang from impetuses that had burgeoned since the 1830s, fuelled particularly by French and English travellers to Spain who became inquisitive about what they saw as a curiously beautiful, wild and dangerous country. Included among these travellers were many who were in some way involved in the operatic productions.[1] First, there was interest in the legacy of Spain's buildings, ancient and modern. Second – and this came later – was an interest in its customs, traditions and ceremonies, which were very different from those even in meridional France, and extremely different from those in London.

For these professional travellers – some earning their keep by the pen, the pencil or the brush – Spain began to romanticise itself, particularly by exporting its image in terms of Andalusia, the region furthest from northern Europe geographically and in many other ways, being, as it was, half-European, half-African. In the scenography of the two Parisian set-designers who fashioned *Carmen*'s first production (1875), and its second staging in 1898 with new sets by Lucien Jusseaume, both features are clear: representation of Andalusian customs is set against the architectural background of Seville and its environs, which opera-goers were invited to travel to in the imagination, aided by realistic sets and, in the outer acts, the ubiquitous tower of the Giralda in the background.

The stage-directions to the opera show a knowledgeable exploitation of the stereotypical customs and costumes documented in jottings and portrayed in images increasingly disseminated from the 1830s onwards. At curtain up, revealing the goings on in an urban plaza, the principal players are the costume-designers and the scenographers, who create an unusually lively *tableau*

1 See Michela Niccolai, '*Carmen* Dusted Down', in Langham Smith and Rowden, Carmen *Abroad* (Cambridge, 2020), chapter four.

vivant of a busy square in Seville, populated with *majos* and *majas* engaging in flirtation and banter, and no doubt some petty crime. The music need not be terribly interesting at this point: more important is the audience's appreciation of this exotic scene: the 'drôles de gens' ('strange people') neither behaving nor dressing like the French or, for that matter, like the people of Spain's more northerly provinces. Bizet appropriately provides a few bars of nothing much to go under the customary applause as the opening set is revealed.

Never mind what was true and what was exaggerated: in the mid-nineteenth century romanticised Spain was becoming ripe for both the balletic and the operatic stages. Even though there were many attempts to portray it before *Carmen*, few could disagree that Bizet's opera was the most durable portrayal of exoticised Andalusia to date. Mérimée had incorporated a great deal of realistic detail into his story of the 1840s, and much of it was retained in the opera thirty years later, to which the librettists added more.

A REVERSE FLOW

As has been outlined in Chapter One, there was a massive exodus of refugees northwards in the immediate wake of critical moments in Spanish history: the defeat of Napoleon, the invasion of the Carlists and persecution around the time of the *trienio liberal* (1820–1823). By contrast, the 1830s began to see a reverse flow: a growing influx of travellers from northern countries attracted by the opening up of Spain, which was gradually transforming itself. Once seen as a barbaric, feudal place it now began to be viewed as an exotic paradise with a rich heritage of historical treasures from Roman, Moorish and, later, Spanish cultures. Travellers who had formerly been fascinated by the Grand Tour through France, via Switzerland and the Italian lakes, and then to the great cities further south, had identified a new must-see destination. It was under the regency of Isabella II (1833–1840) that the Spanish tourist industry really began, founding an infrastructure that flourishes to this day.[2]

Interesting though the English visitors are (and not entirely irrelevant to the background to *Carmen*), it is the French image of Spain on which any study of how *Carmen* came to the stage must focus. Souvenirs of Spain took many forms, from poems, long letters and detailed accounts to large-format books embellished with engravings of varying degrees of detail and luxury as printing technology progressed. Images of Spain became tantalisingly available to would-be tourists.

2 Luis Méndez Rodríguez, *La imagen de Andalucía en el arte del siglo XIX* (Seville, 2008).

Two landmark publications, both weighty tomes, can be staked out at opposite ends of the heyday of Romanticism, well illustrating the changing appeal of Spain for northern Europeans. The first is the three-part travelogue *Voyage pittoresque en Espagne* by the French traveller Baron Taylor, its first volume published in 1826 without illustrations, but the second and third copiously illustrated with engravings done in both Paris and London, from originals by various artists.[3] These largely focus on Spain's architectural heritage – churches, bridges and ruins – though there is an extensive section on the various stages of a bullfight, each part illustrated with an engraving. The second publication is Baron Davillier's *L'Espagne,* first published serially in the periodical *Le Tour du monde* in the 1860s, finely illustrated by Gustave Doré. This was republished as a lavishly produced book that achieved considerable fame in 1874, just before the appearance of Bizet's opera. It soon appeared in Italian, English and American editions, but not until 1949 did a complete (very skewed) Spanish translation appear.[4] Both Taylor's and Davillier's books were celebrated and canonical, yet they trace a distinct change of approach, essentially from a fascination with the monuments of Spain to more of a focus on its present-day customs, its modernity and the vivacity of its people at both work and play.

Mérimée's *Carmen* stood midway between the two, not only in terms of when it was written but also straddling these two broad approaches. His main employment was as an inspector of public monuments, a job to which he had been appointed in 1830, one of his responsibilities being to allocate funds for their restoration and maintenance. Thus it is hardly surprising that the particular interest of the cultured narrator in his *Carmen* is in Spain's buildings, ruins and antiquities: a similar approach predominates in Baron Taylor's *Voyage pittoresque.* The learned narrator in Mérimée's novella, in search of Roman remains, tells his tale with academic footnotes peppered with Ancient Greek and Latin, but he becomes caught up in the intrigues of the stereotypical figures of Andalusian culture so evocatively illustrated by Davillier: soldiers, bandits, smugglers and, above all, gypsies.

More to the foreground in the opera than in the novella is the armed force – the soldiers or perhaps the *Guardia civil,* which was founded just before Mérimée wrote *Carmen* and whose primary purposes were to flush out bandits and quell social unrest, though they were also tasked with keeping order among the *cigarières* and guarding the tobacco factory. Dating is important here, since the foundation of the *Guardia civil* in 1844 was a major event

3 Justin (Baron) Taylor, *Voyage pittoresque en Espagne, en Portugal et sur la côte d'Afrique, de Tanger à Tétouan,* 3 vols (Paris, 1826 [vol. 1], 1832 [vols 2 and 3]); consultable on Gallica.

4 Le Baron Charles Davillier, *Espagne,* illustrated by Gustave Doré (Paris, 1862; rpt. 1874). First published serially from 1860 in *Le Tour du monde.*

responding to a dramatic rise in 'la delincuencia y el bandidaje' ('lawlessness and banditry'), particularly in Andalusia, where more squadrons of the *Guardia* were posted than anywhere else.[5] Their smart uniforms must have attracted a good deal of attention in the major cities.

While Baron Taylor had occasionally paid some attention to more human activities – moving beyond the contemplation of convents and sailing scenes – the majority of his illustrations were fairly static and, although they display an academic interest in the regional variations of local costume, the pictures seem lifeless in comparison with Doré's, which, however romanticised and exaggerated, are always very much flesh and blood. Even in Taylor's sections on the various stages of the bullfight, which describe its horrors in some detail, the accompanying pictures evoke little movement and his prose is uninvolved. How much artistic portrayal had evolved by the time of Doré, who really makes you feel that bullfighters are jumping across the barrier of the bullring in fear for their lives! When Doré portrays buildings – such as the tobacco factory – he populates them, the expression of each and every person carefully crafted to convey their emotions. Contrasting the approaches of Taylor and Davillier also brings to the surface another diametric opposition in nineteenth-century representations of Spain: that of bland, decorative portrayal versus illustrations that imply social criticism and use engaged observation and sometimes caricature. Taylor adhered to the former while Doré was a social commentator in whatever he drew.

In between these landmark publications were several others of considerable interest. For example, in 1830 Alfred de Musset had published his *Contes d'Espagne et d'Italie,* while one of the next reporters was Mérimée himself. His first visit, in 1831, resulted in his *Lettres d'Espagne,* which were a direct influence on his *Carmen* of ten years later. Dealing with an execution, a meeting with a bandit and a bullfight, traces of the *Lettres* infiltrate the opera libretto.

Among the most important travelogues on Spain from organised adventurers was the four-volume *L'Espagne sous Ferdinand VII* by the Marquis de Custine, which came out in 1838; the 1840s then produced a wealth of more realistic memoirs, headed by Théophile Gautier's *Voyage en Espagne* of 1843. A forerunner of the modern guide-book writer, Gautier divides his book into chapters about each of the places he visits. A succession of memoirs postdating Mérimée's novella, but well-known before the librettists' adaptation, can also be added to the inventory; among many others one might mention Edgar Quinet's *Mes vacances en Espagne* of 1846, Alexandre Dumas's *Impressions de voyage de Paris à Cadiz* (1847–1849), and the finely illustrated *L'Espagne pittoresque* of Cuendias and Féréal, dating from 1848.

5 See José María Bueno Carrera, *La Guardia Civil: su historia, organización y sus uniformes* (Madrid, 1997).

THE *COSTUMBRISTAS*

Beside these writers – and certainly no less important – was the increasing interest in regional customs shown by the Spanish artists, and some writers, who have become known as the *costumbristas*, a term implying an interest in local customs, but also an archive of costume and an emphasis of the common activities of daily life, people at work or at play. The movement began to flourish during the 1830s after the death of Ferdinand VII, in part due to liberal reforms and the rise of a wealthier bourgeoisie with money to spend on the arts.

A significant figure in the politics and growing economic prosperity of Spain in the 1830s, including its opening up to travellers, was the economist and politician Juan Álvarez Mendizábal (1790–1853). His reforms encouraged the establishment of art-schools and salons and had a positive effect on Spanish visual art in particular. He had been involved in the financing of cripplingly expensive military campaigns under Ferdinand and several times was forced to flee into exile. But with an ally in the liberal regent Maria Cristina, he was to become in charge of the Spanish treasury in 1835. In the single masterstroke for which he is remembered, he put the heavily indebted Spanish economy back on its feet in what is known as the *desamortización de Mendizábal*. Effectively, he stripped the monasteries of all their assets, forcing many to close, and paid off the national debt; a new measure of prosperity resulted.

In a curious way, the rapid advances Spain underwent during the late 1830s, as well as the memory of its years of French occupation, fuelled the preservation of its ancient customs. The Marquis de Custine remarked upon this change in some detail in his jottings of 1838, referring back to a visit earlier in the 1830s:

> You will find in the descriptions of places and portraits of people I have seen in Spain, a portrait of a society which already does not exist any more. [...] If Spain, as it was six years ago, surpassed all my hopes, the revolution which has just taken place has shown that my view of how it would develop was entirely misguided. The belief in chivalry, the religious faith, the Romantic spirit imposed on everyday life by the old idea of mediaeval honour and by the monastic religion of early Christianity: all of the past is alive, still active, living, in these people – the most independent of all peoples, who refuse to be a part of the new European confederation. [...] these people alone want nothing else than to live according to the ideas handed down from their forefathers.[6]

6 'On trouvera, dans les descriptions des lieux et dans les portraits des personnes que j'ai vues en Espagne, le tableau d'une société qui n'existe déjà plus. [...] Si l'Espagne, telle qu'elle était il y a six ans, a surpassé mon espoir, la révolution qui vient de s'opérer dans

Both writers and visual artists began to produce images of the 'Old Spain', a major impetus behind the *costumbrismo* movement: the representation of people going about their business in their idiosyncratic way – and showing off their clothes.

Knowledge of Spanish painting in France can broadly be divided into two main trends, the first of which is only distantly relevant to *Carmen*. This is the exportation to France of masterworks of pre-nineteenth-century painting – *La Grande Peinture* – particularly by such painters as Murillo, Velázquez, Ribera and Zubarán. Baron Taylor himself sent 464 paintings back to Paris around 1830. An even greater number were exported – often stolen or obtained by threat or extortion – by Maréchal Soult, Napoleon's commander in Andalusia, who, at the end of the war of independence, made off with no fewer than 109 Spanish paintings, gathered through long-term systematic theft. The quality of Spanish painting was no longer in doubt among the French. By the time Louis Philippe founded the Galérie Espagnole in the Louvre in 1838, Spanish masterpieces were well known in Paris. Although their images were a far cry from anything related to *Carmen*, either novella or libretto, they securely identified Spain as a place of culture and considerable interest to the French, not least to painters such as Manet.

More important for the genesis of *Carmen* was the export to France of images by (or after) the *costumbristas*, whether in the form of books of engravings, lithographs, daguerreotypes or paintings. Popularising images of all the stereotypes with which both novella and opera engage, there is hardly a scene in the opera whose essence could not be found in one of these works.

Primarily centred on Andalusia – particularly Seville and Malaga – these painters coincided with that region's becoming increasingly idealised, to the point where its customs came to represent Spain as a whole – a movement now known as *Andalucismo*. Essentially, the region became seen as an exotic paradise, particularly because of its costumes, dances and music, forgetting that it had more illiteracy than the north, and a feudal system ignoring abject poverty. To the outside world Andalusia represented 'Old Spain' more than any other region. Between north and south was the Sierra Morena, which many saw as the meeting place of the occidental with the oriental. Painters contributed to the popularisation of this landscape and its edifices, which

ce pays, a également trompé mes prévisions. La foi chevaleresque, la foi religieuse, les formes romantiques imposes à l'existence sociale par le vieil honneur du moyen âge et par la religion claustrale des premiers siècles du christianisme ; tout notre passé était debout, en action, vivant, chez ce peuple indépendant de tous les peuples, et qui refusait de s'associer à la nouvelle confédération européenne. [...] ce peuple seul ne voulait vivre que des idées qu'il avait reçues de ses pères.' Marquis de Custine, *L'Espagne sous Ferdinand VII*, vol. 1 (Paris, 1838), pp. 65–68.

they often populated so as to present 'moments' of Andalusian life, as had the celebrated *Escenas andaluzas* by Serafín Calderón, a literary *costumbrista* from Malaga.[7] Calderón corresponded with Mérimée, who had met him around 1830 and accompanied him on his first visit to Spain. Mérimée was certainly familiar with Calderón's book, which brought *costumbrismo* in literature together with illustration, since the book was embellished with 125 engravings by the Andalusian artist Francisco Lameyer y Berenguer (1825–1877), who visited Paris several times. However alien some of the *costumbrista* images must have seemed to the French – bulls goring *toreros* or being attacked with exploding picks, garrotted criminals, drunks in inns, Romantic suicides, stagecoaches being robbed – the idealisation of Andalusia as a 'promised land', an earthly paradise, became magnetic despite (or perhaps because of) its darker sides. This paradox runs through Mérimée's novella, and is retained in some of the spoken dialogue of Act I of the opera.

Custine confessed that 'he couldn't write the word Andalusia without his heart missing a beat'.[8] He continues by adopting a theme shared among several of the *viajeros* coming from France, pinpointing the descent from the Sierra Morena as the magical moment of transition into this paradise:

> What surprises one, even if you've visited the most beautiful countries of Europe, is the sudden change of vegetation. [...] suddenly you would think you were in a botanical garden of unparalleled richness: the trees, the flowers, the Mediterranean plants are spread out over the rock formations, as if in a hothouse, each layer forming terraces in which each family of plants finds its own place, its own level, the temperature that suits it and its soil; it is huge and beautiful at the same time: it is a fairy garden.[9]

Gautier records the magic of entering Andalusia at exactly the same place. He adds a comment about the unique light, with which many concurred, and links it with the sudden change in descending from the Sierra Morena (the 'dark Sierra'):

7 Serafín Estébanez Calderón, *Escenas Andaluzas: Bizarrias de la tierra* (Madrid, 1847).

8 '... je ne puis écrire ce nom sans un battement de cœur.' Marquis de Custine, *L'Espagne sous Ferdinand VII*, vol. 2 (Paris, 1838), p. 29.

9 'Ce qui surprend, même après avoir vu les plus beaux pays d'Europe, c'est le brusque changement de la végétation. [...] tout à coup on se croit au milieu d'un jardin botanique d'une richesse sans pareille : les arbres, les fleurs, les plantes du Midi, sont rangés sur des gradins de rochers, comme dans une serre ; ces degrés naturels forment des terrasses, où chaque famille végétale trouve sa place, son élévation, sa température, son terrain ; c'est grand et joli tout à la fois : c'est un jardin des fées.' Custine, *L'Espagne sous Ferdinand VII*, vol. 2, pp. 30–31.

Plate 2.1 Francisco Lameyer's frontispiece to the first edition of Calderón's *Escenas andaluzas.*

Laurels, evergreen oaks, cork trees, figs with their shiny, metallic leaves, have something wild about them, robust and savage, which indicates a climate where nature is stronger than the man who passes through it and can do without him. [...] All this is bathed in a sparkling daylight, splendid, as if one had been entering a paradise on earth. The light glimmered in this ocean of mountains like liquid gold and silver, throwing a phosphorescent mist of streaks on everything it touched.[10]

The lighting plans for the opera demonstrate the considerable care that went into this aspect of the first staging, and in Carré's revival of the opera in 1898 this aspect was further refined.[11]

Another commentator, Cuendias, attributes this elevation of the province to heavenly status to the inhabitants themselves, echoing Custine's visceral response even to Andalusian names: 'As an *Andaluz* would say, it is the country of men living in the country of God.' He adds that 'they are right'. 'Andalucía! Jaén! Sevilla! Málaga! Granada! Córdoba! Cádix! Gibraltar! [...] What glorious memories, what poetry there is in those names!'[12] Mérimée had clearly been reading the memoirs of his predecessors, for he puts a very similar phrase into a dialogue between Carmen and the erudite narrator:

– vous êtes probablement de Cordoue ?	– You're probably from Cordoba?
– Non.	– No.
– Vous êtes du moins Andalouse. Il me semble le reconnaître à votre doux parler.	– Well at least you are Andalusian. It seems to me to be evident from your gentle accent.
– Si vous remarquez si bien l'accent du monde, vous devez bien deviner qui je suis.	– If you're so good at recognising the accents of the world, you should be able to guess who I am.
– Je crois que vous êtes du pays de Jésus, à deux pas du paradis.	– I think you are from the country of Jesus, two steps away from paradise.
(J'avais appris cette métaphore, qui désigne l'Andalousie, de mon ami Francisco Sevilla, picador bien connu.)	(I had learned this metaphor, referring to Andalusia, from my friend Francisco Sevilla, the well-known *picador*).
– Bah ! le paradis ... les gens d'ici disent qu'il n'est pas fait pour nous.	– Bah! Paradise! ... the people round here say it wasn't made for the likes of us.

To his romantic vision, Cuendias adds another pertinent comment, again endorsed by many: 'Once one has left the Sierra Morena behind, the aspect

10 'Les lauriers, les chênes verts, les lièges, les figuiers au feuillage verni et métallique, ont quelque chose de libre, de robuste et de sauvage, qui indique un climat où la nature est plus puissante que l'homme et peut se passer de lui. [...] Tout cela était inondé d'un jour étincelant, splendide, comme devait être celui qui éclairait le paradis terrestre.' Théophile Gautier, *Voyage en Espagne* (Paris, 1843), chapter XI.

11 See Niccolai, '*Carmen* Dusted Down'.

12 'La terre des hommes de la terre de Dieu, *la tierra de loz ómbres de la tierra de Dioz* ... Et les Andalous ont raison.' Manuel de Cuendias and V. de Féréal, *L'Espagne, pittoresque, artistique et monumentale, mœurs, usages et coutumes* (Paris, 1848), p. 316.

of the landscape changes completely', he writes, 'it is as if you suddenly pass from Europe to Africa.'

A further writer who must be mentioned was the American Washington Irving, whose *Tales of the Alhambra* was translated into French twice before 1875 and once soon afterwards.[13] His memories were more of the bleak sierras and vast plains sowed with grain crops but devoid of trees and therefore of birdsong. His enthusiasm was saved for the Alhambra itself. The colours and special light remarked upon by so many travellers could never be captured by black-and-white illustrations, and coloured illustrations were in their infancy (Cuendias's book contains a few). Here is where both the *costumbrista* painters and the theatre designers took over. Light and colour were paramount, though we can reconstruct the colours of Bizet's opera only from piecing together written accounts, a few sketches and a surviving but not comprehensive lighting plan.[14] Certainly the colours and light of Andalusia were in everyone's mind when the operatic venture was planned. Whether the terracottas and ochres of Seville's buildings were evident from the first sets is a matter of conjecture, as coloured records are hard to find.

Another aspect of Andalusia immortalised by the *costumbristas* was less paradisal: the countless images of *ventas* and *posadas* (inns and hostels), ranging from crude bawdy-houses with drunks and brawls going on below, to respectable-looking establishments with well-dressed *majos* and accomplished-looking dancers in a perfectly sedate atmosphere (see Plate III). Shared by both are the ubiquitous balconies, often with available – and sometimes tarted-up but unavailable – women leaning over (see Plate II). In Act II of the opera the first set for the tavern was more salubrious than Mérimée's, which drew upon the many reports of *ventas* being dirty, serving poor food, and being frequented by criminals. His narrator slept in an inn where the bed was rife with bed-bugs, and had his watch stolen there. By contrast, the original set for Act II at the premiere of the opera was adorned with exotic palms and (no doubt aromatic) flowering plants: travellers' accounts often mentioned the flowers hanging from the balconies.[15] They certainly look very Andalusian in the fine engraving of the set by Auguste Lamy in *L'Illustration* (see p. 272). Regional flora are also exploited in the episode of Carmen's throwing of a flower at Don

13 Washington Irving, *Les Contes de l'Alhambra*, trans. Mlle A. Sobry (Paris, 1832); and *L'Alhambra, chroniques du pays de Grenade*, trans. P. Christian Lavigne (Paris, 1843).

14 This is to be found in a *livret de mise en scène* of uncertain date, further discussed in Chapter Nine.

15 See illustrations of maquettes made after the set-designs of Lamy in Hervé Lacombe, 'La Création de *Carmen*', reproduced in *De Carmen à Bizet*, catalogue of exhibition held at the Villa Viardot, Bougival, April–June 2001.

José, a detail often misinterpreted by opera producers, which will be further interrogated when Carmen herself is studied in Chapter Eight.

Among images of tavern-life those by Manuel Cabral Bejarano (1827–1891) stand out. Particularly notable are two sister canvasses of 1850, *Un borracho en un mesón* [A Drunkard in an Inn] (see Plate III) and *La reyerta* [The Brawl]. The *tableau vivant* of Act II of the opera has countless precedents in *costumbrist* paintings, some of which are rather sanitised while others really capture the gypsy spirit and also their physiognomy. Some of the finest depictions of gypsies were by the highly prolific French painter Alfred Dehodencq (1822–1882), whose travels between Andalusia and Paris were important in promoting knowledge of Spanish *costumbrist* painting in France. Dehodencq accurately portrayed their dress. Manet particularly admired them (see Plate IV).

The *costumbristas* are often seen as an important element of what is called Spanish 'Romanticism', but this umbrella term is misleading. In one of its senses, Romanticisation of reality is found in very different degrees among the various painters: the paintings of the Scottish painter David Roberts are an example of paintings with a high degree of Romanticised license, and Doré's celebrated engravings, discussed later, are also very much posed rather than observed, adding a good deal of imagination to their realism.

In Lucien Jusseaume's new sets for Carré's production of 1898 a more realistic, and more up-to-date, approach may be observed. The set for Act IV is now modelled directly on the *Plaza de toros* (bullring) in Seville, with its distinctive red-brick arches. The previous set, from the original 1875 production, had grafted the Moorish 'keyhole' arch from the main entrance to the precincts of the cathedral onto the entry to the arena, whereas the real bullring has no Arabic features. This transfer of the keyhole arch to the *Plaza de toros* can be seen as a background to the image of Carmen's murder on the poster for the first production of the opera. The new set celebrates the new bullring, itself a much-admired landmark of modern architecture and the biggest in the world – so big, in fact, that it could be divided into two, and two simultaneous *corridas* could be mounted.

As the century progressed many books and paintings still concentrated on images of the most famous monuments of Andalusia, but often confectioned rather than drawn accurately from life. Most tantalising were images of the monuments in Andalusian cities, which in themselves demonstrated the region's melting-pot of cultures: the Mezquita at Cordoba; the Golden Tower and Giralda in Seville; and the Patio de los Leones (the Patio of Lions) in the Alhambra in Granada. Such images, as well as paintings, were often mass-produced for the increasing tourist market. Who cared if a few trees and a lake were added to portrayals of the Alhambra, and a little group of gypsy dancers conveniently inserted into one of its patios! Paintings had become opera sets.

Plate 2.2 Plate by Hyacinthe Royet for the illustrated edition of the *Carmen* vocal score (Paris: Choudens, c.1890), showing the scene outside the bullring for Act IV. This shows the transfer of the Moorish arch near the Giralda to the *Plaza de toros*. The sets for Carré's revival dispensed with this and modelled their Act IV set on the actual bullring, revived during the 1880s.

The new set for Act I of Carré's production – like the original set – could be somewhere in the Barrio de Santa Cruz in the old part of the city of Seville, but, however realistic it looks, it is confectioned, cramming in a mixture of stereotypical architecture but retaining the opposition of the Tobacco Factory and the Barracks at the front of the stage. As in the sets for the original staging – and in many *costumbrista* paintings – the tower of the Giralda is seen above in the background.

The *costumbrista* agenda helped the souvenir trade to flourish: everyone wanted to take home a little piece of Andalusia and, as we shall see in Chapter Six, some literally did. The number of painters working in Spain – be they Spanish painters exporting their goods or foreign artists returning with their own works to the cities of northern Europe (or the Americas) – and the vast numbers of Spanish paintings that foreign travellers exported to be sent back home show that the dissemination of images of Andalusia was a thriving concern. The trappings of the budding souvenir industry included a booming trade in genre-paintings in a format small enough to be taken home by visitors or exported *en masse*. Although copying paintings was nothing new for Sevillaños, the scale of mass-produced paintings and reproductions mush-

Plate 2.3 The set for Act IV of *Carmen* in the 1898 revival by Albert Carré. The set is by Lucien Jusseaume and is modelled on the Seville bullring as it was rebuilt in the 1880s, after the 1875 run of *Carmen* at the Opéra-Comique.

roomed vastly as the century unfolded. A hungry market in France helped considerably.

On a deeper level, the *costumbrista* approach coincided with Mérimée's observations of 'moments' in Andalusian life as the basis for *Carmen*: one of the driving forces of his literary technique was the weaving of a narrative around significant moments, just as Calderón had done in his *Escenas andaluzas*. Naturally, unusual occurrences at bullfights were common – a gored *torero* or a horse running loose – but painters began to focus on details of the spectators: excited *majas* in fine dress; a scene in a *palco* (box) with men following the bull; a lady seeing to her toilette. Everyone showed off their class through their attire. The triumphant bullfighter was ubiquitous. We shall later meet Montes, a real-life and highly celebrated bullfighter introduced into the libretto by Halévy.

Another element of everyday life that was crucial to *Carmen*'s *numéros* was costume. By 1875 the operatic costume designers were familiar with historical Spanish dress. One of the best painters of contemporary costume was Eugenio Lucas Velázquez (1817–1870), whose two paintings of finely dressed *majas* from the 1850s were very much admired (see Plate II).[16] These are the top echelons of the *majas*, who walked around the square and sat on balconies in their finery to be admired. Along with published histories of Spanish costume, these images no doubt fed into the work of costume designers involved in the staging of quasi-Spanish spectacles in France. *Majas* with fans and *mantillas* (fine veils or shawls) were complemented by *majos* in tight breeches and embroidered tunics.

As the tourist trade grew, so did its infrastructure, reaching as far as Paris. In Seville the tourist traders centred on the old streets around the Calle Sierpes and the Plaza de San Salvador (now a pedestrianised zone with many shops selling much the same kind of thing). In Paris the *bazars*, particularly along the Boulevard Bonne Nouvelle in the 9th Arrondissement, carried all kinds of souvenirs and guide books for those exploring Spain. Particularly famous was the Bazar de Voyage of Alexis Godillot, which sold everything needed for a Spanish adventure, including saddles and saddlebags for mules, and mementos and prints. Godillot trunks are still collectors' items. Perhaps it was after inspecting prices here that Gautier complained of how, even by the late 1830s, 'castanets were becoming expensive and *tambours de basque* (tambourines) had gone through the roof'.[17]

If the surge of *costumbrist* paintings showed the visual aspect of the Andalusians, later travellers commented on their character, by no means always favourably, even apart from the region's celebrated bandits and smugglers. Before Baron Taylor, the Marquis de Custine had inaugurated a vicious stereotyping of Andalusian women from a French perspective – the 'drôles de gens' of the first chorus of the opera and the subject of José's invective:

> Spanish women in general have strong characters but they lack tenderness. They are seductive but they abuse their charms to please everyone. They have no nobility because they have too much *coquetterie* [...]
>
> They have no calm, no gentleness, no carefree spirit; they are destined by nature to live in extremes, they are in their element with heightened passions:

16 Andrew Ginger, in his *Painting and the Turn to Cultural Modernity in Spain: The Time of Eugenio Lucas Velázquez* (Selinsgrove, PA, 2007), sees this painter as parallel to Manet in inaugurating Modernism, in the sense of a diminished emphasis on subject-matter and a new emphasis on the medium of painting itself. Although he does not claim any cross-influence, there are close affinities between certain of Lucas's paintings and Manet's Spanish paintings of the 1860s.

17 '... les castagnettes deviennent chères, les tambours de basque sont hors du prix.' *La Presse*, 11 February 1839.

> fanaticism in their religion and in love, that's their life; they are creatures who are the most incapable of friendship that I know. Extraordinary in every way, they fight against men instead of helping them in their lives.[18]

By introducing the character of Micaëla, who does not exist in Mérimée's novella, the libretto strengthens the contrast between Andalusians and those of the more northerly provinces.

SOLDATS

Drôles de gens que ces gens là !	What odd people they are!
Drôles de gens ! Drôles de gens !	Peculiar people! Funny people!
Drôles de gens que ces gens-là !	What funny people they are!

A little later, Don José echoes the observations of Custine in a conversation with Zuniga about the factory girls:

DON JOSÉ

Ces Andalouses me font peur. Je ne suis pas fait à leurs manières, toujours à railler ... jamais un mot de raison	These Andalusian girls frighten me. I'm not used to their ways, always mocking ... never a word of sense.

The dialogue quotes Mérimée to the letter, echoing Custine in his emphasis on the uniqueness of Andalusian women, in this case Carmen herself.[19] In the Mérimée novella, the narrator doubts that Carmen was a pure-blooded gypsy, but observes nonetheless that 'Her eyes had above all an expression which was at once voluptuous and wild: an expression I have never seen since in any human being. "The look of a gypsy, the look of a wolf" goes a very accurate Spanish saying.'[20]

18 'Les femmes espagnoles ont en général de grands caractères, mais elles manquent de tendresse ; elles sont séduisantes, mais elles abusent de leurs charmes pour plaire à tous ; elles ont peu de noblesse, parce qu'elles ont trop de coquetterie [...] Elles n'ont pas de calme, point de douceur, point d'insouciance ; destinées par la nature à vivre dans les extrêmes, les passions exaltées sont leur élément ; le fanatisme de l'amour et de la religion : voilà leur vie ; ce sont les êtres les plus incapables d'amitié que je connaisse. Extraordinaires en tout, elles luttent contre les hommes au lieu de les assister dans la vie.' Custine, *L'Espagne sous Ferdinand VII*, vol. 1, pp. 307–308.

19 Prosper Mérimée, *Carmen*, chapter three.

20 'Ses yeux surtout avaient une expression à la fois voluptueuse et farouche que je n'ai trouvée depuis à aucun regard humain. "Œil de bohémien œil de loup", c'est un dicton espagnole qui dénote une bonne observation.' Mérimée, *Carmen*, Chapter II, p. 360.

Later in the same act, Carmen also claims to come from elsewhere and complains about the Andalusians – turning her attention to the false machismo of the men. She may simply be tricking José, but the issue of the contrasting characters of the different regions of Spain has been raised.

CARMEN

On m'a insultée parce que je ne suis pas de ce pays de filous, de marchands d'oranges pourries, et ces coquines se sont mises toutes contre moi parce que je leur ai dit que tous leurs Jacques de Séville avec leurs couteaux ne feraient pas peur à un gars de chez nous avec son béret bleu et son maquila.	I've been insulted because I'm not from this land of crooks and sellers of rotten oranges, and those stupid women ganged up against me because I told them that all their Seville lads swaggering around with knives wouldn't frighten any boy from our parts with his blue beret and *maquila*.

The 'blue beret' signifies José's own homeland and the provinces bordering France, the *maquila* – as indicated in a footnote by Mérimée – is both a traditional Basque walking stick, sometimes iron-shod, and a weapon used in male combat.

As for their reputation for sexual proclivity, it need hardly be said that Mérimée subscribed to the stereotype of the Andalusian female, and not only in his literary works. Of his Malagueño friend Calderón, who had apparently conquered some English girls on a visit to London, Mérimée amusingly wrote to Mme de Montijo of that 'Andalusians find themselves at home everywhere where there are ladies present.'[21]

Travellers had remarked on these differences of character some forty years earlier. Custine emphasised the difference south of Madrid, where 'the desert began'. He is convinced that the Spaniards are 'half-savages': 'they do not know themselves nor examine themselves; their lives admit only passion.'[22] The observation is tempered, however, by his noting the purity of this passion, which he regards as 'pure poetry': the man of the north has to find such poetry in poems', he remarks, 'for the Spaniard, life itself is poetry.' Gautier went further, stereotypically attributing the extraordinary violence and uncontrollable passion of the Andalusians to two factors: the extreme heat, and their Arabic roots. Certainly, the potentially lethal potion of passion and

21 Mérimée, letter to Mme de Montijo, 29 April 1843: 'c'est le propre des Andalous de se trouver *at home* partout où il y a des femmes.' Propser Mérimée, *Correspondance générale*, ed. Maurice Parturier (Toulouse, 1964), vol. III, p. 363.

22 'Les Espagnols, j'en conviens, sont à demi sauvages ; ils ne se connaissent ni ne s'examinent eux-mêmes ; mais leur vie n'est que passion.' Custine, *L'Espagne sous Ferdinand VII*, vol. 1, p. 322.

Plate 2.4 Francisco Lameyer's second illustration for Serafín Estébanez Calderón's *Escenas andaluzas* (Madrid, 1847). Many of Lamayer's plates suggest the undercurrent of criminality for which the region was reputed.

violence underlies the entire framework of the story of *Carmen*, and in the opera is separately exploited in feminine and masculine forms: first between the unruly factions of the gypsy girls in the factory, and in Act III in the set-piece duel with *navajas* between José and Escamillo.

Gautier has quite a lot to say about *navajas*, which he calls 'coutellerie de fantaisie' – a phrase one might translate as 'Romantic cutlery'. He saw some for sale on his way south at Santa Cruz and Albacete, which was (and is) renowned for its *cuchillería* (cutlery) and particularly for its classic *navajas*, which have a strong cultural significance. This long-established tradition of knife-making gave way to a tourist trade in the nineteenth century, still flourishing to this day. Gautier's observation is, as always, detailed, and he notes that these weapons can vary from a few centimetres long to over 3 feet, some sharpened on both sides of the blade.[23] Duels with these weapons are cap-

23 A fine collection of *navajas* varying from the size of flick-knives to that of double-edged swords can be seen in the Museum of Banditry in Ronda.

Plate 2.5 Gustave Doré, *La navaja*, illustration for Baron Davillier's *L'Espagne* (Paris: 1862, rpt. 1874). The image accompanies a discussion of the cutlery town of Albacete (Castilla La Mancha) and its speciality of manufacturing classic *navajas*.

tured in some *costumbrist* pictures and, most tellingly, in two Doré illustrations in Davillier's *L'Espagne*.[24]

The reputation of Andalusia as the province most populated by bandits was clearly established by the time Mérimée made his first visit in 1830. For Spanish consumption, popular illustrated tales – almost *bandes dessinées* – were in circulation by the 1840s, often containing graphic images of torture,

24 All types of *navaja* technique were discussed in great detail in the *Manual de baratero; ó, Arte de manejar la navaja, el cuchillo y la tijera de los Gitanos* [Manual of the *Baratero*; or, The Art of Handling the *Navaja*, the Knife and the Gypsy Scissors] (Madrid, 1849). A *baratero* was a henchman who collected gambling debts, often with threatened violence. The book will be returned to in the discussions of violence in the Seville tobacco factory.

Plate 2.6 Gustave Doré, *L'escrime au couteau – lanzar la navaja*, illustration for Baron Davillier's *L'Espagne* (Paris: 1862, rpt. 1874). This image shows a particular art of *navaja* combat where the knife is thrown.

extortion and even infanticide. Among foreigners and the Spanish alike, 'Banditophobia', as the English traveller Richard Ford called it, became rife. And yet, the idea of meeting a real bandit became an exciting prospect in the over-developed imaginations of some travellers. The young Mérimée was no exception, wanting the excitement (and danger) of meeting one: even in 1831 he regretted not having done so. He writes from Madrid in one of his *Lettres d'Espagne*:

> Here I am back in Madrid, after travelling around Andalusia, in every way for several months: the classic country of bandits, without meeting even one. I'm almost ashamed! I was all prepared for an attack from bandits, not so I could defend myself, but to chat with them and politely ask them about their way of life. Looking at my worn-out clothes and their bare elbows, and my light luggage, I regret having missed these *messieurs*. The pleasure of meeting them would have been well worth the theft of a not very full wallet.[25]

25 'Me voici de retour à Madrid, après avoir parcouru pendant plusieurs mois, et dans tous les sens, l'Andalousie, cette terre classique des voleurs, sans en rencontrer un seul. J'en suis presque honteux. Je m'étais arrangé pour une attaque de voleurs, non pas pour me défendre, mais pour causer avec eux et les questionner bien poliment sur leur genre de

His fantasy of meeting a bandit emerges in the whole narrative of *Carmen*, where the narrator – often seen as a metaphor for Mérimée himself – meets Don José, who is very much cleaned up in the opera but in the novella an infamous *bandolero* about to be garrotted for his crimes.

Although many writers have equated smugglers with bandits – *contrabandistas* with *bandoleros* – both are represented in the paintings of the *costumbristas*, the smugglers generally appearing far more prosperous. In Mérimée's novella the bandits with their blunderbusses, led by Carmen's murderous husband García, are a far more vicious band than the smugglers in the opera, who are treated with a certain amount of levity. Both Mérimée and the librettists were accurate in their references to the south-west corner of Spain in Act III: this was the region where the *contrabandistas* were most active, operating around the coast of Gibraltar, roughly from Algeçiras to Cadiz. Baron Taylor had documented this:

> The smugglers from around Algeciras are, like those from the coast near Malaga, the most famous of the whole of Spain. All those poetic things about smugglers you read in Romantic books, and the picturesque scenes in novels, are true. They are men of the south of the peninsula. They are an extraordinary mixture of nobility and vice. Adventurous and brave, they are true to their word, brilliant at the execution of their business, which they regard as a profession, they confront the tyranny of law with incredible courage when they feel it is unjust: these are the shared principles common to all of this band of brothers which no government could ever destroy.[26]

Taylor's view seems to have been that there was little difference between the romanticised stereotype of the smuggler and the outlook of working-

---

vie. En regardant mon habit usé aux coudes et mon mince bagage, je regrette d'avoir manqué ces messieurs. Le plaisir de les voir n'était pas payé trop cher par la perte d'un léger portemanteau.' Prosper Mérimée, 'Les Voleurs'; dated Madrid, novembre 1830; first published *Revue de Paris*, August 1832; rpt. in *Mosaïque* and *Lettres d'Espagne*.

26 'Les contrebandiers des environs d'Algéciras sont, ainsi que ceux de la côte de Malaga, les plus célèbres de toute l'Espagne. Tout est vrai dans ce que les romances ont dit de poétique et dans ce que les romans ont raconté de pittoresque sur les contrebandiers. Ce type de caractère est celui du peuple dans le sud de la péninsule. C'est un mélange vraiment bizarre de qualités et de vices extraordinaires. Bravoure aventureuse, fidélité à leur parole, finesse dans l'exercice de ce qu'ils regardent comme une profession, adresse incroyable à braver la loi qu'ils considèrent comme une tyrannie : tels sont les principaux traits qui sont communs à tous les membres de cette corporation qu'aucun gouvernement ne pourra jamais dissoudre.' Baron Taylor, 'Contrebandiers des environs d'Algéciras', in *Voyage pittoresque en Espagne*, vol. 1, p. 49.

class Andalusians. Their bravery and defiance were admired by many who saw them as redistributors of wealth in a society made of up a landowning minority and a majority of badly treated serfs. The bandits were willing to risk harsh punishments and were part of the age-old literary stereotype of the honourable thief.

There were obvious reasons why this corner of Spain around Gibraltar was so rife with smugglers: it was in this region that sea-borne trade was most active, much of it from England, not least the trade in tobacco (with the factories in Bristol) and the sherry trade in Jerez. The trade centred on Seville (still at this time a port, before the Guadalquivir silted up), but Cadiz and Huelva were also important centres, as were the Mediterranean ports mentioned by Taylor. Merchant shipping was vulnerable to the turbulent Atlantic weather of the Bay of Biscay, and piracy and wrecking were rife.[27] Thus the libretto's detail on the smugglers' activities with the English had its roots in fact.

In view of this exploitation, and even murder, of the English, it is interesting to read what English visitors had to say about the smuggling trade compared to Taylor's more impartial view. The author of the first guide books, Richard Ford, was ambivalent, on the one hand calling armed bandits the 'weed of the soil of Spain'. He considered this evil to have diminished during the reign of Ferdinand VII because of his social reforms, but he remarks that smuggling remained rife in Gibraltar, 'that hotbed of contraband, that nursery of the smuggler'. On the other hand, like Baron Taylor he sees the activity as a necessity in the face of unfair taxation, and in a beautifully written passage mentions the English not as victims but as fellow sufferers of the Chancellor of the Exchequer:

> The financial ignorance of the Spanish government calls him in [the smuggler] to correct the errors of Chancellors of Exchequers: – 'trova la legge, trovato l'inganno' [wherever there's law there's deceit]. The fiscal regulations are so ingeniously absurd, complicated, and vexatious, that the honest, legitimate merchant is as much embarrassed as the irregular trader is favoured. The operation of excessive duties on objects which people must, and therefore will, have is as strikingly exemplified in the case of tobacco in Andalusia as it is in that, and many other articles, on the Kent and Sussex coasts: in both countries leading to breaches of the peace, injury to the fair dealer, and loss to the revenue [...] In Spain the evasion of such laws is only

27 Visitors to Huelva in particular, an important port for the English wine and tobacco trades, will still be struck by its early twentieth-century Barrio Reina Victoria, an English-style housing estate with a grid of straight roads and half-timbered housing resembling similar ventures in north-west London – Neasden, Acton or Ealing, for example.

> considered as cheating those who cheat the people, the villagers are heart and soul in favour of the smuggler, as they are of the poacher in England; all the prejudices are on his side.

Ford goes on to confirm the popularity of Manuel Garcia's smuggler-song, mentioned in Chapter One:

> The smuggler himself, so far from feeling degraded, enjoys the reputation which attends success in personal adventure, among a people proud of individual prowess; he is the hero of the Spanish stage, and comes on equipped in full costume, with his blunderbuss, to sing the well-known "Yo! que soy contrabandista! yo ho!" to the delight of all listeners from the Straits to the Bidasoa, custom-house officers not excepted.[28]

Little wonder that Bizet echoed this popular song in *Carmen*.

The librettists' dramatisation of the *contrebandiers* is at once accurate, ridiculous and hilarious. Accurate, as we have seen, in pinpointing the hotbed of smuggling; ridiculous because of the scene with the 'breach in the wall' – an obvious ploy to focus on Carmen and her associates as *allumeuses*, wielding their feminine charms. It is a rare moment of humour: the opera's smugglers are a comedy act even though they 'have some business in mind',[29] but Bizet and his librettists take time to underpin a whole chorus philosophising on the appeal of smuggling and *bandolerismo* in general. The extended chorus about 'La liberté' is preceded by the beautiful entr'acte for solo flute. In his film of the opera made in 1984, Francesco Rosi interprets this with a bird flying over the landscape, signifying the freedom of the vagrant – the wanderer, the traveller – before we move into the long trekking chorus ending with cries of 'Liberté' and love of the uncertainty of fortune. Though no musicologist to my knowledge has interpreted its music, Rosi was right in viewing this solo as a prelude to the following chorus, and his symbolism is very apt.

So what is the freedom they sing about so forcefully in Act III, the 'fortune which lies down there' – ambiguous because of the double-meanings of 'fortune' as 'fate' and 'wealth'? They are surely seeking freedom from, for example, the army, military strife, poverty; the dictates of the Church; serfdom. Bizet captures it well, in a chorus whose length is its essence (though it has often been cut). It stresses that freedom comes at a price – the smug-

28 Richard Ford, *Gatherings from Spain* (1846), chapter XVI.

29 'Nous avons en tête une affaire': opening line of the Act II Quintet.

glers constantly look out for the perilous snipers from the army, or perhaps the *Guardia civil*:

La fortune est là-bas, là-bas !	Down there lies our fortune, down there!
Mais prends garde, pendant la route,	But take care as you go
Prends garde de faire un faux pas ! [...]	Mind you don't make a false step! [...]
Et le péril est en haut,	Danger lurks above
Il est en bas, il est en haut,	It lurks below and above
Il est partout.	It's everywhere.

Bizet's musical response is to stress the danger with a series of highly chromatic, descending chords setting the words emphasising the danger: 'Prends garde de faire un faux pas !' ('Be careful not to make a false step!'). This was one of the passages that the chorus at the premiere found difficult to sing, and Bizet had to plead for reinforcement, or perhaps singers better at keeping the tricky chromaticism in tune (see Example 2.1).

The final stereotype of Spanish Romanticism is of course the bullfighter, the matador, the *torero*, the *toréador*. He may be passed over fairly rapidly, not because there was little written about him by the early commentators and Mérimée, but because there was too much. Images of him, even from before the countless *costumbrista* images, present him in many guises, not always triumphant. Chapter Seven will deal with the question in more detail. From the point of view of Bizet's opera, the gory details of nineteenth-century bullfighting in the various regions of Spain, commented upon by visitors, are not of much importance, since in the final act we are outside the arena and do not witness anything until the fight is all over, although it briefly became fashionable over the turn of the century to perform the opera, especially in the Roman *arènes* of southern France, with a live bullfight inserted into the final act.[30]

As the century progressed, interest in historical buildings was supplemented by paintings of the more modern urban landscape: Pharamond Blanchard and Adrien Dauzats, both of whom worked with Baron Taylor, painted the twisting *calles* of Cadiz, Malaga and Gibraltar with their higgledy-piggledy terraces, not so dissimilar from the later impressionist paintings of the streets of Montmartre. Rarer were images of poverty, depravity and violence – subjects which Doré did not shy away from later on. Exceptions were the Sevillian painter Roldán y Martinez, who depicted some of the deprived characters of both of Mérimée's and Bizet's *Carmen*, such as the urchins, in his painting *Los pilluelos de Sevilla* [The Urchins of Seville].

30 Sabine Teulon-Lardic, '*Carmen* in the *Midi* Amphitheatres: A "Tauro-Comique" Spectacle', in Langham Smith and Rowden, Carmen *Abroad*, chapter twenty-one.

Example 2.1 Smugglers' chorus, *Carmen*, Act III, bar 47 et seq. 'Take care not to make a false step!'

Parisians did not always have to travel to see all this. Periodicals presented testimonies of Spain with varying degrees of luxurious illustration and with an international agenda. One such was the *Revue des deux mondes*, where the first three chapters of *Carmen* first appeared; another was *Le Tour du monde*, where Gustave Doré had published his illustrations. Another, more vivid, way in which the Parisian could find Spain on the doorstep was in the *Expositions universelles* that started in 1851 and presented pavilions with reconstructions of Andalusian towns, inhabited by stereotypical citizens in traditional costumes: *majos* and *majas*, *toreros* and perhaps even *bandoleros*. Both *costumbrista* painters and writers catered to the curiosity about what Spanish life had been like in the 1820s and what Spain's inhabitants wore before the fashion for dressing – as Mérimée points out emphatically in *Carmen* – *a la francese*. Several writers also stress advances in mapping the southern peninsula as a catalyst for exploration of its sights, and guide books to the big cities became more widely available. Much of this material found a lucrative export-market in Paris, where the modern Spanish painters were much admired for their technique and use of vivid colour.

Édouard Manet was aware of such ventures, though art historians largely ignore these parallels in favour of his admiration for Spanish art of former generations (the 'other' Velázquez in particular), which is well documented in letters he wrote from Spain to Zacharie Astruc. On his return, however, Manet writes vividly to Baudelaire of Spain's modern customs – particularly the bullfight – and admiringly of the beautiful Spanish women.[31]

31 See *Édouard Manet: Voyage en Espagne*, ed. Juliet Wilson-Barreau (Paris, 1988).

Manet's visit to Spain, and his return to Paris, where he distilled his experiences into several of his most important paintings, coincided with the formative period of Bizet's adult life. In late 1865, the date of Manet's voyage to Spain, Bizet was in his mid-twenties, and it was not long before he conceived both *Carmen* and his unfinished opera *Don Rodrigue,* the real name of the teenage warrior El Cid whose exploits were originally documented in the works by Guillén de Castro (1569–1631), later immortalised by Corneille, reworked several times by nineteenth-century writers, and eventually transformed into operas by Massenet and by Debussy. It might not be entirely inappropriate to describe Bizet's *Carmen* as a *costumbrista* opera, a scenic aspect which is often to the fore in the more traditional of modern productions.

The first of Manet's Spanish paintings to enjoy considerable success, the *Spanish Guitar Player* (1860), was one of two canvasses exhibited in the Salon of 1861, attracting unexpected acclaim from influential critics, among them the established Hispanophile Théodore Gautier. '¡Caramba!', he wrote, 'here's a guitar player not straight out of the Opéra-Comique', going on to stress its authentic Spanish costumes and its roots in Goya and Velázquez.[32] As a result, the painting was moved to a central place in one of the rooms, where it received honourable mention despite its radical style. Although he was later critical of Manet, Gautier delighted in the work's mix of the exotic with the realistic. The painter, at 29, had thus made a breakthrough with a Spanish painting; he followed it up with more works with Spanish themes, or, in the case of the celebrated *Concert in the Tuileries Gardens* of the following year, a Parisian painting with colourful embedded figures from the Spanish dance troupe in which Lola de Valence – the subject of a *costumbrista*-style portrait as well as an admiring verse by Baudelaire – starred in Paris, immediately enthusing Manet to make many sketches and several paintings. Portraits of celebrated Parisian artistic figures – beside a self-portrait – were inserted: Offenbach, Baudelaire, Baron Taylor, Champfleury (a champion of realism) and Fantin-Latour among them.

Another exhibition of Manet's evolving catalogue of Spanish paintings was mounted in an important re-opening exhibition at the gallery of Louis Martinet, a well-known dealer on the Boulevard des Italiens who always had some Manets for sale. Two portraits also resulted from his temporary obsession – one of his brother dressed up as a *majo,* the other of his favourite model, Victorine Meurent, in the costume of a *torera* – at the Salon des Refusés of 1863. Here were two slightly frivolous 'society paintings', indicating bourgeois society's rising interest in Spanish exoticism.

32 Gautier, *La Presse,* cited E. Moreau Nélaton, *Manet raconté par lui-même* (Paris, 1926), vol. I, p. 32.

Manet's short visit to Spain in 1865 was made infinitely easier by the opening of a wealth of new railway lines around 1860: no longer did travellers face the constant threat of assault by bandits. A journey that formerly took weeks was now achievable in a couple of days, and the guide books promoted Spain as a changed country: 'no longer was it necessary to make one's will before visiting', remarked the *Guide Joanne* of 1860, while the next edition of 1866 remarked upon the 5,500 km of track serving all the principal cities of the peninsula. For Manet the excursion confirmed his enthusiasm for the Spanish masters and initiated a new one, namely *tauromachia*: in his rich letter to Baudelaire describing the bullfights he described them as 'One of the finest, the strangest and the most terrible spectacles one could see'. The visit had clearly marked the genesis of an ambitious new painting: 'I hope on my return', he writes, 'to put on to canvas the brilliant, evasive and at the same time dramatic aspects of the *corrida* which I went to.'[33] Perhaps most important was his chance meeting in Madrid with fellow Hispanophile Théodore Duret, who was to become a champion of his work – amidst a wealth of adverse criticism – during the period of Impressionism from 1874. Duret later wrote a monograph on Manet's Spanish period, including detailed memoirs of Manet's visit to Spain.

Did Bizet know Manet's art, we may wonder? A glance at their domiciles in the 1860s reveals their proximity: both in the 9th Arrondissement, in which Bizet moved a few times but never far away from the Batignolles where the painter had his studio. Certainly several of Bizet's intimates, including the pianist Élie-Miriam-Éraïm Delaborde, who went on the fateful swimming escapade in the Seine (which killed Bizet) and was with him at his death, was in Manet's circle, though it is difficult to ascertain at what period exactly.[34] Café society mingled in the nearby Place de Clichy, particularly in the Café de la Nouvelle Athènes, several times painted by Manet. Bizet did not reveal much in his correspondence about his own enthusiasms for the visual arts, but we know that the Halévy family were acquainted with the Manets, as were the Ganderax family, with whom Bizet corresponded. Mme Manet was also a

33 See *Édouard Manet: Voyage en Espagne*, ed. Juliet Wilson-Bareau (Paris, 1988). The French of the quotation from the *Guide Joanne* (Paris, 1866) is cited here: 'Dans l'opinion vulgaire, l'Espagne est encore l'un des pays que l'on ne peut visiter sans au préalable avoir fait son testament' (pp. 15–16). The Baudelaire letter reads: 'Un des plus beaux, des plus curieux et des plus terribles spectacles que l'on puisse voir, c'est une course de taureau. J'espère à mon retour mettre sur la toile l'aspect brillant, papillotant et en même temps dramatique de la corrida à laquelle j'ai assisté' (letter of 14 September 1865, quoted pp. 47–48).

34 See Anne Borrel, 'Geneviève Straus, la "muse mauve"', in Henri Loyette (ed.), *Entre le théâtre et l'histoire: La Famille Halévy* (Paris, 1996), pp. 106–127. Ludovic Halévy, painted several times by Degas, was also in Manet's circle.

possible link since she was a talented amateur pianist, to whom Chabrier dedicated an Impromptu. Personal connections or not, Manet's burst of enthusiasm for Spanish subjects added an important element to the flourishing wealth of hispanomania immediately preceding the genesis of the opera.

Manet's flirtation with Spanish subjects in the 1860s was perhaps the final ingredient added to fertilise the cultural ground from which Bizet's opera sprung: vivid flames of southern reality mingled with northern European imagination, *realidad* combined with *ficción*.[35] This continued – perhaps as a tribute to Bizet – after the composer's death, when in 1879 Manet painted the singer Émilie Ambre (former mistress of King William III of Holland) in the role of Carmen (see Plate XIX), a painting that was bought by the celebrated baritone Jean-Baptiste Faure, one of whose vocal coaches had been François Delsarte, Bizet's maternal uncle. (Faure was also painted by Manet, and in 1873 proposed to Bizet an opera featuring him in the primary vocal role.) It is thus unlikely that Manet did not attend a performance of *Carmen* in its first run at the Opéra-Comique, not least because his picture of Ambre places her in the *venta* in which the *Chanson bohème* opening Act II is sung, Lillas Pastia's tavern.

Manet's picture of Ambre as Carmen has a strange history. In 1879 Manet had left Paris for a new abode, where his neighbour was one and the same Émilie Ambre. She had sung in two Verdi operas in Paris, where she received a cool critical reception. But she received an invitation to sing in performances in the States from the 'Colonel', the celebrated J. H. Mapleson whose Italian Opera Company was mounting *Carmen* there and who describes her as a 'Moorish prima donna of some ability and possessing great personal charms'.[36] The arrangement to paint her was advantageous both artist and sitter, portraying the latter in her title role and providing the former with a ready model for a further *costumbrist* painting. She thus posed for him in Paris. The execution of the painting bears out the aforementioned comparison between Manet and Lucas Velázquez. Manet's use of paint reflects Baudelaire's comment in his essay *The Painter of Modern Life* that 'the pleasure we derive from the representation of the present is due not only to the beauty with which it can be invested, but also to the essential quality of *being present*.' The paint

35 Élie Halévy (the daughter of *Carmen*'s librettist, Ludovic Halévy), in a letter to her family dated 19 November 1892, writes: 'Le familistère Halévy, que fut cette maison, au haut de la rue Fontaine, entre les ateliers de Degas et de Puvis de Chavannes, était proche des Edmond About, de mes oncles Auguste Ohnet et Alfred Blanche, des John Lemoinne, des Manet, de cinq autres intimes de ma mère.' *La famille Halévy*, p. 238. A café named 'Carmen' was established at the end of Bizet's road in 1875.

36 *The Mapleson Memoirs* (1888), ed. Harold Rosenthal (London, 1966), p. 133.

is handled in a fluid, immediate way without clear delineation of detail, and contains tantalising symbols: are the red marks on her dress a foreshadowing of her ultimate violent demise? A discreet marking on her shawl represents a quaver: Manet is perhaps allying himself with his symbolist friends – Baudelaire, Verlaine and Mallarmé – as much as with his colleagues, the Impressionists.[37]

Jottings and sketches (and more developed images) snowballed, as did musical evocations of Spain, often by French musicians who had never ventured beyond the Pyrenees. Rather than sparking French nineteenth-century hispanomania (as it is often thought to have done), Bizet's opera appeared at the mid-point of the craze, which then extended well into the twentieth century in the works of Debussy and Ravel, among others.

37 For further detail on this painting see Therese Dolan, '*En garde*: Manet's Portrait of Émilie Ambre in the Role of Bizet's *Carmen*', *Nineteenth Century Art Worldwide*, 5/1 (Spring 2006) <https://www.19thc-artworldwide.org> (accessed December 2016). The painting is in the Philadelphia Museum of Art.

CHAPTER THREE

Spain on the Paris Stage

NOT until the 1860s was it possible to go from Paris to Spain entirely by train. French railways got near – to Bayonne – by 1856, but it was not until 1864 that the Spanish linked up their railway to Irun, still to this day the frontier junction. After the peninsula wars, the Spanish government had ensured that no French trains could cross into Spain by introducing a wide-gauge permanent way of six Castillian feet, just in case another Napoleonic-style invader harboured any ideas of steaming through the border.[1] Despite this, Spanish theatrical companies (rather than individuals) began to get to Paris by the 1850s and grace its stages. How troublesome it must have been to go by boat, as was previously the way.

Spain was by this time opening up. Import and export became easier. In terms of musical spectacle Spain had become too much of an importer: of Italian opera and French ballet, as Don Preciso had complained. As the century progressed things began to change and, above all, Madrid and Barcelona began to realise they no longer had to rely on imported spectacle; they too could export culture. Opera was out of the question – the Italians and French could hardly be rivalled. But dance became a possibility, and companies were established in these theatres with French dancers prominent in the troupes. The Teatro del Liceu opened in Barcelona in 1847, closely followed by Madrid's Teatro Real in 1850. A fusion of Spanish folk-dances and ballet seemed to be the way forward, and travelling companies were inaugurated, largely under French control, thus forming links with Paris.

The different dance traditions emerging in Spain are often confused. Stemming from the folk dances of the seventeenth and eighteenth centuries was a hybridisation with classical ballet, which professionalised these dances for the stage – they became a spectator performance danced no longer in soft slippers, but rather in proper ballet shoes. Based on what we now call the *bolero*, the style was known as the *Escuela bolera* (Bolero School), and it

1 5 foot 5 13/16 inches to be precise, as opposed to French and British gauge, which, based on the track of Roman carts, is standardised at 4 foot 8½ inches.

underpinned Spanish dance in the mid-nineteenth century, achieving considerable foreign acclaim. The Spanish were known above all for their dance.

In France 'going Spanish' for a couple of ballets became highly fashionable. Referring to the ballet boom in the 1840s, José Blas Vega notes that 'all the grand stars of Romantic ballet would abandon their diaphanous tutus and their Sylphide wings for colourful, flouncy dresses and castanets'.[2] The dances underlying both were the same: the *bolero* with its many regional variants, and *género andaluz* dances such as the *polo* and Fandango-related successors.

THE *ESCUELA BOLERA*

Professionally it was the *Escuela bolera* that reached the stages of Europe, but that is often confused with Flamenco, essentially a type of dance that evolved from gypsy dancing, nearer the end of the century, eventually in venues with a dance-floor or in *ventas* and *posadas* (inns), and also shows in theatres. The dances of the *Escuela bolera* and Flamenco were often muddled in the criticisms of Spanish dance when it came to Paris, and these two distinct performance acts need to be separated. Flamenco was later and essentially a song, dance and literary performative act, not a spectator show. Pure Flamenco remained in Spain and in a sense was not exported until it was fused with staged dance traditions, transformed into a heritage spectacle. Its poetry was often a political, personal or social song of discontent and it was essentially Andalusian. But by the time of Bizet's *Carmen* the public expected some sort of Spanish dancing to be part of the show. They were not to be disappointed: in Act II a ballet, 'La Flamenca', was danced by a pair of female dancers.[3]

In Spain there was a gradually increasing sense of forgiveness for the excesses of the Napoleonic regime, which in 1808 had inflicted terrible brutality, largely centred on Madrid, particularly on the infamous *dos de mayo.* Underneath there was still some support for the French revolutionary agenda of freeing the most deprived regions of Spain from over-localised land ownership and consequent quasi-medieval serfdom. French styles of dress gradually re-emerged, though not immediately after the defeat of the French armies, when any woman wearing French-style clothes would have been punished (by head-shaving, for example).

2 '... las grandes estrellas del romanticismo [...] abandonaron el etéreo tutú y las alas de sílfide por los volantes de encaje carmesí y las castañuelas.' José Blas Vega, 'Escuela Bolera y Ballet Clásico', in *Encuentro internacional 'La Escuela Bolera'* (Madrid, 1992), p. 19.

3 See Stéphane Wolff, *Un demi-siècle d'Opéra-Comique* (Paris, 1953), p. 38. The names of the dancers are given, neither of which is remotely Spanish.

Gradually, southerly winds began to blow northwards again. The traffic became two-way and visiting artists from Spain – above all dancers – began to present their acts in northern Europe, particularly in England and France. Paris, burgeoning and with a multitude of theatres, was a particular draw, perceived as the centre of European culture. Knowledge of Spanish culture had already been growing through travelogues and visual art, as we have observed. But there was now its dance, too, disseminated both live and through the increase in high-quality illustrations in serial publications and books.

CARLO BLASIS

Just as Don Preciso had set up defences against Italian and French appropriation of theatre and dance in Spain, so warnings about the lasciviousness of Spanish dance and the dangers of importing it were given in retaliation by the highly reputed dancing master Carlo Blasis (1797–1878), an Italian who called himself 'principal dancer at the King's Theatre' (London) and published in several languages. His warnings probably had a reverse effect, encouraging rather than discouraging the Spanish dances. In the racially prejudiced manner one encounters in many writings by educated observers of Spanish culture, recurrently biased against Jews, Moors and Gypsies, Blasis over-emphasised the dance's Moorish roots, dismissing it as unrefined and primitive. However, his books reveal that he knew quite a lot about its craft.

In the various editions of his *The Art of Dancing* (1831), Blasis devotes several pages to the details of the principal Spanish dances, though, faithful to his Neapolitan roots, he regarded Italian ballet as supreme. He admired some of the Spanish dances' aspects but saw them as gradually succumbing to over-exaggeration, a view that would be echoed by Sor some twenty years later. Blasis writes that:

> Italian dancing was universally applauded and excited the admiration and imitation of foreigners; among whom the Spanish were the first to follow it. They at first partially succeeded; the use of the castanets, which they added, produced a pleasing effect; but having in the sequel incorporated with it a multiplicity of leaps, capers, uncouth postures, and, in short, the most graceless and extravagant motions; the art of dancing in Spain became a degradation and a vice. [...] This corruption in style and taste [...] must be chiefly attributed to the *chica*, a dance of a very immoral nature which the Moors had brought with them from Africa.[4]

4 Carlo Blasis, *The Art of Dancing: The Code of Terpsichore*, translated under the author's immediate inspection by R. Barton (London, 1831), p. 16. He had published in Milan, but

To add weight to his discouragement of importing it, he later observed that the *chica* 'is now banished from the balls of the white women of South America, being far too offensive to decency'. More racism, but what an invitation: Parisians loved a bit of indecency!

Tracing a line of development from the *chica* to the *fandango*, from which Blasis claims almost every Spanish dance is developed, he cites the *bolero*, *cachucha* and *seguidilla*: 'They are therefore all marked with voluptuousness, I might even say obscenity', he concludes. For him, these dances are dwarfed by the Neapolitan *tarantella*, a similarly seductive dance about 'Love and pleasure', but one of which he approves for, unlike the Spanish dances, 'each gesture is made with the most voluptuous gracefulness'. This courtship dance of 'assault and defence' will be returned to in Chapter Five, for it was originally this very dance, the *tarantella*, that Bizet used for Carmen's entry in the opera, though it was ultimately replaced by the famous Habanera. Curiously, the next section in Blasis's detailed treatise, listing the Spanish dances and codifying their steps and postures, is far more benign, heaping praise on the best of them but constantly warning against those whose additions court vulgarity – those same accretions which Sor would blame on gypsy infiltration.

Those who had visited Spain, and who longed to go there but could not afford it – or pluck up the necessary courage – ensured a continuing, lively French interest in all things Spanish. The *afrancesados* who had fled to London and Paris enjoyed varying degrees of acclaim in the Opera House; one of the first successes was Gomis's *Le Diable à Séville*, premiered at the Ventadour in 1831. This included a lively *bolero* – a fleet duet for two sopranos – as well as a *polo*. Several numbers from this were sold as *pièces détachées* and Gomis also had a side-line publishing gypsy songs with grace notes, and syncopated angular lines, perhaps a model for the vocal line in Carmen's so-called *Séguedille*. Although set in Seville, the music of Balfe's *L'Étoile de Séville*, which followed in 1845, was less Spanish but was quite a success, running to fifteen performances at the Paris Opéra. One of its highlights is a *Chanson mauresque* based on a minor scale with sharpened fourth.

Overall, however, it was dance that dominated Spanish spectacle on the stages of Paris. Ballets such as *La Gitana* (1838), *La Esmeralda* (1844), *Les Contrebandiers de la Sierra Nevada* (1845), and *Paquita* (1846) ensured a continuum of Spanish themes if not Spanish-style music. Dance was perhaps the most direct way of touching the hearts of audiences less adept at unravelling the complexities of opera, bringing realistic *tableaux vivants* to many affordable boulevard theatres, and also to the Opéra balls, which were often masked (see Plates V and VI). The heyday of these highly fashionable events

---

in French, a *traité élémentaire* in 1820 and the *Code complète de la danse* in 1828, which, in translation, largely forms the content of the English volume.

was the 1840s and 1850s, when they were taken over by a director, Mira, whose father had overseen the spectacles at the Variétés centred on the Can-Can. He popularised the Opera Balls by introducing inducements such as tombolas, performances by the *petits rats* (the young trainee dancers), parodies of current political figures, and scenes with Spanish dancers.[5]

The central Parisian press reviewed Spanish dance in several *quartiers*. Venues hosting them included highly esteemed theatres with both fixed and mixed repertoires, for example the Opéra and the Opéra-Comique; but they were also performed in the secondary theatres maintained by the state, such as the Ambigu-Comique, which had both an orchestra and a ballet, as did the Variétés. The Vaudeville was a further state-supported theatre, one that had no resident ballet but did boast an orchestra and singers. Other venues were the Théâtre de la Renaissance, the Folies dramatiques (whose decree originally restricted it to 'Pantomimes-arlequinades' but whose constrictions were gradually relaxed), and the Théâtre Molière. There was also the Hippodrome, a huge arena where Petra Cámara's troupe performed in the interval between bull-running events. And all this is to mention only central Paris, though some of the shows ventured further out. The main point of listing these is to emphasise that they were relatively accessible and cheap, and that they attracted good audiences. More and more people were drawn to Spanish spectacle through its dance.

CRITICAL ANGLES

Viewing dance through the window of the copious criticism produced at the time yields views rather different from the vistas of today. Even so, this outlook is surely the clearest way of charting the infiltration of Spanish dance into Paris and the how it hybridised with French ballet in this era. One dance critic in particular – Théophile Gautier – has deliberately been kept waiting in the wings, not least because of the number of his reviews. Extensively plundered in dance literature, his writings cannot be bettered as regards style, though his angle must be approached somewhat critically.[6] Critics asked themselves whether they were witnessing French ballet with only a touch of Spanish colour, or the real thing. 'Authenticity' became an important issue – nothing better than a lively press and debate about rogue accretions to boost audience figures at the various shows! Was Spanish dance too raw? Or were

5 See *Les Bals de l'Opéra*, exh. cat., Bibliothèque nationale de France, Opéra nationale de Paris (1994).

6 See for example Gerhard Steingress, *... y Carmen se fue a Paris* (Cordoba, 2006); and Rocío Plaza Orellana, *Los bailes españoles en Europa (El espectáculo de los bailes de España en el siglo XIX)* (Cordoba, 2013).

the balletic representations of Spanish dance – often by non-Spanish dancers – too tame? The librettists of *Carmen* also had to weigh up these issues in their composition of a successful show for a major Paris stage. After all, their over-arching aim was success – critical and financial. Subsequent performances have wrestled with this axis. The debate about authenticity continued when Bizet's opera was compared to Mérimée's original.

Gautier was still admired at the end of the century, his criticism several times republished. He was also known as a novelist, and his first novel, *Mademoiselle de Maupin*, concerning the experiences of a man passing as a woman, was not irrelevant to his views on ballet dancers of both sexes. His focus on Spanish dance was nourished by an extended voyage to Spain undertaken in 1840 and immortalised in his oft-reprinted and widely read *Voyage en Espagne*, published two years later.

One of the poles of Gautier's critical standpoint was the attractiveness of female dancers: 'If anyone is rigorously required to be beautiful', he wrote at the beginning of his career as a critic, 'it must surely be a female dancer.'[7] This was an attitude common among critics in England as well as France, and it was one from which he never wavered, though he did modify his initially hostile view of male dancers:

> You know what a hideous sight a common male dancer is: a great awkward lump with a long ruddy neck bulging with muscles, a stereotyped grin that is as irremovable as a judge's, eyes that don't look, like the enamel eyes of mechanical dolls, the thick calves of a parish verger, arms like carriage shafts, making great angular movements with elbows and feet placed at right angles.[8]

The idea is nuanced a few years later when he writes of the Spanish dancer Jules Perrot, dancing in the gypsy opera *Zingaro*. Admitting that 'it is not

7 '... si l'on doit exiger rigoureusement la beauté de quelqu'un, c'est à coup sûr d'une danseuse.' Gautier, 'Les Danseurs espagnols' [The Spanish Dancers], *La Charte*, 18 April 1837. For this and the subsequently quoted reviews by Gautier there are three accessible sources: Ivor Guest's *Gautier on Dance* (London, 1986); his article 'Théophile Gautier on Spanish Dancing', *Dance Chronicle*, 10/1 (1986); and a French version of his book that contains the original French of Gautier's articles, *Écrits sur la danse*, ed. Martine Kahane (Arles, 1998). All translations from Gautier are my own.

8 'Vous savez quelle chose hideuse c'est qu'un danseur ordinaire ; un grand dadais avec un long cou rouge gonflé de muscles, un rire stéréotypé, inamovible comme un juge ; des yeux sans regard, qui rappellent les yeux d'émail des poupées à ressort ; de gros mollets de Suisse de paroisse, des brancards de cabriolet en façon de bras, et puis de grands mouvements anguleux, les coudes et les pieds en équerre'. Gautier, 'Les Danseurs espagnols'.

quite good form these days to show interest in the perfection of a male body', he enthuses about Perrot's legs, deflecting readers from his flirtation with androgyny (in the previously mentioned novel) by asking them to 'imagine that he is speaking of a statue [...] that has just been excavated'.[9] What Gautier admires in Perrot is not his masculine strength or skill but rather reflections of feminine beauty: 'The feet and knees are delicately formed, and counterbalancing the feminine roundness of contour of his legs, which are both soft and pliable, elegant and supple.' Later he calls him 'Perrot the sylph, the male Taglioni', and waxes even more lyrical when he suggests that 'his legs sing most harmoniously to the eye'. Reminding his readers that his praise is all the more 'suspect' because 'he does not like male dancing at all', his final blow is to suggest that 'With the exception of Mabille and Petipa, the male dancers of the Opéra only reinforce the view that women alone should be admitted into the *corps de ballet*.'[10]

Opera-glasses homed in on these dancers – particularly those of the British, who had perfected binoculars and manufactured the most powerful, as was noted both by Halévy and, previously, by Gautier (who, in Guest's English translation, referred to them as 'howitzers').[11] Gautier was obsessed with legs! In one sense any dance critic had to be: how did they move, how skilfully could they execute the steps? Early in his career as a dance critic he frankly was not up to commenting on this vital aspect, but through his relationship with Carlotta Grisi's sister, Ernesta, he later developed a little more critical acumen. Pretty female legs in action were, after all, a major source of the enjoyment in ballet, and surely a major driver for criticism. For testoster-

9 *Zingaro* is a two-act opera with music by Uranio Fontana (1815–1881). 'Il n'est guère dans les mœurs modernes de s'occuper de la perfection des formes d'un homme.' Gautier, 'Théâtre de la Renaissance: *Zingaro*', *La Presse*, 2 March 1840.

10 'Figurez-vous que nous parlons de quelque statue [...] retrouvée tout récemment dans une fouille des jardins de Néron.' [...] 'les attaches du pied et du genou sont d'une finesse extrême, et corrigent ce que les rondeurs du contour pourraient avoir de trop féminine ; c'est à la fois doux et fort, élégant et souple.' [...] 'Ses jambes chantent très harmonieusement pour les yeux' [...] 'À l'exception de Mabille et de Petipa, les danseurs de l'Opéra sont faits pour encourager l'opinion qui ne veut admettre des femmes dans le corps de ballet.' Gautier, '*Zingaro*: Théâtre de la Renaissance', *La Presse*, 23 January 1841. The mention of him as 'a female Taglioni' is perhaps tongue-in-cheek as Maria Taglioni, originally his dancing partner, subsequently refused to dance with him for fear of being outshone. See Gautier, *Écrits sur la danse*.

11 The original read as follows: 'non plus des légères lorgnettes de campagne qu'on met à la poche de son habit, mais ces grosses lorgnettes de siege, ces jumelles monstres, ces mortiers de l'optique.' Guest's delicious translation of the word 'mortiers' into 'howitzers' might seem anachronistic but it was not. *La Presse*, 1 July 1844, in Gautier, *Écrits sur la danse*, p. 162. Guest, *Gautier on Dance*, p. 141.

one-driven males, legs on the stage had a more visceral importance – where else could they be seen, after all? While their shapeliness was there to be ogled, it would be some years before acts involving a whirligig of frothing skirts and high kicks would be admitted to the repertory of variety theatres in such dances as the Can-Can, though by the 1840s this was emerging as the working-class lascivious dance in the back-streets of Paris, and would soon hit the stage.

Though unthinkable today, the overarching focus on physical attributes was an unashamed part of Romantic criticism, not only Gautier's, though few could match his turn of phrase, whether admiring to the point of voyeurism, cruelly vitriolic, or irresistibly amusing. Several of his articles bear testimony to this viewpoint. In a piece entitled 'Gallery of Beautiful Actresses' he singles out the Austrian dancer Fanny Elssler, who despite her nationality was world-famous for her Spanish dancing (see Plate X). He laments other critics' lack of concern with attractiveness, castigating them for their avoidance of this all-important aspect of the spectacle and claiming that 'it is permissible to criticise [them] without any scruples of conscience, to reproach [them] for being ugly just as a painter might be rebuked for faulty drawing.'[12]

One of Gautier's most overt confessions of (or pretences to) sexual attraction was penned in 1838 and is devoted to Fanny Elssler, who, he claims:

> holds in her white hands the golden sceptre of beauty. She only has to appear to draw a passionate murmur from the audience more flattering than all the applause in the world, for it is addressed to the woman, not the actress, and a greater pride comes from beauty which is God-given than from talent that comes from oneself. [...] Your gaze wanders like a caress over those smooth, rounded contours that might have belonged to some divine marble from the age of Pericles.[13]

Phew!

We should not read this, of course, as his personal view. Gautier was a professional writer, a skilled journalist exciting his readers by suggesting tantalising viewpoints to them. He adopted a strategy of default into marble

12 Gautier, 'Les Belles Femmes de Paris', *Le Figaro*, 19 October 1837.

13 Gautier, 'Réflexions sur Fanny Elssler': 'Mlle Fanny Elssler tient dans ses blanches mains le sceptre d'or de la beauté ; elle n'a qu'à paraître pour produire dans la salle un frémissement passionné plus flatteur que tous les applaudissements du monde ; car il s'adresse à la femme et non pas à l'actrice, et l'on est toujours plus fier de la beauté qui vous vient de Dieu que du talent qui vient de vous-même.' [...] 'le regard monte et descend comme une caresse au long de ses formes rondes et polies que l'on croirait empruntées à quelque divin marbre du temps de Périclès.' *Le Messager*, 4 May 1838.

sculpture when he was getting a little hot (or pretending to be), but 'femmes de marbre' were a commonly admired physiognomy – a name even given to a type of prostitute to whom some men were drawn.[14]

What a stir those dancing legs caused! When Fanny Elssler's gauze skirt split in the middle of a performance of the *cachucha* in Paris, the theatre erupted in raucous cries of joy from the men (and of horror from their wives). An anonymous reporter in a column simply entitled 'Legs' in *Illustrated London Life* in 1843 observed the reaction of elderly rakes to the exposure of these 'arrow legs':

> We have seen gentlemen, even elderly gentlemen, deeply affected by this glorious display. We perfectly recollect in admiring the emotion of several ancient aristocrats in the stalls, in the recent appearance of the legs of Fanny Elssler. We thought that we observed one aged and respectable virtuoso shedding tears; another fainted in his satin breeks [breeches] and diamond buckles; one appeared to go mad and bit his neighbour's pigtail in half in sheer ecstasy, Oh! The legs of Fanny displaced a vast deal of propriety, and frightened sober men from their prescribed complacency.[15]

For the anonymous columnist, the Opera was simply 'a bazaar of legs'. Could it be that, like Don José, the old men were polishing rather more than their opera-glasses? Under their 'breeks', their 'priming-pins' perhaps? The Victorian critic's phrase 'fainting in his satin breeks' may allude to this.

Gautier used extravagant comparison (and his richest humour) to contrast those who made it to his 'gallery of erotic beauties' with those *rats* of the Opéra who did not. But there is a deeper point behind his vitriol, since his comments come directly from his comparison with the Spanish dancers. His view, again also shared by other critics, was that Parisian ballet needed revival, perhaps an injection of Hispanic libido:

> What a miserable lot they are! There is enough ugliness, misery and poverty of form to move you to pity. They are as thin as lizards that have been fasting for six months, and when you inspect them without your opera glasses, their bosoms, which are hardly perceptible amid the fragile swirling of their

14 The reiteration of the Pygmalion mythology was the subject of a play, *Filles de marbre*, by Théodore Barrière and Lambert Thiboust, dating from 1853. Its protagonist falls in love with his inert female statues. See Virginia Rounding, *Grandes Horizontales: The Lives and Legends of Four Nineteenth-Century Courtesans* (London, 2003), p. 19.

15 *Illustrated London Life*, 16 April 1843.

> arms and legs, make them look like spiders disturbed in their webs and madly scuttling away. I do not know if you have taken it into your head to make a special study of a ballet girl's head and neck. When lit from below, their clavicles form a ghastly transverse projection, attached to which, like the strings on the bridge of a violin, are four or five tendons stretched to breaking point on which Paganini could easily have played a concerto.[16]

In one sense this was deeply unacceptable. Pontificating from his infamous rose-coloured waistcoat, he wrote engagingly, informatively and perceptively, but it would appear that in the above quotation he was alluding to those so-called 'rats' – the young girls in the *corps de ballet* – and completely ignoring their atrocious social conditions. Abominably paid, worked to the bone during long hours at the *barre,* when walking home at night they were known earn extra money by offering sexual favours to elderly gentlemen, particularly those who were members of the infamous *foyer de danse* or the Jockey Club. The satirist illustrators of the time gave us a deeper insight.

GITANISMO AND DANCE

Another topic of argument among critics was the degree to which the old Spanish dances had been infiltrated by gypsy elements, leading to the much-discussed question of the birth of Flamenco. In Sor's view, for example, the 'corruption' of the steps of the 'Séguedille-Boléro' was the 'fault' of gypsies, in his view not a beneficial development. In his seminal article in the *Encyclopédie pittoresque* he claims that the *gitanas* had added rude stamping and contortions of the body to the steps of the pure tradition, partly because the officers of the invading foreign armies delighted in such things. After a long section on regional variations he adds to Blasis's notions of corruption:

16 'Et les danseuses, quelle triste population ! c'est une laideur, une misère, une pauvreté de formes à faire pitié : elles sont maigres comme des lézards à jeun depuis six mois ; et quand on les regarde sans lorgnette au plus fort de leur danse, leur buste, à peine perceptible dans le frêle tourbillon de leurs bras et de leurs jambes, leur donne l'apparence d'araignées qu'on inquiète dans leurs toiles, et qui se démènent éperdument. Je ne sais si vous vous êtes avisé de faire une étude spéciale du cou et de la poitrine d'une danseuse ; les clavicules éclairées en dessous font une horrible saillie transversale où viennent s'attacher, comme des cordes de violon sur leur chevalet, quatre ` dix nerfs tendus à rompre, sur lesquels Paganini aurait joué facilement un concerto.' Gautier, 'Les Danseurs espagnols'.

> Such was the *Bolero,* and thus it was preserved until the time Spain was invaded by foreign armies. At the approach of French troops to a village, everyone was confused, the theatres were closed and the actors dispersed. As soon as the garrison was installed, the military governor wanted a spectacle [...] no matter what it was like. [...] Mediocre [spectacles] were put on, often at the expense of the governor himself. [...] Above all the *Bolero* was demanded and dancers that otherwise would not have been tolerated by the public performed and not only did they add to the dance all the contortions and crude gestures that [the dancer] Requejo had prescribed, but they added gestures which were only found in certain dances of the *gitanos,* the Spanish gypsies. Somersaults and swerving were added and to debase them further they added steps where they stamped on the floor with flat feet several times in succession.[17]

Although subsequent dance-historians have countered his opinion, claiming that these steps – and the stamping – were already in place in traditional Spanish dances, the opening of a dialectic about modernity and traditional purity of form was a further issue that critics, and the *aficionados* of dance, delighted in.[18] Sor may simply have been rehearsing an anti-Romanist view, a prejudice which will be explored in relation to *Carmen* in Chapter Eight.

THE *CACHUCHA*

Wherever they came from, stamping steps (*sostenidos*) had become a feature of Fanny Elssler's celebrated *cachucha.* The roots, essence and meaning of this dance are crucial to an understanding of why Elssler's performance achieved more fame than any other Spanish dance on the stages of Europe.

17 'Tel était le *Bolero,* et c'est ainsi qu'il s'est conservé jusqu'à l'époque où l'Espagne fut occupée par des armées étrangères. A l'approche des troupes françaises dans une ville tout était dans la consternation. Les théâtres étaient fermés et les acteurs se dispersaient. [...] Dès que la garnison était installée, le gouverneur militaire voulait qu'on donnât un spectacle, [...] il fallait un spectacle quel qu'il fût. Alors on avait recours aux médiocrités qui, très souvent, étaient payées par le gouverneur lui-même, [...] Le *Bolero* fut demandé le premier ; alors, les danseurs que le public n'aurait point souffert autrefois se présentèrent, et non seulement ils ajoutèrent à cette danse toutes les contorsions et les brusqueries dans les mouvements que *Requejo* avait proscrites, mais ils y introduisirent des gestes qui n'appartiennent qu'à certaines danses des *gitanas, bohémiennes* d'Espagne.' Fernando Sor, 'Séguedille-Boléro', in Ledhuy and Bertini's *Encyclopédie pittoresque de la musique* (Paris, 1835).

18 See Marina Grut, *The Bolero School* (London, 2002), p. 8.

Already known for some time in ballet circles, the *cachucha* was not in any way related to the pastel shades of previous Parisian ballet. In the 1830s Elssler sharpened up, more than any other Spanish dancer, the Parisian taste for things Spanish. Narciso (Narcisse) Paz called the *cachucha* an 'American dance familiar with sailors and danced in ports' and includes an example in his Paris-published anthology of 1818.[19] Blasis gives a meaning which is perhaps more pertinent, citing its significance in the Romany language (*caló*), where *cachucha* signifies gold, and a *cachuchero* is a thief who steals jewels.[20] These insalubrious origins perhaps colour Blasis's view of the dance, which, as he viewed it, ended with the '¡*bien parado*!' – the 'frozen moment' when the dancers hold their final position in the Seguidilla-Bolero – which he clearly sees in this dance as the moment of coition or orgasm:

> Alternately do they salute, exchanging amorous looks: they give their hips a certain immodest motion, then they meet and press their breasts together: their eyes appear half closed, and they seem, even while dancing, to be approaching the final embrace.[21]

The meaning of 'final embrace' is thinly veiled. Blasis goes on to admit that the agenda is similar for 'almost every Spanish dance'. Dance is several times introduced into Carmen's activities in the opera, both at her entry (the Habanera) and later in the *Séguedille* and the dance before José, and is part of her characterisation alongside textual and conversational means. *Carmen* does not go quite as far as Blasis – or didn't in early performances, though the climactic conclusion has piqued the interest of several modern 'concept' producers of the opera.

Gautier had wanted to visit Spain long before he ventured there in 1840. His longing to visit may have been partly because, in his words, Spain had become 'à la mode', but it was also because, born in Tarbes, a stone's throw from the Pyrenees, and with southern blood (and looks) inherited from his parents, he felt some magnetic sense of belonging to Spain; it should be remembered that his original title for his *Voyage en Espagne* was *Tras los montes* [Across the Hills], from where he was born.

How did this visit sharpen his critical views on Spanish dancers? Was it a sudden discovery of authenticity at last: a realization that Paris had seen Spain through rose-coloured spectacles? Did he want to bring back the real

19 '... danse américaine. Familières aux gens de mer sur les Ports'. Narcisse Paz, *Première collection d'airs espagnols, avec accompagnement de piano ou guitare* (Paris, 1818).

20 Carlo Blasis (premier danseur au théâtre de Covent Garden), *Code complet de la danse* (Paris, 1830), extracts from his *Code de Terpsichore* (Milan, 1820).

21 Blasis, *Code complet de la danse.*

thing? The answer is no. Quite the reverse! To summarise his conclusions, he considered the fusion between the somewhat raw, unrehearsed *bailes* he witnessed in Spain and the immaculately trained adaptations of the *Escuela bolera* dancers in France a fortunate advance for French dance spectacle, a process of productive hybridisation. In the best of the Spanish dancers who visited Paris – Serral and Comprubí above all – he acknowledges a vital catalyst to French spectacle's imitating Spain, but some of those to whom they imparted their skills (such as Elssler and, later, Marius Petipa) could do it better, not least because they had rehearsed all their lives in what Gautier called the 'torture chambers at the bar'.

Spanish dancing in Spain was ultimately a deep disappointment. He wrote hilariously of his first encounter with a *baile nacional* in Vitoria in his *Voyage en Espagne*, throwing the full force of his lexicon of invective at the unfortunate dancers:

> No cheapskate theatre could ever have brought on to its woodworm-riddled boards a more worn-out, decayed, toothless, rheumy-eyed, bald, or dilapidated couple. The poor woman, who had plastered herself with cheap white powder, had a sky-blue complexion that called to mind the not very fresh corpse of a victim of cholera or drowning, and the two red splotches that she had daubed on her bony cheeks to give a little life to her eyes – resembling those of a cooked fish – particularly contrasted with the blue. With her veiny, emaciated hands she shook her cracked castanets that chattered like the teeth of a fevered man or the joints of a rattling skeleton.[22]

Elsewhere Gautier was thwarted for a different reason: he was admitted to *tertulias* – soirées given in people's homes – but found that well-brought-up girls were far happier engaging in European social dances than *boleros, fandangos* or *cachuchas,* which were associated with the lower classes and gypsies, and, as has been seen, were considered distinctly unladylike. He was

22 '… le théâtre à quatre sous n'a jamais porté sur ses planches vermoulues un couple plus usé, plus éreinté, plus édenté, plus chassieux, plus chauve et plus en ruine. La pauvre femme, qui s'était plâtrée avec du mauvais blanc, avec une teinte bleu de ciel qui rappelait à l'imagination les images anacréontiques d'un cadavre de cholérique ou d'un noyé peu frais ; les deux taches rouges qu'elle avait plaqués sur le haut de ses pommettes osseuses, pour rallumer un peu ses yeux de poisson cuit, faisaient avec ce bleu le plus singulier contraste ; elle secouait avec ses mains veineuses et décharnées des castagnettes fêlées qui claquaient comme les dents d'un homme qui a la fièvre ou les charnières d'un squelette en mouvement.' Théophile Gautier, *Voyage en Espagne* (Paris, 1843), chapter IV, 'Le Baile nacional'.

more fortunate when attending theatrical performances where some dancing was interspersed, giving him a direct point of comparison with similar spectacles mounted in the theatres of Paris. Overall, he concluded that it was in Paris that the best Spanish dance was to be seen. He was not alone. Europe preferred Spanish dance tamed, hybridised with ballet, and presented in adapted costumes.

Although his views of a particular dance-team often changed when they returned to the stage several times, Gautier too-often returns to the well-worn refrain about 'hot-blooded passionate southerners'. By 1837 he had developed sufficient critical acumen to recognize the extra streak of authenticity in Dolores Serral's *cachucha*: 'For Dolores the *cachucha* is a faith, a religion. [...] Fanny Elssler and Mlle. Noblet dance it a little like unbelievers.' But unbeliever or not, it was Fanny Elssler who captured the limelight with this dance, taking it not only to the stages of Europe but also to the Americas.

Elssler's dance was originally part of a ballet, *Le Diable boiteux*, developed from a tale by Lesage published in 1707 and known in English as *The Devil on Two Sticks*. It was created in 1836 by the choreographer Jean Coralli (1779–1854) for the Paris Opéra, where he had studied and for which he later produced several successful ballets, including *Giselle*. *Le Diable boiteux* became a landmark in several ways, causing many critics to see Elssler's cameo *cachucha* as embodying the essence of Spanish dance, more definitive, in fact, than those of Serral and Comprubí, who had taught her.

A theme central to *Carmen* the opera – though not the novel – is prominent in *Le Diable boiteux*, intensified by the introduction of Micaëla into Bizet's opera. This is the conflict between the 'ideal wife', the family childbearer, and the exciting, exotic lover, probably not from home, highly attractive to all the men around, and suggesting sexual pleasure away from the home hearth.[23] The context in which Fanny Elssler danced the *cachucha* in this ballet is striking, because her character dances it before guests in her own home: she was no angel of the fireside.

This complicated fantasy-ballet begins with a masked ball in the Teatro Real in Madrid, where rival men are attracted by three masked ladies. In the second act, set in an apothecary's laboratory, one of the men who figures prominently, Cleophas, hears a groan coming from a large bottle. Smashing it, a black vapour exudes and turns into a devil leaning on a crutch, who thanks Cleophas for liberating him and promises to serve him. Cleophas asks him to unmask the three ladies from the ball, thereby revealing Paquita, a simple working girl; Florinda, a dancer; and Dorotea, a young widow. Subsequent intrigues set in rehearsal and dressing rooms involve Florinda (played by

23 See Baudelaire's poem *Le Jet d'eau*.

Elssler) feigning a sprained ankle to avoid dancing with her partner, who would upstage her *pas*. While she is recuperating on a sofa, Cleophas enters and Florinda shows her affections. Other men appear and Cleophas, hiding behind a screen, observes her showing similar affections to all comers. In Act II she has invited all her suitors to dinner in her own house, but not Cleophas. The assembled company move to the drawing room so that she can teasingly dance for them. So that he can watch too, the devil lifts the roof of the house. Cleophas gazes down, realising her fickleness. Encouraged by others persuading him that she is nothing but a flibbertigibbet, he ceases his pursuit of her, and after many more sub-plots have been enacted, he and Paquita, the simple working-girl, are united in a final festive scene accompanied by *tambours de basque* and castanets.

The music, by Casimir Gide, clearly served the ballet well. Among extracts published in several versions, the piano reduction of the *cachucha* ran to over thirty editions. From a manuscript in Elssler's own hand, probably written as an aide-memoire, we know the music she originally danced to. Authentic transcriptions exist but so do other versions elaborating upon, or simplifying, Gide's music with its characteristic turns of phrase and *fioriture*. Other composers 'frame' it with evocative introductions; for example, F. J. Klose spun it out into a Fantasy for piano. A version for guitar published on New York's Broadway adapts the music with slithery chromatics, while Henry R. Bishop arranges it as a 'Rondo for the Pianoforte' and robs it of its characteristic acciaccature. A piano reduction of 'The Original Castanet Spanish Dance', claiming to have been 'performed with unbounded applause' by the Boston Brigade Band, was published there shortly before 1841.

The piece's enormous appeal to music publishers worldwide is hardly surprising, especially in an era when considerable money was invested in the fancy presentation of sheet music. Elssler's picture, often with her dance in full swing, was commonplace on covers. Sometimes a melody stave would be added – flutes were particularly favoured. Piano parts occasionally indicated the intervention of a *tambour de basque* and castanets.

The parallels between *Le Diable boiteux* and the story of *Carmen* hardly need be pointed out. Among them are the similarity not only in the woman delighting in her role as an *allumeuse*, but also in her using dance as an agent to excite multiple men. Her sexuality is employed to climb in society. If only José had seen through Carmen and married Micaëla – audiences would think – the librettists' equivalent of Paquita![24]

24 See Joellen A. Meglin, 'Fanny Elssler's Cachucha and Women's Lives: Domesticity and Sexuality in France in the 1830s', *Dance Reconstructed*, October 1992, pp. 73–96.

The popularity of this spectacle, which in some ways subverts the benign traditions of early nineteenth-century Opéra-ballet yet also employs many of its well-tried tricks – masked-balls; pink and white dominos; the formula of the hidden, observing rival – was certainly enhanced by Elssler's appearance dancing the *cachucha*. She was succeeded by other star dancers and the moment became engrained as a key-moment in Romantic, exotic ballet: a formula to stir audiences into questioning contemporary mores many times repeated on theatre stages.

In Gautier's discussion of Elssler's *cachucha* he opened a further topic of criticism: a comparison between the 'Christian' dancing of Maria Taglioni and the 'Pagan' dancing of Elssler, despite her 'German' looks (she was actually Viennese).[25] He isolates that dancing as the most powerful, sexual spectacle to have graced the Parisian stage:

> The dancing of Fanny Elssler is entirely free of academic principles. It has a unique character which sets it apart from every other dancer. Hers is not the virginal, ethereal grace of Taglioni, it is something much more human which more vividly engages the senses. Mlle Taglioni is a Christian dancer, if one can use such an expression for an art proscribed by Catholicism. She floats in like a spirit in a translucent mist of white muslin in which she likes to envelop herself, resembling a contented soul scarcely flexing the petals of celestial flowers with the tips of her rosy feet. Fanny Elssler is an entirely pagan dancer. She makes one think of the muse Terpsichore with her tambourine, and her tunic slit to reveal her thigh, held up with gold clasps. When she fearlessly arches her back, throwing her voluptuous arms behind her, she conjures up a vision of those beautiful figures from Herculaneum or Pompeii, standing out in white relief against a black background, accompanying their steps with sonorous, resonating crotales.[26]

25 According to one writer her face had 'the angularity of German script'.

26 'La danse de Fanny Elssler s'éloigne complètement des données académiques, elle a un caractère particulier qui la sépare des autres danseuses ; ce n'est pas la grâce aérienne et virginale de Taglioni, c'est quelque-chose de beaucoup plus humain, qui s'adresse plus vivement aux sens. Mlle Taglioni est une danseuse chrétienne, si l'on peut employer une pareille expression à propos d'un art proscrit par le catholicisme : elle voltige comme un esprit au milieu au milieu des transparentes vapeurs des blanches mousselines don elle aime à s'entourer, elle ressemble à une âme heureuse qui fait ployer à peine du bout de ses pieds roses la pointe des fleurs célestes. Fanny Elssler est une danseuse tout à fait païenne ; elle rappelle la muse Terpsichore avec son tambour de basque et sa tunique fendue sur la cuisse et relevée par des agrafes d'or ; quand elle se cambre hardiment sur ses reins et qu'elle jette en arrière ses bras enivrés et morts de volupté, on croit voir une de ces belles figures d'Herculanum ou de Pompéi qui se détachent blanches sur un fond

Elsewhere he signals the 'joyful' *cliquetis* of the castanets; no wonder the *cachucha* was dubbed a 'castanet Waltz' in English translations of the title of the dance.

In support of Gautier's isolation of the erotic qualities of Elssler's performance was another critic, Charles de Boigne, who was better than Gautier at pinpointing how she projected her sexual appeal. He estimated that Taglioni (who never danced a Spanish ballet) was her arch-rival, and was preferred by women *balletomanes,* while Elssler was always preferred by men; in general, however, the prudish lorgnettes ('pudique lorgnettes') of the Parisian public were not ready for Elssler's revelations:

> That swaying of the hips ... those provocative gestures, those arms which seemed to reach out for and embrace an absent being, that mouth which asked to be kissed, the body that thrilled, shuddered, and twisted, that seductive music, those castanets, that unfamiliar costume, that short skirt, that half-opening bodice, all this, and, above all Elssler's sensuous grace, lascivious abandon, and plastic beauty were greatly appreciated by the opera-glasses of the stalls and boxes. But the public, the real public, found it difficult to accept such choreographic audacities.[27]

Such commentary is more than mere indulgence: it isolates a sea-change in ballet, which is no longer a mere cameo to be observed, but a spectacle in which the audience is drawn into the action – not only by Elssler's embracing gestures, but by the whole episode, in which everyone watches her flirtatious dance, including Cleophas, from the rooftops. The *grand public* becomes just as much part of her audience as are the players on the stage. This new inclusivity is something also inherent in *Carmen,* where several scenes go out of their way similarly to draw in the audience, in particular in the abandoned 'Scène et Pantomime' discussed in Chapter Six.

The steps of Fanny's *cachucha* were still of interest forty years after she danced them and were supposedly immortalised in 1887 by the German

---

noir et accompagnent leurs pas avec les crotales sonores.' Gautier, *La Presse,* 11 September 1837; Gautier, *Écrits sur la danse.*

27 'Ces déhanchements, ces mouvements de croupe, ces gestes provocants, ces bras qui semblent chercher et éteindre un être absent, cette bouche qui appelle le baiser, tout ce corps qui tressaille, frémit et se tord, cette musique entraînante, ces castagnettes, ce costume bizarre, cette jupe écourtée, ce corsage échancré qui s'entr'ouvre, et pardessus tout la grâce sensuelle, l'abandon lascif, la plastique beauté d'Elssler, furent très-appréciés des télescopes de l'orchestre et des avant-scène. Le public, le vrai public, eut plus de peine à accepter ces témérités chorégraphiques, ces excès de prunelles.' Baron Charles de Boigne, *Petits Mémoires de l'Opéra* (Paris, 1857), p. 132.

choreographer Friederic Albert Zorn, transcribed into Laban notation by the dance historian Ann Hutchinson, though some doubt has been cast upon the accuracy of Zorn's transcription.[28] The music of a *cachucha* is driven by its poetic form: essentially it is a song with an introduction, *coplas*, characteristic refrains (*estribillos*), and a short coda. Its musical characteristics are that it is in 3/8 time, the major key, and its vocal range is no more than a minor sixth. While there was certainly no particular *cachucha* melody used by Bizet in *Carmen*, a study of its musical characteristics in relation to its extreme popularity may solve the riddle of Carmen's dance-song at the end of Act I, which Bizet calls *Séguedille* but in fact is nothing of the sort.

A year after Elssler's popularisation of the *cachucha* another piece of Gautier's contains an interesting paragraph about costume. This sows seeds for the importance of dress in such spectacles, which would grow as the century progressed. Both opera and dance were to recognise the increasing importance of costume – both its realism and its symbolism. In 1834, reviewing a Spanish dance evening at the Palais Royale, Gautier pronounces that:

> The way Spanish dancers dress is far preferable to that of the French dancers, who seem to be addicted to white muslin in the style of Mademoiselle Taglioni. The sequins have a charming effect, they attract the light, sparkling suddenly and unpredictably and flooding your vision; however, they seem to have for a long time been relegated to the costumes of suburban acrobats, of Harlequin suits and those of ridiculous Marquises. What dancers need is feathers, tinsel, artificial flowers and little gold bells: all the silly, fantasy make-up of wandering actresses.[29]

28 See Ann Hutchinson Guest, *Fanny Elssler's Cachucha* (London, 2008).

29 'La manière de se costumer des danseuses espagnoles est de beaucoup préférable à celle des danseuses françaises, qui paraissent vouées à la mousseline blanche depuis Mademoiselle Taglioni. Les paillettes sont d'un effet charmant ; elles accrochent la lumière par points brusques et inattendus, et fourmillent vivement à l'œil ; cependant, elles sont reléguées depuis longtemps sur les jupes des saltimbanques de Carrefour, les habits d'arlequin et de marquis ridicule. Ce qu'il faut à une danseuse, ce sont des plumes, du clinquant, des fleurs fausses, des épis d'argent, toute la folle et fantasque toilette de comédienne errante.' Théophile Gautier, *Histoire de l'art dramatique en France* (Paris, 1858), vol. 1, p. 14.

FURTHER DANCERS

There were some performers who seemed to follow Gautier's extravagant suggestions (which were surely somewhat tongue-in-cheek). Among them was the infamous Lola Montez, a dancer claiming to be a Spanish noblewoman but whose appellation 'Irish Slut' was, in terms of Victorian hypocrisy, nearer the truth. After a trial for adultery in London, she had strings of lovers (including Liszt) and became talk of the town in Paris when she danced there in 1844. Certainly, she kept the flames of Spanish dance alive, though her *succès de scandale* in Paris was rather short lived.[30]

To summarise her rather eventful life, it might be remarked that she decided on a stage career in her early twenties, far too late to learn the techniques of classical ballet. Realising the potential of Spanish dance, she first found a teacher in London and then sailed to Cadiz to learn more, perhaps visiting Seville but certainly not dancing on the stage of Teatro Real there, as she claimed. On her return to London in 1842 her skill at what we would now call 'networking' ensured her introduction to no lesser stage than that of Her Majesty's Theatre. The critics rained plaudits on her, the public, bouquets.

Several new lines of criticism appeared. The *Evening Chronicle* proclaimed Lola Montez's dancing 'to be what we have understood Spanish dancing to be – a kind of *monodrama* – a representation of various emotions succeeding each other with great rapidity, but always with coherence and consistency'. This success ensured a tour in Germany and, in 1844, she hit the stages of Paris. Her act was no longer derived from the Bolero School but, as several reviewers testified, was centred on the communication of strong emotional states. *Gitanismo* – the attributing of everything Spanish to gypsy influence – had taken hold and critics saw her dance, in contrast to the Italian-French school of ballet, as full of gypsy energy. At first denied a debut at the Paris Opéra, critics came to her rescue, their *feuilletons* asking why she was denied a performance there. *Le Corsaire* complained that she 'dances the most voluptuous boleros and is perhaps the only woman who can perform this dance of the gypsies in all its romantic energy'. Sor would have shuddered at this identification of a bolero as a gypsy dance.

By now the Paris public (especially those from the Jockey Club, which Montez had infiltrated) would expect nothing less than corporeal exposure and lasciviousness from any Spanish dance performance. They were not to be disappointed. *Le Siècle* described how:

30 For a brilliant and concise account of the life of Lola Montez and her relationship with Liszt see Alan Walker, *Franz Liszt*, vol. 1: *The Virtuoso Years*, rev. ed. (London, 1988), pp. 392–394.

> After the first leap, she stopped on the point of her foot, and with a movement of prodigious agility, she detached one of her garters. The lorgnettes were riveted to the sight. Mlle Lola moved once more towards the footlights, waving between her fingers the ribbon which had just encircled her leg, and, fortifying herself with her most rebellious graces, she threw this ribbon to the spectators.[31]

Attributing this to an 'Andalusian style', the review nonetheless considered that she had over-stepped the mark (she never repeated the stunt), but her driving a coach and four through all the values of the Italian-French school of dance put paid to her career in France. Lola Montez, who acquired the taste for smoking small, strong cigars mentioned by Mérimée, was a *Carmen avant l'heure,* but only just – her appearances almost coincided with the publication of the novella in the 1840s. As her biographer, Bruce Seymour, claims:

> Her beauty was reputed to conceal a physical courage as great as any man's, and the cigarettes she constantly smoked characterized her disdain for conventional femininity. She could ride like an Amazon, was deadly with a pistol, and had horsewhipped more than one man who had dared to impugn her character.[32]

Preparing the stage for *Carmen,* a few other dancers deserve a mention. One such was the Andalusian dancer Petra Cámara, whose activities were at their peak a decade after Montez; she created a storm in Paris in 1851. As principal dancer in a Spanish troupe of twenty-eight, she performed at the Hyde Park 'Great Exhibition' in London before moving on to the Gymnase-Dramatique in Paris and to Versailles. A short biography of her, appearing in 1855 after her second season in Paris, sketches a highly romanticised picture of Seville, contrasting the gypsy quarter of Triana with the more prosperous main town; the contention is that Cámara carried all the exoticism of the gypsy ghetto into her art, which she eventually took north. The little biography already recognises Andalusia as 'French and poetic': 'notre poétique Andalousie!' Its unidentifiable author spends an inordinate amount of lyrical prose on the female costumes of the gypsies and fantasises about singers 'accompanied by a hundred guitars', before surmising that 'La Petra knew how to dance the *bolero* while still at her mother's breast.'

Amidst such exaggerated tosh, it was certainly true that Cámara's origins lay in Triana and that her art was built on Triana's gypsies, their looks and

31 Quoted Bruce Seymour, *Lola Montez: A Life* (New Haven and London), 1995, p. 73.
32 Seymour, *Lola Montez,* pp. 1–2.

their ways. But she also acquired technique, having been noticed at an early age by an impresario (she was only 13 at the time, according to her biography). She received a rigorous training at the Teatro Real in Seville, where the troupe that Spain exported to northern Europe was formed. Undisputedly, it was the first ever large-scale exportation of live Spanish spectacle.

Gautier, who by now was writing with more authority about technique (and ogling less), noticed both the skill of this 'pearl of Seville' – her nickname – and her fire, though he for some reason did not cover her 1851 performances. Of an 1853 performance in the opera-ballet *Le Lutin de la vallée*, after having praised the French dancer Mlle Guy-Stéphan, he described the way Cámara brought 'savage Andalusian imagery of *tambour de basque*, castanets, fan, sombrero and cape' to the stage, speaking also of her 'disturbing charm, as irresistible as death itself'.[33] Such accoutrements were recent additions to exported Spanish dance spectacle.

Two months later Gautier waxes yet more lyrical about her insertion of Spanish dances into a vaudeville, recalling for us that sense of *costumbrista* spectacle considered in Chapter Two. Focussing no longer on the female dancer but rather on the pairing with her *majo*, he begins his article as follows:

> When Petra Cámara comes forward to the footlights and raises the lace of her mantilla and the dark fringes of her eyelashes, the true sun of Andalusia lights up the theatre ... Her head voluptuously rests on the shoulder of her *majo*, who wraps his cape around her like a curtain.

He returns to the importance of Spanish costume and his love of what we would today call 'bling':

> Imagine a sparkling jumble of filigree buttons, folderols, silk tassels, ornaments, *soutaches*, fringes, embroidery and every fancy decoration that a delirious haberdasher might sew on a bodice.[34]

33 '... tout cette ardente, gracieuse et pourtant sauvage poésie andalouse du tambour de basque, des castagnettes, de l'éventail, du sombrero et de la cape'. Gautier, 'Le Lutin de la vallée etc.', *La Presse*, 1 February 1853.

34 'Lorsque la Petra Cámara, s'avançant près de la rampe, soulève les dentelles de sa mantille et les franges noires de ses paupières, le vrai soleil d'Andalousie a illuminé la salle ... La tête voluptueusement penchée sur l'épaule de son *majo*, qui lui fait un rideau de sa cape [...] imaginez un étincelant fouillis de boutons en filigrane, de passequilles, de houppes de soie, d'agréments, de soutaches, de franges, de broderies et de tout ce qu'un passementier en délire peut coudre d'ornements fantasques après un corsage'. Gautier, 'Théâtre du Gymnase: Petra Cámara, Danses ajoutés dans les «Folies d'Espagne»', *La Presse*, 7 July 1853.

Gypsy costume had become imperative in Spanish spectacle for the French.

Following Petra Cámara with the Royal Ballet from Madrid was the dancer who created the most powerful ripples in the artistic world of Paris: Lola de Valence, as she was known there. Her real name was Lola Menea. Not only were her shows acclaimed, but she was also immortalised in paintings (and a subsequent oil-sketch) by Manet, and in a quatrain by Baudelaire, who went to see her with the painter. Manet's companion Zacharie Astruc composed another poem for her and set it to music, publishing his *mélodie* with an ornate cover depicting the *danseuse* (see Plate 3.1). Closest in time to the composition of Bizet's opera, and with Manet's biographical proximity to Bizet, she was perhaps the most vibrant influence on the *Carmen* team. She captured Parisian audiences in 1862 with a season beginning in April at the Odéon and continuing from August to September at the Hippodrome. She danced with the veteran dancer Mariano Comprubí. Manet was moved to ask her to sit for him in the grand studio owned by the English painter Alfred Stevens. The results were several, but first was a large portrait in oil (123 cm × 92 cm) that hung in Manet's atelier after its completion in 1863 until 1870, when it was put up for sale by the well-known art dealer Duret; it was bought by the singer Jean-Baptiste Faure in 1873.[35] Between these times it had been exhibited in the salon of 1865.

This portrait's companion piece was a less formal painting, the *Ballet espagnol*, where Manet depicts a dance from one of the ballets in their programmes, *La Flor de Sevilla*. Lola de Valence is seated, and Comprubí dances some kind of *Escuela bolera* dance with Anita Montez. The men are dressed in Andalusian costumes, and in the final oil version virtually everyone holds castanets. Although essentially a studio painting (it contains accessories from Manet's own studio and also models the subsidiary figures on Goya), it captures the two dancers' movements and costumes above all, as was observed by several of its critics. Giving the semblance of a performance, or the end of one, Manet throws in a paper-wrapped bouquet.

The portrait of Lola de Valence is frequently misunderstood as a gypsy portrait. As Mario Bois has observed, it is nothing of the sort: the dancer's 'cone' skirt, bolstered with underskirts, is that of a ballet dress, not the long skirts of gypsies depicted by many of the *costumbrist* painters. She wears classical ballet shoes, not the heeled shoes associated with Flamenco.[36] Her legs are in classic fourth position. Yet, although this is not a real gypsy-style costume at all, it is noticeably adorned with the very accoutrements Gautier had listed in his comparison between French and Spanish dance costumes, and

35 See *Manet–Velázquez : La Manière espagnole au XIXe siècle* (Paris, 2002), p. 380.

36 Mario Bois, *Manet : Tauromachies et autres thèmes espagnols* (Paris, 1994).

its colours are those typical of Andalusian shawls. Her left hand is placed on her hip – one might say proudly – in the stereotypical position sometimes known as the 'Carmen elbow.'

Baudelaire, when faced with the painting, saw in its subject 'the beauty of a character at once tenebrous and playful.'[37] Certainly audiences would imagine they were being transported to Triana when she danced, but this was *gitanismo* – a gypsy-ballet, not the real thing, and certainly not Flamenco, as is so often assumed. Manet was perhaps catering to a growing appetite among the well-to-do Parisian bourgeoisie for paintings of costumed actresses, singers and dancers: Chassériau had painted Petra Cámara; Courbet, the Spanish actress Adela Guerrero; and there were, of course, various portraits of Fanny Elssler.

Still more attention was drawn to Manet's painting by the quatrain Baudelaire penned, originally hoping Manet would use it as a caption:

Entre tant de beauté que partout on peut voir	Amongst so much beauty that one can see around
Je comprends bien, amis, que le Désir balance.	I well understand, that Desire is measured.
Mais on voit scintiller dans *Lola de Valence*	But you see shining in *Lola de Valence*
Le charme inattendu d'un bijou rose et noir.	The unexpected charm of a pink and black jewel.

Exhibited at the same time as Manet's *Olympia*, which was seen as highly provocative if not obscene, Baudelaire's reference to a 'pink and black jewel' was viewed in a similar vein, becoming part of the *succès de scandale* surrounding Manet in this year. The memory of Lola's performances continued to excite artists even up to the time of Picasso, who sketched her several times.

On the cover of Zacharie Astruc's *mélodie* is another representation of Lola, from a lithograph Manet executed in 1863.[38] The song went into countless editions – she invaded the salons of the bourgeoisie all over Europe.

It is hard to be precise about what her shows were like. What we do know is that she displaced the earlier shows of Spanish dancing, entirely based on *boleros*, which had captured Paris audiences up to her appearance in the 1860s. Up to that time, about thirty dancers had been celebrated in the city – a fair number. Costume and colour were important features of the Parisian

37 'Une beauté d'un caractère à la fois ténébreux et folâtre.'

38 There are two other representations as well: a watercolour with black crayon, indian ink and gouache (1862), and an eau-forte and aquatint from the following year. See Bois, *Manet*.

Plate 3.1 Elaborate cover of the sheet music for Zacharie Astruc's *Sérénade* for Lola de Valence. Note the unusual fonts and the detailed portrait by Édouard Manet.

production, but Lola de Valence's appearances changed the whole perception of Spanish prowess in dancing on the stage.

By now the mechanisms of the press and the entrepreneurs behind the dance profession had learnt how to keep the enthusiasm burning, not least so that the next Spanish shows could be profitably rolled out, attracting even larger audiences and further good criticism in the press. Successful artists such as Elssler were followed across the world, and the triumphs of their

American performances in particular were reported in detail by the Paris press. It was not unusual for the many illustrators, who employed varying degrees of satire, to portray dancers with one foot in Europe and one in the New World. America was of particular interest to the cultivated French at this time, and they devoted a long-running periodical to it: the *Revue des deux mondes*. Paris was proud of those whose careers it had helped on their way.

Another benefit of prolonging the memory of the most celebrated dancers was that it provided music publishers with a lucrative market in the domestic sphere. They brought out all kinds of follow-ups that could be played on the piano at home, among them selections of the hottest numbers from the dancers' shows, fantasies on their themes, arrangements for all kinds of instruments, and plenty of gypsies. French composers vaguely modelled their Spanish-style compositions on authentic Spanish exemplars. A common strategy in such publications was to market sheet music with a picture of the celebrated dancer on the cover, and an 'as danced by' etiquette appended. The plethora of sheet music claiming to have been danced by one or another celebrated performer sometimes leads one to doubt the truth of the claims on the covers, and it is difficult to ascertain what music accompanied which performer. What is clear, though, is that Spanish stage-shows had become an immensely important growth area of the Parisian music industry once Spain opened up after its conflicts of the 1820s.

This chapter has concentrated on dance, but other Hispanic spectacle also graced the stages of Paris. There was 'higher' music, if that hierarchy can be drawn, deemed superior less from any aesthetic evaluation than from the social classes who attended it. Such was opera, and there were hints of Spain in French opera before *Carmen* – many of them. They will be interrogated in Chapter Eight to yield a view of why Bizet's Spanish opera 'made it', while its predecessors have been rather left to obscurity.

PART II

FICTIONS, REALITIES, STRUCTURES

CHAPTER FOUR

From Novella to Libretto

On 27 June 1830, as the result of a broken love-affair, Mérimée, aged 27, embarked on a visit to Spain. 'Les voyages font la jeunesse', so the French saying goes ('Travels form your youth'). Certainly, this voyage was to prove crucial: its resonances never left him. As he himself confessed, the final straw was rejection by one Mélanie Double, daughter of a celebrated physician. Mérimée's attraction to her is documented in letters to Stendhal with whom (among others) he shared intimate details of his sex life. She never married but a chain of letters, now as a *confidante*, followed. Essentially Dr Double had decided that Mérimée's financial stability was insufficient for him to marry his daughter.[1] His unluckiness in love, however, turned out to be fortuitous: he admitted that his journey to Spain was 'the best thing he ever did'.[2] Had he remained in Paris, licking his wounds, we would never have had Bizet's opera.

Mérimée's trip turned out to be curative Hispanotherapy, although the Spanish official who had issued his passport had feared that his liberal allegiances, atheism and anti-clericalism might have made his entry into Spain somewhat risky.[3] Just in case, his close friend Stendhal had proposed to Mérimée a Plan B, which was to go to Italy instead. In the end his entry into Spain went smoothly and he soon found himself in the south. Although he visited Spain on several subsequent occasions he was never to visit Andalusia again. This is an important point, since by the time he wrote *Carmen* he would be drawing upon details of this visit of over ten years before, or else reminding himself of it through reading some of the already-mentioned travelogues. This he certainly did.

1 On this episode in Mérimée's life see A. W. Raitt, *Prosper Mérimée* (New York, 1970), pp. 76–78.

2 'C'est une des belles actions de ma vie'. Letter to Jenny Daquin, 25 September 1832, Mérimée, *Correspondance générale*, vol. 1, p. 184.

3 See Mérimée, *Correspondance générale*, vol. I, p. 66n2, letter from A. Tourguéniev: 'un libéral et athée de sa notoriété courait grand risque en entreprenant ce voyage' ('a liberal and atheist of his standing would run a great risk in undertaking this journey').

Largely by happenstance, he met plenty of like-minded liberals in Spain, not least the Montijo family, to whose children he became known by the pet-name Don Prospero. He had met the brother of the Count of Teba by chance when travelling in a shared diligence, and through this became friends with this famous family, particularly the Count's wife, Mme de Montijo, with whom he corresponded intimately and frequently, in an entirely Platonic way. Her daughters sat on his lap and loved him. Little was he to know that one of them, Eugénie, would later become Empress of France by marrying Napoleon's cousin and subsequently settle in England – in Chislehurst, to be precise.

LETTRES D'ESPAGNE

Mérimée wrote only a couple of personal letters back from Spain but he wrote four essays, later collected as *Lettres d'Espagne* and published in the *Revue de Paris* in the early 1830s, then added to and reprinted in book form.[4] Two are from Madrid and two from Valencia. It is often forgotten that aspects of these are incorporated in the opera libretto in addition to its basis in the 'story' of José and Carmen, though the libretto's relationship to the two texts is very different. It would be a simplification to say that the *Lettres* provided the contextual underpinning of the action while the later novella provided the story, but there is a grain of truth in it.

The librettists of *Carmen* had clearly read these letters very closely, extracting details to incorporate directly, sometimes by-passing Mérimée's later novella. Although he had not yet been appointed to his esteemed position as inspector of public monuments, Mérimée's eye for significant detail in events and places he witnessed emanates from every page of these early writings. His relaxed travelling agenda allowed him the time to achieve this: his aim, after all, was not to 'see the sights' but to become a professional writer, unlike the authors of guide books who followed in his footsteps, packing in the principal edifices and moving rapidly on from place to place as they wrote their travelogues. As Xavier Daros remarks, 'The eye of the storyteller (i.e. Mérimée) was incessantly on the look-out. The slow pace of diligences allowed him the time to observe both the people and the places he would later incorporate into his works.'[5] In his way he was a committed *costumbrista* even if he was a foreign visitor.

4 'Les Combats de taureaux', *Revue de Paris*, January 1831; 'Une exécution', ibid., March 1831; 'Les Voleurs', August 1832 (republished in book form in *Mosaïque* [Paris, 1833]); and 'Les Sorcières espagnoles', *Revue de Paris*, December 1833, added to editions of *Mosaïque* after 1842.

5 'L'œil du conteur est sans cesse aux aguets. Le pas lent des diligences lui laisse le temps d'observer des physionomies et des sites qu'il placera plus tard dans ses œuvres.' Xavier Daros, *Mérimée* (Paris, 1998), p. 99.

Underpinning his visit was a desire to get to the heart of the true Spanish spirit, to capture its authenticity and idiosyncratic ways. These early essays are consequently much deeper than mere travelogues, and nothing like the more idealised writings of many French visitors. He went straight for the jugular, choosing subject-matter that sometimes showed Spain at its most cruel and vengeful, sparing nothing in its details despite knowing these might be repellent to his readers (the librettists later took pains to avoid them). His own responses betray an ambivalent mixture of attraction and distaste, but mostly the former: he many times displayed an interest in seemingly barbaric Spanish traditions.

However much these essays stem from observations there are clearly embroideries and exaggerations: Mérimée's was not a sanitised Spain, but nor was it an embroidered Romantic one. Even so, in Meilhac and Halévy's transformation of the novella into a libretto many closely observed details either filter through directly, or are assigned to other characters or places. Essentially Mérimée's aim was to tell things as he experienced them. It was in the transfer process from novella, and the earlier *Lettres*, that the real Spain – a first glimmer of nineteenth-century realism – filtered through into the opera.

One of Mérimée's most fortunate attributes was his ability to befriend all manner of classes. On the one hand he could drink in *posadas* with the working class and even criminals; there were also the so-called 'easy-ladies' for whom he had already developed a taste in Paris, and he wrote back to Stendhal with precise details about the cost of the girls he procured: 15-year-olds, guaranteed virginal, could be had for only 42 francs apiece (a *doublon*).[6] On the other hand, he could hobnob with high-society Spanish liberals in Madrid, and the future empress he would dandle on his knee.

In the first letter back, Mérimée detailed some of the horrific practices of the early nineteenth-century *corrida*: he mentions the exploding *banderillos* employed when a bull refused to move from his *querencia* – the place in the ring constantly returned to by the animal. Their use, he notes, were egged on by the crowd's shouts of '¡Fuego! ¡Fuego!' ('Fire! Fire!). He notes the gored horses in their death throes, dragging their entrails around the arena, and he gives a detailed description of the exact way in which a skilled *torero* delivers the vertical, mortal blow to the 'cross' in the bull's back. Although in the opera a metaphorical safety curtain is lowered (in that the bullring itself is heard but not seen), some realistic details of the tauromachic spectacle make their way directly in, not least the way in which music was employed to signal 'la hora de la verdad': the moment of truth. Mérimée had observed the drum-roll

6 Mérimée, letter to Henry Beyle (Stendhal), 30 April 1835, *Correspondance*, vol. 16, pp. 88–89.

signalling this moment: 'Un roulement de tambours se fait entendre.' Similarly, he remarked upon the fanfare sounded when the bull is dead, and both these devices are employed by Bizet in the last act of his opera. At the outset of the essay Mérimée had proffered the oft-repeated arguments in favour of bullfighting: its reinforcement of national identity; its barbarisms being modest compared to that of the Romans; its economic benefit to agriculture; and the fact that out of twenty bulls, only one will be brave enough for the ring.

The *cuadrilla* (procession) in the opera may well have been taken from this first essay. It is enacted in detail in Bizet's work (though it does not feature in the novella) and is transferred exactly into the stage directions for the final act. We learn much about costume: the adjuncts, for instance, wore the 'costume de Crispin' – that of the valet from the *commedia dell'arte* and the subject of a well-known play by Lesage, *Crispin rival de son maître.* Mérimée also mentions the Andalusian clothes worn by most of the attendant men, 'resembling Figaro in the *Barber of Seville*'. Also described are the costumes of the *majos* and *manolas* who make up much of the audience. He noticed that the best seat, ornately decorated, was reserved for the archbishop, but that, in general, priests from lower orders were not allowed to attend, though some were to be seen in disguise. He tells us about the taunting processes carried out by the *picadors* and *chulos* (the matador's assistants – now an archaic term), who confuse the bull by waving brightly coloured draperies. The ubiquitous ritual of the matadors' receipt of a useless key (auspiciously to open the *toril* – the stable where the bulls are kept) is also detailed.

In terms of soundscape Mérimée's essay mentions the crowd's cries of '¡Viva! ¡Viva!' – cries several times put into the mouths of the opera chorus – and the constant whistling and jeering. Enriched by an appendix added in 1842, Mérimée pays his respect to the *torero* Francisco Sevilla, who had recently died of liver disease. Mérimée had the pleasure of meeting him, 'the most jovial companion whom you could ever meet'.[7] At least he had fulfilled his aim in encountering a representative of at least one of the country's principal national stereotypes. He was less fortunate as far as meeting a bandit was concerned, as he laments in his third essay.

He also witnessed a hanging, the subject of the second *lettre* and the background scenario of the novella, in which the narrator listens to José-Maria's life-story the night before he awaits the noose or perhaps garrotting. Here Mérimée's liberal and anti-royalist political stance is thinly veiled. He clearly sympathises with the condemned man, 'delicate to the point of honour', who had not realised that upsetting an *alguazil* (an agent of the state) could be a

7 '… c'était le plus gai compagnon qui se pût rencontrer'.

capital offence ('un cas pendable').[8] Whereas hanging remains only a threat in the opera, the execution Mérimée witnesses is a grim reality: the poor man is paraded to the scaffold on a mule. Typically, Mérimée also notices a proliferation of pretty young women who have come to enjoy the execution from the comfort of chairs on a balcony.

The barbarisms of Spanish punishments form a nagging background to *Carmen*. 'Danger lies with every step', sing the trekkers in Act III ('Et le péril est en haut, il est en bas, il est partout'), reassuring themselves that they are 'Unafraid of the soldiers who lie in wait down there, waiting for us to pass' ('Sans souci du soldat qui là-bas nous attend Et nous guette au passage'). By the end of the opera José is a man wanted for murder – perhaps two.

Another Spanish humiliation involving a parade through the town on the back of a mule is described in the second letter, and it too emerges in the libretto, in the gypsies' banter during the fight in the factory, this time imbued with obscene sexual connotations as the squabbling girls taunt Carmen:

CHŒUR DES CIGARIÈRES	CHORUS OF CIGAR GIRLS
La Manuelita disait Et répétait à voix haute, Qu'elle achèterait sans faute Un âne qui lui plaisit.	Manuelita said, And repeated it in a loud voice, That she could buy a good donkey Which would give her pleasure.
Alors la Carmencita, Railleuse à son ordinaire, Dit : « Un âne pour quoi faire ? Un balai te suffira. »	So Carmencita replied, Mockingly, as usual, 'A donkey, for what reason? A broom would be enough for you.'
Manuelita riposte Et dit à sa camarade : « Pour certaine promenade, Mon âne te servira ! »	Manuelita replied And said to her friend: 'For a certain type of walk My donkey would be perfect!'
« Et ce jour-là tu pourras À bon droit faire la fière ! Deux laquais suivront derrière, T'émouchant à tour de bras. »	'So on that day You'd have a right to be proud! Two lackeys would follow behind Swatting off the flies.'

The librettists are careful to preserve Mérimée's double-entendres. The primary sense is of the mule used to parade women identified as witches through the streets (the reference signified by the mention of the broomstick), with the lackeys following behind to whip their bare shoulders. A sec-

8 '... homme délicat sur le point d'honneur'.

ond meaning is more transparently obscene: the opposite end of the broom. The librettists' verses on this threatened ritual expand upon this local custom that Mérimée had observed in the *Lettres* and reworked in a scene in the novella. Also treated in this way – another dirty metaphor – is the focus on José's working on his priming pin.

Adept at flitting between muleteers and aristocrats, Mérimée's first experiences were nothing to do with all those '*ismos*' that have become dismissive critical terms among Spanish commentators on the nineteenth century. His interests may be segmented into *andalucismo* or *gitanismo, alhambrismo* or *majismo,* among many of the other Spanish terms implying a mild incursion of these elements into the tide of Romanticism; but if there is an underpinning term which can be applied it is *casticismo, castizo* meaning 'authentic', from a lineage or long-standing tradition.

MÉRIMÉE'S COMPANION, CALDERÓN

The crucial encounter with the *costumbrista* writer Calderón reinforced Mérimée's desire to experience Spain at close quarters. Mérimée had met him through Mme de Montijo's husband and they became lifelong friends. Essentially Mérimée saw him as distilling the Andalusian temperament ,and that caused him to forgive unanswered communications and unpaid debts.

Calderón, who shared Mérimée's liberal views, was at this time writing under the name of 'El solitario en acecho' ('The wanderer at the ready'). The pseudonym 'El Solitario' was used for his most important legacy: his celebrated book, already mentioned, *Escenas Andaluzas* [Andalusian Scenes]. This was not yet published at the time of his first meeting with Mérimée, but it was forming in his mind. The first paragraph of chapter fourteen of this classic book distils his *credo,* which he allies with the *casticismo* movement. Entitled 'Toros y ejercicios de la gineta' [Bulls and Exercises on Horseback], the chapter begins with a typically nineteenth-century 'spiral' sentence. It is a long-winded paragraph (saying the same thing in every sub-phrase), but it distils the approach he instilled into Mérimée:

> In a publication such as the present, which prides itself for its exactitude since its aim is to narrate and reveal the habits and customs of Spain in the most authentic way possible, characteristic of our lands, it would seem wrong and bad mannered to discuss the subject any further without mentioning

> something related to the national spectacle of Spain, which is none other than the bullfight.[9]

A committed *aficionado*, Calderón had clearly taught Mérimée to appreciate the details of every possible moment in a bullfight, and in the first *lettre* Mérimée delights in showing off his newly acquired knowledge. In an account that presages Hemingway's *Death in the Afternoon*, where the text is similarly peppered with the Spanish vocabulary of the bullfight, Mérimée outlines the customs of the *corrida* with his customary pausing to analyse its significant details. One of the more astute reviews of the premiere of the opera, Henri de la Pommeraye, recognised that the spirit of Calderón as well as Mérimée had been preserved in Halévy's libretto, quoting a poem by Alfred de Musset (who had himself done the tour of Spain):

L'un, comme Calderón, et comme Mérimée,	One, like Calderón and like Mérimée,
Incruste un plomb brûlant sur la réalité,	Encrusts reality in burning lead,
Découpe à son flambeau la silhouette humaine,	Cutting out in its flame the silhouette of humanity,
En emporte le moule et jette sur la scène,	Taking away its outline and throwing on to the stage,
Le plâtre de la vie avec sa nudité.	The naked model of life.

Prominent at the outset of the third *lettre* is Mérimée's lamenting that he never met a real bandit. Instead he is forced to turn to hearsay, and to his own imagination. The final story, about witches, is written in the format of an imaginary conversation between Mérimée and his guide. A young gypsy girl called Carmencita serves the pair food and drink. But his guide, Vicente, warns him against the family, believing that she is the daughter of a witch. She is important as one of the sources pointed to by commentators seeking the literary roots of Mérimée's 'pretty gypsy.' In his short description of her in the *lettre*, the two things he seems to like most are her fairish skin ('pas trop basanée') and the *gazpacho* she brings them. Maybe her seductive eyes and pretty feet really did bowl him over – he was certainly sufficiently distracted to misremember *gazpacho* as a kind of salad (it is actually a cold

9 'En publicación como la presente que presume de muy castiza por lo mismo que su principal propósito se cifra en relatar y revelar los usos y costumbres españolas por el modo más peculiar de nuestro suelo que posible sea, parecería ya malsonante y peor visto si dejáramos andar más allá el asunto sin sacar á plaza algo que frise y toque con el espectáculo nacional de España, que no es otro que las corridas de toros.' El Solitario [Serafín Estébanez Calderón], *Escenas andaluzas* (Madrid, 1847), p. 183.

soup), though he usually records the food and wine he enjoyed in Spain in his customary precise way.[10]

He naturally commented in detail on the Andalusian women he encountered in his correspondence, 'the secrets of the mantilla', as one commentator suggests, and those doe-eyes and tiny feet. Mérimée himself remarks on their uncut tresses 'which would have dragged along the ground were they not tied to their heads with combs of enormous length.'[11] Was this Carmencita real or was she one of the girls in his *bordel imaginaire*? Difficult to know.

Among other significant details that recur in both novella and libretto are the characteristics of the bandit. In the second *lettre* Mérimée is struck by the 'honour' of these men, which filters through into José's characteristics in the libretto. In the third *lettre* it is clear that he takes the side of those who regard banditry as an 'honourable profession' in a country seriously afflicted by inequality in the distribution of wealth; this is the 'Robin Hood' aspect, already touched on in Chapter Two. So much for the realities of the true Spain.

Other details from this *lettre* feed into Mérimée's later construction of the character of Don José. Note the prefix, 'Don'. José was a downfallen *hidalgo*, a descendant of a noble family, which entitled him to use it; indeed, several mentions of his previous nobility are scattered through the novella. A detail developed in the novella but only just making it into the libretto is the stealing of his expensive watch, developed from a scene in the third *lettre* about the 'montre de Bréguet'. The *plantation* (layout) for the scene indicates that in the plaza, opened at curtain up, a young Spaniard (who is crucial in the scene to be discussed in Chapter Six) is pacing up and down looking at his watch (which he might have stolen).[12]

One question that needs to be asked is why Mérimée wrote his *Carmen* story in the format of a novella – not really a short story, and not long enough to be a proper novel. The answer lies in the infrastructure of French publishing in the nineteenth century. The text first won acclaim though its publication in the *Revue des deux mondes* – the 'two worlds' being Europe and America – and because of its success was accepted to be published as a book, so popular that it was republished in several anthologies before the end of the century. This was one of the ways in which the publishing industry in France worked: if a book was well received in a *Revue* (often in series form) it would

10 Mérimée, *Lettres d'Espagne*, IV (1831), pp. 434–435.

11 M. Bataillon, 'L'Espagne de Mérimée d'après sa correspondance', *Revue de Littérature Comparée*, January–March 1948, p. 41. 'Leurs cheveux qui traîneraient à terre si on ne les rattachait sur le haut de tête avec un peigne de dix-huit pouces de haut' (Mérimée, *Correspondance générale*, vol. I, pp. 74–78).

12 Typed notes to the *livret de mise en scène*, see Chapter Nine.

later re-emerge as a proper book. A short novel fitted this periodical format. Such was the fate of Mérimée's *Carmen*, which is hardly surprising since it is a masterpiece of its genre. Had Bizet's opera not intervened, with its 'offprints' of the most popular numbers illustrated with black-and-white covers drawn from the operatic scenes to which they pertained, there would surely have been several versions of Mérimée's text with illustrations by the most celebrated book-illustrators of the time: Doré perhaps, the Rouargue brothers … or even Manet. His friend Calderón's book had been published in this way.

MÉRIMÉE'S BORROWINGS

The ingredients that went into the novella itself have long fascinated literary scholars, and there is no doubt that Mérimée took details from quite a few literary sources, some of which he had worked on himself as editor, prefacer or translator. Paragraphs of *Carmen* have been put alongside those of many other writers but, persuasive though many of these are, ultimately Mérimée's novella was a product of his own hyperactive imagination, fertilised by the Spain he so closely experienced. His was an imagination catalysed by detail. If 'realism' is a term applied to his work, or to *Carmen* the opera, that is one aspect of its genesis.

A few of these comparisons with previous literature merit attention but the roots of the story Mérimée himself acknowledges in an oft-quoted letter:

> I've just spent eight days locked away composing a story which you told me fifteen years ago and which I fear I have spoiled. It's about a *jaque* ('young blood') from Malaga who had killed his mistress.[13]

However scrupulous he was as an observer, documenter and travel-writer, by now he was also an aspiring professional writer seeking a place in the higher echelons of French *hommes de lettres*. At the time he wrote *Carmen* he was in the middle of a run of novellas. The extent of his borrowing is dwarfed by the skill with which he marshalled his material.

One writer who influenced him (one whom we have encountered already in another context) was Théophile Gautier, whose *Voyage en Espagne* stemmed from a tour he undertook in the same year as Mérimée, but a few months before; they never encountered each other on their trips. Extracts from Gautier trickled out in the French press between 1840 and 1843 and in book form in February of the latter year. Jean Pommier, in exhaustive articles on sources that influenced Mérimée, considers Gautier the most important

13 Mérimée, letter to Mme de Montijo, 16 May 1845.

of his models. But this may be more complex a process than it seems, for Gautier himself would no doubt have had knowledge of Mérimée's earlier *Lettres*. And, after all, they went to the same places.[14] There are similarities between their descriptions of the gorges in the *sierra*, but so there would be: Gautier describes them as 'well-prepared theatres for a murder' and notes the 'enclaves of gypsies'.[15] The similarities between their descriptions of the girls in the tobacco factory are striking:

Gautier:

Entrons quelques instants à la manufacture de tabac … L'on nous conduisit aux ateliers où se roulent les cigares en feuilles. Cinq à six cents femmes sont employées à cette préparation. Quand nous mîmes le pied dans leur salle, nous fûmes assaillis par un ouragan de bruits ; elles parlaient, chantaient et disputaient tout à la fois. Je n'ai jamais entendu un vacarme pareil. Elles étaient jeunes pour la plupart, et il y en avait de fort jolies.
Le négligé extrême de leur toilette permettait d'apprécier leurs charmes en toute liberté.

Let us enter the tobacco factory for a minute … We were led to the workrooms where the cigars are rolled in leaves. Five to six hundred women are employed for this task. When we set foot in their room, we were met with a storm of noises; they were talking, singing, and arguing all at the same time. I've never heard such a din. They are mostly young and some of them were very pretty.
The skimpiness of their dress meant that one could appreciate their charms as much as one wanted.

Mérimée:

On me mit de garde à la manufacture de tabacs de Séville … Il y a bien quatre à cinq cents femmes occupées dans la manufacture. Ce sont elles qui roulaient les cigares dans une grande salle, où les hommes n'entrent pas sans une permission du Vingt-Quatre, parce qu'elle se mettait à leur aise, les jeunes surtout quand il fait chaud. Je monte [dans la grande salle des cigares] … Entré dans la salle, je trouve d'abord trois cent femmes en chemise ou peu s'en faut, toutes criant, hurlant, gesticulant, faisant un vacarme à ne pas entendre Dieu tonner.

I was put on guard at the cigarette factory in Seville … Some four to five hundred women working in the factory. Some of them rolled the cigars in a large room where men are not allowed to enter without a permission from the *Vingt Quatre*, because they strip off, especially when it's hot. I go up [to the large cigar room] … On going in, I found about three hundred women just in their blouses or less, all shouting, crying, gesticulating and making a din which would make you fail to hear God's thunder.

14 See Jean Pommier, 'Notes sur *Carmen*', *Bulletin de la Faculté des Lettres de Strasbourg*, November and December 1929; February and April 1930.

15 '… théâtres tout préparés pour un meurtre' ; 'une *tertulia* de Bohémiens'.

The description of the factory is probably partly invented. As the historian of the factory and the dissemination of tobacco in Spain has shown, the *fábrica* was well run and its atmosphere was generally quiet, although there were occasional uprisings as documented in various images of the time (see Plates 5.1 and 5.2).[16] Essentially Gautier is the root of the sexualisation of the factory and this is imitated by Mérimée, who even plunders Gautier's vocabulary. It is very possible that Mérimée never even visited the factory but was content to take Gautier's word as to what it was like. Whatever the case, in the opera, its exact (or imagined) details are incorporated into José's description of it in his first dialogue with the newly arrived Zuniga, and it is memorably fashioned into two lengthy choruses, one on the heady pleasures of smoking, and the other portraying the dispute between Carmen's supporters and her enemies.[17]

Further sources that influenced Mérimée are to be found in Le Sage's *Histoire de Gil Blas de Santillane*, from where the holes in Carmen's silk stockings seem to have originated, and also her red attire – her ribbons and shoes – which one Melchior Zapata brings out of his haversack at the moment of encounter with Gil Blas in Book 2.[18] The borrowing is evident at two key moments in the novella: first when the narrator meets Carmen, and second in José's extended description of his meeting with her, which forms chapter III. This rather suggests that Carmen's appearance was neither a reminiscence of the Carmencita whom Mérimée had encountered while journeying in Andalusia, nor entirely his own invention.

Also borrowed were some details from Musset. Hardly surprising! Musset and Mérimée were close. Openly plundered is an episode in Musset's *Mimi Pinson* where Mlle Pinson suggests cracking a plate to substitute for castanets:

16 See José M. Rodriguez Gordillo, 'El personal obrero en la Real Fábrica de Tabacos', in *Sevilla y el Tabaco* (Madrid, 1984), pp. 84–92.

17 Pommier, 'Notes sur *Carmen*' (April 1930), p. 211 et seq. is persuasive on this connection and expands his argument to details that have only underlying relevance to the libretto.

18 We should recall that Lesage, author of *Le Diable boiteux*, discussed in the previous chapter, was an important dramatist and author portraying Spanish customs in French. The lengthy adventures of Gil Blas around Spain were an obvious source of detail, along with Cervantes's *Don Quixote*. The passage in chapter VIII reads 'il tira de son havre-sac un habit couvert de vieux passements d'argent faux, une mauvaise capeline avec quelques vieilles plumes, des bas de soie tout pleins de trous et des souliers de maroquin rouge fort usés.' For a full account of how Carmen's appearance is blended with quotations from Gautier see Pommier, 'Notes sur *Carmen*' (1930), p. 209 et seq.

Musset:	
Mlle Pinson prit une assiette et fit signe qu'elle voulait la casser, ce à quoi Marcel répondit par un geste d'assentiment, en sorte que la chanteuse, ayant pris les morceaux pour s'en faire des castagnettes, commença ainsi …	Mlle Pinson took a plate and signalled that she wanted to break it, at which point Marcel signalled his agreement so that the singer, using the bits as castanets, could begin …
Mérimée:	
Où trouver des castagnettes ? Aussitôt elle prend la seule assiette de la vieille, la casse en morceaux, et la voilà qui danse la Romalis en faisant claquer les morceaux de faïence aussi bien que si elle avait eu des castagnettes d'ébène ou d'ivoire.	Where can the castanets be? At once she took the only plate the old lady had left and thus danced the *romalis* by clacking the bits of china together so well that they could have been castanets made of ebony or ivory.

One further source of Mérimée's *Carmen* must be mentioned: Pushkin's narrative poem *Tsygany* [Gypsies], which not only has a similar storyline to *Carmen* – it is the tale of a gypsy girl stabbed to death by a jealous non-gypsy – but also contains a passage which may have been at the root of the librettists' idea for the interrogation scene. Carmen's 'la-la-la' replies to Zuniga's questioning, saying 'she's singing her songs for herself' are strikingly similar to a scene where the gypsy girl, Zemira, refuses to disclose the name of her new gypsy lover to her *payillo* (non-gypsy) husband. The idea of the gypsy as a carefree bird that permeates the text of the Habanera may also have come from this source.

In the libretto Carmen's lack of cooperation during her interrogation indicates that nothing will make her talk: 'You can cut me or burn me, I still won't talk!' ('Coupe-moi, brûle-moi, je ne te dirai rien !'). Although no such phrase is to be found in the novella, it does appear in Pushkin's text. Mérimée was not fluent in Russian when he wrote *Carmen* and had not yet translated *Tsygany*, but when he did a very similar phrase would appear in his translation. It is difficult to see all this as a coincidence. By the time Meilhac and Halévy were writing the libretto they had access to Mérimée's Pushkin translation, and the librettists were clearly familiar with other Mérimée works.[19] The idea of gypsy resiliance to fire and pain is captured in the emblematic salamander,

19 Alexander Pushkin, *Gypsies*, trans. Roger Clarke, in *Eugene Onégin & Other Stories* (London, 2005).

which appears in all three texts and was widely associated with this aspect of gypsy character.[20]

The Mérimée translation reads as follows at the crucial point where Zemfira, the gypsy girl, confronts Aleko, her previous lover, to tell him she is in love with another man:

ZEMFIRA	
Vieux jaloux, méchant jaloux, coupe-moi, brûle-moi ; je suis ferme, je n'ai peur ni du couteau ni du feu.	You're old and jealous, evil and jealous, cut me! Burn me! I'm strong and have no fear of your knife or fire!
Je te hais, je te méprise, j'en aime un autre ; je meurs en l'aimant.	I hate you, I despise you, I love someone else and I am dying of love for him.
ALEKO	
Finis. Ce chant me fatigue. Je n'aime pas ces chansons sauvages.	Shut up. Your song is tiring. I don't like these gypsy songs.
ZEMFIRA	
Cela ne te plaît pas ? que m'importe ! je chante la chanson pour moi.	Oh you don't like it? What do I care: I'm singing it to myself.
Elle chante :	She sings:
'Coupe-moi, brûle-moi, je ne dirai rien ; jaloux, méchant jaloux tu ne sauras pas son nom.	'Cut me and burn me, I won't say a word; jealous old man, evil old man: you'll never know his name.
Comme je l'ai caressé quand tu dormais la nuit ! comme nous avons ri tous les deux de tes cheveux blancs.'[21]	How I've caressed him while you were asleep in the night and how both of us have laughed at your grey hair!'

The passage confirms the librettists' skill at transformation and reallocation in several ways. The non-gypsy husband is reflected in José's noble birth but ultimate unsuitability for the *vie errante*. Mérimée's translation of Pushkin reads: 'You like us even though you were born rich. But that doesn't make you well-suited to freedom, for you are acquainted with comforts.'[22] The passage also demonstrates the librettists' art of carrying the implications of borrowed texts into their libretto. The idea of the gypsy's being resistant to any

20 Alexander Pushkin, *Gypsies*, trans. Roger Clarke, in *Eugene Onégin & Other Stories* (London, 2005). See also David A. Lowe, 'Pushkin and *Carmen*', *19th-Century Music* (Summer 1996), pp. 72–76.

21 Mérimée, 'Les Bohémiens' (*Tsygany* traduit de Pouchkine), *Nouvelles* (Paris, 1852), pp. 279–300. Quote from pp. 287–288.

22 'Tu nous aimes toi, bien que né parmi les riches ; mais celui-là ne s'habitue pas facilement à la liberté, qui a connu les délices du luxe.'

kind of torture is brought over into the interrogation scene, as is her insolence in singing gypsy songs to the authorities. The sentiments from Pushkin also metamorphose into a dialogue with José at the end of the opera, when Carmen confronts him with her burning passion for her new love, Escamillo: 'Je l'aime et devant la mort même, je répéterai que je l'aime !' ('I love him and in the face of death itself, I repeat that I love him!') Even Zemfira's laughing at her previous lover's jealousy is incorporated into José's inflamed dialogue: 'Ainsi, le salut de mon âme je l'aurai perdu pour que toi – pour que tu t'en ailles, infâme, entre les bras rire de moi !' ('So I sold my soul so that you, you devil, could fall into his arms and laugh at me!') Carmen is unafraid of torture or death to the last: 'Frappe-moi donc – ou laisse-moi passer !' ('Kill me or let me leave!') Here is a focussed example of the librettists' transference of both ethos and detail into sung dialogue.

TRANSFORMING THE NOVELLA

The question of evaluating transformations from literary sources to a libretto is a favourite of critics wanting to pour scorn on deviations, simplifications, and downright contradictions of an original text. There is a view – and it was rehearsed in several of the reviews of the first production of *Carmen* – that any sort of deviation from the original, or watering down of its characters, is a fault: Bizet's *Carmen* was not Mérimée's. Alan Raitt expresses this view:

> To appreciate *Carmen* at its true worth, it is of course necessary to forget all about Bizet; whatever the musical and dramatic merits of the opera, it is in its basic schema no more than an emasculated and prettified version of Mérimée's tale. What Mérimée wrote has a savage power that the more conventional picturesqueness of Bizet's adaptation cannot match.[23]

Although Raitt will have heard only the recitative version of the opera, *Carmen* enthusiasts may justifiably disagree with this view. Subsequent performances may have consciously reverted to its Spanishness (even Albert Carré's of 1898), but on probing the premiere production one finds that even then there was plenty of earthiness, and downright sexiness, in Galli-Marié's performance – many thought a bit (or a lot) too much.

23 Raitt, *Prosper Mérimée*, pp. 191–192.

To counter Raitt's argument it should be asserted that although the opera can lose many of the novella's harsher qualities (the liberal use of his blunderbuss by Carmen's hideous one-eyed husband García, for example), the best of its productions – and above all the music, scenography, dance and costume – put this back, albeit in a different way. Mere libretto-knocking displays ignorance of the skilled art of fashioning a story into musical theatre of one sort or another, which is a profession in itself. The celebrated 'duos' – in this case Meilhac and Halévy – had somehow to turn their sources into forms which could be set to music, and in *Carmen*'s case provide some rhymed numbers (airs, duets and choruses) and spoken dialogue, as was required at the Opéra-Comique. In addition, the dance-songs in the opera are an effective way of replacing narration, especially when they contain explicit movements that advance the action.

Another criticism aimed at the opera was that it was too simplistic. Halévy quotes a detractor (an elderly admirer of the librettist Scribe and a friend of Meilhac, with whom he played billiards). He claimed:

> It's not a play … There's a man who meets a woman … he likes her: that's the first act. He loves her, she loves him: that's the second. She doesn't love him any more: that's the third. He kills her: that's the fourth. You call that a play? In a real play you have to have surprises, quid pro quos, adventures, things that make you wonder what's going to happen in the next act.

'Père' Dupont, as Halévy calls him, predicted that *Carmen* would last for only twenty-five performances. The old boy lived until the age of 97, and Halévy remarks sardonically that on the day he died the opera celebrated its 307th performance![24]

But the question of the suitability of the novella for transformation on to the stage was addressed by every other critic of the premiere, too. Some admired the librettists' capturing of Mérimée's original, especially the libretto's retention of direct quotations from the novella. Others thought it did not work. Arthur Pougin, one of the most perceptive critics of the day – and one of the wittiest writers – posed the question 'Are there in Mérimée's masterpiece, the elements of a staged play, and above all an *opéra-comique*?' He

24 'Et votre pièce, ça n'est pas une pièce … Voilà un homme qui rencontre une femme … il l'a trouvé jolie, c'est le premier acte. Il l'aime, elle l'aime, c'est le second. Elle ne l'aime plus, c'est le troisième. Il la tue, voilà la quatrième. Et vous appelez ça une pièce !! Dans une vraie pièce il doit y avoir des surprises, des quiproquos, des péripéties, des choses qui font dire : " Qu'est-ce qui va passer à l'acte suivant ?"' Halévy, 'La Millième representation de *Carmen*', *Le Théâtre*, January 1905 (I), p. 10.

went on to remark on Mérimée's essence: 'With his literary technique, as cold as a pair of scissors, as brief as a flash of light, as implacable as death itself, Mérimée triumphed in gripping effects.' He concluded that the operatic transformation failed because the characters had become uninteresting. However, he admired its 'episodes'.[25] Raitt's antipathy was presaged in several of the early criticisms: 'Where is that acrid scent, that violent smell of the ferocious that you get when you read Mérimée's masterpiece?'[26] Some other critics were simply revolted by the character of Carmen onstage at the bourgeois Opéra-Comique: *Carmen* the novel was good to read but Carmen herself became 'odious and unacceptable' when transferred to the stage.[27]

HALÉVY AND MEILHAC

Ludovic Halévy's relations with Bizet were historical in that he was the son of the writer Léon Halévy and nephew of the composer Fromental Halévy, in whose composition class Bizet had studied at the Conservatoire. In 1863 Fromental had been in the audience for Bizet's *Les Pêcheurs de perles* and written admiringly in his *Cahiers*: 'Remember this name: it is that of a musician!' He spoke of a 'remarkable performance' and a score of 'the highest order'. Regarding it as the first masterwork of the composer, he found 'an assurance, a tranquillity and an ease of writing with a strong handling of both chorus and orchestra'.[28] The connection later became familial when Bizet married Geneviève Halévy, Fromental's niece.

Ludovic Halévy's output was prolific and by the time he embarked on the conversion of Mérimée's novella into an *opéra-comique* he had twenty year's experience and over forty works behind him, his greatest successes having been collaborations with Henri Meilhac. Many of these were transformations of previous literature into libretti. The exact division of labour between the two librettists remains a matter of speculation. Many of their librettos were for Offenbach, *La Belle Hélène* and *La Vie parisienne* being the

25 'Avec son procédé littéraire, froid comme un ciseau, bref comme un éclair, implacable comme la fatalité, Mérimée atteignait des effets saisissants […] c'est qu'aucun des personnages n'est intéressant'. Arthur Pougin, *Le Ménestrel*, 7 March 1875. Quoted Wright, *Dossier* (Weinsberg, 2001), p. 20.

26 'Où est cette saveur âcre, ce violent arôme de férocité qui vous vient au lèvres à la lecture du chef-d'œuvre de Mérimée ?' Simon Boubée, *Gazette de France*, 8 March 1875. Quoted Wright, *Dossier*, p. 39.

27 Paul Bernard, *Revue et Gazette Musicale*, 7 March 1875. Quoted Wright, *Dossier*, p. 24.

28 'Retenez bien ce nom, c'est celui d'un musicien […] exécution remarquable […] d'un ordre supérieur […] une assurance, une tranquillité, un maniement facile et puissant des chœurs et de l'orchestre qui annoncent certainement un compositeur.' L. Halévy, *Cahiers* (1863) (MS), BnF.

most successful. Commentators see Meilhac as the wittiest of the two, with a particular talent for biting parody, while Halévy was more concerned with the overall narrative. Meilhac's literary beginnings had been in satire, writing under the pseudonym Talin for the *Journal pour rire*. Halévy, by contrast, had more understanding of the theatre, having first obtained a junior post at the age of 18. Jean-Claude Yon estimates that he had 'a familiarity with the "wings" [*les coulisses*]' and a 'solid classical understanding' of theatre.[29] It was perhaps the structure that Halévy added; certainly the distillation of Mérimée's twice-narrated novella involved some process of reduction to render it down to the original libretto of three acts and four tableaux, though there were many possibilities for scene changes within these basic divisions. *Carmen* was not at all typical of their earlier work, though one or two of their familiar targets of parody will be found, especially foreigners (above all the Englishman discussed in Chapter Six), but also the differences between José's Basque habits and those of the gypsy Carmen and her Andalusian companions. Also from Meilhac may have come the satire on the military in general, both their ineptitude and their continual associating with the very criminals they are meant to be rooting out.

In May 1872 Bizet had announced to his friend the composer Paul Lacombe that the Opéra-Comique had commissioned three acts from him and that Meilhac and Halévy would write him something 'light-hearted' which he would treat 'as succinctly as possible, not an easy task but I hope to manage it'.[30] So far no subject seems to have been proposed, but the words 'gai' and 'serré' (compact), one suspects, echo advice from the directors at the Opéra-Comique. The often-recited account of the directorate's reaction to the proposal of *Carmen* as the subject of an *opéra-comique* will be saved for the next chapter; suffice it here to assert that using Mérimée's story seems to have been Bizet's idea.[31] One more important directive came from the house: in 1873, probably after performances of Gounod's *Roméo et Juliette*, an article in the statutes was passed forbidding the performance of entirely sung works and stipulating the inclusion of spoken dialogue.[32] *Carmen* had

29 'Cette familiarité avec les coulisses vient compléter une très solide formation classique'. Jean-Claude Yon, 'Le Théâtre de Meilhac et Halévy : Satire et indulgence', in *La Famille Halévy, 1760–1960* (Paris, 1996), pp. 162–177.

30 'De Leuven et Du Locle m'ont commandé trois actes. Meilhac et Halévy seront mes collaborateurs. Ils vont me faire une chose *gaie* que je traiterai aussi *serrée* que possible.' Bizet to Paul Lacombe, May 1872, in *Lettres, 1850–1875*, ed. Claude Glayman (Paris, 1894), p. 241.

31 See Halévy, 'La Millième représentation de *Carmen*'.

32 Article 24: 'Sont interdits les ouvrages exclusivement lyriques et sans dialogue parlé.' See Hervé Lacombe, *Georges Bizet* (Paris, 2000), pp. 622–623.

to have substantial dialogue in its original version for the Opéra-Comique whatever has been done to it since.

Returning to the style of criticism typified by Alan Raitt, it is illuminating to build upon the methods of comparison between source and libretto explored by Christine Rodriguez, which are much more based upon similarities of structure than differences in detail or characterisation.[33] She follows a series of semiologists who have focussed upon theatre, but concentrates upon the process of transfer from a text into a libretto in a series of analytical stages beginning with an underlying template that might underpin countless narratives. For the *Carmen* libretto her most fundamental structure (what semiologists call a macrostructural level which is non-specific to the text) is in three parts:[34]

Order – Disorder – Restoration of Order.

At first glance the novella does not follow this pattern, since when it begins José has already abandoned the order to which he once bore allegiance, and has turned to lawlessness. If, however, we regard his soliloquy in chapter III as the 'source', with details rather than the structure taken from the entire novella, then Rodriguez's pattern can be discerned.

Rodriguez identifies a kernel, a 'noyau irréductible', which has to be preserved in the transfer of a text to a libretto if comparisons are to be worth drawing. She also identifies processes of truncation, simplification and clarification as essential qualities in the fashioning of a libretto. A charting of the essential structure of the novella and libretto in *Carmen*, reveals much more underlying similarity than approaches based on character studies might reveal (Table 1).

A further approach – through the aural and visual procession of signs that appear and sometimes recur – gives insight into the transfer processes of these highly skilled librettists. Signs in opera may be seen (as part of the stage-business) or heard (not just musically, consider gunshots or mass shouting, for example), or both at once. Table 2 perhaps reveals a fundamental technique of libretto formation, where the narrative is structured by establishing a number of 'pillars', aural or visual signs supporting the forward-moving storyline and holding the action when a purely musical number intervenes.

33 Christine Rodriguez, *Les Passions du récit à l'opéra : Rhétorique de la transposition dans 'Carmen', 'Mireille', 'Manon'* (Paris, 2009).

34 See Anne Ubersfeld, *Reading Theatre* (translation of *Les termes clés de l'analyse de theatre*) (Toronto, 1999), p. 33 et seq (original Paris, 1996).

Table 1 The Structure of *Carmen* (Novella and Libretto)

Novella

	Introduction: *topos*/ characters/themes	José meets Carmen	Series of transgressions: Prison defection etc.	Murder of Carmen	Impending execution of José
Method of Introduction	Narrator meeting José and Carmen 1st narrative (Chapters I and II)	—	José's *récit* in Chapter III 2nd narrative (Chapter III)	—	—

Libretto

	Introduction: *topos*/ characters/themes	José meets Carmen	Series of transgressions: Prison defection etc.	Murder of Carmen	Impending execution of José.
Method of Introduction	Musical genre, numbers, Carmen's 'motive' and physical display (dance-song), scenery/costume, 'foil' character of Micaëla	Spoken dialogue and elements from *Lettres d'Espagne*	Series of transgressions lessened but opera follows 2nd narrative (Chapter III) Introduction of Escamillo.	Murder of Carmen	Impending execution of José suspected but not present in opera.

STRUCTURAL TRANSFER

In the process of libretto construction the nature of transfer is central, differing between the several professionals active within the field – often working in pairs, as in *Carmen*. Some important scenes are transferred directly, for example the whole episode of José's allowing Carmen to escape, his imprisonment and cashiering, and the smuggling of a file and a coin baked inside a loaf of bread (which his honour prevents him from using). All this is incorporated in exact sequence in the libretto, reinforced as part of Carmen's armoury when she turns against him (Table 2).

The copious spoken sections left considerable scope for incorporation of many details from Mérimée's sources, both the novella and the *Lettres*, as well as retention of the underpinning structural contrarieties, over-arching themes, and their reinforcement in the music. Most notable are the binary

Table 2 Structural Transfer: Sounds and Props

Novella	Libretto	Remarks
	ACT I	
	Lances with red and yellow pennants (Scene 1 overall stage direction).	From 1st *Lettre d'Espagne.*
Cigarette smoking. Narrator smokes **cigar** with José; ***papelitos*** with Carmen.	Transferred to soldiers and factory girls, scenography and chorus.	
Watch ('Montre de Bréguet').	In the typed *plantation* preceding the *livret de mise en scène*, the instruction is for the young Spaniard to be looking at his watch.	Incorporated into costume and action in the Scène de l'Anglais.
	1st **Bugle** fanfare ('Changing of the guard') (Scene 2).	Diegetic aurally and visually: soldiers are seen as well as heard.
	Soldiers parade **lances** with red and yellow pennants and are commanded to present arms.	
	2nd **bugle** fanfare, now with miming on fifes. (Old guard depart).	
	Factory **bell**. **Cigarette** smoking by factory girls. Chorus about 'ivresse' of smoking (Scene 4).	
Priming-pin dialogue; throwing of **flower**.	Retained little altered in extended dialogue and melodrama (Scene 5).	
	Letter from José's mother brought by Micaëla.	
Knife I (in factory).	Transferred into chorus and following dialogue (Scene 8).	
	Rope first used to tie Carmen's hands (Scenes 9–11).	
	Arrest warrant introduced.	
	Rope used for Carmen's escape in original stage directions.	

Novella	Libretto	Remarks
	ACT II	
Tavern accoutrements.	Elaborated in stage directions, dialogue and scenography (Scene 1).	
	Torchlights.	*Candelas* from *Lettres d'Espagne*?
Gold coin.	Retained in dialogue and action. Spent in Lillas Pastia's tavern in Triana (Scene 5).	A stereotypical reference to a gypsy attribute: gypsies would do anything for a gold coin. See Chapter Eight.
Details of Andalusian **oranges**, **confectionery** and ***frutos secos*** purchased by Carmen in Sierpes (rue de la Serpent).	Retained in detailed dialogue, but ordered from Pastia's bar in Triana instead of in Sierpes. The episode is used to distance Carmen's gypsy eating habits from José's more conventional northern ways, and the meals in the barracks.	
Castanets, broken plates.	Transferred into musical number and action in Carmen's *la-la-la* dance for José.	
	Bugles (clarines) (from *coulisses*).	
2nd appearance of **flower**.	Transferred into extended musical number (José's flower aria).	
Fight with **swords** (José and officer).	Retained in altered version in sung scene with Zuniga.	
Bandages and **curative drink** (*chufas*, now called *horchata*).	Eradicated from libretto.	

Novella	Libretto	Remarks
	ACT III	
Bundles (*gros ballots*).	Incorporated into initial stage direction (Scene 1).	
Breach in the wall.	Retained in dialogue.	
Fire.	Retained in stage direction (Scene 2).	
Playing cards.	Transferred from García to Carmen, Frasquita and Mercédès in musical number. Their meaning is intensified: they are now the 'pitiless cards ('cartes impitoyables').	
Castanets.	Incorporated into dialogue.	
Gun shots (Remendado shot first by the soldiers, then finished off by García).	Transferred to José aiming a shot at Micaëla (Scenes 5–6).	
Navaja (José kills García).	Transferred to fight between José and Escamillo (Scene 6).	
Dagger (drawn by English soldier, threatening José). Carmen saves him.	Transposition of characters. Carmen draws dagger on José, Micaëla interposes herself and offers herself as victim.	
	ACT IV	
	Oranges developed from previous mentions in novella. Cigarettes also sold alongside water, etc. (Scene 1).	
	Fanfares, now from bullfight.	
Bell at hermitage where José prays.	Religious ending eradicated.	
Final killing with ***navaja***.	Final knifing preserved but location altered from mountains to outside the bullring (Scene 2).	
Execution of José arranged by **garrotting machine**.	Execution of José presumed?	

oppositions, which form a criss-cross of themes and images in text and libretto. These opposing axes are another important feature preserved in the transfer process: not only the contrast between José's Basque roots (and Micaëla's) and the Andalusians, but also the issue of 'pure' lineage and as opposed to those of mixed race. We learn, for instance, that José-Maria is clever enough to self-accompany himself on the mandolin, has a pleasant voice, and that the narrator is clever enough to recognise his *zortzico* (the Basque dance in the unusual rhythm of 5 beats in a bar). As we shall see, Carmen's lineage is ambiguous: is she Basque or is she Andalusian? Certainly, the opposition of north (Navarre) and south (Andalusia and Gibraltar) is a major theme stressed in both the novella and the opera (Table 3).[35]

Another way of looking at the story would be more dynamically: as a series of journeys interacting to some extent by happenstance. By her nature, Carmen – as a gypsy – is a rootless vagrant. José, by his defection, has become one. The narrator (and the Englishman who will be examined in Chapter Six) have come from afar. The soldiers are constantly on the move to intercept the journeying criminals. Escamillo, as a *torero*, travels from bullring to bullring.

Retained from the novella is the scene where Carmen comes, tambourine in hand, to dance for the colonel, 'decked out like a shrine, dolled up and rigged up with gold and ribbons all over. Her dress was sequinned and so were her blue shoes. She had flowers and gold braid all over.'[36] Her subsequent visit to Lillas Pastia's tavern in Triana is also shared between novella and libretto, with many details retained. Mérimée's detailed description of her attire becomes a gift for opera costumiers; elsewhere in the libretto (when she appears at the bullfight) a stage direction indicates that she should be dressed 'radieuse et très bien nippée' ('radiant and very well turned out'). Any director using a traditional setting might well light upon the extraordinary transformation of her usual red into sequinned blue, and transfer it to her entry into the bullring. José must have been doubly taken aback to see her dressed in the colour he so much admired in the girls of his homeland. Sequins were ubiquitous in elaborate Spanish clothes at this time, their glinting on the jackets of *toreros* was used to confuse the bull during the *corrida*.

Commentary on the principal characters will be left for Chapter Eight, though characterisation is of course an important issue in the transformation

35 See Lola Saint Martín Arbide, 'Carmen at Home: Between Andalusia and the Basque Provinces (1845–1936)', in Langham Smith and Rowden, Carmen *Abroad* (London, 2020) chapter twenty.

36 'Elle était parée, cette fois, comme une châsse, pomponnée, attifée, tout or et tout rubans. Une robe à paillettes, des souliers bleus à paillettes aussi, des fleurs et des galons partout. Elle avait un tambour de basque à la main.'

Table 3 Structural Contrarieties in Novella and Libretto

Novella	Libretto	Remarks
North–South provinces/dress/custom. José's Basque roots/Carmen's Andalusian roots.	Retained substantially in dialogue and scenography. Trifurcated in scene with Englishman.	See Chapter Six.
Law versus lawlessness. Christian state law versus Gypsy law. Obedience/transgression. *Guardia civil*/soldiers to curb mutiny in the factory and hunt down smugglers and bandits.	Retained substantially in dialogue and scenography. Reinforced with 'gamins' imitating soldiers. Climax in José's defection from law to lawlessness in 'hinge' scene.	Opposition captured many times in musical genres. See Chapter Five.
Marriage versus alternatives: prostitution, short-term relationships. Carmen/García, Carmen/Zuniga, Carmen/English soldiers.	Micaëla added to introduce status quo of bourgeois marriage. 'Kept' woman introduced in scene with elderly Englishman. Opposition of long-term and short-term relationship stressed in José's pleas to start a new life with Carmen.	Opposition captured many times in musical genres. See Chapter Five. Character of Micaëla and unseen mother emphasised early in the opera, returning just before the dénouement.
Gypsy versus *payillo*/mixed race versus 'old Christian stock' (Carmen/José). Theme introduced early in novella with narrator.	The first mention of Carmen's race is delayed until after the establishment of Micaëla as a potential wife for José (in the dialogue during Carmen's interrogation). José's pure blood – he is a *vieux chrétien* from Navarre – is introduced in the first dialogue of the libretto, with Zuniga.	Carmen's recurrent motive brands her as a gypsy in its dramatic appearance in the unexpected final section of the Prélude.
Hierarchically structured profession versus *vie errante*. Church or military versus 'travelling life'. José's failure in structured professions is recounted in his chapter III narrative.	José's first consideration for the Church mentioned in first dialogue. Progression from military to vagrant life a central scene in the libretto. Rank is stressed.	Stress on military music in stage directions (changing of the guard; bugles etc.).
Political freedom versus subjugation. Mutiny to escape exploitative factory work.	Emphasis in extended musical numbers in libretto (factory girls fighting; trek in hills towards 'La liberté'.) Time-keeping of factory bell.	–
Superstition/magic versus reality. In the novella Carmen tells the narrator's fortune with a dead chameleon.	José and Carmen met on a Friday, the day of Venus. The flower has persistent 'magic' qualities.	–

from novella into libretto. It is difficult to see how the character of the narrator – transparently identified as Mérimée himself – could have been retained, though it is in some of the films.[37] In the novella the whole story is introduced by a narrator, an erudite lover of classical remains; he meets the bandit, and in turn Carmen herself, and then the bandit tells him his life story and why he is about to be put to death. This is quite different from the opera. The double-narrative, with the narrator both as someone to whom José recounts his story and someone who is for a moment suspected of direct involvement with Carmen, is too complicated for any opera, let alone the Opéra-Comique. Thus Mérimée's novella is turned into a simple, evolving story principally derived from chapter III of the novella.

GAINS AND LOSSES

Lost in the metamorphosis of novella into libretto are the narrator's erudite references to classical antiquity, Carmen's husband, and several other minor characters, though some aphorisms derived from the narrator's paraded wisdom do make their way through into the libretto (the qualities of a beautiful woman, for example, and the comparison between women and cats). Women have to have several features to be beautiful, Mérimée claims in the novella: 'the Spanish say, combine thirty *si*'s [*si* is Spanish for *yes*]; you must be able to define her by ten adjectives that are each applicable to three parts of her person.' As for the wisdom about cats: 'women and cats don't come when you do call them, and do come when you don't.'[38] This latter statement finds its way directly into the libretto; the former does not, but its spirit remains in many encounters between José and Carmen.

Essentially the librettists' formula was to adopt the well-established operatic convention of pairs of protagonists, and although it is often asserted that both Micaëla and Escamillo are additions, both these characters are latent in the novella, the former mentioned in direct contrast to the argumentative, self-willed Andalusian women José has encountered in his posting to Seville (an angel of the fireside); the latter developed as a macho man (and a rich one) not only from the character of Lucas in the novella, but also from the first *Lettre*.

None of the first reviews recognised that Micaëla might have been developed in the novel from a passing mention of Basque girls, traditionally reli-

37 The narrator appears in Vicente Aranda's celebrated film of *Carmen* of 2004.

38 '… suivant l'usage des femmes et des chats qui ne viennent pas quand on les appelle et qui viennent quand on ne les appelle pas.' *Carmen*, chapter III.

gious, and typically with blonde tresses and unrevealing costumes. More than half of these reviewers, many of them well-versed in the repertoire of *opéras-comiques* and clever with the pen, saw in Micaëla an 'Alice Navarraise', referring to a Norman country girl in Meyerbeer's *Robert le diable.* There are indeed many similarities apart from their both being the innocent girls from the country (Alice is 'une paysanne normande'): like Micaëla, Alice brings news of the death of Robert's mother and prays in the final act. Such parallels in the Opéra-Comique did not go unnoticed if they were successful – and will be further remarked upon with reference to Gallet's memory of how well spoofs at the expense of the English had gone down in *Fra Diavolo* (Chapter Six).

Moreover, Alice's entry into the opera may well have been a model for Micaëla's encounter with José in Carmen. Compare the two:

Meyerbeer, *Robert le diable*:

ALICE	
J'y viens pour remplir un devoir. Avec mon fiancé j'ai quitté ma chaumière. J'ai suspendu l'hymen qui devait nous unir …	I've come to fulfil a duty. I've left my cottage and my fiancé Postponed my marriage which would have united us
ROBERT	
Pourquoi ?	Why?
ALICE	
Pour accomplir l'ordre de votre mère !	To carry out your mother's orders!
ROBERT	
Ma mère bien-aimée ! Ah ! Parle, à son désir Je m'empresserai de me rendre.	My beloved mother! Ah! Tell me for her sake. I need to know now.

***Carmen* Act I: Duo**

MICAËLA	
[…] C'est votre mère qui m'envoie …	[…] It's your mother who sent me …
JOSÉ	
Ma mère … Parle-moi de ma mère ! Parle-moi de ma mère !	My mother? Tell me about my mother! Tell me about my mother!

Bizet skilfully exploits this moment as a transition from speech to song. At 'Parle-moi de ma mère !' José suddenly bursts into song, the moment intensified by the phrase's repetition on a higher note but with a wider leap down.

Plate 1 Manuel Cabral Aguado Bejarano (1827–1891), *The Death of Carmen* (1890). Oil on canvas, 37.5 cm × 56.5 cm. Private collection. © Sotheby's / akg.

Plate 11 Eugenio Lucas Velázquez (1817–1870), *Majas al balcón* [Ladies on a Balcony] (1862). Oil on canvas, 108 cm × 81 cm.

Plate III Manuel Cabral Aguado Bejarano, *Un borracho en un mesón* [A Drunkard in an Inn] (1850). Oil on canvas, 60 cm × 74.5 cm. Note the details indicating the extreme drunkenness of the main character, whose shirt is falling off. He is clearly singing. He has a wineglass in his hand and there is a broken bottle on the floor. He has lost a shoe. Other drunks are in his audience, many of whom seem bemused. The work's sister painting, *La reyerta* [The Brawl], depicts a scene of even more destruction, with broken furniture and crockery and a man ready for a fight with a drawn *navaja*.

Plate IV Alfred Dehodencq (1822–1882), *Un baile de gitanos en los jardines del Alcázar* [Gypsies Dancing in the Gardens of the Alcázar in Seville] (1851). Oil on canvas, 111.5 cm × 161.5 cm. Dehodencq was a Parisian painter who worked in Spain and North Africa and was employed by the Dukes of Montpensier. The scene is set outside the Pavilion of Carlos V, and the gypsy is dancing to the song of two women in the background as well as guitars and clapping. Representative of the *costumbrista* school, the painting depicts both custom and costume with an accuracy typical of the movement, and also the physiognomy of the North African dancer and singers. The use of black in the surrounding characters throws the vivid colours of the dancers into relief.

Plate V Illustration of an Opéra ball with Spanish dancers. From *Universal und Europaisade Modenzeitung*, 'Le Progrès: Modes de Paris pour l'Académie européenne des modes'.

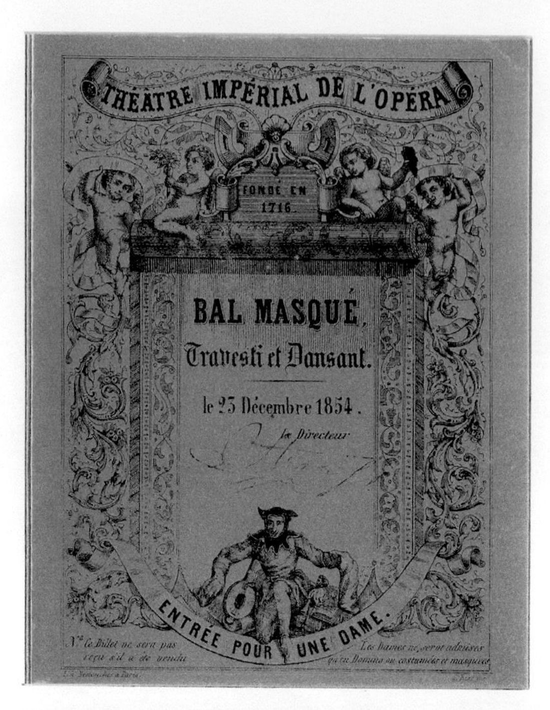

Plate VI A lady's entry ticket for a masked ball (*en travesti*) at the Paris Opéra (1854). These balls were increasingly graced by Spanish dancers as the craze for Spain burgeoned through the 19th century. The small print indicates that women will not be admitted unless dressed in the traditional 'domino' (a masked black cape) or in costume and masked. ('Les dames ne serot [*sic*] admises qu'en Domino ou costumes et masquees [*sic*].')

Plate VII Life-size model of a *banda taurina*, the signalling band employed at the *Plaza de toros* in Seville. These bands, consisting of percussion and *clarines* (a type of bugle), signalled to the bullfighting team the actions they should make, for instance proceeding from the capework to the 'moment of truth': the killing of the bull.

Plate VIII Juan Mata Aguilera, model of the bullring in Alcalá (1843–1846). Detail showing position of the banda taurina as in Seville, with the drummer and clarines. Behind is another drummer with a larger drum, perhaps to execute the drum-rolls sounded at particularly emotive moments. These are mentioned by Mérimée in his account of a bullfight in 1830.

Plate IX Entry of the *cuadrilla* (procession into the bullring). From *Tauromachia; or, The Bullfights of Spain* [...] drawn and lithographed by Lake Price; with preliminary explanations by Richard Ford (London, 1852).

Plate x The Austrian dancer Fanny Elssler as Florinda in *Le Diable boiteux*. 19th-century engraving. In this role Elssler immortalised the Spanish *cachucha,* which she danced to phenomenal acclaim all over Europe.

Plate XI Rouargue brothers, illustration of gypsies dancing in Triana (the gypsy quarter across the river from the main town of Seville). From Émile Bégin, *Voyage pittoresque en Espagne et en Portugal* (Paris, 1852). Note the ubiquitous cask of sherry.

En Espagne « aux taureaux » on fume à tous les étages.
(Liv. III, ch. iii.)

Plate xii Gustave Fraipont, 'En Espagne "aux taureaux" on fume à tous les étages' ('In Spain at the bullfight one smokes at all levels'). From Spire Blondel, *Le tabac* (Paris, 1891).

Sortie des « cigarellas » à la manufacture de Séville.
(Liv. III, ch. iii.)

Plate xiii Gustave Fraipont, 'Sortie des "cigarellas" à la manufacture de Seville ('Exit of the *cigarellas* from the factory in Seville'). From Spire Blondel, *Le tabac* (Paris, 1891).

Plate XIV D. Antonio Chaman, 'Cigarreras'. Lithograph from his *Costumbres andaluzas* (Seville, [1850]). An early image showing the sexualisation of the factory workers, with a 'peeping-Tom' looking up one girl's skirt.

... Y ASÍ GRANIZARON SOBRE ELLA CUARTOS, QUE LA VIEJA NO SE DABA MANOS Á COGERLOS.

Plate XV Carlos Vazquez, '... y así granizaron sobre ella cuartos, que la vieja no se daba manos á cogerlos' ('... and so many *cuartos* were thrown down for her, that the old *gitana* had not enough hands to pick them up'). Illustration of a young gypsy woman dancing in a public place, while an older gypsy gathers up the coins thrown down for her. From *Ilustración Artistica* 1902.

Plate XVI Carlos Vazquez, 'La gitanilla, por otro nombre La Preciosa' ('The gypsy girl, otherwise known as La Preciosa'). From *Ilustración Artística* 1902.

Plate XVII Front cover of Catulle Mendès and Rodolphe Darzens, *Les Belles du monde : Égyptiennes*, illustrated by Lucien Métivet (Paris, [1890]). This section refers to real Egyptians (not the early word used for gypsies); there is a separate section on *Gitanas*, who are included as *belles du monde*.

Plate XVIII Charles Auguste Steuben, *La Esméralda* (1839). Oil on canvas, 195.3 cm × 145 cm. Note the tambourine resting against the bed.

Plate XIX Édouard Manet, *Portrait of Émilie Ambre as Carmen* (1880). Oil on canvas, 92.4 cm × 73.5 cm.

José's emotion, 'pausing to control [*maîtriser*] his emotions', is caught in the music in another way, though Mérimée's text is still the driver. Micaëla is surely one of the 'pretty girls with blue skirts and plaits falling down to their shoulders' whom Mérimée's José mentions in contrast to the 'mocking Andalusian girls who never utter a sensible word'.[39]

Also added are Carmen's partners in crime, Mercédès and Frasquita. These girls are too lowly to be called *confidantes* but essentially, in a common way, that is what they are. They are developed a little in their own right and are important in the transfer process. Events in the novella are loaded onto other characters, because some of those in the novella have been excised.

It is a mistake to assume that José is 'given a mother', as some commentaries have it. She too is developed from a significant passage in the novella where, just before his execution, José asks the narrator to deliver a silver medallion to a 'good woman' in Pamplona, if by chance he finds himself there. 'You can say I'm dead', he adds, 'but don't say how'.[40] His French, reinforcing his lineage – also mentioned on other occasions – is entirely correct and

39 '… je pensais toujours au pays, et je ne croyais pas qu'il y eût de jolies filles sans jupes bleues et sans nattes tombant sur les épaules.' (I thought of the countryside and did not believe there was any such things as pretty girls without blue skirts and plaits down to their shoulders.')

40 *Carmen*, chapter III:

– Oserai-je encore vous demander un service ? … Quand vous reviendrez dans votre pays, peut-être passerez-vous par la Navarre, au moins vous passerez par Vittoria qui n'en est fort éloignée.

– Oui, lui dis-je, je passerai certainement par Vittoria ; mais il n'est pas impossible que je me détourne pour aller à Pampelune, et à cause de vous, je crois que je ferais volontiers ce détour.

– Eh bien ! si vous allez à Pampelune, vous y verrez plus d'une chose qui vous intéressera … C'est une belle ville … Je vous donnerai cette médaille (il me montrait une petite médaille d'argent qu'il portait au cou) vous envelopperez dans du papier … (il s'arrêta un instant pour maîtriser son émotion) … et vous la remettrez ou vous le ferez remettre à une bonne femme dont je vous dirai l'adresse. Vous direz que je suis mort, vous ne direz pas comment.

– Can I dare to ask you for another favour? When you go back home, perhaps you'll go through Navarre, or at least you'll go through Vitoria which isn't far away.

– Yes, I said to him, I'll certainly go through Vitoria but it's not impossible that I can make a detour and go to Pamplona, and because it's you who ask, I will willingly make this detour.

– Good! If you go to Pamplona you'll certainly find more than one thing which will interest you … It's a fine town … I'll give you this medal (he showed me a little silver medallion which he wore around his neck), you can wrap it up in paper … (he paused for a moment to control his emotions) … and you can either deliver it or have it delivered to a good woman whose address I'll give you. Say that I'm dead, but don't say how.

refined to the point of exact politeness. Mérimée's style for José's speech is copied by the librettists. One thing neither the novella nor the libretto does is delineate characters or class by the style of language – there are no 'common' elisions or *argot* even for the smugglers, although on the 1911 recording they speak in characteristically nasal voices and act up deliciously!

MÉRIMÉE AND THE SIGNIFICANT MOMENT

A further process illuminated by the above-mentioned scenes is the librettists' desire to focus on the impulses behind Mérimée's observations – key moments – and to relocate them somewhere else in the libretto, now devoid of its narrator and Carmen's husband, García. José's steadfast respect for his mother, and the feeling that he has let her down, are cleverly retained and straddle the libretto. The scenario is re-enacted still more emotionally a little later on when Micaëla delivers him a kiss from his mother over an intensely chromatic few bars from the orchestra. Text, stage directions and the dynamics are crucial to this moment. Little Micaëla (who, we have learnt, is only 17) stands on tip-toe to give him a maternal peck ('un baiser bien franc, bien maternel'). He promised himself he might marry her, but nothing was said between them; those who refer to her as 'his fiancée' are slightly over-egging the cake.

In terms of directly transferred details, the most interesting and least understood is the detail about the *fleur de cassie* thrown at José at his first encounter with Carmen and clasped to his breast for days. On the stage it is often represented by a red rose or carnation – both cultivated flowers which Carmen could not possibly have afforded (but might have stolen). In translations the flower is often termed an 'acacia' (which is plain wrong – acacia is *acacie* in French) or, worse, described as a bunch of blackcurrants (*cassis*)! Who would throw bunch of blackcurrants at someone they fancy? Nor should it be a rose, as Ernest Reyer commented in his review.

To horticulturalists the *Cassia* is a problematic genus of which there are hundreds of varieties. Some have now been reclassified as *Senna*, one in particular known as the 'Sen of Spain'. Many varieties are common in Andalusia, and the flowers are profuse and always yellow. This is our *fleur de cassie* – any gypsy could pull a bunch of these from a tree. As Mérimée notes, they have a pungent and persistent smell that is almost overpowering – José remarks that even when it dried up, his flower kept its perfume. Touching though it is, his drooling over this wilted local flower (almost a weed) in an extended sugary aria could be seen as ironic. In both the novella and the libretto the crowd are already laughing at José as Carmen has made an extended joke about him making lace with his priming-pin. When she takes the flower from between her teeth and throws it to him, the laughing continues as he is so overcome by the moment: 'it had the same effect as a bullet hitting him', he recalls, 'and he stood there stiff as a plank of wood'.

As a Basque only recently encountering life in the south, José is clearly unaware of the commonness of this bunch of tree-flowers and misinterprets Carmen's gesture of mockery as a come-on. Would it be too much to over-interpret this moment in terms of the medical qualities of the plant? The pods of the genus *senna* had been used as a powerful laxative for years. Perhaps Carmen thought José needed a little help with his evacuation system, bearing in mind the precision of his diet of 'hake and rice', and used her gypsy knowledge of herbal medicine to offer a little advice and raise a laugh from her entourage?[41]

DOUBLE- (AND TRIPLE-) ENTENDRES

Tantalising excursions into triple meanings are among Mérimée's specialities. The priming pin which José constantly polishes is prime example. It has both realistic and symbolic meaning, as well as a suggestive undertone – when it comes to smutty jokes in nineteenth-century writing, Mérimée is right up there with the best of them. The crowd is laughing about José's pin even before Carmen throws him the (common, smelly) flower, which provokes further mirth. His *épinglette* ('priming-pin') is a finely polished rod that is constantly moved up and down in the barrel of a gun to remove detritus from previous firings. Out of this reference Mérimée extracts several other meanings to be laughed at by the crowd. First, it is a 'pin' with which he could make lace. Everyone laughs – a man making lace? Second it is 'black' lace, lace perhaps being a metaphor for semen, but black presaging death. Third, he is constantly working on it, polishing it, surely for the sex-mad Mérimée a reference to José's virginity. The undertone is that so far he only masturbates and has never had real sex, rather explaining his reaction when Carmen – a

41 See also Matthieu Heim, '*Carmen* : L'identité espagnole en question', *Revue Musicale de Suisse Romande*, June 2014, pp. 4–24. Heim, again to my mind mistakenly, identifies the plant as an acacia, the *araucaria farnesiana*, which he concludes may be a reference to Carmen's gypsy origins since the tree is a native of Egypt, and the term 'égyptienne' was commonly used for a gypsy woman. Mérimée, as usual, has identified the plant exactly and for a simpler reason: it was a plant found everywhere and was readily available to be picked for nothing.

real woman (and how!) – suddenly comes on to him, offering the real thing. The two triple-entendres of the flower and the priming pin are vital in the formation of José's character, or lack of it.

The elaborately modelled tavern (*posada*) of the first production was much admired, immortalised in an engraving in *L'Illustration* which nicely portrays the lawlessness of the establishment with a look-out placed stage left (see Chapter Nine). The only major character kept out of the inn is Micaëla. She has other functions, one of them being as a go-between with José's mother, to whom the background theme of religion is relegated. In the novella reference to religion is minimal but is just kept alive, first by the mention that José was once destined for the Church, second in the one instance where he 'goes into a hermit's chapel and weeps bitter tears' after flaring up at Carmen's first mention of taking a lieutenant to Dorothée's *baisade*, something he does again when he catches Carmen red-handed, about to take Zuniga to her bed in the opera.[42] This has more drastic results later as the two soldiers fight, effectively sealing José's fate as he passes the point of no return. Here the music puts back into the opera the nitty-gritty lost in transfer from the novella, where there is a fierce duel between José and Carmen's husband, the one-eyed García. In the libretto the three smugglers help out with this scene, holding the officer hostage to give José time to escape: this is, after all, his crucial moment. The final reference to religion in the novella is when José-Maria hears the church bell and asks the narrator to have a Mass said for him. Once again details lost from the novella are subtly put into the music: as Micaëla mentions José's mother going to church we have a moment of *stile antico* – old-style polyphony and a kind of Palestrinan cadence in a few bars interlude (see Example 4.1).

THE WANDERING LIFE

Freedom, which is the over-arching gypsy *credo* of Carmen and her criminal entourage, is distilled into a long chorus in the libretto rather than being a subject of conversation, though she also reinforces it several times, most notably just before José stabs her. In a prominent outburst with staccato interjections from the orchestra (allowing her voice to sing out) she utters the words of her conviction: 'Libre elle est née et libre elle mourra !' ('Free she was born and free she will die!')

42 'J'errai quelque temps par la ville, marchant deça et delà comme un fou ; enfin j'entrai dans une église, et, m'étant mis dans le coin le plus obscure, je pleurai à chaudes larmes.' For *baisade* cf. Flaubert, 'scène d'amour physique'.

Example 4.1 *Carmen*, Act I, No. 6 (Duo: José and Micaëla), bars 36–41, modified 'Palestrina-style' accompaniment for the reference to José's mother attending church with Micaëla. The religious overtones are augmented with a harp.

Purposefully long because it is a long trek into the mountains, the chorus in Act III is the first of two set-pieces to do with the wandering life. Once again, the sentiments of the novella are rhymed and turned into a chorus. Before this, and before José's reappearance, another show-stopping minor masterpiece has been created by the librettists and responded to brilliantly by Bizet. Because several sources have been destroyed we do not know to what extent they worked on it together, but it is highly likely that much collaboration went on; certainly they were in daily contact. This masterpiece is the Quintet, whose rhythm owes much to *opéra-bouffe* (above all Offenbach), as the smugglers bolster their spirits for a new and potentially dangerous 'business' ('affaire'). It is difficult to sing precisely, as the 1911 first recording proves. Whatever the various soloists made of it, the choral singing in the first run was terrible, according to the critics. Bizet's acid harmonies imbue the movement with the appropriate grit for the journey on which this crew is about to embark, though some critics equated chromaticism with that ubiquitous term 'Wagnerism' – an umbrella term of abuse too liberally and unthoughtfully applied by French critics of the time.

More important is that the libretto is careful to preserve an idea found earlier in the novella: that this quintet of smugglers is only a small part of an organised network stretching down to Gibraltar, with English victims largely in mind. Again the theme of the economic north–south divide is touched upon: why not murder English officers for their gold, and lead English ships on to the rocks, the better to plunder them? Surely it is just a moral redistribution of wealth? For one critic this was Carmen's essence: 'Married in the gypsy fashion, her pastimes included the seduction of rich Englishmen whom her companions robbed and then killed.'[43]

Overall, the relationship between novella and libretto is a fruitful avenue to explore: the opera retains a lot, rejects some things, but skilfully transforms the novella for the musical stage. *Carmen* is, after all, now remembered more – far more – as an opera than as a novella. 'Now', however, is the key word, for the novella was much remembered by audiences in the nineteenth century and it should not be forgotten that its remembrance was to a large part responsible for the appreciation (or the reverse) of Bizet's opera in its early days. Everyone knew the tale and many were eager to see it transformed for the operatic stage. Nowadays opera audiences have to be prompted to read Mérimée's delicious little original.

In the opera the music contributes in many brilliant ways: the flirtatious music in the *plaza*; the seductive, body-led dances with which Carmen introduces herself, using the fashionable Latin American dances popular in the 1870s when *Carmen* was first produced; the fierce music for the fight between José and Escamillo. This is immediate opera! And that is not to mention those last lines – 'Ah Carmen, my beloved Carmen' – which would fail to ring tears only out of a heart of stone. But that is the next chapter ...

In the nineteenth century, scenography and costume – and, by *Carmen*'s time, the accuracy of these elements – were *de rigueur*. Thus the novella, with its distinct images of places, gave a clear message to operatic set-designers. These places had to be introduced. Curtain-up was a crucial moment. In exotic opera it was a moment of glory for costumiers and scenographers. With the music playing, the staging had to whisk the audience out of their seats into another place. A good production of *Carmen* will do this.

Let us for once return to the old school, before narratology, semiotics and the 'new musicology'. In his 1948 biography of Bizet for the Master Musicians series, Winton Dean (to whom we owe a lot) sums up the excellence of *Carmen*'s libretto as follows:

43 'Mariée à la mode égyptienne, son passe-temps consistait à séduire de riches Anglais que ses compagnons pillaient et assassinaient ensuite', 'Némo': *Paris-programme*, 11–18 March 1875, p. 2.

> The libretto of *Carmen* has been criticized for diametrically opposite reasons. To most contemporaries it was so shocking that it ought never to have been staged; later writers have damned it as a timid watering down of Mérimée's novel. Both criticisms fail for the same reason: they neglect the angle that most matters – the dramatic. Considered thus, *Carmen* has one of the half-dozen best libretti in operatic history.[44]

Nicely put.

44 Winton Dean, *Bizet*, The Master Musicians (London, 1948), p. 212.

CHAPTER FIVE

Libretto into Opera

In the formation of their libretto the two writers had plundered many sources, taking their cue from Mérimée, who had also borrowed freely. Bizet – transforming the libretto into an *opéra-comique* – did much the same. He found models in libraries, sheet music, anthologies, previous ballets and operas, possibly concerts, and perhaps consulted acquaintances who knew about Spanish music – there were, after all, plenty around in Paris. His over-arching aim was surely to succeed in writing a piece that would become standard repertoire.

For anyone to succeed as a composer of *opéras-comiques*, using a serious story like *Carmen* meant steering a precarious course, on the one hand somehow preserving the text's *casticismo* – the Spanish 'authenticity' (particularly the passion and violence, which are the essence of the tale) – and on the other satisfying Opéra-Comique audiences' unquenchable thirst for the formulaic (and sometimes saccharine) numbers they knew and loved. Warning shots had been fired across Bizet's bows by the directorate, particularly by the co-director du Locle, but he had managed to appease them. The underlying commitment of the librettists to Mérimée's original has already been established. Certainly the process was not as simple as the chapter plan of this book might imply: that the novella was turned into a libretto, then the libretto turned into an opera. There must have been meetings, collaborations, arguments one suspects, and eventually joint results, though we have few extant documents with which to chart this process.[1] There was also literary input from Bizet himself, for example in the revision of the text for the Habanera.

The 'number opera' formula (the *opéra à numéros*) helped Bizet considerably. He could use the gaps provided by the intervening acted sections to move effortlessly from numbers full of 'local colour' to music more familiar and intimate, confections in the styles loved by the bourgeois audiences and the chaperoned-betrothed who were the central part of the Opéra's livelihood. Structure was as important as it was to the librettists and Bizet's

1 See René Stricker, *Georges Bizet* (Paris, 1999) for discussion of Halévy sources.

choices between genres were crucial for the opera's success. The musical ways of structuring the story from the libretto, and fashioning it into numbers preserving its Spanishness while still satisfying Opéra-Comique conventions, required considerable skills; luckily, Bizet had several at his disposal.

He utilised five in particular. First was the 'framing' of the whole opera between the opening Prélude and the bullfight at the end. The music of the Prélude, at first employing an 'out-of-doors' orchestration not too far from a military band, but returning at the end of the opera on cornets-à-pistons, imitates the ring-side bugles used as signalling tools in actual bullfights, accompanying the death of the bull and presaging that of Carmen. This implies a method, perhaps developed from the already fashionable practice of writing an overture including themes from the rest of the opera. Bizet does this more tightly and with deviations from the norm.

Second, he had to choose between genres, some of them modelled on the set dance forms of the *Escuela bolera* dances, but many of them stock-in-trade forms of lighter opera: the 6/8 ensemble rhythms of Offenbach, or the easy lyricism of the Gounod-esque sentimental aria. There was also the nature (distinguishable from genre) of each number, again often hybridised: the solos over a chorus, or the sung rather than spoken dialogue. Should he insert a chorus at a particular point in the dialogue, or an unaccompanied solo, a melodrama, an ensemble or sung dialogue? Or should he soften the tone with an orchestral interlude, as is so brilliantly done in the flute solo introducing the third act? No French operatic composer before had fused such a wide variety of styles.

Third there was key-structure. Bizet certainly considered this carefully, harking back even to some of the conventions of Baroque opera in the polarity between F minor as the flattest and darkest key, and E major as the sharpest, reserving a final sharpening to F sharp major as the ultimate twist. The A major of the opening Prélude is the first pillar in an over-arching structure without which the last words of José would not make their point, as Bizet's hesitations about how the opera should end clearly demonstrate.[2] In between, Bizet plunges to the 'heritage' baroque key – the *chant lugubre* tonality of F minor – for the Toréador song (proudly boasting about the bullfighter's dicing with death), and also for Carmen's reading of the tarot cards predicting her own imminent death in Act III, while José's lovely song in adulation of the senna-flower is in D flat major, a traditional key for romantic arias in the French nineteenth-century tradition.

2 A version by Michael Rot has attempted to add sketch materials to the end of the opera, to my mind unsuccessfully and flying in the face of Bizet's own decision to stick to his original when proofreading the vocal score published for the first run of the opera.

Fourth, there was the technique of Carmen's unifying motive, which could be seen as a fate-, gypsy- and death-motive all rolled into one. And fifth, the periodic introduction of musical reminders that we are in Andalusia, through occasional use of scalic and cadential devices typical of the music of that region.

NUMBER BY NUMBER

As we have hinted, the Prélude is crucial not only for its launching of the opera but also for its re-appearance at the dénouement. How many of the audience would have recognised it as a *pasodoble,* or even as a *pasodoble taurino*? The composer and ethnomusicologist Raoul Laparra, in his *Bizet et l'Espagne* of 1935, was the first to notice that it was a *pasodoble,* writing that it has 'a luminous quality apt for a meridional drama just as much as for a Flemish *Kermesse*'.[3] Laparra's critical approach to the opera is of some interest, first because he was one of the most important experts on the regional music of Spain, having published a richly illustrated and lengthy study of it, and, second, because he reprimanded Bizet for not using more of that music.[4] The *pasodoble* rhythm was originally that of the 'military two-step', or 'quickstep' used for training soldiers to march in double time, and also for show-horses to trot to, long before it became a showpiece in international ballroom dancing. Unsurprisingly, plenty were composed during the Napoleonic era, for example by Cherubini, who in 1814, having been director of the band of the National Guard under Bonaparte, published a collection of *pas redoublés* for the 'Régiment des Chasseurs de la garde du Roi de Prusse' once Napoleon was exiled to Elba. Similar forms were to be used in operas; for example, Rossini's *Guillaume Tell* has a 'Pas de soldats' with a vamping bass similar to Bizet's, and also a similar orchestration including bass drum, cymbals and timpani underpinning.

What has not been noticed about Bizet's Prélude is that it is in the tripartite form of the typical *pasodoble taurino* – the principal music performed by the larger military bands who played at bullfights, quite distinct from the signalling bands already mentioned. They were often barrack or police bands and their staple repertoire was *pasodobles.* The hallmark of the *pasodoble taurino* was its

3 'Il est d'ambiance lumineuse, et constitue, *a priori,* une couleur d'atmosphère à laquelle une action méridionale est aussi susceptible de s'adapter qu'une joyeuse kermesse flamande.' Raoul Laparra, *Bizet et l'Espagne* (Paris, 1935), p. 11.

4 Raoul Laparra, 'La Musique et la danse populaires en Espagne', in *Encyclopédie de la musique et dictionnaire du conservatoire* (Paris, 1920), pp. 2353–2400. Laparra had also written seven operas on Spanish themes, three of which enjoyed success at the Opéra-Comique, in particular *La Habanera,* which ran to 120 performances after its premiere in 1908, the last being in 1947.

A-B-A form where the central section is more lyrical, sentimental even, and invariably named after a bullfighter – alive or dead. All the famous bullfighters had them – Pepe Illo and Montes, for example, who are both mentioned in the libretto. 'Bullfight pasodobles' were beginning to emerge in Spanish *zarzuelas* immediately before the composition of *Carmen*, a striking example being in *Pan y toros* (1864) by Francisco Asenjo Barbieri (1823–1894). The second number in this nationalistic fantasy incorporating Goya and two celebrated bullfighters, and centring on the historical period of Godoy, the governor who appeased Napoleon, exploits the *pasodoble taurino* to the full, with lively outer sections melting into a lyrical tune for the *torero*'s section. The Empress Eugénie admired Barbieri's works and organised some performances in France. More importantly, extracts from *Pan y toros*, in the form of its numbers with piano accompaniments, were published very soon after its premiere.

Were these, perhaps, among the many sources Bizet plundered for *Carmen*?[5] Mariano Sanz de Pedre is precise about the lyrical section of the form: 'In the bullfights, a principal element of the *pasodoble torero* [*sic*], grandly harmonious, is a joyful but emotional melodic theme.'[6] He stresses the importance of this central section – the bullfighter's lyric tune – in many moments of the 'liturgy' of the *corrida*: 'An attraction for those who feel it essential to attend from the beginning of the *cuadrilla* until the dragging out of the last bull [...] it feels as if the *pasodoble torero* is the manager and master of the spectacle.'[7] It is an appropriate description of the theme's function in *Carmen*.[8] Bizet inserts Escamillo's tune into its rightful place in two *pasodobles* (the Prélude and the Toréador song in Act II), as well as in Escamillo's two exits, in Acts II and III. It is extremely effective and is the tune which the audience come out singing – despite Bizet's opinion that it was a mere piece of 'cochonnerie' ('rubbish').[9]

Into this first section of the Prélude, Bizet immediately inserts recurrent reminders of Andalusia – scalic, harmonic and cadential devices reminding us of place. The immediately recognisable feature of this musical *andalucismo* is a

5 See Francisco Asenjo Barbieri, *Pan y Toros* [*zarzuela*] (1864). Critical edition by Emilio Casares and Xavier de Paz, Musica Hispana 33 (Madrid, 2001).

6 'En las corridas de toros el pasodoble torero, de armoniosa grandeza, alegre y sentimental tema melódico es un elemento principalísimo, de indudable interés y utilidad.' Mariano Sanz de Pedre, *El pasodoble español* (Madrid, 1961), p. 80.

7 Alicientes por los que se hace imprescindible su colaboración desde el desfile de las cuadrillas hasta el arrastre del último toro, o sea desde el principio hasta el final del popular festejo. En esos momentos, en la plaza, el pasodoble torero se siente dueño y señor del espectáculo. Sanz de Pedre, *El pasodoble español*.

8 Its metronome marking is only slightly slower than that of the Prélude, crotchet = 108 instead of 116 in the Prélude.

9 Laparra, *Bizet et l'Espagne*, p. 11.

scale whose second note is flattened and whose third is flexible – creating an interval between a major or minor third – and whose seventh is inevitably flattened. Sanz de Pedre reminds us that insistent, twisting and turning motives characterised the *pasodoble taurino*, 'often adorned with graces or rapid flourishes in imitation of the traditional songs of the south of the Peninsula.'[10] This is an apt description of both the Prélude and the Toreador song.

The first surprise of the opera follows immediately in the form of an unexpected postlude. Ominous tremolando strings in the 'requiem' key of D minor accompany a strangely chromatic motive extended downwards through repetition. It is so well known that it hardly needs quoting, yet it is perhaps worth revisiting, not least because of the gypsy scale on which the motive is based. Laparra found in it a 'strongly African gust', sometimes identified as 'the minor gypsy scale' ('le mode mineur tsigane') contrasting with the conventional harmonic languages associated with the non-gypsy characters.

It should not be forgotten that Liszt was celebrated in the literary world as well as the musical, having written lengthy study of gypsies, published in French in 1859; this, coupled with the first audience's knowledge of Liszt's *Hungarian Rhapsodies* and Sonata in B minor, may well have sprung to mind when they heard Bizet's music in the opera house. Liszt would seem to be the most likely source of Bizet's gypsy language, either directly from his music or from his description of the usual 'gypsy' scale in his study of gypsies, where he states that it 'usually takes the augmented fourth, the minor sixth and the sharp seventh.' He goes on to point out that in gypsy music it is 'above all through the use of the sharpened fourth that the music obtains a peculiar shimmering and off-putting brightness.'[11] This can hardly be said of Bizet's use of it, however, where it is subsumed into a formulaic extension into the relative major – essentially D minor to F major – and a typically sugary *opéra-comique* cadence whose approach dwells on the ubiquitous dominant thirteenth. Unlike in Liszt, the unconventional scale steps do not attract unconventional harmonies, and they are relegated only to passing-notes. It might be added that the two reiterations of the motive, with its augmented second, are separated by two hammer-blow bass-notes underpinned by timpani and sounded as rasping open notes from the unvalved natural horns (who have quickly changed their crooks to D) in the very lowest register, and the double-bass: a carefully manipulated and unusual texture. Do these

10 '… sus incitantes giros melódicos; éstos muchas veces recargados de graciosos adornos o agiles floreos, a imitación de los tradicionales cantos del sur de la Peninsula.' Sanz de Pedre, *El pasodoble español*, p. 79.

11 'D'ordinaire, elle [la musique bohémienne] prend dans la gamme mineure la quarte augmentée, la sixte diminuée et la septième augmentée.' Liszt, *Des Bohémiens et de leur musique en Hongrie* (Paris, 1859), p. 223.

Example 5.1 'Le mode mineur tsigane' ('the minor gypsy scale') and Carmen's motive.

perhaps represent the *sostenidos* – stamping steps – associated with gypsy dancing as mentioned in Chapter Three, or do they, coupled with the 'masculine' register of the whole motive, underline Carmen's power, anger and rebelliousness, distancing her from the conventional female heroine, and still more from Micaëla? By 1911 the Opéra-Comique was deepening the feeling of foreboding in this section by adding timpani rolls as well.[12] There is one noticeable discrepancy between the sources in the harmony employed in this passage, where one chord is different in the manuscript and copied orchestral score from that used in the vocal scores.[13]

Had any opera before used such extreme musical means to emphasise a difference of race? One is hard-pressed to think of any. Bizet's identification of this gypsy scale in Schubert and Liszt can be reinforced with a quotation of its exact use as the opening motive of Liszt's celebrated Sonata in B minor for piano:[14]

Example 5.2 Franz Liszt, Sonata in B minor for piano, opening, making use of the gypsy scale.

12 These are clearly audible on the 1911 recording.

13 See Peters vocal score, p. 4.

14 See Steven Huebner, '*Carmen* de Georges Bizet: Une *corrida de toros*', in P. Prévost ed., *Le Théâtre lyrique en France au XIXe siècle* (Metz, 1995), pp. 181–218.

The orchestration of this passage, with its use of the horn's lowest register to add to the 'gothic' tremolando strings and the division of the motive into a scary opening and a warmer, lyrical complement, is typical of Bizet's thematic invention. Throughout he chooses his crooks with great care and focusses on the horn as one of his most important obbligato instruments with which to accompany the voices. Most noticeable, however, is the way that the three themes of the Prélude provide a scaffolding in the opera, as well as interlocking character-motives and signifiers of deeper ideas, such as fate, death and male rivalry.

Segue into 'curtain-up'. For Bizet, a few bars of pedal-point twaddle do the trick nicely, while the audience have time to take in the variety of the passers-by in the square: 'strange people' – 'drôles de gens'. One of them is a young Spaniard in pursuit of the young wife of an elderly beau, pacing up and down and looking at his watch, an object which is a central focus in the novella, where an expensive watch is stolen from the narrator. Chapters Six and Nine, on the sceneography and staging, will examine this section and its extras more closely.

Opéras-comiques of this epoch typically use a variety of spaces for the unfolding of the drama, with music appropriate to each space – full orchestra (and choirs) for open spaces, and reduced forces for closed and intimate spaces. *Carmen* is no exception, moving from the bustling open plaza and barracks, to closed spaces such as the guard-room, the cigarette factory, and later the *baisade* where Carmen rewards José by dancing the *romalis*. There are also moments which are less clear-cut: the intimate dialogue between Zuniga and José about the girls in the tobacco-factory, for instance, and the important revelation about José's noble background (he is the only one of the soldiers who can boast the appellation 'Don', signifying a gentleman).

STANDARD FORMULAE

Hervé Lacombe has written at length on the formulaic elements of *opéras-comiques* and finds a typical model in the old stalwart of the house, Boieldieu's *La Dame blanche*.[15] To summarise, the opening formula is as follows:

A Chorus and open-space
B Characters detaching themselves and moving into focus
C Arrival of hero(ine)
D Presentation of characters

15 Hervé Lacombe, *Les Voies de l'opéra français au XIXe siècle*, chapter four, 'Espace ouvert et espace clos', p. 94 et seq.

Carmen essentially employs exactly this formula, especially with the various characters receiving their first focus through the 'detachment/focus' process, highlighted musically by key-change, new textures and new motives. The first focus is on Moralès lamenting the boredom of the soldiers guarding the tobacco factory. He is there for a purpose: to converse with Micaëla, who soon enters asking for Don José and is surrounded by soldiers suspiciously inviting her into the guard room (a closed space, forbidden to women). Their intentions may not be honourable: virgins were, after all, precious commodities – as has been seen in Mérimée's letters to Stendhal. This significant moment is projected well in Bizet's music, which employs a device that goes beyond that of the librettists: repetition. In this case it is allied to a sort of choral stretto with Micaëla's 'Non pas' set against a crescendo of the soldiers increasingly insistent 'Vous resterez !' A director's dream, these days heightening the tension as if something dreadful would have occurred had not the 'bird flown' – in a flurry of unaccompanied *grupetti*. The chorus reprise.

The next scene, whose significance is discussed in the next chapter, has – as we have seen – been linked to the stage action in the plaza, presumably by the stage-director, at that time one of the *régisseurs*. If omitted it reduces the 'detachment' process and butts two 'open-space' scenes together, and two choruses – a good enough reason in itself for including the scene, quite apart from its humour. This is to a certain extent defused by the first example of what Lacombe calls 'zoom sonore' and the first of several uses of the *coulisses* – the wings – an all-important unseen stage of age-old importance in the Opéra-Comique tradition. Here trumpets (or *cornets à pistons*, or even simple bugles) start in the wings and are taken over by an identical military fanfare in the orchestra, employing only rudimentary harmonics. It is the first of several diegetic indicators of important moments: apart from its immediate repetition in the changing of the guard, the sound of trumpets recurs at the crucial moment where José hears them sound the retreat, while he is in the *baisade*; and at the end of the opera trumpets announce – with the initial *pasodoble* themes – the death of the bull and Escamillo's victory.

The characteristics of the tobacco factory will be explored more deeply in Chapter Seven. At this point, however, the *raison d'être* of the urchins' chorus might be sketched in and a question posed about its interpretation. Illegitimate children of the tobacco girls are depicted in many illustrations of the factory – prominent in Doré – and these children were eventually provided with schooling. How should the actions of the urchins be interpreted: as a mischievous parody of the soldiers, or as boys who would like to grow up to be soldiers? Both ways have been convincingly staged, but the evidence of the first production suggests the latter interpretation. The ritual of changing the guard is prolonged to give time for the audience to appreciate the realistic costumes, which had been designed by the celebrated painter of military events Édouard Detaille, thus the extended postlude after the street-urchins have departed (often cut even in early performances).

So far, Bizet has introduced José only through his spoken voice. In accordance – again – with established principles, no solo tenor voice has been heard, and no soprano. In terms of keys, he has – and will again – employ a favourite device of mediant side-slips. The Prélude ended with a diminished seventh creating suspense, but essentially the A major – important as Bizet's 'bull-fight' key – is raised by a semitone for curtain up, via a protracted dominant preparation, prolonged while the audience take in the set and the wealth of characters who populate it. An F major/D minor area is used for the urchins, and another dominant pedal is used – this time on G leading to C – for the entry of the factory girls. For their paean of praise for smoking, Bizet employs them *divisi* in high-register close harmony and in the heady, intoxicating key of E major – about as far sharp as French music went at this time. Uncut, this version has extremely full, *divisi*, versed chords to end the number, with the sopranos divided into 5 and the tenors into 3.

CARMEN'S ENTRY

There is much to say about Carmen's entry, known mostly as a short introduction to her singing of the Habanera; indeed, a whole book has been dedicated to this celebrated number.[16] It is this very *tube* – French for a 'hit' – that has perhaps delayed much research into this crucial operatic moment. Bizet's first biographer, Charles Pigot, tells us in no uncertain terms that:

> The highly popular Habanera that Carmen sang at her first entry was written during rehearsals. Bizet had originally composed a song with chorus in 6/8. The chanson had been learned and rehearsed but Galli-Marié didn't like it. She wanted her first appearance to produce a great effect and to identify her definitively as a gypsy. To do this she wanted a characteristic aria, something like a *chanson du crû* – a Spanish song or a slightly disturbing

16 The sequence of publications drawn upon for this section detailing the rediscovery of the early versions of Carmen's entry are as follows: Hervé Lacombe, 'La Version primitive de l'air d'entrée de Carmen', in *Aspects de l'opéra français de Meyerbeer à Honegger*, ed. Jean Christophe Branger and Vincent Giroud (Lyon, 2009), pp. 34–55; idem., 'Célestine Galli-Marié et la Habanera', in programme book for *Carmen*, Opéra-Comique, June 2009, pp. 58–63; idem. and Christine Rodriguez, *La Habanera de Carmen : Naissance d'un tube* (Paris, 2014).

> vivid pastiche where she could show off at her will the entire arsenal of what I without hesitation call her 'artistic perversities': smiling vocal caresses with voluptuous inflections, killing looks and menacing gestures.

She eventually got what she wanted – thirteenth time lucky according to a footnote.[17]

The first part of Carmen's discarded entry number was a *tarantella* that arises out of the short chorus of young men – 'Carmen ! sur tes pas nous nous pressons' – at her stage entrance, where the second version of 'her' motive – from the postlude to the Prélude – is heard, now like a fleeting bird-call. The text of the abandoned number reads differently from the text which ended up in the Habanera, the most important difference being in a verse conserved in a manuscript in both Bizet's and Halévy's hands:

Hasard et fantaisie,	By chance and on a whim
Ainsi commencent les amours !	That's how love affairs begin!
Et voilà pour la vie	And that's it for life
Ou pour six mois ou pour huit jours !	Or for six months or a week!
Un matin sur la route	One morning on the road
On trouve l'amour – il est là !	You find love – there it is!
Il vient sans qu'on s'en doute	It arrives when you're not expecting it
Et sans qu'on sans doute il s'en va !	And when you're least expecting it, it goes away!
Il vous prend, vous enlève,	It takes you over, carries you away,
Il fait de vous tout ce qu'il veut !	It does with you what it will!
C'est un délire, un rêve	It's delightful, a dream
Et ça dure ce que ça peut.	And lasts as long as it can.

17 'L'Habanera si populaire que dit Carmen à son entrée en scène, fut écrite pendant les répétitions. Bizet avait d'abord composé une chanson à *six-huit* avec chœur. La chanson avait été apprise et répétée, mais Galli-Marié ne la trouvait pas à son gout. Elle voulait dès son apparition produire un grand effet, camper fièrement et définitivement le personnage de la bohémienne, et, pour cela, elle désirait un air caractéristique, quelque chose comme une chanson de crû – chanson Espagnole ou pastiche très coloré, légèrement troublant, – où elle pût à loisir déployer l'arsenal complet de ce que j'appellerai volontiers ses *perversités artistiques* : caresses de la voix et du sourire, inflexions voluptueuses, œillades assassines, gestes troublants.' Charles Pigot: *Georges Bizet et son œuvre*, Paris, 1886 p. 243. The footnote reads 'La chanson d'entrée de Carmen, fut refaite treize fois ; ce ne fut que la 13e version, l'*Habanera*, qui fut adoptée. In the undated revised edition of his biography Pigot claims that this information was communicated to him by Guiraud. The pagination in the revised version occurs on pp. 211–212 but is virtually unaltered.

Bizet himself conceived the refrains beginning with the word 'L'amour' and asked Halévy to intersperse sections of eight lines in between, without altering his model verses. These sections transferred into the final Habanera. An orchestrated section of this version made its way into the collection of folios making up Bizet's original orchestral score (Source A)[18] but subsequently a complete manuscript of the early version of this number turned up in Choudens's archives and was recorded by EMI.[19] Lacombe has raised the question of which of the thirteen versions of Carmen's entry this is, pointing out that it is most unlikely to be the first, and is possibly the twelfth – the last version before the composer changed his mind and wrote the Habanera. The number is of considerable interest, presenting Carmen as a sentimental, rather conventional, heroine at first sight. But ultimately it is hard not to agree with Galli-Marié that something earthier was needed, and to feel she was right to pressure Bizet into rethinking the number. Had he lived to write another opera, he would probably have recycled the abandoned version, for the middle section has a rather beautiful, haunting melody emphasising the word 'amour' (Example 5.3).

The score eventually acknowledged that the Habanera was based on 'El arreglito' [The Betrothal], a piece by the Basque composer Sebastian Yradier (1809–1865). Yradier had visited the Americas in 1857 with the composer and pianist Louis Moreau Gottschalk, ending up in Havana, where he began to add Latin American dances to his already copious catalogue of *canciones* and waltzes. During the early 1850s Gottschalk had himself made a considerable impact in Spain with his Creole pieces and compositions in an American style. For Yradier this was a fortuitous meeting, and he evolved the *Habanera de salon,* infusing it with the strong current of *andalucismo* which had begun to pervade his songs, both in their use of Andalusian inflections and in the texts on stereotypical figures. Examples include *El contrabandista,* various *sevillanas* and *canciones jitanas.* Like Mérimée, Yradier was adept both at the bohemian life and in Parisian high society, being friendly with many of the Spanish dancers as well with the Empress Eugénie. It was to Paris that he returned from his American voyage, and he subsequently enjoyed considerable success with publishers in Paris, London and Germany who brought out his works, most famously his *habaneras,* in collections. Bizet possessed more than one of his scores.[20]

18 See the orchestral score by Fritz Oeser, Vorlagenbericht, pp. 805–809.

19 EMI CD 7243 5. Gheorghiu, Alagna, Orchestre de Toulouse conducted by Michel Plasson, 2003.

20 The inventory of Bizet's library of scores, held in the Bibliothèque nationale de France, included five sheet-music songs by Yradier: 'La colosa', 'El jaque', 'El curro', 'La calasera'

Example 5.3 Extract from the middle section of the abandoned version of Carmen's entry, 'L'amour, l'amour !'

The process of adaptation from Yradier's 'El arreglito' to Bizet's Habanera is best demonstrated by a comparison of the first sections of the two pieces. Many sources have printed both scores but some comments on the nature of Bizet's alterations need to be made, though they are hardly surprising. Recent research by Hervé Lacombe into Galli-Marié's insistence that the initial version of her entry be abandoned has rather changed the picture. Essentially it would seem that Bizet found Yradier's Habanera, saw how he could use it, composed some new words, asked Halévy to compose some more, and then refined Yradier's Habanera to incorporate them.[21] This process of refinement was clearly driven by the need to make the number into something which would go down nicely at the Opéra-Comique. The awkward beginning was smoothed out and the approach to cadences mollified – once again by way of the ubiquitous dominant thirteenths – to comply with Opéra-Comique

(a *chanson andaluza*) and 'Aÿ Chiquita'. Collections containing the *habanera* 'El arreglito' were published by Heugel in collections of 1864 and 1870 but neither of these appears in Bizet's inventory.

21 The original Yradier song is recorded on a CD by Axivil Criollo: *En un salón de la Habana: Habaneras y contradanzas (1830–1855)*, rtve musica: 64073 (Madrid, 2000).

cadential conventions. But the lack of modulations, and the insistent 'tango' rhythm sectionalised into an alternation of tonic major and tonic minor, were preserved. Here was an important novelty: a vernacular music – not a folk music but one used in Cuban and perhaps Spanish salons – imported directly into an opera.

Example 5.4 Opening of Sebastian Yradier, 'El arreglito' [The Betrothal], the model for the Habanera in *Carmen*.

Bizet's friendships with the Spanish violinist Sarasate and the composer Édouard Lalo were particularly important at the time he was working on *Carmen*. He had given the premiere of Lalo's Sonata for violin, accompanying Sarasate in November 1873, and although its premiere was not until a month or so before the premiere of *Carmen*, Bizet must have known that the Habanera in Lalo's *Symphonie espagnol* was also based on one of Yradier's

Example 5.5 *Carmen*, Act I, the opening of the Habanera.

habaneras, in this case 'La Negrita', described on the sheet music as a 'Tango americano'.

The scene which follows is again one which was for several reasons rethought, but is unified dramatically by José's seeming nonchalance at what is going on around him and his concentration on working at his priming pin (his *épinglette*). Here the third transformation of Carmen's motive is heard, with the 'stamping' interjections that first introduced it. Dramatically it seems that it is José's apparent obliviousness to her which proves to be the fatal attraction. The whole scene changes rapidly between speech (or melodrama) and song, depending upon which version of the 'flower-throwing' music – both of which have sinister reiterations of Carmen's motive – is used. It was clearly the longer version of this important moment which was used in the first run, since this is the version in the performing *matériel* and there are no marks indicating its deletion. It is difficult to support Winton Dean's dismissal of this version as 'Wagnerian – indeed Tristanesque', which in the context of French music of this period was a term of considerable abuse, both stylistically and politically.[22] For a production which requires longer stage business at this juncture the extended version has no stylistic jolt.

22 See Winton Dean, 'The True *Carmen*?', in *Essays on Opera* (Oxford, 1990), p. 294 (a first version was printed in *The Musical Times*, November 1965).

Bizet's final version of this scene must have also been reworked to include the recapitulation of the Habanera by the 'laughing sopranos' after the flower fiasco, and Bizet also improved the exit tune.[23] Accompanying the sopranos' giggles, a riot of ambient noise finishes off this scene as their mirth crescendos to general laughter ('éclat de rire générale'); the factory bell clangs, signalling the end of their fag-break; the romantic melody swoops above and is counterpointed with the fourth entry of Carmen's ominous theme. José is left alone picking up the loose cassia petals. The girls enter the closed space we never see while José links to the next scene with a pithy speech taken directly from Mérimée. He has intuitively understood the reason for Carmen's attention: 'So, just like women and cats who don't come when you call them and come when you don't, she came up.'[24]

The subsequent link to José's duet with Micaëla is almost comic in its branding of José as a mummy's boy when he bursts into song as soon as she is mentioned: 'Parle-moi de ma mère !' Transition to a sharper key has been facilitated by the interruption of speech: Bizet can advance his carefully thought-out key structure. We are in happier climes, moving sharpwards to B flat and introducing hints of the bourgeois bliss which results from adhering to conventional Catholic values. If Carmen's motive has so far had an earth-pull, Micaëla's tends to draw us sharpwards.. There is a hint of parochial religion as she talks about going to church with José's mother: four-part, *stile-antico* counterpoint accompanies for a few bars. Harps accompany Micaëla's extended solo about José's mother, always trying to move sharpwards and denying the E flat of the key signature in favour of E naturals. Impossible slurs covering whole phrases are found in the violin parts: legato marks not bowings where Bizet asks for an especially seamless texture. The style of this number was known as 'Saint-Sulpicien', referring to its use at society weddings for tear-jerking numbers in the fashionable churches in the *quartiers aisés* of Paris.

Laparra disliked the number intensely but his observations are astute; he finds Micaëla's style 'Rossino-Gounodesque' but lacking in any true Basque quality.[25] He even draws a diagram of what her Basque dress should have

23 Dean, 'The True *Carmen*?', presents the two versions for comparison.

24 'Tout ça parce que je ne faisais pas attention à elle ! … Alors, suivant l'usage des femmes et des chats qui ne viennent pas quand on les appelle et qui viennent quand on ne les appelle pas, elle est venue.'

25 Some biographies of Bizet give credence to a remark which the society painter Jacques-Émile Blanche claimed to have heard Gounod make after the premiere, to the effect that he considered Bizet to have stolen this number from him. Blanche would have been only 14 at the time and his memoirs date from the end of his life.

looked like, ultimately finding her 'as if cut out of a picture-postcard'.[26] Having been one of the first writers to document the idiosyncratic styles of Basque dances – including the five-in-a-bar *zortico* which Mérimée mentions José singing – he laments the fact that Bizet did not employ Basque music for her. This is Laparra's overall agenda: why did Bizet not write a properly Spanish opera? (He had written several himself, after all!) However perceptive his remarks are, Laparra failed to realise the bridge Bizet was building between the conventions (and audience) of the Paris Opéra-Comique and the perceived customs of Spain. In their ways, José and Micaëla were very deliberately French. Laparra is right when he complains that José's flower song is a typical Parisian salon Romance.

Even within Laparra's 'Rossino-Gounodesque' conventions, José and Micaëla are not strong enough to have motives of their own: they are the bourgeois couple who should not have ventured as far as the dangerous territory of Andalusia. They spend their time together singing nice tunes and melting into cadences by way of the aforementioned dominant thirteenths, crooning away in ever sharper keys with only a brief, fifth, introduction of Carmen's motive in its 'bird-call' version. When with Carmen, José's music is quite different.

Bizet repeats both Micaëla's lovely B flat music and the G major duet music, satiating the audience who will shed a tear as José reads his mother's letter. This is the first crux of the opera. José is 'about to' throw away those malodorous flowers thrown at him by the witch, and his reading of the letter just about matches the length of his previous summation of Carmen's attitude to him. 'If only he'd chosen this way and married her', think the audience! But then they wouldn't have had an opera.

This reflective quietude is an effective device for throwing into relief the first episode of transgressional violence, introduced by high-registered, screaming strings. It was longer in its original version, too. The sopranos take sides and Mérimée's obscenely triple-meaning text is subsumed into their lines, though not very audible to the audience. (The significance of the donkey and the broomstick has been discussed in Chapter Four.) We still do not see inside the workplace, but the two sides come out to lobby the

---

See Michel Poupet, 'Gounod et Bizet', *Cahiers de l'association des amis de Ivan Tourguéniev*, 12 (1988): pp. 113–130.

26 'Si les librettistes ont vraiment désiré un contraste, ils l'ont obtenu avec ce rôle de la quasi-suissesse Micaëla où Bizet, plaisant accommodeur, va s'amuser à une sorte de ragoût Rossino-Gounodesque. [...] Micaëla semble avoir été découpée dans un chromo, alors que Carmen émane de la vie.' Laparra, *Bizet et l'Espagne*, p. 24.

Plate 5.1 Anon., illustration of a mutiny in the tobacco factory in Seville (19th century).

soldiers. Cuts were copious in this number during the first production, but the full version allows time for both factions of bellicose *cigarières* to turn on the soldiers before they resume fisticuffs with each other. Carmen's motive is clearly heard in the lengthy orchestral continuum which accompanied this riot.

The interrogation dialogue which follows has Zuniga's glad eye for Carmen tucked in – he addresses her as 'Mademoiselle' and 'la belle', preparing us for a future episode. Its musical sequel, the interrogation scene, is informed by the Pushkin tale, as already examined. Edgar Istel finds its origins in a folksong from Ciudad Real and puts forward the idea that, as in other numbers, Bizet adapted this melodically and rhythmically, although its text had nothing to

Plate 5.2 Anon., 'Jealousy in the Factory', a further image of female disputes.

do with interrogation.[27] Bizet's original orchestral score (A) makes it clear that this was to be murmured (*fredonné*) and the *piano* dynamic in the vocal score is mirrored in *pianissimo* directions for the orchestra, reduced to solo strings. Gradually these indications became ignored in subsequent scores, most fatally in the most widely distributed second Choudens edition, which omitted the *piano* marking for Carmen altogether. Sung too heftily it loses its impertinence.

The score giving the most precise indications of the gypsy's insolence – annoyingly singing a repetitive folk tune with no modulation, really just repetitive ululations with a few words thrown in – is the copied score used for the first run (B). In that score Carmen's second phrase is marked 'un peu moins *p*' whereas all other scores omit the 'un peu', resulting in a destruction of the murmured folk song. The English and American editions compound the problem: the 1895 Schirmer score mistranslates *fredonnant* as 'singing' while the Metzler edition (subsequently Cramer) is even worse, indicating 'defiantly'. Many editions corrupt or omit the later indications of Carmen's insolence, for example the instruction to sing (again *piano*) 'with the greatest

27 Edgar Istel, *Bizet und 'Carmen'* (Stuttgart, 1927), pp 126–127.

insolence' ('avec la plus grande impertinence').[28] There are many suggested cuts in all of the sources – the scene does go on rather! But perhaps this was the point, to portray Carmen's persistence in annoying the authorities. Only in her last phrase, just before José ties her 'pretty hands', does she sing defiantly, in her lowest tessitura, a zig-zagging, descending phrase which is a rare instance of a flamenco-like flourish.

The advantage of the Opéra-Comique tradition is utilised to the full after this scene, where the skill of the script-writers comes to the fore in the spoken sections. In the dialogue between Carmen and José when he is guarding her is a key passage, directly borrowed from Mérimée, introducing the idea that Carmen, like José himself, is from the north. Do we believe her when she claims to come from Etchalar, in the Basque country, at the other end of the valley from Elizondo, where José comes from? No he says. Surely she is Andalusian?[29]

BIZET'S *CANCIÓN ANDALUZA*

Several Yradier songs could be regarded as models for Carmen's Act I number 'Près des remparts de Séville'. Its 3/8 time is typical of his songs, and indeed many Spanish songs of the period. Bizet exploits the idea of octave leaps – gypsy virtuosity – more than any of the Spanish models. He also uses considerably more key-changes than Yradier and Soriano Fuertes, even though they sometimes employ more unusual juxtapositions of chords and particularly dwell on the 'Andalusian' hallmark of the flattened supertonic.

This *Séguedille* is baffling in another way, too. First, there is the question of why Bizet titled it so, because it is in no way a *seguidilla* in musical terms, as Bizet surely knew. He would undoubtedly have been familiar with the Seguidilla-Bolero which Sor had detailed in his articles, and also with the rich corpus of music composed by the immigrant Spaniards in classic *seguidilla* form – 3/4 with the song beginning on the second quaver of the bar, and the last three quavers emphasised. Yet 'seguidillas' may just mean 'rhymes'. One or two examples of pieces entitled *Seguidilla* in 3/8 time can be found in the Spanish repertoire, but essentially the number is more of a waltz ('vals').

28 The new Peters Edition is based on the indications in source B, which is closest to the Pushkin model.

29 See Lola San Martin Arbide, 'Carmen at Home: Between Andalusia and the Basque Provinces (1845–1936)', in Langham Smith and Rowden, Carmen *Abroad* (Cambridge, 2020) pp. 320–334.

It is the first piece in a gypsy style, an Andalusian moment, remembering that Bizet's first, more conventional, ideas for Carmen's entry had none of these qualities, though there were hints in the interrogation scene. Bizet carefully hybridises his *canciones*, imbuing the traditional forms of the Opéra-Comique with Andalusian characteristics. Dramatically, it forms a promise from Carmen to dance with José and get drunk on manzanilla. After his criminal release of her, this promise will have to be fulfilled to preserve her gypsy honour: 'I pay my debts', she will remark. For the moment, under arrest, she comes on strong to José: 'Qui veut mon âme ? Elle est à prendre !' she sings ('Who wants my soul: it's here to take'). She continues, 'It's just the right time: I can't wait any longer, With my new lover at my side.'[30] Essentially it is a promise that she will make love to him, or he to her. Probably the former – he may need to be 'shown the way'.

The two-sharp key signature becomes comprehensible only some way into the piece. In typical Andalusian fashion the dominant is prolonged as if it were the tonic, thus we have a waltz rhythm emphasised on an F sharp major chord for the first fourteen bars. The other chord highlighted is C major – the major chord on the flat supertonic, a further Andalusian device. You can hear these clearly, and audiences even only a little educated in listening would know by now that this device evoked Spanish music. There seem to be two points of tonic attraction, and often the dominant is more prominent. Both attract the flattened supertonic above and Bizet dwells on these in a repetitive section at the bottom of Carmen's tessitura, perhaps a reason why Bizet chose this key for the number. Carmen sings in a strange, exotic way using octave leaps in one section, a technique used in several Spanish *canciones* with gypsy texts. The song, even though not in a *seguidilla* rhythm, does end with one of its essential features: the ¡*bien parado*! This was the final moment of the dance, where the two dancers freeze for the admiration of the audience, in this case achieved with an extraordinary stretching of the mezzo's tessitura. She shrieks the final notes in a flourish that ends on a high B.

This song – like the dances which have already been interrogated – demonstrates female sexual display, deliberate attraction of a male audience (like Montez's famous garter trick), *gitanismo*, *andalucismo*, and the marriage of a Spanish *Escuela bolera* favourite (some sort of 3/8 dance) with a more modern waltz. Furthermore, it transforms a seductive solo into an intimate duet as José intervenes.[31]

30 'Vous arrivez au bon moment ! Je n'ai guère le temps d'attendre, Car avec mon nouvel amant.'

31 See Felix Salzer, *Structural Hearing* (New York, 1952; rpt. 1962), p. 408. For another analysis which comes to similar conclusions, but with different diagrammation, see Huebner, '*Carmen* de Georges Bizet, une corrida de toros', in P. Prévost, ed., *Le Théâtre lyrique en France au XIXe siècle*, Metz, 1995, pp. 181–215.

Example 5.6a *Carmen*, Act I 'Séguedille' from the first Choudens vocal score, bars 1–11, showing ambiguity between F sharp major opening and eventual B minor tonic.

As in the illustration of gypsies by the Rouargue brothers (Plate XI), the dancing in Lillas Pastia's *venta* is fuelled by a barrel of manzanilla (which usually weighs in at about 15% alcohol). Carmen offers sex: 'Voici la fin de la semaine : Qui veut m'aimer ? je l'aimerai !' ('It's the weekend, whoever is up for it, I am too.')

Example 5.6b *Carmen*, Act I 'Séguedille' from the first Choudens vocal score, bars 12–23, emphasised flattened supertonics and submediants give Andalusian inflections.

WINDING UP ACT I

Bizet's use of a 'learned-style' – a number with a fugal opening – for Carmen's arrest is no doubt to emphasise the re-imposition of order, the opposite of those 'nice gypsy songs' she sang to Zuniga, José and the surrounding interrogators. The F minor key marks the first of two of Carmen's 'low' points in this key: the second comes after the black tarot cards have been dealt to her in Act III. What a breath of fresh air, and a triumph for the anti-establishment brigade when the dismal fugue subject turns major as Carmen is freed in an athletic act, originally by jumping over the side of a bridge! Bizet carefully manages closure to Act I in a return to the opening A major. The first act of violence has been committed, but the subsequent punishment is deflected on to José – Carmen's enemy, lover or rescuer? The librettists have ended the act – as good librettists do – with a question mark.

The tableau which opens Act II is carefully described in the stage direction: people are smoking and drinking, clearing the tables, strumming guitars, dancing. It is a *costumbrista* image from a *posada*. Musically it is a dance number in the guitar key of E minor – it would hardly be out of place for the strumming guitars indicated in the stage-direction to add a few E minor chords. Unlike the previous *Seguédille* this *Chanson bohème* is in the correct rhythm: a real *seguidilla bolero* with a few Andalusian turns of harmony. Its formula is a pedal point without too much modulation but replete with crescendos and a slowly climaxing accelerando. Its text is full of gypsy references, such as 'peaux bistrées' ('dark-skinned'), and swirling, striped materials 'd'orange et rouge zébrées'. Ululation alternates with melody. The text emphasises the actuality: the intoxication of dance from distant lands, its exoticism exuding from the text. 'Les tringles des sistres tintaient, avec un éclat métallique' ('The jingling sistrums rattled with a metallic ring'), we learn from this self-referential song. Metallic percussion had by now become a standard signifier of the exotic, whether worn on (or as) clothes or sounded on folk instruments such as the *tambour de basque*.

Bizet uses another gypsy trademark, distancing the music from conventional harmony. This is the use of the descending Andalusian tetrachord without real modulation. Carmen is allowed only one operatic cadence. The 1911 Opéra-Comique recording effectively adds castanets, at first on the offbeat, later intensified by trilling. A screeched 'Olé' – not notated in the score – concludes.

In his first draft orchestral score Bizet included a notated part for castanets in the Act II scene where Carmen seductively dances for José (to 'repay her debts'). Choudens signalled two options for its performance: either these could be played by a percussionist in the pit, or Carmen could play these herself, in which case she was allowed to improvise freely.[32]

A possible model for the *Chanson bohème* is Casimir Gide's music for Le Sage's *Le Diable boiteux*, which had been such a resounding success in the 1830s (not least, as we have seen, because of Fanny Elssler's legs). Gide's full score was deposited in the library of Paris Opéra in 1854 and contains a lengthy *bolero*, also in E minor, with many Andalusian inflections. Any composer inquisitive about the prodigious success of this piece might well have sought out this score.

32 Cette partie sera executée ; soit à l'orchestre, par l'un des instrumentistes de la batterie, soit sur le théâtre, par l'artiste chargée du rôle de Carmen. Dans ce cas le rythme pourra être modifié au gré de la cantatrice. A similar instruction exists in all the early scores.

Example 5.7 Casimir Gide, *bolero* for *Le Diable boiteux* [The Devil on Two Sticks], whose *cachucha* achieved worldwide fame.

TOASTING THE *TORERO*

The entry of Escamillo was carefully crafted by both librettists and composer to portray another stereotypical Spanish scene: the 'promenade aux flambeaux' is none other than a *candela* procession. No one can outdo the Spanish at processions – for all kinds of reasons – and *candela* processions or dances were a favourite subject of the *costumbristas.* Traditionally these used lamps, here the idea is more flaming torches. While the 'amis d'Escamillo' praise his boldness and skill, 'un coup plus beau' captures the attitude of the true *aficionado*, for whom the *corrida* is an art not a blood-sport – 'le grand art de la tauromachie', as Zuniga calls it. A little bullfighting background is added with the mention of two of the most famous *toreros* in Spanish history: Montes and Pepe Illo.

If true, Bizet's sense that his so-called Toréador song was nothing but 'cochonnerie' is surely one of the best examples of composers failing to understand the worth of their own work. The central melody itself divides into three sections, perfectly capturing the essential character of a bullfighter.

There are clear parallels between Escamillo's verses and those Carmen and her accomplices sang in the gypsy song: essential qualities of *fiesta*, trance and cumulative crowd hysteria. The verses spare no details: Seville was the centre of bullfighting on horseback and perhaps the line about 'the horse falling,

Example 5.8 Three sections of Escamillo's Toréador song, his middle section a *pasodoble taurino* characterising the different aspects of the *torero*'s art. How wrong was Bizet! This was much more than a piece of 'cochonnerie'.

dragging a picador behind' ('Un cheval roule, entrainant un Picador') has its roots in Mérimée's first *lettre*, where he admits to taking pleasure not from the killing of the bull, but quite the reverse: when the animal triumphs over the matador. At this juncture the minor key is replaced, first by its relative major and subsequently by the sudden sharpwards movement to E major as Escamillo departs. The tiny stage direction indicating that Carmen and Escamillo look at each other as they sing 'l'amour' to swoony sevenths is a masterstroke never to be ignored. It would appear that this was originally a stage-direction in the libretto itself, responded to by Bizet.

THE *CONTRABANDISTAS*

The dialogue which follows, introducing the smugglers, is hilarious. Listening to the 1911 recording is a must, where their silly voices, especially that of Le Remendado (which means 'The Dishevelled'), give an idea of how hammed up the dialogue may have sounded in the first run. The recording is an invaluable document of how *opéra-comique* speech was done, raising a further laugh about the English in the reference to Gibraltar, where 'you can see English people. Nice people, the English; a bit cold but distinguished' – lines which are amusingly delivered, especially the clipped word 'froid', contrasted with the satirically elongated 'distingués'.[33] Rather more violent activity was hinted at in Mérimée's original, where Carmen was employed to be an accomplice to robbery and even the pre-meditated murder of English soldiers. One caution has to be signalled in respect to this recorded source, since it is unclear whether the singers also deliver the dialogue – it is very possible that actors were imported to record these sections. Nonetheless, I know of no other convincing source to give us an idea of how these dialogues might have been delivered.

The Quintet which follows was clearly a test for the first cast, not least because of its D flat major key and acerbic harmonies. This was a challenge, and remains one even now – only the best recordings and superlative stage performances get it right. The 1911 recording, for instance, has plenty of gypsy and smuggler spirit, but very little accuracy of pitch. While the Quintet's rhythm may be Offenbach's, its harmonies are brilliantly advanced, crafted carefully for the moment in the opera when we are told that in 'business matters' it is always good to have women around ...

For a moment we rejoin the musical language of the *opéra-comique* as Carmen refuses to accompany the smugglers on their mission because – a real

33 'Jolie ville Gibraltar ! ... on y voit des Anglais, beaucoup d'Anglais, de jolis hommes les Anglais ; un peu froids, mais distingués' (libretto).

surprise – 'she's in love!' It is the only time in the opera when she sings in this voice, with a heartfelt dominant ornament on a sentimental cadence. 'Don't be silly', says Le Dancaïre, and he and Le Remendado sing an aphoristic duet about love and duty.

The evocation of a third unseen space is of particular importance in *Carmen.* We have had the guard-house, whose inside we never saw, and we have never seen the inside of the factory. Now José's prison is invoked with a double motive: he has suffered behind bars for the love of Carmen, but in the gypsy's eyes he was a coward for not trying to escape – after all, she had smuggled him a file and money to change his clothes. The *coulisses* are now mobilised for a dramatic function: José comes in from afar, singing his dismal song. Laparra tells us that the music, though given new words, is like a Basque 'Noël' and is clearly from the north. Certainly in comparison to Escamillo's fleet-footed horsemanship, this number has more of the plod of a mule.

DON JOSÉ'S DILEMMA

Scene 5, which follows, initiates the opera's gradual moving away from the *opéra-à-numéros* concept to variegated scenes where diverse musical and spoken items are united into a narrative sequence. Thus the feasting on whatever Pastia has in his larder, washed down with manzanilla, flows naturally into Carmen's seductive dance for José, their row, his showing her the flower, and his pleading aria – as if a bit of D flat major and a sentimental aria will put everything right. Carmen's 'nons', in her best chest voice, counter José's lyrical pleas. Unified by the final section recalling the Quintet, this is all in all the first continuous scene in the opera, ending with a stretto of oppositions of love and duty, and of honour against gypsy values.

In the novella Carmen 'repays her debts' by using Dorothée's *baisade* to give José her body. In the opera this is softened and sent up more than a little as Carmen prepares to dance for José an extended diegetic dance-song, employing a perfectly conventional operatic *récit* beginning and ending with formulaic musical gestures and 'with a comic solemnity'. The accompanying picture in the illustrated edition of the Choudens vocal score rather amusingly emphasises José's innocence.

Whatever is done (and the illustration captures nothing of the moment's essence), this is a crucial scene crystallising the conflict between the soldier and the gypsy.[34] Musically it is brilliantly effected as the bugles are heard approaching from the distance: a wake-up call for José's 'honour' and an ironic moment for Carmen as she infuriatingly remarks 'how nice it is to have

34 https://www.youtube.com/watch?v=grRzcTs5NVc

Example 5.9 *Carmen*, Act II, No. 16 (Duo: José and Carmen), bars 7–12, Carmen's humorous operatic *récit*.

N° 7 ACTE II — CARMEN, DON JOSÉ « Je vais danser en votre honneur! »

Plate 5.3 Plate by Hyacinthe Royet for the illustrated edition of the *Carmen* vocal score (Paris: Choudens, c.1890), showing José watching Carmen dance the *romalis*.

an accompaniment'.[35] The *coulisses* are used to maximum effect as the band approaches and passes the inn where the couple are. Mimicking the urchins' 'ta-ra-ta-ras', Carmen's fury at José's rejection of her in favour of his duty rises to a peak. He tries to calm her with his flower song (recycled from an abandoned opera, *Grisélidis*) but they argue again, and José wavers.

Too late! There is a knock at the door which will seal his fate. His superior Zuniga appears for an assignation with Carmen. His ordering José to leave is firmly rebutted, and swords are drawn. The gypsy men appear, disarming Zuniga and restraining him at pistol point. Having threatened his commanding officer, this is the point of no return for José. Foreshadowing the sentiments of the trek into the mountains in the next act, Carmen reassures José about the freedom of 'la vie errante', which he now has no option but to adopt. Interrogating Zuniga's past, what ensues is a repeat of the mortal combat between two Basque rivals (Zúniga – or Zuñiga – is a Basque name) that had caused José to join up in the first place. José has swapped sides, changing his role from hunter to hunted. Carmen then asks whether he has defected, and he replies in the affirmative: 'I have no choice.' The chorus prolong the sentiment of freedom.

Francesco Rosi's unparalleled filmic interpretation of the entr'acte to Act III suggests that the subsequent music, with its prominent flute solo, represents this sentiment of freedom by coupling it with an image of a bird in flight. Commentators have used the word 'exquisite' for this entr'acte (and quite rightly), but few have offered interpretations. It has been suggested that its opening comes from a religious song later quoted by Felipe Pedrell in his *Cancionero musical popular español*, and that, somehow – perhaps through one of the Spanish community in Paris – Bizet borrowed it.

The opening chorus of Act III – darkly trudging through the mountains in a new minor key – is purposefully long and relentless. It has an eerie chromaticism which the Opéra-Comique chorus had difficulty singing; Laparra thought it sounded Russian. Certainly, it gets colder up in the Sierra Nevada, and this was the transposed place – ripe for a murder – where in the novella José kills Carmen. Nothing much Spanish about it, but the stage directions are very prescriptive of a wild landscape, for which Bizet adds minimal music: just two prolonged unisons on two horns in E flat, with *pianissimo* pizzicatos and a short roll on the timpani, the motive underpins the whole chorus. The smugglers enter with their contraband. Again, it is a carefully contrived curtain-up moment.

35 'Il est mélancolique de danser sans orchestra … Et vive la musique qui nous tombe du ciel !

Example 5.10 ‘Canción de cuna’, from Felipe Pedrell’s *Cancionero musical popular español* (Valls, 1918–1922), vol. 1. Bizet may have borrowed the opening of this Asturian song for the flute melody of the entr’acte to *Carmen* Act III.

After the next pithy dialogue between José and Carmen, further emphasising the growing rift between them as she angrily clicks her castanets, the card game ensues. Bizet introduces rhythmic motives for cutting and shuffling: a cue for synchronised movements from the gypsy girls on the stage. Humour *à la Offenbach* prepares for its opposite, with a little hint of Carmen's motive (in bird form) as the cards are dealt. Carmen's black prediction is in the key of F minor, singing for the first time a heartfelt, operatic aria – her heavy heart reflected in the offbeat rhythms. For the first time in her appearances there is certainly nothing 'gypsy' about it: she has suddenly been promoted to the status of a thinking, feeling human being, rather than a gypsy whore. Laparra calls it a 'funeral march'. A recap of the girls' banter, flirting and the business of smuggling temporarily defuse the situation, but José's constant jealousy is rising again. He is notably absent for the rest of the scene.

Micaëla's reappearance was originally presented in spoken dialogue, but at the Opéra-Comique this was the sole instance where one of the recitatives with which Ernest Guiraud replaced the spoken dialogue became standard usage, the reason perhaps being to accelerate the action towards the dénouement with music, without further interruption from speech. A few details about the payment of the *guide* are lost but are of little importance. Micaëla's dark, frightened aria, memorably accompanied euphoniously by four horns with carefully chosen crooks (E flat and low B flat) turns into a prayer for protection as José – unseen to her – toys with his gun. Laparra – of course – hated this movement! He called it 'the worst *longueur*' of the opera and 'like a *pièce de concours* [competition piece] [...] worthy of the epithet Bizet applied to his toreador song [*cochonnerie*] [...] Let's quickly turn over from this soporific page', he suggests. Many will disagree.[36]

The fight between José and Escamillo which follows was radically shortened in the second Choudens vocal score, and it loses a lot of its power in this compression. Both versions employ harsh harmony, sounding an accelerating repeated motive in unison, diads, open fifths and diminished chords, punctuated by *sforzando* brass. Tension is built through the use of dotted rhythms and syncopation. It was surely for reasons of staging that the original fight was shortened (by 77 bars). A great deal of effort had clearly been put into it in the first run (as it was the first staging of a new opera after the 1874 fire in the Salle Favart). The second version seems to take the steam out of the duel almost before it has begun, quite apart from reducing the alternation between the characters as each has the other at his mercy. In the finale José's jealousy has to be restrained by the smugglers as Escamillo exits to a rather sophisticated, contrapuntal rendering of his *toréador* tune.

36 Laparra, *Bizet et l'Espagne*, p. 54.

Laparra waxes lyrical about this scene, as always from his uncompromisingly Spanish point of view:

> The scene between José and Escamillo constitutes excellent *opéra-comique*, light, correct in its emphases, but which, right up to the final duo, justifies the definition which was attributed to Bizet himself: '*Carmen*? An operetta which ends badly.'
>
> No, no! It's not that: *Carmen*, a magnificent *zarzuela* with wonderful lightness and unfathomable depths: the finest Spanish *zarzuela*, written by someone who never went there; *Carmen*, an intuitive masterpiece; a miracle![37]

Micaëla's reappearance, reprising her heavenly Act I aria, is a masterstroke – *pace* Laparra. Carmen and Micaëla are for the first time staged together in opposition, both counselling José to leave. The double text of the chorus turns the moment into opera, intensified by the sound of Escamillo singing his song in the wings, the *coulisses* again employed to maximum effect. A crucial moment occurs: José leaves for his 'home village' with Micaëla ...

The source for the tune of the following entr'acte has been the object of many researchers, the earliest being Tiersot, but the best being the expert Laparra, who is essential reading on this borrowing, having discovered how Bizet bound Carmen's 'fate' motive together with the well-known source used to form the cadence of a melody partly borrowed from a celebrated *polo* by Manuel Garcia, 'Cuerpo bueno, alma divina' from his light opera *El criado fingido* [The Man Masquerading as a Servant]. What can be deduced from Ralph Locke's painstaking study of all the manuscript and printed sources of this song is that it was extremely well known and had probably been popular in concerts ever since its first appearance in a collection called *Regalo lírico*, published in Paris in 1831.[38] One suspects that performers kept it alive

37 'La scène entre José et Escamillo (p. 287), constitue de l'excellent opéra-comique, aisé, juste d'accent, mais qui, au duo final, justifierait sur ce point la définition attribuée par quelqu'un à Bizet lui-même : "*Carmen*, une opérette qui finit mal". Non, non ; bien autre chose : *Carmen*, magnifique zarzuela avec d'adorables légèretés et d'insondables profondeurs ; la plus belle zarzuela d'Espagne, écrite par un musicien qui ne vit jamais le pays ; *Carmen*, chef-d'œuvre d'intuition : miracle !' Laparra, *Bizet et l'Espagne*, p. 55. Laparra's citing of the page number shows that he was referring to the second Choudens vocal score with Guiraud's *récits*, but without the 'Scène de l'Anglais' on which he makes no comment. This was the standard score when he wrote his book, the original Opéra-Comique score having already become scarce.

38 *Regalo Lírico : Colección de boleras, seguidillas, tiranas y demás canciones españolas por los mejores autores de esta nación* (Paris, 1831). See Julian Tiersot, 'Bizet and Spanish Music',

Example 5.11 Theme of final entr'acte in *Carmen*, woven around Carmen's motive.

– certainly the García sisters did later on in the century. Some of the Hispanophiles in the audience would have been delighted to recognise it turning up in *Carmen*. Bizet did not need to alter it one jot to fashion it around his 'fate' motive, as Laparra showed in a succinct diagram which could hardly be bettered.[39]

Locke assumes it was the later version, from *Échos d'Espagne*, which Bizet used as a model – he possessed a copy of this anthology. But, as has been seen in Chapter One, this model presented the *polo* in a highly romanticised form, with a little story grafted on. It is not at all impossible that his model was the plainer version in the *Regalo lírico*. Whatever the case, Bizet stripped the inappropriate hushed C minor piano accompaniment away, and turned it into street-band music, assigning the vocal line to a solo oboe and producing a brilliant number for a bullfight band. The semiquaver runs, which Bizet orchestrates in a standard 'oriental' way (perhaps Moorish here), had become a commonplace device for signalling the near-African exotic. For example, they appear as early as the 1830s in Gide's score for *Le Diable boiteux* (Example 5.12).

Bizet evokes the Andalusian atmosphere – perhaps in its strongest ritual – on a low clarinet with piccolos doubling two octaves above, the 'gapped' sound topped with shrill flutes particularly evoking the exotic. They would seem to come from orchestral music or piano accompaniments rather than the vocal *fioriture* of Garcia, as some commentators have suggested. As far as the opening pizzicato introduction is concerned, this came from another Garcia model reprinted in the *Regalo lírico*, *El contrabandista*, although as has been seen in Chapter One, this song was so famous that Bizet probably knew it from elsewhere.[40]

trans. Theodore Baker, *Musical Quarterly* 1927, p. 581; Laparra, *Bizet et l'Espagne*, pp. 58–66; and Ralph Locke, 'Spanish Local Color in Bizet's *Carmen*', in *Music, Theater and Cultural Transfer: Paris, 1830–1914*, ed. Annagret Fauser and Mark Everist (Chicago and London, 2009), pp. 316–360.

39 See Raoul Laparra, *Bizet et l'Espagne*, p. 63.

40 There is an 1838 edition with Spanish, French and German words 'chanté dans tous les concerts' par Mme Malibran (Schlesinger, Berlin), and a London edition (n.d.). Its version in the *Regalo lirico* titles it 'El caballo'. The introduction to this song contains 4 bars of a turning semiquaver figure from which Bizet may have developed the wind flourishes in this movement.

Example 5.12 *Fioriture* in Casimir Gide's *bolero* for *Le Diable boiteux*, resembling a similar passage in Bizet's final entr'acte for *Carmen*.

Example 5.13 Bizet, woodwind motive in final Entr'acte to *Carmen*.

Possible models for Act IV of *Carmen* may be found in various 'bullfight' spectacles which had been staged in Paris, or published. One of the most successful works of the *zarzuela* composer Francisco Asenjo Barbieri, *Pan y toros* [Bread and Bulls – a Spanish catch-phrase], premiered at the Teatro de la Zarzuela in Madrid in 1864. It opens with a *bolero* overture succeeded by a scene with various street-sellers (*vendedores*) onstage. Barbieri was well known in Paris, which he had visited in the late 1850s, most importantly to visit the Opéra-Comique for the purpose of modelling his Teatro de la Zarzuela on it – a hugely important act of cultural exchange possible only because the wars with the French had faded into the past. Scores of *Pan y toros*, in the form of sheet music extracts, following the customary way of disseminating *opéras-comiques* in France, were published at the time of the Madrid premiere, as was the libretto. News of this lavish spectacle no doubt reached the Spanish community in Paris, and certainly reductions for guitar or piano would have been welcome, since the original had three separate bands of musicians: a full orchestra (including obbligato folk instruments such as the *piporro* and *pandera*); a 'strumming' band of six each of guitars and *bandurrias*; and a backstage band with two trumpets. Other ideas for the act – including the *cuadrilla* – may also have come from *zarzuela* sources. Bizet's movement reasserts the setting in Seville: the libretto uses a Spanish word for the first time (*cuartos*), and the sellers are purveyors of typical Andalusian produce exploiting the *aficionados* around the arena by selling oranges, tobacco goods, fans and wine.

The recapitulation of the opening motive from the Prélude clearly identifies the theme as a *pasodoble taurino* for those who had not realised at the outset. Bizet's assigning it to the trumpet shows that he knew about the importance of high brass instruments at all stages of the bullfight, from the procession to the '*hora de la verdad*' and the triumphant *brindis* (toast) of the *torero* throwing his hat into the air after his moment of victory. The use of these instruments as signals had formed an important part of another *zarzuela*: *En las astas del toro* [On the Horns of a Bull] by Joaquín Gaztambide, premiered two years before *Pan y toros*. This shorter and less lavish piece used the technique of signalling the changes between the three stages of the *corrida* (the *tercios*) with different fanfares (*toques*). In the *Diccionario de la zarzuela* the process is described thus: 'The work consists of a prelude in which the trumpet fanfares are used to signal the changes of episode in the bullfight, plus five musical numbers' (see Plates VII and VIII).[41]

41 'La obra consta de un preludio en el que utiliza el toque de cambio de tercio de los clarines en las corridas de toros, y cinco números musicales', Ramón Sobrino, entry in *Diccionario de la zarzuela*, Vol I, p. 700, ed. Emilio Casares Rodicio, 2nd ed (Madrid, 2006).

Bizet uses the brass to convey the diegetic music of the marching band accompanying the *cuadrilla*, playing their ubiquitous *pasodobles*, but he also seems to have known about the use of *toques*, as in the development of this compressed bullfight: he intersperses trumpet signals into the orchestra during the final (and brilliant) confusion of ideas where Escamillo moves to the final stage of the *tercio* – at the moment of truth when the bull is killed – while José and Carmen wrestle emotionally in front of the arched entrance. D major trumpet fanfares are heard in the background.

The ground is prepared for this by way of recapitulation – a sure sign of Bizet's concern for structure within the opera. Not only does the overture now underpin the processional chorus, but there is also a fine unison anthem: 'Et puis saluons au passage [...] les hardis Chulos'. A strong sense of growing excitement and *fiesta* builds up as the chorus draw attention to the finely embroidered costumes. They also sow the seeds of the violence which will ensue, pointing to the blades of the picadors' lances, now wounding the bulls' flanks ('Harceler le flanc des taureaux'). The climax of the procession is the entry of Escamillo, who appears with Carmen close at his side. We return to the opening A major as he comes into sight with the fatal *espada*, the killing sword. It would seem – from the A major return – to be the end of the story, but Escamillo breaks the tension for a while with a declaration of love for Carmen, with a new melody and a sentimental cadence before the gypsy girls appear to warn Carmen of José's return, a warning which she ignores.

Bizet uses unstable key centres to propel the dénouement, though much of the music is centred on A flat, one semitone beneath the A major ending for which the music seemed to be on course. José, in repeated declarations of love, is accompanied first by a minor version of a new motive of entreaty, then by a lyrical major version of it, 'À quoi bon ?' Carmen, in a solo outburst, repeats her credo of freedom: 'Libre elle est née et libre elle mourra.' The key jerks up to G major and, in a state of intoxication, the chorus burst in telling us of the carnage in the ring: the bull is down and bleeding. Over a stooging chromatic bass the orchestra stabs at chords. After Carmen has confirmed – to José's face – that she loves Escamillo, her fate motive interrupts, heard on full orchestra as never before, suddenly in a remote key. Any secure tonal ground has been swept from under the audience's feet. Fanfares from the ring accompany a final singing of the Toréador song, in the sharp key of F sharp major – never heard before. Then, 'José strikes her, she falls and he kneels before her body.' 'Ah ma Carmen, ma Carmen adorée !' The opera ends in this key of heightened emotion. Whatever certain editors have tried to refashion from rejected passages, the version in the vocal score corrected by Bizet is what should stand.

Act V is unwritten, uncomposed, unseen and unheard. As Carmen predicted, José will die. In the novel he awaits his capital punishment. Not hanging or the firing squad, but the garrotting machine, deemed to be a kinder punishment than hanging and reserved for those of noble class. This emblematic machine was to Spain what the guillotine was to France: examples can be seen in the Museum of Banditry in Ronda and they were chillingly portrayed in Goya's *The Disasters of War*.[42] Mérimée does not go into the details but several productions have reminded the audience, through nooses and even a firing squad, that José too will die. However much we have been entertained, at this point we realise that Bizet's transformation of Mérimée's tale into opera was no light *espagnolade*, but a gripping tale of love, transgressional violence, and legal, violent, retribution.

42 Don Francisco Goya, *Los desastres de la guerra* (1863), Colección de ochenta láminas inventadas y grabadas al agua fuerte, Madrid.

CHAPTER SIX

The Forgotten Englishman

ONE of the principal differences between the first Opéra-Comique vocal score of *Carmen* and subsequent editions was that it contained a soon-abandoned 'Scène et Pantomime' placed after the opening chorus, which disappeared from the stage around the time of Bizet's death. It appeared in the copied conducting-score used at the Opéra-Comique and in the hand-copied orchestral parts used in performances until printed parts were produced in the 1890s.

Many commentators have written about it, but only a few recent editions have included it either within their main text or as an appendix.[1] Most subsequent writers, from Pigot in his *Bizet* of 1886, to Macdonald in his biography of 2014, have expressed the view that cutting it improves the opera, largely without considering the case for its inclusion.[2] Important biographers in between these gave it short shrift: Mina Curtiss mentions it as a 'a typical little opéra-bouffe pantomime in which a young woman on the arm of her elderly husband flirts with her lover as they cross *la place* while the brigadier, Moralès, describes the episode in song'.[3] Yet it certainly was not 'typical', and nor does Moralès really sing much! Malherbe and Winton Dean briefly mention it, but Streicher, Maingueneau and Lacombe fail to give it time of day. Most influential in its subsequent demise was probably Pigot in his first biography of Bizet.

Pigot had not changed his mind about the scene in his revised and substantially altered edition of 1911. Quite the reverse, he expanded his critical section on the scene, possibly influencing twentieth-century producers of the opera by suggesting that they forget it, and advising them not even to muse upon its meaning.[4] It was duly forgotten until late into the twentieth century. The

1 Oeser's Bärenreiter full score of 1965 includes it as an appendix in his separate *Vorlagenbericht* but nowhere prints its matching vocal score, done by Bizet himself. Didion's Schott vocal score includes it, as does its matching miniature score. The Peters vocal score includes it, as does the matching orchestral score. For full details of these scores, see Bibliography.

2 Charles Pigot, *Georges Bizet et son œuvre* (Paris, 1886). Hugh Macdonald, *Bizet* (Oxford, 2014).

3 Mina Curtiss, *Bizet and His World* (London, 1958), p. 383.

4 Charles Pigot, *Georges Bizet*, rev. ed. with preface by A. Boschot (1911).

trouble was, no-one remembered or understood what it was really about, and only a few recorded it.[5]

The scene unfolds as follows, arising out of a focus on two characters in the plaza. It begins with a detailed stage direction both in the score and libretto (which is unusual), setting the scene:

> The movement of the passers-by now resumes with some liveliness, having stopped during the scene with Micaëla. Among those coming and going is an elderly gentleman (a mime) with a young lady on his arm. The old gentleman wants to continue his walk but the young lady is doing everything she can to keep him in the square. She appears to be nervous and anxious. She looks to the left and the right, looking for someone who does not appear. The miming of these characters must coincide exactly with the following couplets.[6]

As can be seen from the printing in the first Choudens vocal score, the commentary on the action of the scene is precisely indicated and printed above the musical staves, with Moralès's commentary and gestures coinciding with particular musical ideas. As a dramatic idea the scene is remarkable from the outset. Moralès, 'presque parlé' in this case ('almost whispering'), addresses the audience with an imperative 'Taisons-nous !' and tells them not to talk, and to watch what happens carefully. It is a clever and unusual idea, more common in the music hall than the opera-house, drawing the audience in and demanding that they and the passers-by watch the physical movements of the mime.

The audience are asked to notice the man's 'suspicious look' ('œil soupçonneux') and 'jealous gait' ('mine jaloux'). When Moralès remarks that 'the lover can't be far away' ('L'amant, sans doute, n'est pas loin') the soldiers gleefully repeat his phrase as if they are used to similar scenarios, heightening expectation of what is to come. The gestures that precede his entry char-

5 At the time of writing this, there are two commercially available recordings of the scene. The first is the audio recording conducted by Michel Plasson, starring Gheorghiu and Alagna as Carmen and José (EMI Classics, 2003). The second is the video recording of an Opéra-Comique staging of 2009, conducted by John Eliot Gardiner and produced by Adrian Noble (Théâtre de l'Opéra Comique / FRA Musica, 2009).

6 *Livret*, 'Le mouvement des passants qui avait cessé pendant la scène de Micaëla a repris avec une certaine animation. Parmi les gens qui vont et viennent, un vieux monsieur (mime) donnant le bras à une jeune dame (danseuse) ... Le vieux monsieur voudrait continuer sa promenade, mais la jeune dame fait tout ce qu'elle peut pour le retenir sur la place. Elle paraît émue, inquiète. Elle regarde à droite, à gauche. Elle attend quelqu'un et ce quelqu'un ne vient pas. Cette pantomime doit cadrer très exactement avec le couplet suivant.' The direction in the Choudens vocal score is only slightly different.

Example 6.1 Opening bars of the 'Scène de l'Anglais', *Carmen*, first vocal score (1875).

acterise the old man and his wife, beginning with an almost balletic note: a trilling flourish continuing with a brisk walking vamp in the bass, rendered more than a little foppish by the marked syncopated rhythm with its finicky across-the-beat phrasing, accented and staccato alternately. Bizet gives us time to observe the couple visually before we listen to Moralès's commentary.

The story begins, seemingly a frequent occurrence well known to the soldiers, who join together in predicting what's going to happen:

MORALÈS	
Voici venir un vieil époux	Here comes an elderly husband
Œil soupçonneux ! mine jalouse !	Looking suspiciously with a jealous gait!
Il tient au bras sa jeune épouse	On his arm is his young wife
L'amant sans doute n'est pas loin,	The lover is no doubt not far away,
Il va sortir de quelque coin !	He'll appear from somewhere!
SOLDATS	
Il tient au bras sa jeune épouse	On his arm is his young wife
L'amant sans doute n'est pas loin,	The lover is no doubt not far away,
Il va sortir de quelque coin !	He'll appear from somewhere!

And indeed, to a more lyrical musical idea, he does! An elegant young Spaniard appears and once again the score reminds Moralès to time his gestures precisely with the actions of the *figurants*, the miming characters.

The young *majo* makes an extravagant gesture as he greets the couple ('un salut empressé'), which Moralès imitates. He goes on to imitate all three: the grumpy old man, the flirtatious smiles of the young lady and the obsequious gestures of the young man, who is now referred to as the *galant.* Skilled mime-artists could render this scene hilarious. As the three take a turn round the square, Moralès points out that he is trying to give a *billet-doux* – a note – to the girl while distracting the old man by pointing up at something with one hand ('Le jeune homme d'une main montre quelque chose en l'air au vieux monsieur'), while with the other he slips the *billet-doux* to the girl. An ironic little gesture, with three-note *gruppetti,* tells us the deal is done: 'le tour est fait !' 'We'll see what happens', sing the soldiers, laughing aloud again.

The questions that need to be answered about this forgotten scene are why Bizet included it and why it was eventually cut, and, most importantly, what is it all about? It was certainly unusual to include a Pantomime in an *opéra-comique,* though there were some operatic precedents, the most notable being the role of Fénella in Auber's *La Muette de portici* (famously played by Fanny Elssler). They were more common in *opéra-bouffes,* operetta and more comic forms. That dancers were trained in the art is confirmed by Carlo Blasis in his widely distributed treatise of 1830. His chapter 'On Pantomime and the Studies Necessary for a Pantomimic Performer' begins with a succinct French quotation from Brebœuf summarising the art: 'art ingénieux de peindre la parole et de parler aux yeux' ('The ingenious art of painting words and speaking with the eyes'). He continues in a substantial analysis of the art – 'undoubtedly the very soul and support of the ballet' – to describe its unique power, which sometimes surpasses words: 'Independently of the natural gestures, it is known that the figurative and symbolical language of motions, composed of regulated signs, or signs of intelligence, is sometimes

Example 6.2 *Carmen*, Act I 'Scène et Pantomime', bars 77–93. From Peters Edition (2013), ed. Richard Langham Smith, trans. David Parry.

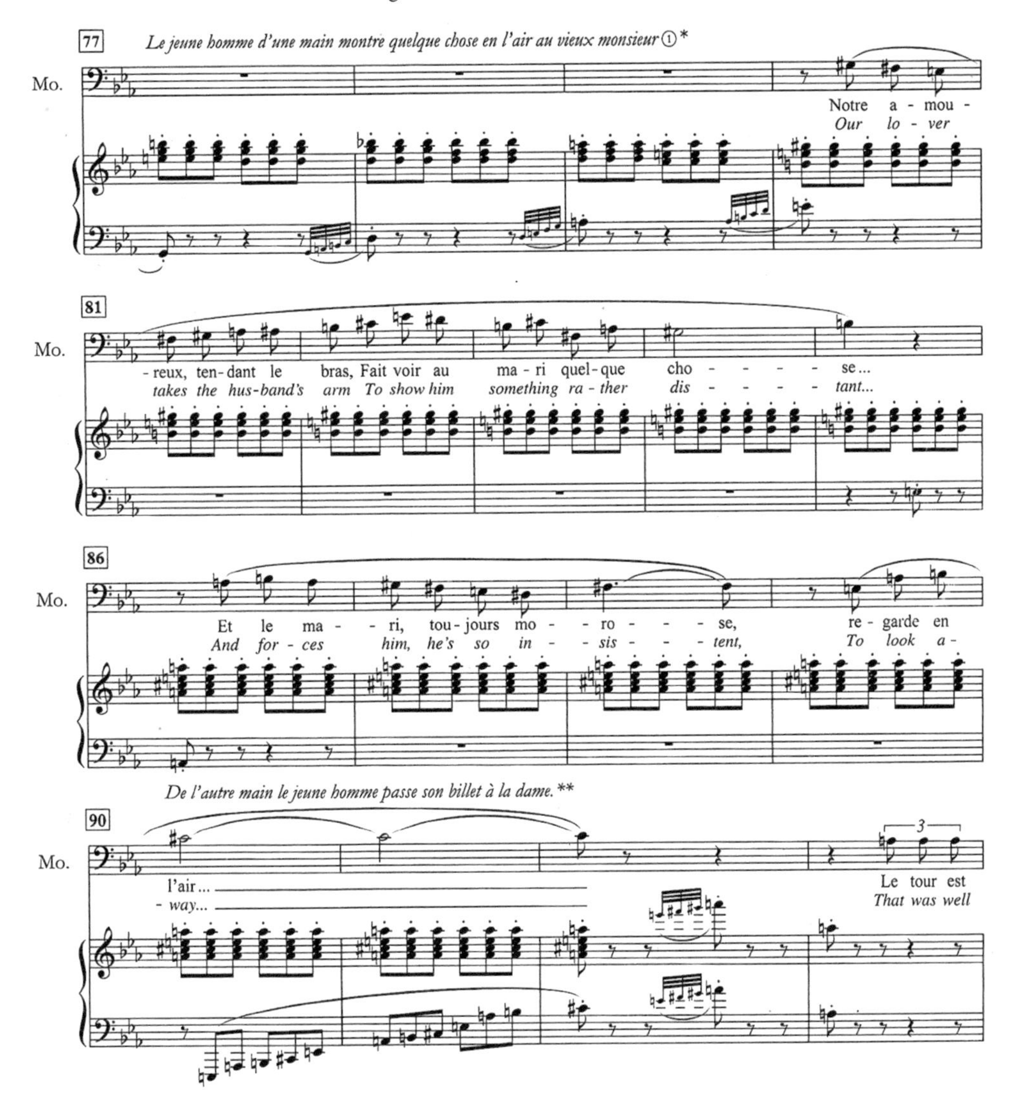

more striking than the slower and systematic language of words.'[7] Was it merely to satisfy the singer Duvernoy, who took the part of Moralès and, some recent biographers claim, was dissatisfied with the insignificance of his role in the early version of the opera?[8] The implication is that he threw a tantrum and demanded a more important scene, the better to display his

7 Carlo Blasis, *The Code of Terpsichore*, trans. R. Barton (London, 1830), p. 111 et seq.

8 Lacombe makes this assertion but gives no evidence and Didion, in the preface to his vocal score repeats this claim.

vocal prowess and dramatic skills. Credible though this may be, there is no firm evidence to support such a theory and it seems an unlikely hypothesis when compared with the music Bizet wrote for the scene, which emerges not at all as a scene to display Moralès's vocal prowess, much more as a vehicle to display his skills as a comic actor and mime.

From another angle the scene can be viewed in the context of the Mérimée novella, its setting in Seville and, not least, its musical and dramatic interest. There are ways in which it enhances several subtexts of the opera, and also its dramatic structure, even though one reason put forward in favour of the scene's excision is that it further prolongs the already overlong first act. Whether or not Bizet (and his librettists) buckled under pressure from Duvernoy, it is clear from a close reading of the staging sources that Bizet reconsidered Mérimée's inclusion of references to the English in the Iberian peninsula and capitalised on previous traditions for a mild lampooning of the English 'milord' on the French theatrical stage. Even Pigot admits it is a nice little scene and admires the music. In short, we do not really know much about Bizet's motivation for adding it, but some suggestions can be made.

The music for the scene was printed only in the first Choudens vocal score, where the genre of the work is clearly stated to be *opéra-comique*. The common second score, which calls the work an *opéra*, cuts out the scene altogether because, by the time of the reprinting, it had been abandoned. This score had already been lengthened by the addition of Guiraud's *réçits*, its main purpose being to render the opera suitable for opera houses where only fully sung performances were admitted, eschewing the dialogue required in an Opéra-Comique and vastly increasing the opera's marketability.

As was customary, the first score, even though it is described as an *opéra-comique*, gives us only the *répliques* (cues) for the ins and outs of the text, and it gives no hint of what the scene is all about. For its meaning we have to look elsewhere. The libretto, published to coincide with the premiere, prints the text but again gives us no clue as to its significance. No wonder subsequent commentators have dismissed it, not understanding the reasons for its composition and inclusion! At first sight it is simply an irrelevant distraction, delaying the entrance of the principal characters and holding up the progress of the first act. It has also been suggested that *restaurateurs* around the Opéra-Comique would have welcomed a shorter act in an opera whose timings were rather top-heavy – not such a ridiculous suggestion for those who know Parisian priorities and the habit of having the separate components of a French *dîner* in between the acts of a theatrical performance.

Because of the unusually full stage directions for the scene, the vocal score gives us more clues than most vocal scores of that period about its meaning. The libretto only prints the bare text and stage direction, telling us little about the two miming characters, who were only once to reappear in the first production. Luckily the staging sources are more revealing. From a page indicating the extras in the first scene in the plaza, referring to the 'Ancienne mise en scène' – the first run – it is clear that these characters have appeared already in the stage business immediately after curtain-up. The set was later altered, abandoning the central fountain which, although it was a nice piece of local colour, probably got in the way of the stage action.

C A R M E N

Ancienne mise en scène

Au lever du rideau, le marchand d'eau est assis à droite sur la margelle de la fontaine.
2 Fleuristes vont et viennent.
Un couple d'amoureux est assis sur la margelle de la fontaine à droite.
Un jeune homme courtise une jeune fille sous les arcades(fond cour)

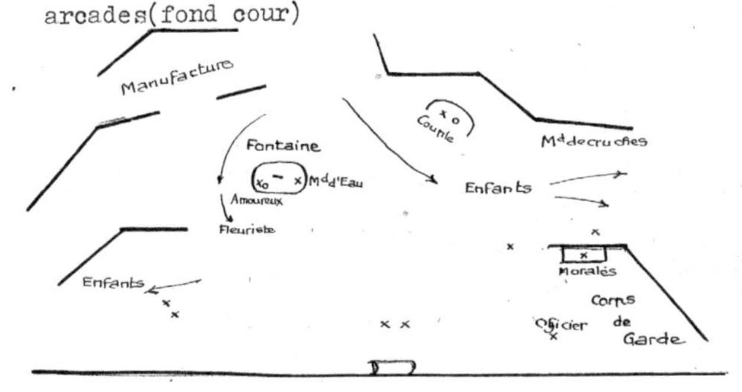

2 Figurants porteurs de soupe
I Mendiant
8 Danseuses,dont une marchande de cruches
I Jeune homme,consultant sa montre arpente fébrilement la scène,il sort 2e Plan cour.
Les enfants sortant de l'école entrent en trombe
I Couple de Bourgeois entre par 3e Plan cour
I Jeune femme vient du fond jardin,elle est suivie d'un Vieux beau qui la suit jusque devant la fontaine.
Le Jeune homme parait à nouveau,rejoint sa compagne regardant le vieux beau d'un air significatif,celui-ci s'excuse et remonte au fond jardin.Le Jeune homme et la jeune femme sortent par le 4e Plan cour.
Le vieux beau aborde une autre dame et lui offre des fleurs que vend la marchande,la dame accepte en riant,pendant que le vieux beau paie un jeune homme venant du 2e Plan jardin prend la dame par le bras,ils s'éloignent par 2e Plan jardin.
Ayant payé,le vieux beau se retourne et se trouve nez à nez avec une bonne bourgeoise qui prend le bouquet en remerciant Le vieux beau dépité,suit le couple par le 2e Plan jardin.

Plate 6.1 *Plantation* for the opening scene in Act I, including directions for the staging of the 'Scène de l'Anglais'. Typescript from a folder in the collection of the Association de la Régie Théâtrale in the Bibliothèque historique de la ville de Paris.

The characters detailed in the typed *mise en scène* portray the square as a place for both business and amorous intrigue: a young man 'pacing up and down looking at his watch' and then making an exit is undoubtedly a young *majo* waiting for his assignation. Then a young lady enters followed by the 'elderly beau'. A moment of humour is introduced as he finds himself 'nose-to-nose' with a 'bonne bourgeoise', suddenly presenting her with a bunch of flowers he has just bought. Is this perhaps a ruse to make his young wife jealous?

Both the staging sources confirm that the following scene zooms in on a corner of the stage action and is about an Englishman, a stereotype of the English 'Mylord' whose wealth has enabled him to undertake the long journey to Seville, not forgetting to wed a pretty young wife before he left. He may be a tourist doing the Spanish version of the Grand Tour, or just one of the many English businessmen who went to the city in connection with the two flourishing trades of the region – tobacco and sherry.[9] Most interesting is the way in which the librettists turn him into a figure who combines both roles.

Mérimée mentions the English traders in one of his academic footnotes in the novella, the footnotes being an innovative idea in the novella format, used to give factual weight to precise elements of reality in his narrative, which is partly imaginative and partly observed. He footnotes Englishmen as predominantly cloth-traders, rather irrelevant to the operatic plot, for which the agent who goes into the factory would have been better cast as a representative of the English tobacco trade, most likely from Bristol or one of the other British ports licensed to trade in tobacco. (Licenses were necessary as rigorous customs facilities ensured appropriate taxes were paid.) Although the factories in England dealt with the importation of raw tobacco from the Americas, and from Australasia, where taxation was lower for British-owned plants processing tobacco, from Spain the trade was more in high-class ready-processed tobacco-goods, primarily cigars, which were imported for connoisseurs.

The undisputed capital of the industry was Seville. After its discovery in America, soon after Columbus's voyage in 1492, the pleasures of smoking tobacco began to be appreciated in the Iberian peninsula. Seville was the only port in Spain granted a royal warrant to trade with America, and it was because of this that it flourished as the centre of the tobacco industry. From well before the nineteenth century (and well into the twentieth) the English

9 At this time, before the Guadalquivir silted up, Seville was a thriving port, particularly important for the Bristol tobacco industry and its wine-importing firms; many of both exist to this day. Some of our previous generations will have enjoyed Wills cigarettes (their tower in Bristol still stands) and a rather sweet sherry in Bristol is still widely marketed. Because of these important trades and the British love of cigar-smoking, traders were common in Seville long before the tourist trade flourished. They either travelled overland or by boats to the ports of Huelva and Cádiz from where these products were exported.

were closely connected with the industry in many ways. Bizet and his librettists adapted Mérimée's (and other writers') descriptions of the place with a grand spoof of an English businessman visiting it with a young wife, an element lost if this scene is cut.

In fact the British tobacco trade had been enormously catalysed by a Spanish family of apothecaries who were highly influential in encouraging the flourishing market for smoking in England in the nineteenth century. This was the company founded by José Carreras in the late eighteenth century, continuing until well into the twentieth century and eventually produced such world-famous brands as Craven-A, the first cork-tipped cigarette. It was originally named after the Third Earl of Craven, who was particularly enamoured of tobacco and for whom Craven Mixture had been blended in the 1860s, subsequently becoming internationally renowned.[10] Carreras (the father) was another casualty of the Peninsular wars, though not an *afrancesado*, quite the reverse. He had to leave because of his over-close associations with Wellington, under whose command he fought. Moving to London, he founded an international business for the importation of cigars and all tobacco-related goods, and, followed by his son, José Joaquín, later became involved in the brokering of processing machinery introduced into Spain. He had shops all over Europe, but his centre was London, where he opened prestigious shops near Leicester Square and later in Regent Street arcade, and his skills as a tobacco-blender were unequalled. Among his patrons were both British and Spanish royalty, and in 1853 he had been granted a warrant as the sole supplier of cigars and tobacco to the Spanish Legation in London.

Although tobacco was a very small part of English trade with Spain, within its own industry trade-relations with England were a vital link as far as the international tobacco industry was concerned, not least because Spain was interested in British and American developments in tobacco-processing machinery. No wonder an Englishman should have visited the celebrated Seville factory in this little scene where reality was so important! In the first production he stayed in the factory for quite a long time, to be precise from bar 57 in the 'Marche et chœur des gamins' until the sounding of the factory bell at the beginning of Scene IV.

The narrative *mise en scène* describes the action in much the same terms as the score and confirms that the old man is English, though it is likely that the audience would have spotted this already from his first entry and would have had a laugh because of his characterization through costume and demeanour. Especially interesting is the *livret de mise en scène* (claiming to be the *mise en*

10 Craven Mixture was singled out for praise by J. M. Barrie, author not only of *Peter Pan* but also of a book on tobacco, *My Lady Nicotine* (London, 1860). On Carreras and his exploits see Maurice Corina, *Trust in Tobacco* (London, 1975).

scène from before the character was dropped), which weaves the English couple into the action, and also has some fun at the old man's expense because the street urchins knock him over on the steps. The source is hard to date, but it includes red-ink sections marked 'Ancienne mise en scène', indicating sections abandoned after the first run. This almost incontrovertibly suggests that the movements detailed are how the scene was originally conceived.

In a later stage direction, not found in the scores or libretto, the Englishman comes out of the factory before the chorus of cigar girls, perhaps giving

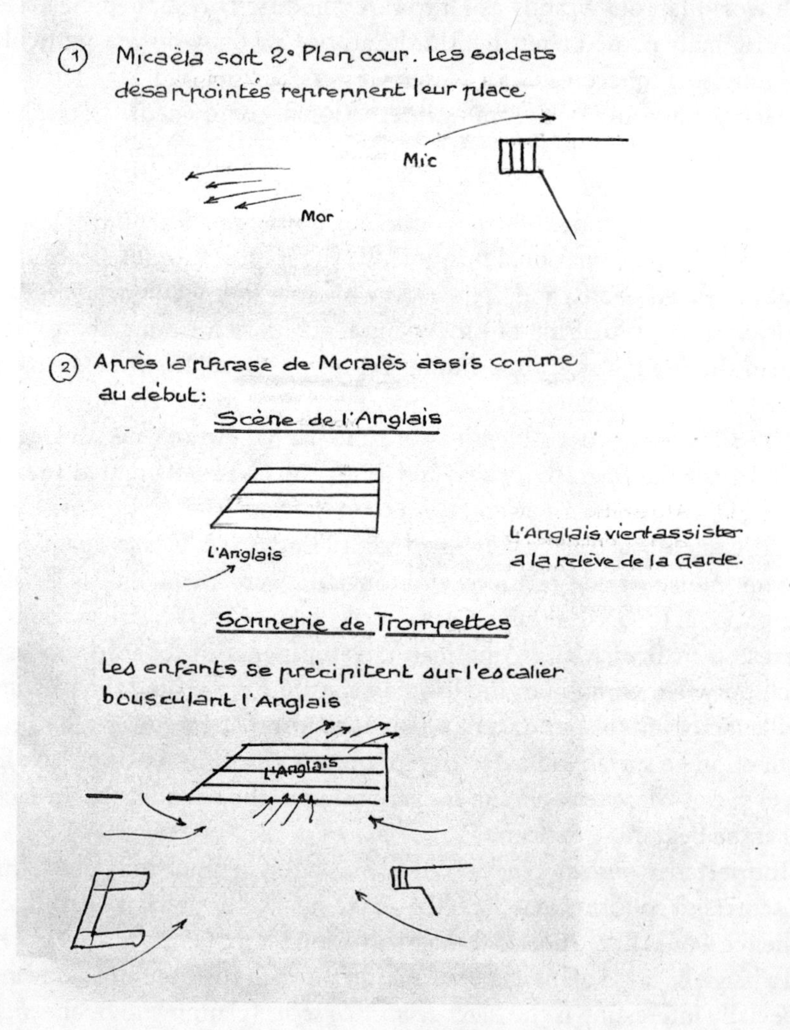

Plate 6.2 Page from the *livret de mise en scène* indicating the 'Scène de l'Anglais' and the children knocking him over on the steps, marked 'Ancienne mise en scène' ('old production') in red ink. Collection of the Association de la Régie théâtrale, Bibliothèque historique de la ville de Paris.

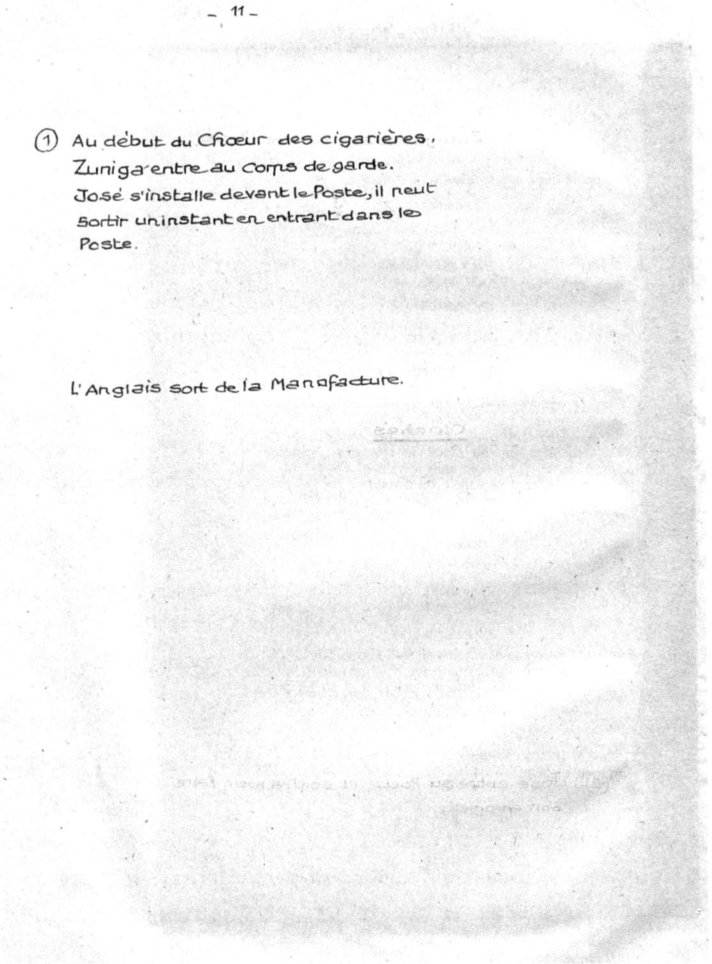

- 11 -

(1) Au début du Chœur des cigarières,
Zuniga entre au Corps de garde.
José s'installe devant le Poste, il peut
sortir un instant en entrant dans le
Poste.

L'Anglais sort de la Manufacture.

Plate 6.3 Page from the *livret de mise en scène* showing the exit of an Englishman, marked 'Ancienne mise en scène' ('old production') in red ink. Collection of the Association de la Régie théâtrale. Courtesy Bibliothèque historique de la ville de Paris. The text translates: 'At the beginning of the chorus of factory girls Zuniga comes into the guard-house. José sits down in front taking a breath of air before going inside. // The Englishman comes out of the factory.'

some credence to the supposition that he may be a businessman. Since he is with his wife he is hardly likely to have come for a less salubrious reason hinted at in both novella and libretto – namely to ogle the young *cigarières*, who often worked bare-breasted (an illicit voyeurism for which black-market passes could be bought).

What becomes clear from these sources is the meaning of Bizet's music, with its foppish opening. No doubt the Englishman appeared with ruddy make-up – to imitate what the French call 'le teint anglais' – with the trills of the first note perhaps signifying the shaking of that ubiquitous English fashion accessory, the handkerchief, and the cross-beat motive over the swaggering bass introducing him as a haughty milord (and a bit of a nancy-boy). Music and attire (check trousers perhaps, rather too short) parody English taste as the French saw it. It is a pity that no sketches of the first-run costumes for the Englishman and his wife survive, though we do have a pictorial source and some documentation on what Halévy thought of the English (see Plate 6.7).

Another factor which lay behind the introduction of this character was that the Opéra-Comique was well-practised at parodies of *le rosbif* and their audiences well-accustomed to laughing at them loudly. A rival librettist to the Halévy–Meilhac partnership, Louis Gallet, had identified this potential many years earlier, remembering in his memoirs of the 1890s an occasion where Mérimée's *Carmen* was recognised as a possible opera-subject. He recalled a conversation after sitting on a jury, although the precise date is not mentioned:

> Would you like me to recommend a subject? proposed one of the judges: I'll give it to you for I'm only a critic myself. It's *Carmen*, for there you have an opera in the same genre as *Fra Diavolo* with a part for an Englishman, think about it![11]

The anonymous jurist's recommendation clearly stems from the English references in Mérimée's *Carmen*. The presence of the English in one form or another is felt throughout the novella.

When the narrator first meets Carmen, she mistakes him for an Englishman.[12] Further encounters – at which Carmen pronounces herself to be well experienced – are with English soldiers in Gibraltar. Once again to stress how well known they are, Mérimée introduces one of his academic footnotes to

11 'Voulez-vous que je vous donne un sujet ? me proposait un de nos juges : je vous le donne ; je ne fais plus que de la critique, moi. C'est *Carmen* ; il y a là un opéra dans le genre de *Fra Diavolo* avec un rôle d'Anglais. Songez-y !' Louis Gallet, *Notes d'un librettiste : Musique contemporaine* (Paris, 1891), p. 267.

12 To stress the accuracy of his account of Andalusia and the learned quality of his narrator, as well as to translate certain Romany terms, Mérimée adds footnotes to the novella. At the point where Carmen suggests that the narrator is English he adds the footnote:

> Every traveller in Spain who does not carry about samples of calicoes and silks is taken for an Englishman (*inglesito*). It is the same thing in the East. At Chalcis I had the honour of being announced as a Μιλορδος Φραυτσεσος [phonetically, a 'Milordos Franntzesos'].
>
> En Espagne, tout voyageur qui ne porte pas avec lui des échantillons de calicot ou de soieries passe pour un Anglais, *Inglesito*. Il en est de même en Orient. A Chalcis, j'ai eu l'honneur d'être annoncé comme un Μιλορδος Φραυτσεσος.

inform the reader that such soldiers, who wore red uniforms and had plumed headgear, were popularly known as *écrevisses* (crayfish). The third part of the novella presents an extended episode where Carmen teases English soldiers with sexual promises, subsequently trapping them with her companions and robbing them.[13] None of these exploits find their way directly into the *Carmen* libretto, but the omnipresence of the English was an element of the novella which Bizet himself – as much interested in the libretto as in the music – perhaps felt was under-exploited. Also of interest is the reference of Gallet's anonymous fellow jurist to *Fra Diavolo* (an opera to a libretto by Scribe, music by Daniel Auber), which was premiered in 1830 and subsequently enjoyed resounding success at the Opéra-Comique, running up its 283rd performance in 1848 and its 500th in 1863. Duvernoy had sung in these two revivals, though not in the role of the Englishman, Cockburn, whose young wife, Pamela, is similarly seduced by a young Spaniard.

Like Mérimée's English milords, Cockburn and Pamela are victims of Latin brigands, though this time in Italy. Cockburn (Lord Kokbourg in the *distribution*, but merely marked 'Milord' in the text), is a figure of fun from the outset, as is clear from the printed French libretto where his dialogue is turned into a parody of an English couple speaking French, amusingly aspirating the 'h' syllable in front of verbs in the wrong tense:[14]

MILORD
Je havais l'honneur d'être Anglais ; je havais enlevé, selon l'usage, miss Pamela, une riche héritière que je havais épousée par inclination.

I 'ad the honour of being English; I 'ad brought, has is the custom, Miss Pamela, a rich widow who I 'ad fancied to marry.[15]

PAMÉLA, soupirant
Oh oui ! A Gretna Green !

(sighing)
Yes! At Gretna Green!

13 José, in the account of events he tells the narrator in the novella, hears the voice of a woman pretending to be an orange seller. 'I looked up and saw Carmen on the balcony, leaning over with an officer dressed in a red uniform with gold epaulettes, curly hair, and the look of a fat milord.' The Englishman, in broken Spanish, shouts for José to come up, and he and Carmen dupe him by speaking Basque to each other, hilariously mistranslating for the Englishman what they are saying. 'The lobster's guineas will soon be mine', boasts Carmen.

14 Eugène Scribe, *Fra Diavolo*, in *La France dramatique au dix-neuvième siècle : Choix de pièces modernes* (Paris, 1847), pp. 3–4.

15 Translation strategy taken from Joyce Carey's role in David Lean's iconic film *Brief Encounter*, where 'h's and their dropping are reversed: hence, 'My H'Aunt in 'Ove'.

In a subsequent scene Cockburn is angry that Pamela has been willingly receiving the attentions of an elegant cavalier, and has taken a detour to try to shake him off:

PAMÉLA Je ne pouvais pas empêcher lui de faire la même route.	I couldn't stop him from taking the same route as us.
MILORD Vous pouvez empêcher vous de la regarder et de chanter, comme hier au soir, ce petit barcarolle qui amusait pas moi de tout.	You could stop him from looking at you and singing, like last night, that little Barcarolle which I didn't like at all.
PAMÉLA (avec humeur) On peut pas faire la musique ?	(cheekily) Surely one is allowed to make music?
MILORD Vous faisiez pas la musique, vous faisiez le coquetterie avec lui.	You weren't making music, you were flirting with him.
PAMÉLA Moi, la coquetterie !	Me, flirting?
MILORD *Yes*, milady ; je l'avais vu, et je déclare ici que je ne voulais pas.	Yes milady, I saw you and I have to say I don't want any more of that!

This must have brought the house down! The similarity of an elderly Englishman, perhaps no longer very adept at exercising his wedding-tackle, and rather grumpy because of that, duped by the young *majo* is clear. It is impossible that Bizet was unfamiliar with this scene.

The English are a somewhat serious omission in the opera for other reasons, too. First that they are very much to the fore in Mérimée's novella, and second because Seville, at the time when he visited in the 1840s, and still more by the time Spain was established in the French mind when the opera was produced, was flooded with English visitors as well as the tradesmen mentioned by Mérimée when Carmen mistakes the narrator for an Englishman. Any scene in a plaza in Seville would have been a falsification if it failed to include a few English visitors. The extra scene gave Bizet an opportunity to rectify this omission, and apart from this no Englishman ever makes an appearance in Halévy's libretto, though they are amusingly referred to when the smugglers are talking about Gibraltar in Act II, just before the Quintet:

LE DANCAÏRE (addressing Carmen, Frasquita and Mercédès)

Taisez-vous alors. Nous arrivons de Gibraltar, nous avons arrangé avec un patron de navire l'embarquement de marchandises anglaises. Nous irons les attendre près de la côte, nous en cacherons une partie dans la montagne et nous ferons passer le reste. Tous nos camarades ont été prévenus ... ils sont ici, cachés, mais c'est de vous trois surtout de que nous avons besoin ... vous allez partir avec nous.	Now listen. We've just come back from Gibraltar where we've fixed up something with a sailor bringing a consignment of English goods. We're going to wait for them near the coast, hiding them in a place in the mountains and we'll bring the rest back. All our accomplices have been forewarned ... they're here hidden, but it's you three we need above all ... so you're coming with us.

Earlier on in the same scene comes a more conventional joke exploiting the English stereotype of the Anglo-Saxons in Gibraltar, clearly aimed at the gallery:

LE REMENDADO

Jolie ville, Gibraltar ! ... on y voit des Anglais, beaucoup d'Anglais, de jolis hommes les Anglais ; un peu froides, mais distingués.	Nice town Gibraltar! You see English people there, a lot of English people, nice chaps the English; a bit cold, but distinguished.

The 1911 recording includes this latter passage of dialogue, and it is most amusingly delivered, with a stress on the last line, slowed down and amusingly elongating the word 'distingués'. As has already been pointed out, this, an invaluable source, is testimony to how dialogue was delivered in the Opéra-Comique tradition. The exaggerated enactment of this particular scene gives us a rare example of how caricature was done – to use English jargon, it was considerably 'hammed up'.[16] Ridiculing an English milord was an opportunity not to be missed.

16 The reader is strongly urged to listen to this piece of dialogue in the extant recording of 1911. *Carmen* (Opéra-Comique version). Marguérite Mérentié (Carmen); Agustarello Affre (Don José – sung sections). Orchestra of the Opéra-Comique conducted by François Ruhlmann. Originally recorded in 54 parts by French Pathé for a cycle of operas entitled 'Le Théâtre chez toi'. Reissued 1999 by Marston in The Pathé Opera Series, vol. 3 (Marston, USE, 52019–2).

The inclusion of the scene, however, may have had deeper motives, more to do with retaining what might be called Mérimée's structural counterpoints in his finely constructed novella. Good writers, after all, know that one of the best ways to increase the visceral power of a tragedy is to introduce a contrary element, to make the audience laugh before they are faced with the bloody dénouement. In the novella, Mérimée uses the Englishman and his poor knowledge of languages to fashion a farcical scene which is at once very funny and contrapuntal in that it weaves three developing elements together: the lampooning of the Englishman, the developing rift between Carmen and José, and the omnipresent sense of violence of one sort or another.

Contrasted with Carmen's fluency in her gypsy language, Andalusian Spanish and Basque, and also no doubt with a smattering of milord's tongue, is the Englishman's total lack of understanding of Carmen and José's dialogue. Mérimée, who was quite an anglophile and visited England on several occasions to see friends in elevated positions – no doubt observing British manners with some amusement – was well qualified to lampoon the British and he peppers *Carmen* with quotations from languages ancient and modern, often adding footnotes to explain their nuances. He included English scenes in three works in particular: *Columba* (1840), *Carmen* (1845), and the later *La Chambre bleue* (1871).[17] In Mérimée's *Carmen* the significant element of farce is introduced towards the end of the real story (meaning chapter III).

This farcical scene is juxtaposed with one of the nastiest moments in the novella, after Carmen's one-eyed husband, García, has joined the smugglers in the mountains. This character, much too horrible for the stage of the Opéra-Comique, is described by José (who had no idea Carmen was married) as 'quite the ugliest monster the gypsy world has ever bred, his skin was black and his soul blacker'.[18] On his first escapade with El Dancaïre and El Remendado – described as a 'handsome lad' ('un joli garçon') – this young lad is wounded in the small of the back by their pursuers, perhaps members of José's former regiment. José goes to help him but García is merciless, shouting that there is no point 'in doing anything with a corpse. Finish him off, and don't lose his cotton leggings.' He proceeds to shoot straight into the young lad's face with his blunderbuss at point-blank range. 'It would be a clever man who could recognise him now', he gloats, 'looking down at the face that twelve balls had blown to shreds'.[19] Straight after, García gets out a pack of

17 See Thierry Ozwald, 'Une figure propitiatoire : Le Touriste anglais, dans trois nouvelles de Mérimée', *French Studies Bulletin*, 95 (Summer 1995), pp. 8–12.

18 '… c'était bien le plus vilain monstre que la bohème ait nourri : noir de peau et plus noir de l'âme'.

19 'Imbécile ! me cria García, qu'avons-nous à faire d'une charogne ? achève-le et ne perds pas les bas de coton.'

cards and plays the card game with El Dancaïre, memorably retained in the opera but totally transformed and recast.

Immediately this dark scene turns into comedy, 'deliberately *tragi-comique*', as Ozwald remarks. Carmen is heavily disguised and announces that she has heard of two English milords who are leaving Gibraltar for Granada, and she knows when and by what route. All are after their 'good guineas' but García – as is his way – wants to finish them off. In the end they are merely relieved of their money and watches – and their shirts, of which the smugglers had great need. José briefly goes away but on his return, posing as an orange-merchant, a more developed episode with an Englishman descends into a hilarious farce. In this instance the Englishman is a cross between an 'écrevisse' and a milord: he is a soldier in red with gold épaulettes, 'plumage', and curly hair, but still a 'milord' (with all his pomposity) underneath. Carmen flirts with him on a balcony. Seeing José's wares, the Englishman shouts at him in his broken Spanish (hints of *Fra Diavolo* here) to come up as Madame Carmen fancies an orange. She prompts José but in Basque, telling him not to speak a word of Spanish, and then turns to the Englishman with the following most amusing pretence:

> I told you so! I saw at once that he was Basque; you'll hear what a funny language it is! Doesn't he look stupid? He looks like a cat caught up to mischief in a larder!

Their dialogue continues in Basque, and as always when Carmen is using her charms on anyone else, José's jealousy rises:

> – 'And as for you', I said to her in my own language, 'you look like a total slapper, and I've half a mind to slash your face in front of your lover-boy.'
> – 'My lover-boy indeed!' she said, 'did you guess that all by yourself? You can't be jealous of this buffoon? You're even more naive than you were before our nights in Candelejo.[20] Can't you even see, idiot that you are, that I'm up to gypsy business, and really good business too. This house is mine and the crayfish's guineas will be mine; I've got him round my little finger; and I'll lead him into a trap he'll never get out of.'
> – 'As for me', I said to her, 'if you do your "gypsy business" in this way again, I'll see to it that you never do any ever again!'

20 This is clearly a dig at José's sexual inexperience, though over a few nights at Candilejo Carmen no doubt showed him the way. The calle Candelejo is a street in Seville where Carmen entertained her lovers. Her jibe is clearly designed to inflame José's mounting jealousy further.

– 'Is that so? Since when have you been my *rom*, telling me what to do? One-eye thinks it's a good ruse, so it's none of your business. Can't you just be satisfied that you're the only one who I can call my *minchorró*?'[21]

It is at this point that the linguistic farce begins:

– 'What is he saying?' asks the Englishman.
– 'He's saying he's thirsty and could do with a drink', replied Carmen, collapsing on a sofa in peals of laughter at her translation.

No doubt she's pleased to have squeezed a drink out of the Englishman for José. José continues, addressing the narrator:

> Sir, when this girl was laughing there was no way anyone could be sensible! You just laugh with her. And the tall Englishman began to laugh too, just like the imbecile he was, having ordered me something to drink!
> While I was drinking:
> – 'Do you see that ring he's wearing?', she said, 'if you want it I'll get it for you.'
> I replied:
> – 'I'd give one of my fingers to get your milord up in the mountains, each of us with a *maquila*!'

The Englishman pipes up, not understanding:

21 Mérimée explains *minchorró* in a footnote as 'my lover, or rather, my whim' ('Mon amant, ou plutôt mon caprice'). The passage reads thus in the original:
– Je vous le disais bien, je l'ai tout de suite reconnu pour un Basque ; vous allez entendre quelle drôle de langue. Comme il a l'air bête, n'est-ce pas ? On dirait un chat surpris dans un garde-manger.
– Et toi, lui dis-je dans ma langue, tu as l'air d'une effrontée coquine, et j'ai bien envie de te balafrer la figure devant ton galant.
– Mon galant ! dit-elle, tiens, tu as deviné cela tout seul ? Et tu es jaloux de cet imbécile-là ? Tu es encore plus niais qu'avant nos soirées de la rue du Candelejo. Ne vois-tu pas, sot que tu es, que je fais en ce moment les affaires d'Égypte, et de la façon la plus brillante. Cette maison est à moi, les guinées de l'écrevisse seront à moi ; je le mène par le bout du nez ; je le mènerai d'où il ne sortira jamais.
– Et moi, lui dis-je, si tu fais encore les affaires d'Égypte de cette manière-là, je ferai si bien que tu ne recommenceras plus.
– Ah ! oui-dà ! Es-tu mon *rom*, pour me commander ? Le Borgne le trouve bon, qu'as-tu à y voir ? Ne devrais-tu pas être bien content d'être le seul qui se puisse dire mon *minchorró* ?

– '"Maquila", what does that mean?' asks the Englishman.
– '"Maquila"', says Carmen still in peals of laughter, 'means an orange. It's a funny word for an orange, isn't it? But he said he wants to eat a *maquila*.'
– 'Ah yes!', says the Englishman, 'Very well. Bring me some more *maquilas* tomorrow!'[22]

What farce! Everyone knows a *maquila* is the hallmark of macho Basque males – a stick with a sharpened metal spike. Even the jealous (and condemned) José chuckles remembering this exchange as he recounts it to the narrator.

The whole passage is cleverly constructed because it advances several threads in the novella: the fading of Carmen's admiration for Don José, the increasing threats of violence arising from José's jealousy, and the omnipresence of military threats to banditry, both from the *Guardia civil* and from the English soldiers still hanging around in Andalusia. After all, to the surprise of the smugglers, it turns out that our Englishman has not only good guineas up his sleeve, but also immaculate weaponry: good guns which are certainly a match for the smuggler's blunderbusses.

All this at first sight seems weakened in the opera libretto: simplified, and with its background of impending bloodshed watered down. But there is a sort of redistribution. The Englishman becomes simply a milord, with the jealousy element retained, but any military presence, and armed robbery, removed. Humour is introduced into the game of cards played in the dark, not now by One-Eye (who is totally eradicated), but by Frasquita and Mercédès, who dream of what money will bring them if they turn up a good hand,

22 The French original reads:
– Qu'est-ce qu'il dit ? demanda l'Anglais.
– Il dit qu'il a soif, qu'il boirait bien un coup, répondit Carmen.
Et elle se renversa sur un canapé en éclatant de rire à sa traduction.
Monsieur, quand cette fille-là riait, il n'y avait pas moyen de parler raison. Tout le monde riait avec elle. Ce grand Anglais se mit à rire aussi, comme un imbécile qu'il était, et ordonna qu'on m'apportât à boire.
Pendant que je buvais :
– Vois-tu cette bague qu'il a au doigt ? dit-elle ; si tu veux je te le donnerai.
Moi je répondis :
– Je donnerais un doigt pour tenir ton mylord dans la montagne, chacun un maquila au poing.
– Maquila, qu'est-ce que cela veut dire ? demanda l'Anglais.
– Maquila, dit Carmen riant toujours, c'est une orange.
N'est-ce pas un bien drôle de mot pour une orange ? Il dit qu'il voudrait vous faire manger du maquila.
– Oui ? dit l'Anglais. Eh bien ! apporte encore demain du maquila.

all to a catchy tune in 6/8. Frasquita sees a young lover who will be constant ('Moi, je vois un jeune amoureux / Qui m'aime on ne peut davantage'). Mercédès sees an old man who proposes marriage. While Frasquita is whisked away into a Romantic dream on a trusty steed, Mercédès's old man dies and she inherits a fortune.

The momentary humour – exploiting a similar dramatic contrast to the Scène de l'Anglais – serves to throw Carmen's dealing herself the black cards of death into higher relief. The threat of violence from the whole scene is distilled into the confrontation between José and the newly invented Escamillo, where they fight with *navajas*. It would seem that Bizet and his librettists learned a lot from this pre-dénouement passage from Mérimée's chapter III, though we will probably never know whose idea the scene really was.

To understand his importance, the Englishman merits a little more attention in the context of Mérimée's substantial inclusion of him both as a ubiquitous merchant figure and a soldier lingering from the Napoleonic wars. Doré, in his illustrations for Davillier, includes him in several guises, first as a vandal, chipping out priceless Arabic tiles from the Alhambra palace in Granada. Doré's cartoon immediately identifies the thief as an Englishman by his height, frock coat and milord hat. What seems to have been an enhanced Spanish translation of Davillier's text, from some time later, reinforces – one could say embroiders – this with a passage I have not found in any of the nineteenth-century editions or translations:

> We arrived not yet knowing anything about the beautiful ceramic tiles. One day, in one of the rooms of the Alhambra we saw an Englishman amusing himself by gouging some out from a wall, not in the least put out by our arrival, as if it was the most natural thing in the world to do. This rival of Lord Elgin seemed to be well-practised in his art.[23]

More conscientious English milords would content themselves with ogling pretty young Spanish dancers. The stereotype of the ruddy-faced Englishman, too fond of an excess of strong liquor, and with an eye for the Continental girls, became quite a favourite in illustrations and cartoons. Indeed, lampooning the English milords in this way was a sport not only for the French but also for the English themselves. In 1871 Doré was commissioned to illustrate

23 'Llegará el momento en que ya no quede ni uno solo de estos bellos azulejos de cerámica. En una de las salas de la Alhambra vimos cierto un inglés que se divertía en arrancarlos del muro, y que no se turbó por nuestra llegada, como si estuviera haciendo la cosa más natural del mundo. Este rival de Lord Elgin parecía tener gran práctica en esto.' Davillier, *España*, Spanish translation (Madrid, 1949), R. 1957.

Despoilers of the Azulejos of the Alhambra

Plate 6.4 Gustave Doré, *Despoilers of the Azulejos of the Alhambra*, illustration for Baron Davillier's *Spain* (English edition), showing an Englishman stealing precious decorative tiles from the Alhambra palace in Granada.

a satirical book on the English in Paris, and its frontispiece exploits this stereotype. His caricature had hallmarks of the stereotype no doubt imitated in theatrical costumes of Englishmen: the lorgnettes, curly hair and top- or bowler-hats.

Halévy was by no means averse to joining in with lampooning *le rosbif*, and in his case there was an undercurrent of disgust stemming from his experiences of the English during the Paris Commune, particularly their insouciant attitude to watching the city burn from the safe distance of the prestigious Hôtel des Réservoirs at Versailles. He was clearly incensed. A page of his diary for 24 May 1871 records his disgust:

MI LORD ANGLAIS AT MABILLE.

He is smiling, he is splendid, he is full of graceful enjoyment ; on the table are a few of the beverages he admires ; but above all he adores the ease of the French ladies in the dance.

Plate 6.5 Gustave Doré, *Mi Lord Anglais at Mabille*, illustration of an English gentleman in Paris for Blanchard Jerrold's *The Cockaynes in Paris; or, Gone Abroad* (London, 1871). 'He is smiling, he is splendid, he is full of graceful enjoyment, on the table are a few of the beverages he admires; but above all he adores the ease of the French ladies in the dance.'

> Two English people were dining beside me in the great dining-room of the Hôtel des Réservoirs and I picked out of their conversation the following phrase, uttered with perfect calm:
> – Montretout is the best place to see Paris burn.
> While this Englishman was communicating to me this precious observation, a newspaper boy was shouting out 'Ask for the latest edition of the *Petit Moniteur* ... Only a sou: "The Great Fire of Paris"'.

Plate 6.6 Gustave Doré, *A Dancing Academy, Seville,* illustration of English tourists being entertained at a Spanish dance academy, for Baron Davillier's *Spain* (English edition).

Let's go to Montretout then since it's the best place to see Paris burn. The English are practical fellows and know the best places. There was an Englishman settled in at Montretout with three lorgnettes ... three! ... a large pair ... a small one ... and a long-range one on a stand ... Every now and again he'd look at a plan of Paris and take notes in a little notebook. His face was glowing, as much as an Englishman's can. He was happy there, it was nice weather and his lorgnettes were good – and Paris was on fire! From time to time, he sat on a folding stool ... He hadn't forgotten anything ... and he had his folding stool. Nothing could be more irritating than this Englishman, smiling and happy. It made you want to see London a little on fire.[24]

Earlier in the same memoirs, Halévy recounts how he had met the celebrated satirical cartoonist Cham near the same hotel, 'with his eternal companion Toutou [a little dog] in his arms, his precious little jewel'. Cham was clearly a close companion and the two memoirs curiously come together when, some years later, Halévy edited and collected his favourite satirical drawings by Cham, including a picture of an Englishman in Paris during the Commune, just as in the memoirs. An urchin remarks that he need not have bothered coming all the way to Paris, as he could get a bunch of bother-boys together to set London on fire. Note the caricatured appearance of this Anglais: tall (the English had more tall people than the French); bold checked trousers, rather too short (checks were considered bad taste in France); little bowler hat; tombstone teeth; and, of course, the ubiquitous lorgnettes and umbrella.

In his sketches (rather than engravings) for Jerrold's spoof on the 'Cockaynes in Paris', Doré – immensely popular on both sides of the Straits of Dover – seems to have been fixated on another physical stereotype, possibly derived from the physiognomy of the English royal family: that of 'chinless wonders' and the Habsburg lip. He had employed this already in the engraving of the tile-stealer in the Alhambra, and his Englishman wandering the Paris boulevards is cast in a similar mould (Plate 6.5).

24 The original reads:

Deux anglais déjeunent, à côté de moi, dans la grande salle à manger de l'Hôtel des Réservoirs, et, de leur conversation j'ai saisi cette phrase, dite du ton le plus calme :

– Montretout is the best place to see Paris burn. (Montretout est la meilleure place pour voir brûler Paris.)

Pendant que cet Anglais me donnait ce précieux renseignement, un gamin crie sous les fenêtres de l'hôtel : « Demandez la dernière édition du *Petit Moniteur* ... L'incendie de Paris ... Un sou, le grand incendie de Paris. »

Allons donc à Montretout, puisque c'est la meilleure place pour voir brûler Paris. Les anglais sont gens pratiques et connaissent les bons endroits. [...]

Un anglais est installé là, à Montretout, il a trois lorgnettes ... trois ... une grosse jumelle ... une petite ... et une longue-vue avec un pied ... De temps en temps, il consulte un plan de Paris et il prend des notes sur un petit calepin ...

Sa figure rayonne autant que peut rayonner la figure d'un Anglais. Il est au bon endroit, le temps est clair, ses lorgnettes excellentes, et Paris brûle ! De temps en temps, il s'assied sur un petit pliant ... Il n'a rien oublié.

Rien de plus irritant que la vue de cet Anglais épanoui et souriant ... Cela donne le désir de voir un peu brûler Londres. Ludovic Halévy, *Notes et souvenirs, de mai à décembre 1871*, (Paris, 1888) p. 43.

— Mylord, faut pas vous gêner ! si ça vous amuse, on peut aller faire ça chez vous,

Plate 6.7 Cham [Amédée Charles Henry Noé], cartoon depicting an Englishman observing the aftermath of the Paris Commune.

All in all, Bizet's little Pantomime scene went down well enough in some quarters but was passed over by most of the critics who reviewed the first run. One rare admirer was the critic of the *Revue dramatique*, Jules Guillemot, who advised his readers:

> Look out in particular for a meaningful pantomime between an elderly husband, his young wife, and a lover, commented on by Brigadier Moralès who makes up the words of these characters which we don't hear: the idea is original and witty and its interpretation left nothing to be desired.[25]

25 'Remarquez particulièrement une pantomime significative entre un vieux mari, une jeune femme et un amant, commentée par le brigadier Moralès. qui prête à chacun des personnages les paroles que nous n'entendons pas : l'idée est originale et spirituelle. l'exécution

Plate 6.8 Gustave Doré, *On the Boulevards,* sketch of English couple wandering around Paris, Blanchard Jerrold's *The Cockaynes in Paris; or, Gone Abroad* (London, 1871).

Several critics took the line of criticising the opera because of what it left out as well as what it added. Eugène Gautier, in the *Journal officiel,* took this approach and thought the transformation of Mérimée's novella into an *opéra-comique* had missed a trick precisely because it failed to exploit the important English undercurrent:

n'est pas en reste avec elle.' Jules Guillemot, *Le Soleil, Revue Dramatique*, 9 March 1875, pp. 1–2. Quoted Wright, *Dossier* pp. 90–91.

> In its transformation it has omitted a certain type of English officer who could have brought a touch of comedy to a work in which humorous effects are not very common! There's no doubt that a red costume with gold-embroidered frogs and loops was all that was needed to make the public of the Salle Favart double up with laughter, always welcoming the English officer in *Le Domino noir* with hoots of laughter.[26]

This is an interesting comment, since Auber's *Le Domino noir* is another example of an *opéra-comique* with an inserted spoof Englishman, in this case chasing a Spanish girl to no avail. His appearance is a minor sub-plot to the main action but is based on his mistaking another woman at a masked ball for his wife. Becoming a figure of ridicule, one imagines he would have raised quite a laugh, again reinforced particularly by costume and gait. In fact, Duvernoy had sung the part of Lord Eldon (in the opera an attaché at the British Embassy in Spain) at the Opéra-Comique in 1854. If the story about him demanding more to sing in *Carmen* is true, he might even have had a hand in advising Bizet and his librettists about the winning formula of including a little scene in which the Opéra-Comique audience – well used to such episodes – could have a laugh at the English.

Whatever the case, for most commentators Bizet's scene did not work, and there are clear indications in the orchestral parts that there were several attempts to move it around into different positions in Act I. Pigot, Bizet's first biographer, subsequently summed up the objections and merits:

> After the dialogue between Micaëla and Moralès and the short reprise of the chorus, the authors of the libretto have placed a strange scene: the famous Pantomime that we've seen or rather heard – because its appeal stems entirely from the fine, descriptive music Bizet has given it, and from the pleasant monologue of Brigadier Moralès, heard at the first performances of *Carmen* at the Opéra-Comique in March 1875. Bizet, despite his deep understanding of the demands of the theatre, no doubt had not quite got the courage to get rid of this useless scene and to nip it in the bud. The admirable symphonist saw a pretext for a richly coloured sparkling musical tableau so he kept the scene, trying to liven it up and make it inter-

26 '... il a perdu dans cette transformation un type d'officier anglais qui pouvait amener un peu de comique dans un ouvrage où les effets comiques ne sont pas nombreux ! nul doute qu'un habit rouge à brandebourgs d'or n'eut suffi à dérider le bon public de la salle Favart, qui accueille toujours avec de si francs éclats de rire l'officier anglais du *Domino noir*.' Eugène Gautier, *Journal officiel*, 16 March 1875, pp. 2006–2007; quoted Wright, *Dossier* p. 132.

esting scenically and he succeeded, because the musical tableau is full of charm and movement, gracefulness and the witty monologue of Moralès which accompanies the scene and underlines the action. But in spite of all this, it remains outside the plot and acts only as a brilliant hors-d'oeuvre. Its most serious weakness is that it puts the spectators totally off course, onto a false path, putting them off the scent by focussing their attention on transitory, secondary characters while the main characters still remain entirely unknown. What is more, as we have already said, it brings nothing new to the action and remains totally alien to it, having not the slightest relevance and it slows down, if not stops, the action. M. Carvalho, in the role of a ruthless controller of the *mise en scène*, suppressed this Pantomime, the lovely music of Bizet failing to please him. Despite our respect for the best intentions of the Master, and our admiration for this lively page, we are forced to admit that the first act, free of this overlong and useless scene, gains considerably in speed and vigour.[27]

27 Pigot's original reads as follows:
Après le dialogue de Micaëla et de Moralès et la courte reprise du chœur, les auteurs du livret ont placé une scène étrange : c'est la fameuse *Pantomime* que nous avons vue ou plutôt entendue – car elle tire tout son attrait de la belle musique descriptive écrite par Bizet et du plaisant monologue du Brigadier Moralès, – lors des premières représentations de *Carmen* à l'Opéra-Comique en mars 1875. Bizet, malgré son sens profond des exigences scéniques, n'eut sans doute pas la force de faire disparaître cette scène inutile, de couper dans le vif. Symphoniste admirable, il vit là un prétexte à tableau musical chatoyant, riche en couleur : il conserva donc cette scène, essaya d'animer, de la rendre intéressante scéniquement, et il réussit, car ce petit tableau musical est plein de charme et de mouvement grâce au spirituel monologue de Moralès qui l'accompagne et le souligne : mais, malgré tout, il reste en dehors de l'action et ne constitue qu'un brillant hors-d'œuvre. Son tort le plus grave est de dérouter complètement le spectateur, de le mettre sur une fausse voie, de lui donner le change en attirant et fixant son attention sur des personnages épisodiques très secondaires, dont la plupart ne reparaîtrons pas dans l'action, tandis que les personnages principaux, les acteurs du drame, sont encore complètement inconnus. De plus, nous l'avons déjà dit, il n'apporte rien de nouveau dans le drame, auquel il reste complètement étranger, avec lequel il n'a même pas le moindre point de contact, et qu'il ralentit, ou plutôt qu'il retarde, car il n'a pas encore commencé. M. Carvalho, en impitoyable metteur en scène, a supprimé le *Pantomime* ; la musique savoureuse de Bizet n'a pas trouvé grâce devant lui. Malgré notre respect profond pour les moindres intentions du Maître et notre admiration pour cette page si alerte, nous sommes forcé d'avouer que le premier acte, dégagé de cette scène un peu longue et complètement inutile, a beaucoup gagné en rapidité et en vigueur.

Pigot, *Georges Bizet*, pp. 238–239. The second edition (Paris, 1911) slightly alters this passage (p. 208), but its viewpoint remains unchanged.

His view only reiterated the view of the management, the restaurateurs and most of the critics.

Having examined its roots, however, it may be suggested that despite these objections there are strong arguments for the inclusion of the 'Scène de l'Anglais': it adds a counterpoint of humour; it exploits a parodistic element well tried at the Opéra-Comique; it rectifies the disappearance of the English in the transfer of Mérimée's novella to the stage; it bridges the awkward (and unusual) juxtaposition of two crowd scenes in Act I; and it introduces yet another way of conducting male–female relationships (the young wife 'bought' by the rich old gentleman). Having this little sideshow in the plaza brings in a further element of the reality that was striven for in the first stagings of the opera, and indeed its conception. And, last but not least, the scene that is half-mime, half melodrama, was a novel element which today might be termed 'interactive' – involving the audience in the action by pointing out details for them to look at.

It ultimately failed, generally considered too much of an interruption to the plot although it chimes in with themes of the English elsewhere (particularly in the references to Gibraltar). What is undeniable is that it created an imbalance, overweighting the first act. Lovely music, though, and it did have its advocates in Gallet before, and one or two critics after.

PART III

CHARACTERISATION, MUSIC AND THE STAGING OF PLACE

CHAPTER SEVEN

Carmen's Places

Returning to a reading of Mérimée's *Lettres d'Espagne*, less for details that infiltrated both the *novella* and the libretto, and more for an overall impression of the Spain he visited in the 1830s, we realise that an over-arching sense of the text's cultures of violence emanates from all four acts of the opera. The extraordinary number of weapons mentioned in the novella, and those retained in the opera, were clearly deliberately inserted to maintain the threat of violence throughout. There is also a sense of the unjust distribution of wealth in Andalusia, which was seen as justifying banditry, smuggling and wrecking. Above all it is clear that this constant background of imminent violence, along with its unpredictability, excited northern travellers to Spain rather than repelling them, and that Mérimée was no exception. He captured this undercurrent in his *Lettres* and skilfully injected a similar character into his *Carmen* of ten years later. Study of the libretto reveals that the librettists made some attempt to preserve these darker sides, even though detractors see the opera as a trivialised transformation of Mérimée's original. In each of the four acts of the opera there are moments of violence either spontaneous or premeditated. Listen to Bizet's music in that context and maybe the opera appears a little more sinister.

IMMINENT VIOLENCE IN MÉRIMÉE'S VISITS TO SPAIN

As the *Lettres* evolve there is a distinct move from observation to imagination.[1] Yet even in the description of the bullfight in the first *lettre*, Mérimée details his emotions as he approaches his first *corrida*, moving from a fear that he will not be able to endure the 'free-flow of blood' to his confession that after he had witnessed the death of the first bull 'he never looked back'. Of the different types of tauromachic spectacle, he immediately sided with the fully

1 The various views of commentators on the balance between travelogue and invention are discussed at length in François Géal, *Relire les Lettres d'Espagne de Mérimée* (Paris, 2010), p. 44 et seq.

fledged bullfight – which he terms 'la tragédie' – rather than the bull-running, such as was (and is) done in Pamplona and the south of France, where there was only minor danger to the men.

Before travelling to Madrid in November 1845, Mérimée had written to his companion and guide Calderón asking him to reserve him a place 'surrounded by informed *aficionados*' at a *corrida* (if there were to be one during his stay).[2] The essay finishes with a modulation from factual observation and a parade of bullfight vocabulary into an exciting (but possibly fictional) account of a triumphant moment when a *picador* of unparalleled bravery usurped the role of a *torero* and killed a raging bull by jumping on its back. Mérimée had met this man of considerable charm, one Francisco Sevilla, but the boundary between reportage and invention is blurred.[3] What is clear is Mérimée's desire to glamorise extreme acts in the *corrida*.

VIOLENT PUNISHMENT FOR VIOLENT CRIME

While the first letter began with a listing of the arguments in favour of bullfighting, the second begins with a defence of Mérimée's attendance at a public execution, based on the premise that 'In a foreign country one is obliged to see everything, and one should beware of moments of laziness or disgust which could cause you to ignore one of its curious customs.'[4] In both these letters one senses the influence of Mérimée's aforementioned travelling companion, the writer Estébanez Calderón, both in his role as an *aficionado* of every detail of the bullfight, and in his *casticismo* interest in the old customs – the *mœurs curieux* – of old Spain, which – several commentators agreed – were fast disappearing.[5] This was in part motivated by a nostalgia for Spain before the French invasion and occupation during the *era Josefina*, when northern tastes had eroded the old habits of the peninsula – a possible reason, too, for the librettists situating the action back in 1820. Dating *Carmen* will be examined more closely later.

2 Mérimée to Estébanez Calderón: 'S'il y a des taureaux, tâchez que je puisse trouver une place dans quelque loge honnête avec des personnes doctes en *tauromaquia*'. *Correspondance générale*, vol. IV, p. 394.

3 Mérimée appended a tribute to him on his death, in his re-edition of the *Lettres* in 1842.

4 'En pays étranger on est obligé de tout voir, et l'on craint toujours qu'un moment de paresse ou de dégoût ne vous fasse perdre un trait des mœurs curieux.' *Lettres d'Espagne II.*

5 Custine, writing just before Mérimée's *Carmen*, estimated that 'One finds in the descriptions of places and in the portraits of people I have seen in Spain, the picture of a society that no longer exists.' ('On trouvera dans les descriptions des lieux et dans les portraits de personnes que j'ai vu en Espagne, le tableau d'une société qui n'existe déjà plus.') Custine, *Mémoires d'un touriste* (Paris, 1838).

Even by the early 1830s the fashion for English and French costumes was a major force in obliterating a sense of the 'Old Spain' which Calderón was so anxious to preserve. In the first *lettre* Mérimée remarks on this: 'In the boxes you can observe a few elegantly dressed people, but few young women. Recently French and English novels have corrupted the Spanish and taken away their respect for their old customs.'[6] For Gautier, Andalusia was the last refuge: 'In general', he notes, 'national customs are preserved only in Andalusia, in Castile there are hardly any old customs.'[7] Both writers shared Calderón's *casticismo.*

Mérimée soon plunges into his imagination to recount in detail a part-imagined story of an unfortunate condemned young man, claiming that he wanted to see what the condemned looked like and was happy to test his own nerves.[8] An unexpected escalation of violence had flared up between the condemned man, whom Mérimée presents as the kindest and most honourable of men, a perfect *majo,* and his friend, a volunteer royalist. A fortnight later the volunteer was despatched to hunt out some smugglers in an isolated inn and was ambushed. He was shot a dozen times in the chest. An over-zealous *alguazil* (a bailiff) seems to have taken an interest, not least because a woman he was pursuing preferred the *majo.* Thus the *majo* was blamed and condemned. Mérimée asks us to agree with him that he was 'a victim of *fatalité malheureuse*', an unfair justice system.

As was Mérimée's way, every detail is charted – from the construction of the scaffold, to a hideous painted crucifix displaying Christ's tortured flesh in graphic detail, which the condemned man is forced to contemplate. Having remarked that the Spanish 'go out of their way to emphasise terror in their religion' ('Les Espagnols, qui cherchent à faire la religion terrible'). Mérimée prolongs his detailed description of the various religious rituals – confessions, prayers, public readings – that put off the terrible moment. Descriptions of the bound, condemned lad are supplemented by descriptions of his confessor, and the hangman who walks behind as he is led to the scaffold on a mule. The final blow comes as the sentence is read out: he is to be dragged behind a mule before his execution: 'Pendu après avoir été "trainé sur la claie."'

Mérimée's order of play in this *lettre* was 'Punishment and Crime', rather than the reverse. He was frustrated in his desire to meet a hardened criminal, in particular one of the legendary Spanish bandits. So, once again, he returned to informed reportage from all kinds of sources. The use of mules for

6 'Dans les loges on remarque pourtant quelques toilettes élégantes, mais peu de jeunes femmes. Les romans français et anglais ont perverti depuis peu les Espagnoles, et leur ôtent le respect pour leurs vieilles coutumes.' *Lettres d'Espagne I.*

7 Gautier, *Voyage en Espagne* (Paris, 1843).

8 '... je voulais voir sa physionomie ; enfin j'étais bien aise de faire une expérience sur mes nerfs.' Mérimée, *Lettres d'Espagne* II, p. 402.

public humiliation is given space in the opera's libretto, and the overhanging capital punishment of José is omnipresent in the novella and often suggested in modern stagings of the opera. The third *lettre* advances to imagined narrative nourished by factual reports, enhanced by a Romantic imagination.

NORTH AND SOUTH

While there are many elements of alterity between the north and south of Spain, and more widely of Europe, in both the *Lettres* and the novella, the libretto expands the divide considerably. The personification of Micaëla as the religious, honest, girl from José's home village is perhaps the most conspicuous way in which this is done, but there are many others. Even Carmen, if she is telling the truth about coming from Etchalar, may be a migrant to Andalusia just like José. His mother, hinted at in the novella but distantly personified in the opera, adds to this regional difference. Exploitation of the English soldier's misunderstanding the Basque language, made fun of in the novella, has already been discussed in Chapter Six. As regards the geographical divide, there is a deeper recognition of the distinction between the 'African' deep south of Spain and influences from northern Europe running as an undercurrent throughout the libretto.

In the novella, the mention of the English traders in textiles was an important cultural issue, since the adoption of northern ways of dressing – both French and English – was a trend of which many educated visitors disapproved. Many French visitors – like Mérimée – had gone South specifically to experience 'Old Spain' before it became diluted by northern fashions, customs and politics. Bartolomé and Lucile Bennassar put it nicely: 'Custine, Mérimée, Gautier and Alexandre Dumas are not interested in signs of statistics of progress: quite the contrary! They were in search of a 'different' Spain and delighted in the archaisms of that country, playing at making themselves afraid.'[9]

An aspect of the attraction was Spain's ability to mirror the past; Spain, to some extent, showed how northern countries used to be. Custine and Stendhal saw Spain as a window on the Middle Ages, viewing it through the rose-coloured spectacles of dreaming Romantics and ignoring the injustices of its feudalism: 'at every step you think you are interrogating time', wrote Custine, 'How can one not respect a country covered with relics from the past which

9 'Custine, Mérimée, Gautier ou Alexandre Dumas ne s'intéressent pas aux signes ou aux indices du progrès [...] au contraire ! Ils cherchent une Espagne « différente », se délectent des archaïsmes du pays, jouent à se faire peur.' Bartolomé et Lucile Bennassar, *Le Voyage en Espagne : Anthologie des voyageurs français et francophones du XVIe au XIXe siècle* (Paris, 1998).

are still alive?'[10] As the century progressed, visitors began to see Andalusia as the only bastion preserving the old customs and costumes.

Regional difference is expanded into a major issue in the libretto, elaborated in terms of combative customs: the *maquilas* of the Basque country versus the *navajas* of Andalusia. Overall it can be concluded that the north was crude in manners but in some ways more organised and richer; the south was more elegant, having on the one hand better manners but on the other an ingrained addiction to violence.

VIOLENCE AND TRANSGRESSION IN THE LIBRETTO

The sense of unpredictable violence from the *Lettres* is carried through into Mérimée's *Carmen*, and this perpetual threat was clearly perceived by Meilhac and Halévy in their libretto transformation. Weapons are repeatedly mentioned, and *Carmen*'s armoury is impressive:

Maquila (Basque: *makila* or *makhila*); a Basque walking stick with hidden metal spike, symbolic of ethnicity and power. José fought and murdered with this weapon, as is mentioned in the spoken dialogue.
Cigar girl's trimming knife (used to slash the face of an insulter)
Scissors (*tijeras*, particularly associated with gypsies)
Rope (used by the *Guardia* to tie up Carmen's hands – perhaps too tightly)
Swords (military issue, *épée* and *sabre*)
Glove (in the novella used by the unnamed officer whose first gesture against José is the traditional Spanish slap in the face)
Pistols
Guns (military issue)
Blunderbuss
Media luna (used for trimming tobacco goods)
Navajas (of all sizes)
Daggers (José's and Carmen's) and Escamillo's *puntilla*
Picas (the picks used by picadors to taunt the bulls)
Banderillos (both normal and exploding)
Lances (Spanish lancers were particularly important)
L'Espada (the matador's killing sword to be used in one vertical blow into the *croix* of the bull – a vital moment in *la hora de la verdad* – the moment of truth, i.e., the killing of the bull)

10 '... à chaque pas que l'on fait on croit interroger le temps. Comment fouler sans respect une terre couverte des reliques encore vivantes du passé ?' Custine, *L'Espagne sous Ferdinand VII* (Paris, 1838).

To this list can be added the *garrotte* – the method of execution awaiting José the day after his visit from the narrator in the novella. It had been introduced during the Peninsular wars and was the standard method of execution in Spain throughout the nineteenth century. Mérimée details the introduction of its use in a footnote. Whether it was less cruel than hanging, which it replaced, is debateable. The Spanish machines were designed to replace strangulation with a metal bar breaking the spinal cord, but the exact positioning of the victim seems to have been crucial. There are tales of the bribery of executioners who knew the least painful positions and could be persuaded to use them for a fee. Copious images of these machines, at first used publicly, were circulated to discourage resistance to the Napoleonic regime during the *era Josefina*. Gentlemen (*hidalgos*) and bandits were executed by this method. Its gruesome imagery no doubt augmented the sense of impending violence that permeated the *Lettres*, novella, opera and, indeed, Spain itself.

The way in which the librettists ensured constant reference to the violence lurking beneath the surface throughout the opera can be seen in a diagram isolating the essential structural transference of violent scenes between novella and libretto.

Novella and other sources		**Libretto and Opera**
	ACT I	
José's previous murder over game of *pelota*		Transferred to libretto (Highlighted in spoken dialogue)
(fight with maquilas)		
Carmen's attack: riot in factory	(strengthened)	Transferred to spoken dialogue
(Carmen's trimming knife)		Converted to musical number (split Chorus, Carmen v. Manuelita)
Actualities not in novella about which Mérimée and Halévy may have known		Added interrogation scene with impertinence (tra-la-las) (Pushkin: Gypsies) (Hands tied with rope)

Novella and other sources		**Libretto and Opera**
	ACT II	
Fight with lieutenant in Dorothée's *baisade*.	(weakened) →	Musical number: (Recitative, sung dialogue and air)
(Swords) José wounded by his superior, drugged and recovers. But receives permanent scar.		Softened as lieutenant (Zuniga) is threatened and bound but not attacked.
		(Slap with glove—a standard Spanish warning—drawing of sabre and pistols)
	ACT III	
Guardia civil pursue smugglers and gypsies.	(strengthened) →	Constant threat distilled into chorus text: 'Le péril est en bas, en haut, partout, qu'importe !'
Remendado badly wounded.		(Not in libretto)
García finishes off Remendado with a blunderbuss at point blank range—has a smoke, plays cards).	(altered but weakened) →	Card-game transferred to female gypsies. Remendado's wounding and death omitted.
	→	Shot in mountains transferred to a 'pot-shot' from José at Micaëla whom he does not recognise.
Duel from Lettres II and novella.	(strengthened) →	Central Stage Fight: José and Escamillo. Duet and orchestral music.
		(Navajas, hand-to-hand fight)
Recurrent arguments and jealousy between José and Carmen	(incorporated with much quoted directly from novella) →	Carmen and José argue. He threatens her. She draws her dagger from her belt to wound José. Micaëla interposes herself, offering herself as a victim. Carmen bursts out laughing.
		(Gypsy dagger)

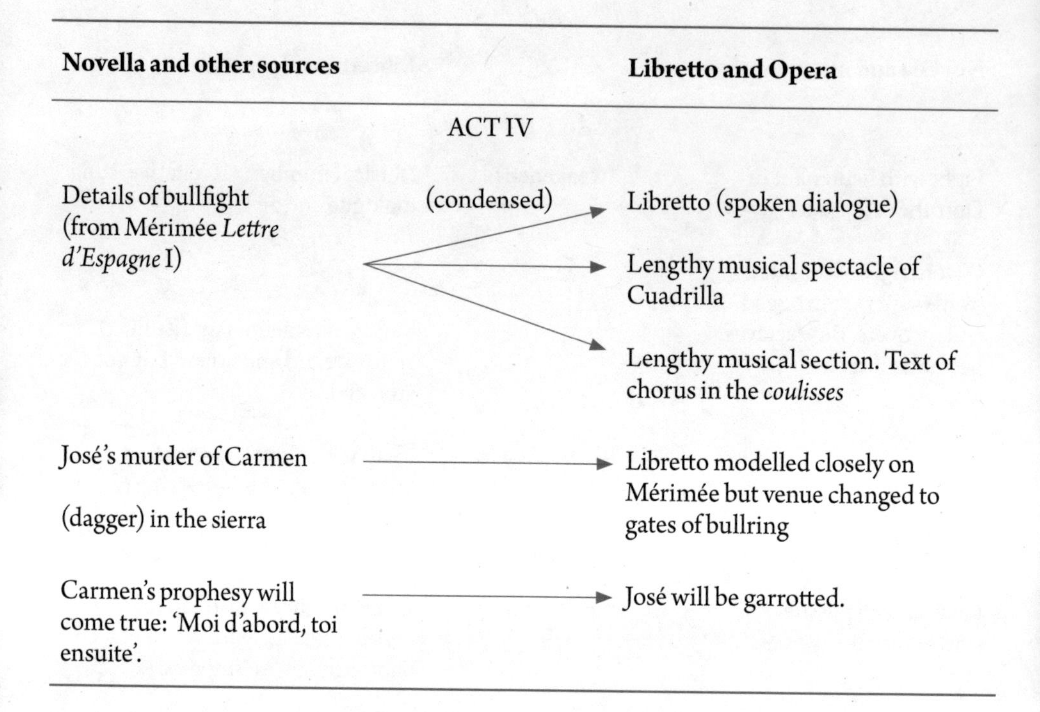

Novella and other sources		Libretto and Opera
	ACT IV	
Details of bullfight (from Mérimée *Lettre d'Espagne* I)	(condensed) →	Libretto (spoken dialogue)
	→	Lengthy musical spectacle of Cuadrilla
	→	Lengthy musical section. Text of chorus in the *coulisses*
José's murder of Carmen (dagger) in the sierra	→	Libretto modelled closely on Mérimée but venue changed to gates of bullring
Carmen's prophesy will come true: 'Moi d'abord, toi ensuite'.	→	José will be garrotted.

DATING *CARMEN*

Dating Carmen is a necessary process to explore before a thorough examination of its places can be made. The libretto unequivocally sets the action in Spain around 1820 ('En Espagne vers 1820'), eleven years before Mérimée's first visit. In the intervening ten years, Spain had changed a good deal and had undergone a period of oscillating turbulence between northern-inspired liberalism and meridional Catholic conservatism. While Calderón may have instructed Mérimée about the changes, both places and customs were documented by many writers, predominantly French and English. To prepare himself for his journey, Mérimée would have had much to read, not only the many travelogues but also press reports on the unstable political situation – especially regarding the Carlist wars and the changing fortunes of the liberals.

Fifteen years further on – when he wrote his novella – the country had evolved even further and opened up considerably. Unlike the libretto, the novella bears no dating, although because of José's long narration of the events of his life on the eve of his death, it covers quite a long period. Another thirty years pass until the fashioning of the libretto and the composition of the opera in the 1870s. Certainly no-one knew about Habaneras around 1820. But there are other details of characters and places that are also clearly anachronistic to that period. The all-female workers in the factory were not introduced until 1828, and the imposition of order by the *Guardia civil* was not in place until the early 1840s, though it was no doubt something Mérimée knew about when he wrote *Carmen*. In the 1820s policing was chaotic – landowners had their own henchmen, the ratio of soldiers to the areas of land was low, and the system disorganised.

With the great influx of tourists during the 1830s and 1840s, entertaining and catering for them had considerably improved and was an enhancement for the economy, hence Mérimée's ice-cream shops (*neverias*). Bars had smartened up and gypsy dance had become a spectacle for all classes of people, a feature exploited in both novella and opera, partly as a further provocation to José's jealousy. The Sierra had changed little, though some roads had been improved, and railways began to link the prosperous ports of the Mediterranean to the cities of the north. In the 1820s the bullfight would have involved horses rather than the combat on foot which would soon replace it. Montes, one of the two classic bullfighters who is mentioned in the libretto, had been director of the most-esteemed bullfighting school in Seville in the early 1830s and had a significant influence on the classic style of bullfighting throughout Spain in the nineteenth century. Essentially, he made it more theatrical and ornamental, introducing the *habit de lumière* (the matador's jacket of sequins) and the *verónica*, the typical cape on a stick used for stylised cape-work. This more entertaining style of *corrida* had a considerable effect on the *fiestas* of the later nineteenth century. No doubt Escamillo's musical and textual swagger reflect this late, more glamorous style. But in terms of dating the content of the opera, the conclusion is clear: the opera libretto is a hotch-potch of customs and elements from different times, and the simple indication of 1820 is not really credible. *Carmen* resists dating.

Some of Mérimée's correspondents kept him up to date with developing events. One feature which continued unchanged – and which he would no doubt have noticed – was that banditry was as strong as ever. In his third *lettre* he had already remarked on the many attempts to eradicate the scourge of banditry, and how they all failed, because of public support for them: 'Stealing on the roads, in the eyes of many, was a means of forming an opposition, to protest against tyrannical laws', he remarks.[11] As soon as one band was destroyed, another sprang up in its place. Act III of the opera projects this sense of the fearless alliance between the gypsies and the bandits, in terms of both text and music.

In the novella (and this is carried forward even more strongly in the opera) there is a focussed opposition between order and disorder. The dragoons

11 'Voler sur les grands routes, aux yeux de bien des gens, *c'est faire de l'opposition*, c'est protester contre des lois tyranniques.' *Lettres d'Espagne III*.

police the factory in Act I and in Act III they set off after the smugglers. (Admittedly in Act II they somewhat erode the clear opposition by trying to pull the gypsy girls in the tavern.) It would be ridiculous to state definitively that the *corps de garde* in the opera are the *Guardia civil,* but it is equally improbable that they were not modelled on the robust new initiatives to combat smuggling and brigandage of the early 1840s, initiatives which Mérimée had found lacking on his first visit and were certainly not in place around 1820. The underlying problem was the system of landownership, *latifundismo,* where enormous estates were controlled by extended families, thus preserving a system akin to serfdom. While Mérimée might have been correct to observe in the 1820s that combatting the ingrained violence of banditry was impossible, the case was decidedly less hopeless by the time of his novella. In *Carmen,* Mérimée notes that older soldiers who had fought in the Peninsular wars were recruited into this recently founded movement. This detail is incorporated into a lengthy dialogue in the libretto, where the older Zuniga asks the new recruit José what the factory is all about.[12]

Mérimée's excitement at the ever-present sense of danger is transferred directly into his *Carmen* right from the outset. When the narrator encounters José-Maria for the first time, he builds this sense of fear, as usual, through significant detail: the narrator's horse neighing as he senses the presence of another animal in a leafy glade from which the narrator and his guide seek refuge from a 'leaden sun'; the mien of the man he has woken has a skin 'darkened by the sun to the point where it was blacker than his hair'; his copper blunderbuss is polished and ready for action. The narrator persuades himself not to be perturbed by this last accoutrement, though his unease comes through clearly in Mérimée's description of this encounter, exacerbated when he sees that his guide has gone pale. What has emerged from this first meeting is a place at once beautiful and dangerous. Each of Carmen's places projects similar contrarieties, transferred into all four acts of the opera.

THE TOBACCO FACTORY

Mérimée's recurrent technique in the novella was to tell his story within a scaffolding of realities. The Fábrica de Tabaco was (and still is) one of sev-

12 ZUNIGA (to José): Qu'est-ce que c'est que ce grand bâtiment ? JOSÉ: C'est la manufacture de tabac. ZUNIGA: Ce sont des femmes qui travaillent là ? JOSÉ: Oui, mon lieutenant. Elles n'y sont pas maintenant ; tout à l'heure, après leur dîner, elles vont revenir. Et je vous réponds qu'alors il y aura du monde pour les voir passer. Act I, Peters vocal score, p. 39.

eral edifices in Seville of considerable historical importance. At the time of his publication of *Carmen* tobacco smoking – particularly in cigars of various shapes and sizes – had become extremely fashionable. In 1844 an extended poem – *L'Art de fumer*, 'in the form of three songs' – had been published by Barthélemy instructing on all aspects of smoking decorum.[13] No doubt Mérimée, who was a smoker himself, knew the poem, which was supplemented by illustrations of the new craze that arrived with the era of Louis-Philippe.[14]

Quand, au Palais-Royal, l'homme heureux se pavane,	When a happy man struts about at the Palais Royal
En semant les parfums de son noble Havane;	Exuding the perfume of a good Havana –
Complément obligé des dîners de Véfour	*De rigueur* as a complement to dinner at Véfour's;
Quand, après une nuit de champagne et d'amour,	When after a night of champagne and love,
De nos lions fumeurs la troupe évaporée Déborde avec fracas de la Maison-Dorée	Our fuming lions descend on the Maison-Dorée
Qu'ils ne se baissent pas, si glissant de leur main	Let them not bend down and let slip
Un trésor allumé tombe sur le chemin ...	One of their lighted treasures on to the road ...

POLICING THE FACTORY

The guard-house protecting the factory was probably a fabrication of the librettists but reflected important historical issues, most importantly the escalation of a black market in contraband in Andalusia, and the need to keep the girls in the tobacco factory under control. The various places evoked in the libretto testify to a knowledge of the geography of Seville around the tobacco factory. Its prison for miscreants can still be seen, and only a short walk away are the barracks from where the crucial bugle calls for the operatic José to return would have been heard. The Calle Candilejo, detailed by Mérimée as the place where Carmen entertained her lovers, is not far away, up the wandering old street of S. Maria la Blanca. All this is in the *barrio Santa Cruz* in the old quarter of Seville.

The factory itself, now part of the University of Seville, still retains the old signs for the various rooms of production and its history has been carefully

13 Barthélemy, *L'Art de fumer* (Paris, 1844).

14 'Avec Louis-Philippe arriva la période triomphale du cigare'. Spire Blondel, *Le Tabac : Le Livre des fumeurs et des priseurs* (Paris, 1891), p. 146.

preserved in collections of documents and implements. It had been world news when it first went into production in 1758, and in its evolution over the turn of the eighteenth century, when fashions in taking tobacco radically changed towards smoking it as cigars, rather than inhaling it as snuff or smoking it in a pipe. 'La pipe est du vieux temps, le cigare est nouveau' (The pipe is old-fashioned, the cigar a novelty), wrote Barthélemy. In the early years of the nineteenth century demand for smoking tobacco mushroomed as it became cheaper and 'democratised', with all classes of people using it. Despite this, the type of 'smoke' used became an indicator of class: cigars were aristocratic (both for men and women); long, thin cigars smoked by women became a sign of their availability.

Seville, however big and famous its factory, had to keep abreast of competition from other factories – notably Cadiz and Madrid – and later from Havana, where the cigars were works of art categorised not only by their shapes – Londres, Medianitos, Trabucos, Cazadores Regalias de la Reina, etc. – but also by the varieties of plant, some of which – like the *cépages* of wine – were more esteemed than others. Some Cubans were such expert smokers that, like the experienced wine-connoisseur, they could tell the *terroir* from which a particular smoke emanated; sophisticated *aficionados* of cigars began to appear.[15] Blondel lamented the fact that Europeans were not yet as knowledgeable of the different *crus* as were Latin-Americans.

Mérimée's guide offers a cigar to the bandit he meets in the novella, stressing the fact that it is a genuine Havana – a typical Mérimée detail. This expensive offering is a bit of a give-away, indicating that he is rich and perhaps well worth robbing, presaging the theft of his expensive watch. Paper-wrapped cigarillos and eventually cigarettes came in, and tobacco usage became even more common. In the first production the 'Chorus of cigarières' – not the singers but especially-employed extras – were put on stage to create a wall of cigarette smoke, exhaled during the appropriately spaced rests provided by Bizet. Unthinkable today, but all in the cause of realism.

Next in the history of the factory was its employment of women as the predominant force: a fact which is turned into a crucial element of the novella and a whole scene in the opera. Various reasons for this radical change have been put forward – that women could be paid less, or that the whole initiative was philanthropic (to save the women, who often had children, from prostitution), but the real reason seems to have been that they were better at rolling cigars. There was a rivalry with other factories who made neater smokes. Pictures of cigars from the period rather show uneven roll-ups which would hardly grace a gentleman, especially a foreign one who could peruse cigars

15 See Blondel, *Le Tabac*, p. 160.

from both Havana and Seville's rival factories in Spain. The tobacco industry was crucial commerce in the mid-nineteenth century. In April 1811, 700 male workers had been sacked, and in October 1812 some women were admitted; after a turbulent period of transition during which where they worked alongside men, the factory became completely staffed by women by order of a controversial decree passed in 1829, on the eve of Mérimée's visit to Seville.

The production workshops were divided into *ranchos* (tables) of between six and ten girls, supervised by *una ama de rancho* ('the table nurse'), officially entitled a *maestra* (mistress). Silence was maintained during working hours and control mechanisms were put in place both to monitor quality and to maintain discipline. Photographs rather contrast with the reports of French observers, which describe vast halls of unruly female workers. But while Mérimée's account of the riot in the factory is invented, and centred on an insult to Carmen's morals, disputes of one sort or another were common for several reasons. Pay was by piece work, but there was a scale of pay for each cigar produced dependent on experience. The quality of the leaves issued to each worker also affected the time it took to roll a cigar: crumbly leaves took longer because joins had to be made and there were accusations of favouritism in the handing out of raw leaves. There was also a constant and sometimes wide fluctuation in demand, and also variation between the seasons in the work that could be offered.[16] A further source of discontent was the system of apprenticeship, where a novice worked beside a more experienced worker who took a third of her salary. Changes in the design of the cigars were also frequent as competition with other factories was constant and the uniformity of the cigars necessitated a rigorous system of quality control. Petty pilfering had to be monitored because of the black market – smuggling is a major theme in both novella and opera. Siphoning off a little tobacco each day was punished with instant dismissal after a spell in the factory prison before a trial.

Personal quarrels and fights such as occur in Mérimée's story were also common. After each dispute there would be an inquest, which often became inflammatory – another feature focussed upon in both the novella and the opera. Apparently catalysed by the invention of the card-index, each worker was documented from admission to resignation (or dismissal) – age, build, colour of hair, dependents, etc. – and these records exist to this day, often giving insubordination as a reason for the firing of an *obradora* (worker). Vidal

16 The information in this section is predominantly gleaned from José M. Rodriguez Gordillo, 'El Personal obrero en la Real Fábrica de Tabacos', in exh. cat., *Sevilla y el Tabaco*, 28 April–27 May 1984, and from an interview conducted with this author in 1997.

gives an amusing example of a record coincidentally detailing a flare-up by a teenage Carmen, daughter of another Carmen and a José:[17]

María de Carmen García, hija de José y Carmen, natural de Sevilla, en Santiago; soltera, de edad 15 años, pequeña de cuerpo, color claro, ojos negros. Decreto 9 septiembre 1822	Por decreto 12 de agosto de 1825 es expulsada para siempre por haber proferido palabras insultantes a las compañeras, y escandalosas, y tirado las tijeras a Concepción Vegue, y diversos atados de tabaco que halló a mano, atemorizando a la maestra con su furia. Habilitada el 31 de enero de 1826
María de Carmen García, daughter of José y Carmen, born in Seville, in the Santiago district; unmarried, aged 15, petite body, fair-skinned, dark eyes Decreed 9 September 1822	By a decree of 12 August 1825 she is expelled permanently for having addressed insulting and quarrelsome words to the staff and thrown her scissors at Concepción Vegue, as well as various packets of tobacco which were found in her hand, frightening the *maestra* in her rage. Re-admitted 31 January 1826.

Sounds like Carmen! It is just possible that Mérimée had heard of this incident, perhaps from Calderón, perhaps through a local newspaper report.

The new opportunities offered by the tobacco factory – and other factories of the era – slowly resulted in a newly emancipated type of woman, no longer reliant on the income of a man. She was an important ingredient of the Carmen myth. Sexually free, economically independent, she could live a new life-style, dress in her own way. If she had children, they too could be employed in their early teens.

The factory in Seville inaugurated three levels of schooling in the 1840s: a nursery (*lactancia*) where the infants would be looked after all day, with their mothers allowed visits to breastfeed; a preparatory school (*escuela de párvulos*), which catered for children aged two to six; and segregated primary schools for the older children, in part oriented towards admitting them to the factory later on. These are not mentioned by Mérimée in any source, but it is clear from the several entries of the children's choir in the opera that knowledge of the *gamins* surrounding the factory inspired their introduction in Act I, and their return later on. They are mentioned in several visitor's accounts between 1840 and the composition of the libretto. Many of the images and photographs from the middle of the nineteenth century show the *cigarreras*

17 José Pérez Vidal, *España en la historia del Tabaco* (Madrid, 1959).

Plate 7.1 Gustave Doré, *Cigarreras au travail*, illustration for Baron Davillier's *L'Espagne* (Paris, 1874). Note that these tobacco-factory workers have their children with them.

with their children – the reason why, no doubt, the urchins' chorus of *gamins* is so prominent in the opera.

Antonio Flores, another reporter on Andalusian customs, who published a lengthy two-volume book of essays on professions, ended his pieces with advice under a heading in bold type indicating the moral to be deduced from his articles ('Moral que resulta de este articulo'). He castigates those who do not smoke 'properly', who prefer sage, aniseed or vervain, calling them 'criminals of the highest order who demoralise society' by preventing the female tobacco workers from earning an honourable crust.[18] Historians of the factory have treated Mérimée's account of it with some caution. It was clearly not full of pretty gypsy girls; indeed, older, experienced workers were vital. And the evidence does not suggest frequent turbulence, but rather quite the reverse.

18 'Que cuantos más cigarros consuman los fumadores, tantas más mujeres pueden ganarse el pan honradamente; y que si el fumador de Tabaco (fumador noble) es eminentemente filantrópico, por este concepto, los que fuman salvia, anís o yerba luisa, son criminales en alto grado, y queda probado que tienden á desmoralizar la sociedad.' Antonio Flores, *Los Españoles pintados por si mismos* (Madrid, 1843–1844), vol. 2, p. 337.

Plate 7.2 E. Beauchy, photograph of older women workers in the Seville tobacco factory, with their wrapped bunches of cigars and the *maestra* behind.

Certainly Mérimée, along with Gautier, was among the first to sexualise the factory, including through the mention of the permits issued to men as a pretext to ogle the young girls, who loosened their clothes in the hot weather. That story may have come more from Madrid. But as he penned his novella, peeping-toms eyeing the legs of *cigarreras* were not Mérimée's sole prerogative; it was already an established pastime, as can be seen from one of Santigosa's illustrations to another book on Andalusian customs (see Plate XIV). This is another an early example of the sexualisation of the young factory girls, a major ingredient of the first act of the opera.[19]

There is no evidence that a squadron of dragoons was in constantly in place directly outside the factory, and the idea of these may be transferred from Mérimée's second *lettre*, where he notices dragoons guarding the prison from which the prisoner is led to the scaffold. 'There was nothing to predict that anything out of the ordinary was going to happen, except the presence of a dozen dragoons near the prison door', he writes.[20]

19 D. Antonio Chaman, *Costumbres andaluzas* (Seville, [1850]).

20 'Rien n'annonçait que quelque chose d'extraordinaire allait se passer, si ce n'est une douzaine de dragons rangés auprès de la porte de la prison.' *Lettres d'Espagne II.*

Plate 7.3 Anon., a *cigarrera* in the traditional pleated skirt and shawl – *mantón de Manila* – that the girls wore when not working. They typically owned a wardrobe of these in different colours.

SOLDIERS, BANDITS AND THE *GUARDIA CIVIL*

The early 1840s saw a considerable rise in banditry, already detailed in Chapter Two, in the province of Andalusia. Eventually the authorities decided, nationally, that a force to counter this pest had to be formed. An example of Andalusian localities formalising this is given by Henk Driessen. Intolerance of local banditry had come to a head:

> when all districts of the *campiña*, the richest and finest part of our province, are infested by bandits who are excellently armed, have horses and keep the working population in a constant state of terror; while nobody is

> safe even in his own house; when private properties are robbed in the most cruel and violent ways and the population has to suffer incalculable damage; while the infamous behaviour of those perverts leads to the painful and terrible trial of young girls being raped in the presence of their parents; when the army cannot assist with cavalry, the only instrument for pursuit in the *campiña*, because of lack of horses; we cannot remain passive in the view of so many crimes and disasters. The time has come for active and effective measures to exterminate banditry and free the inhabitants of the *pueblos* from terror and violence. The Provincial Deputies have decided the following measures: in each district there shall be organised an armed force consisting of twelve men on horseback and a commander. All municipalities to provide the necessary arms, the costs of which are spread over the inhabitants; each *pueblo* shall contribute according to the size of its population.[21]

This recognition of crisis was particularly Andalusian but also agreed nationally. It gave rise to the inauguration of a modern police force, still operant to this day, but in its initial stages was tied to the military. To what extent this force was in Mérimée's mind when he fabricated the character of José is unclear, but without doubt he would have been up to date with the initiative. The libretto, however, is precise in indicating that the dragoons are 'dragons du régiment d'Almanza' and their ritual of the 'changing of the guard' is not something the *Guardia civil* would have engaged in.[22]

The *Guardia civil* was inaugurated in 1844, just when Mérimée was penning his *Carmen*. Whether he conceived José as a member of this force is doubtful (he had the wrong hat: a *shako* rather than a *tricorne*), but the opera's inclusion of a moral, Christian force to counter the various crimes of banditry was highly topical. If anything, the librettists magnified this opposition in their libretto, and Bizet augmented it further in his brilliant and crucial 'turning-point' scene where José is alone with Carmen and hears the bugles of his force of ex-colleagues going off on an escapade. Missions into the countryside to hunt out bandits were predominant among the activities of the state forces – whether dragoons or the newly founded *Guardia civil* – during the early 1840s.

As Mérimée was writing *Carmen*, a lengthy set of guidelines for admission to the newly founded *Guardia civil* was published. Severe demands were written into its statutes: you had to be a Catholic and go to Mass to show it; to

21 Cited Henk Driessen, 'The Noble Bandit and the Bandit of the Nobles', *European Journal of Sociology*, 24 (1983): pp. 96–114.

22 See stage direction to Act I scene 1, Peters vocal score, p. 5.

obey its regulations under pain of instant dismissal; and you had to be able to swim. But most important was its first statute, demanding *honor* – a fundamental theme at the heart of the opera. At the head of a list of thirty-four requirements for admission, it reads unflinchingly as follows: 'Honour [...] is the first principle of the *Guardia civil* and it has to be preserved without stain. Once lost it can never be recovered.'[23] This over-arching statute developed an obvious fact of life: the concept of masculine honour was a given for every male Spaniard, but honour to the force added a further dimension. The statute explains José's reaction – though he is feasting his eyes on Carmen's sexy dance – when he hears the sound of the bugles in Act II. It also explains her extreme anger: how can a potential lover, on the brink of a mutual sexual encounter, reject her?

This first history of the Guardia also tables the distribution of *tercios* (divisions) throughout the country. Andalusia had 2,130 men and 345 horses: far and away the most in the country (for example, Galicia had 563 men and 30 horses). Criminality was predominantly meridional. The guard-house in the opera may be an invention, but it is an invention founded on fact. The libretto emphasises its corruption on several occasions. For example in the first act, where the soldiers surround Micaëla and try to force her into the guard-house – certainly compromising their sworn *honor*; and in the second, where several of the senior officers turn up in Lillas Pastia's tavern, trying to lure the girls into a visit to the theatre.

SOCIAL SPACES

One major difference between France and Spain was Spain's more democratic treatment of class, perceived in both its spaces and its customs. Mérimée imbues his narrator with similar openness, quite the opposite of the stuffy French. He meets Carmen with ease. It was the custom to 'offer a light to those who did not have one', says Vidal, or to ply women with *papelitos,* as the narrator does Carmen. Three of the acts of the opera go out of their way to portray public spaces where the various classes mingle comfortably: the plaza, Lillas Pastia's tavern and the bullring. The exception is the dangerous Sierra of Act III.

23 'El *honor,* [...] ha de ser la principal divisa del Guardia Civil: debe por consiguiente conservarlo sin mancha. Una vez perdido no se recobra jamás.' Quoted José Sidro y Surga and Antonio de Quevedo y Donis, *La Guardia Civil: Historia de esta institución y de todas las que se han conocido en España con destino á la persecución de malhechores ...* (Madrid, 1858 [1859]).

While it was not unusual for an opera to open on a public space, the plaza seems to have been particularly rich in its conception of a *costumbrista* setting filled with a number of people going about their daily business. It has already been noted that the lighter side of Spanish painting in the mid-century delighted in scenes of this sort, with tradesmen alongside elegantly dressed *majos* and *majas*, a few gypsies perhaps, and maybe some men doing illegal-looking deals. While the stage directions indicate something of this, the typed page seen in Chapter Six gives us further details of how this typical 'crowd' scene in an *opéra-comique* was at one time done – essentially with quite a lot of 'extras' in addition to the chorus (see p. 167). This was the 'curtain-up' scene – so much a part of the delight of going to the opera at this period, giving time for the audience to appreciate the sets for each tableau.

Careful attention had been paid to this list of extras to ensure it had not only a wide variety of ages and social classes but also some features which branded it as Andalusian: the water-sellers and, even more typically, the orange- and fan-sellers, as well as the emphasis on courtship involving the offering of flowers. The costumes would, of course, also place the scene in the south of Spain. Categories of wealth are introduced through the specification of the 'vieux beau' and the 'bourgeoises' with the beggar. One wonders about the watch as a symbol of wealth, for it may be more to do with goods stolen by bandits and sold on the black market. As has been seen in the young man's dealings with the Englishman, he is a bit of a chancer. As for the overall scenography (the *plantation*), the original intention was to centre the action around a fountain, ubiquitous in meridional climes. The idea seems to have been quickly abandoned, probably because it hindered movement on an already cluttered stage; all this to be discussed in Chapter Nine.

LILLAS PASTIA'S TAVERN

Commentators intent on pointing out the libretto's weakening of Mérimée's novella have rather missed the point when they suggest that Lillas Pastia's tavern in the opera is but an over-prettified parody of the sordid *venta* where the narrator stays with Don José. It is perhaps more modelled on the wayside *cabaret* where the real Carmencita served Mérimée with *gazpacho*, described in the fourth *Lettre d'Espagne*.[24] Nobody in the opera seems to be residing at Lillias Pastia's tavern; they are there rather for drinking, smoking, eating, strumming guitars, banging tambourines and dancing, though it may have elements of Dorothée's *chambres particulières* – off the balcony. The place is

24 'Cabaret' in this sense means a small roadside restaurant.

in post-prandial disarray but is an ideal place for a gypsy *fiesta*. While the activity in the *plaza* acted as a springboard for further action, one aspect of Pastia's tavern focusses more clearly on the endemic corruption between those in authority and those who defy it: the soldiers try to get Pastia to break civil licensing laws; the officers flirt with the gypsies and serve them drinks;[25] the smugglers mingle with the very men who are employed to hunt them. In the *livret de mise en scène* Moralès (who has already given both Carmen and Micaëla the glad eye) has now turned his attentions to Mercédès, who is sitting on his knee.[26]

Pastia somehow has to steer a path between these factions, as the following dialogue makes clear: on the one hand there is the *corregidor* (magistrate), who knows well that the tavern is populated by smugglers; on the other, the soldiers go there to get drunk and pick up girls. When Escamillo arrives with his torchlight procession ('promenade à flambeaux'), despite Pastia's protestations about closing time, Zuniga pulls rank and demands another round of drinks to toast Escamillo. At least his arrival defuses the situation about the licensing laws.

The long opening number with its unrelenting *seguidilla* rhythm provides an opportunity for a gypsy dance, one certainly more related to the mid-century fashion for gypsy dancing than to any gypsy dances of the 1820s, before they had become entertainments laid on for tourists. In the first – and many subsequent – performances of the opera in France, dancers who were either Spanish, or who had learned from native Spaniards, were the mainstay of this number.

Although we are not yet in the bullring we hear all about it from Escamillo's lengthy series of couplets. By the time he finishes, Pastia is at his wits' end, wanting to shut his doors. At last they leave and we realise that Pastia's respect for the licensing laws was a cover-up for the arrival of the smugglers, who immediately turn their attentions to reports of goings on in Gibraltar (the area which, as has been discussed in Chapter Two, saw the most activity in terms of wrecking, smuggling and armed robbery, particularly of the English residents and military protectors). As yet, the inn has not quite exhausted its purpose, for it is to serve as a backdrop to a scene directly taken from the novella, exploring the gypsy side of Carmen's character.

The tourist office in Seville has devised a '*Carmen* trail' – an itinerary around the city which is half-factual and half-imagined. It imagines Lillas

25 'Les officiers vont et viennent offrant à boire aux femmes et buvant eux-mêmes. ART C27 IV.

26 'Lillas Pastia, aidé d'un garçon, circule entre les tables, servant des clients. Mercédès est assise sur le genou droit de Moralès.' ART C27 I.

Pastia's inn to be half-way between the tobacco factory and the prison of the Puerta de la carne.[27] The latter is factual and still exists as a barracks. The inn they have – quite imaginatively – situated in the Callejón de Agua, an ill-lit alley that runs along the walls of the Jardines del Alcázar. There is no evidence that Mérimée had any particular location in his mind. However, the positioning of the imagined inn between the factory and the barracks, and not far from the Calle Candilejo where Carmen entertained her lovers (possibly Dorothée's), is apt. If Carmen had not been making such a racket with her castanets, José would have clearly heard the bugles at the barracks. 'He thinks he can hear the bugles, but Carmen's castanets are clicking very loudly', according to a rather important stage direction in the libretto, indicating his actions rather than the way he should sing.[28]

The move from the public space of the inn to a private space in 'a corner of it', which is the indication in the libretto, was further explained in the staging sources.[29] With the stage clear of other characters, a table on stage right serves as the centrepiece around which the scene where Carmen dances the *romalis* for José is enacted. In the *livret de mise en scène* José's first action is to take off his belt and place it on the table.

The inn has one more function, as the location where the final nail is hammered into the coffin of José's commission. Zuniga turns up for an assignation with Carmen. Remember there are perhaps rooms off the balcony … In the novella there is more violence than in the opera: José is clipped with the unnamed officer's sword and is administered a pain-killing, healing potion by Dorothée to aid his recovery. A common feature of bandits is a permanent scar, and this clip leaves José with one. The infliction of scars, or crosses on the face, were common in Andalusian culture. In the opera this is softened a little, though there is clear reference, elsewhere in the dialogue, to Carmen carving a 'Croix de Saint-Jacques' on the face of a cigar-girl who insults her. After the scuffle Le Dancaïre and Le Remendado disarm Zuniga and hold him for an hour to give the others time to get away, but there is no real violence. Up they all go to the mountains, where the fresh air of freedom dispels all cares.

27 *Sevilla, ciudad de ópera* [tourist trail], Junta de Andalucia; Ayuntamiento de Sevilla etc. n.d.

28 'Don José prête l'oreille. Il croit entendre les clairons, mais les castagnettes de Carmen claquent très bruyamment.' Peters vocal score, p. 198.

29 The libretto indicates that 'Carmen sits José down in a corner of the stage and performs a little dance.' This is a cushioned version of his 'reward': sex for setting her free. In the novel she takes him to Dorothée's *baisade*. The original operatic production is less explicit – she dances in a corner of the stage: 'Elle fait asseoir Don José dans un coin du théâtre.' Peters vocal score, p. 198 (see Plate 5.3).

THE *COULISSES*

The inside of the barracks becomes one of the two unseen places in the opera (the other being the *Plaza de toros*). Both admirably exploit the tradition of the *coulisses* (backstage action, heard but not seen). We hear the procession come out of the barracks and approach the inn. Bizet clearly indicates the slow approach of the soldiers with detailed indications of the dynamics of the brass, reaching a climax as they pass the inn, and then fading as they pass by, without José joining them. Although he physically tries to hold Carmen's arms he is unable to free himself of his fascination with her dance.[30]

Processions were – and still are – highly popular in Spain in general and particularly in Andalusia. There are four in the opera: this is the third, the other three being the changing of the guard, the 'procession des flambeaux', and the procession of the *cuadrilla* (the taurine 'team') into the bullring (see Plate IX). While the other three are seen and heard, this one is projected entirely musically, with Carmen amusingly remarking that it is nice to have an orchestral accompaniment to her singing and clacking – a *plaisanterie* which clearly aggravates José.[31] Also important is Carmen's anger when José hears the bugles, and his words are written in bold letters in the *mise en scène*: 'Tu n'as pas moi compris', he shouts ('You have not understood'). Carmen has thrown her castanets on the table, rather sulkily, one suspects.

DANGERS OF THE SIERRA

At the root of the third *lettre* is the most infamous of Andalusian bandits of the nineteenth century: José María, known as El Tempranillo. Legends of banditry are also behind the third act of the opera. In real life José Maria came from Lucena, to the south of Cordoba, but fled further south to escape the death penalty for murderous crimes. Mérimée clearly chose him as a model because of his fame, and he is both the subject of the third *lettre* and the centrepiece of the novella. On his first visit to Seville he would have seen José Maria's picture everywhere on a 'Wanted' poster all over town.

Although Mérimée was perfectly acquainted with the provenance of the actual José María, both novella and libretto turn him into a Basque but retain the idea of his fleeing his homeland to escape the death penalty. Both the real-

30 'Nouvel effort de Don José pour s'arrachera cette contemplation de Carmen ... Il lui prend le bras et l'oblige encore à s'arrêter.' Peters vocal score, p. 201.

31 CARMEN: 'Bravo ! Bravo ! j'avais beau faire : il est mélancolique de danser sans orchestre.' Act III Duo. Peters vocal score, p. 200.

life bandit and the fictional Don José started out with the intention of taking religious orders. It is as if Christian charity, justified by higher moral principles, had propelled them into crime as the only hope for a fairer distribution of wealth. Mérimée invents José's past crime: killing a rival over a game of *pelota*. The event is embroidered with a description of how it escalated into a duel with Basque *maquilas*, which all men carried, a symbol of national pride already detailed by Mérimée.

In his third *lettre*, regretting never having met a real bandit, he recounts tales told by innkeepers and coachmen of all kinds of abductions, murdered travellers, captured women, and travellers left naked on the road and returning thus to nearby villages, 'like angels.' These attacks, he adds, 'had always happened just the day before on the stretch of road on which one was about to travel.'[32] Fuelling the sense of danger, Mérimée emphasises the suddenness of nightfall in these meridional climes, and the cold wind of the Sierras. For the first time in the *Lettres* he invents dialogue, dramatising the scene of a band of six highwaymen, all armed with guns. Mention is made of a young Englishman deliberately wounded by a bandit in the novella, repeating that Andalusian custom already demonstrated by Carmen: the bandit has slashed a cross on the lad's forehead.

The appearance of Micaëla in this 'lieu sauvage' (wild place), trying to persuade herself that she is not scared but in fact praying for protection, is only the second reference to religion in the opera. In her aria, her prayer is now cushioned by four euphonious horns instead of the harps in her Act I duo with José, but still in that *style Saint-Sulpicien*: the sentimental Gounod-esque aria style shared between the opera houses and the fashionable churches of Paris. This was the type of music which Laparra railed against so strongly, precisely because it failed to project Micaëla's Basque roots and because its comfortable ending, with the echoing horns, was in the most saccharine style of formulaic, Opéra-Comique tear-jerkers. Whatever the case, it must be admitted that it sets up a brilliant dramatic moment, when the E flat major comfort is shattered by the appearance of José cocking his rifle and firing a shot at her. It also projects her offering the prospect of a respectable life by the fireside back in José's 'home village'.

THE PLAZA DE TOROS

In the opera, Carmen's final place – rest her soul – was the bullring, or, to be precise, just outside, though in the novella José murders her in the moun-

32 'L'événement qu'on raconte s'est toujours passé la veille et sur la partie de la route que vous allez parcourir.' *Lettres d'Espagne III*.

tains. How could the opera, beginning with its focus on the tobacco factory, not end with Seville's other world-famous and ground-breaking edifice: the bullring? It is a brilliant touch by the librettists. But 'bullring' is a misleading word, failing to incorporate all the other essential cultures it housed: the training of the matadors; the breeding of the bulls; the training of the horses; the supporting team of those who 'prepared' the bulls; the rituals of the *fiestas* themselves; the participation of the various performers in the ritual, through assistants, *picadors* and *bandarilleros*, and fully fledged matadors. The music is also of considerable interest, evoking the peripheral trades surrounding the *fiesta* days – something absent in the novella but reinstated to some extent by the libretto (Plate VIII).

In Act IV of the opera we are essentially taken on a visit to a live *fiesta de toros*, starting with the merchants plying their wares outside the arena, and in the shaded and spacious walkway around the ring itself. From this we progress to the procession of the *cuadrilla*, and, finally – with the personal action of the protagonists interwoven – to the bullfight itself and the triumph of Escamillo: the climax, which is heard but not seen.

The preliminary events were pertinent to the spectacle of the mid-nineteenth-century *corridas* and were in a way the essence of its subculture. Understanding them leads to a deeper penetration into the character and esteem of Escamillo. From the outset there was a division of ideas about bullfighting. Some saw it as the heart and soul of Spain, right up to the writings of Lorca. Some, including many senior Catholics, the predecessors of animal-rights activists, and many from overseas, opposed the whole notion. Catholic opposition never managed to wipe bullfighting out though, not least because it allowed many to make instant and considerable profits. Rings housed many spectators, *aficionados* from all ages and classes were attracted, and the whole thing worked well financially. In 1754 Madrid had given over its bullring to its hospital; any church in need of restoration or new bells would stage a fund-raising *corrida*; and even the award of university doctorates would be celebrated with a taurine *fiesta* in some places.

If the Seville tobacco factory achieved world-wide fame for its building, its products and its social innovations, the city's *Plaza de toros* was no less celebrated. Its predecessor, the eighteenth-century arena in Ronda, played an enormous role in developing the classic method of *fiestas*, which became the norm in the nineteenth century, but Seville's enormous bullring and its ornate, theatrical spectacles became the model for the Hispanic taurine world.

This classic nineteenth-century *cuadrilla* is presented in both sung and spoken libretto, and its costumes and accoutrements process into the bullring in the first part of Act IV, after the audience have witnessed another crucial feature of any day at the *fiesta*: the various sellers of goods (water, wine, oranges, figs, fans etc.). The scene is presented in its classic form, for Halévy had done his homework. The initiator of this tradition, with its rituals of opening the door to the ring and its old-fashioned costumes, had been initiated by Montes, who had taken over the important school of bullfighting outside Seville (an institution which trained boys for positions in the ring, and also was concerned with the raising of the horses, which were particularly involved in the spectacle up to the middle years of the century).

The bullring was another place where class divisions became irrelevant. Whether the *aficionados* could afford seats in the shade or only in the sun, they all came to rejoice in the fine art of the *toreros,* or protest when they found it mediocre. Everyone smoked at every level (Plate XII), a fact illustrating the links between Seville's two great edifices. Music resounded as well as the sounds of animals. Mérimée remembered this from his first visit and detailed it in his first *lettre.* A good performance of *Carmen* introduces extraneous sounds of shouting as well as the 'Vivas' in the score, and the roars of excitement when one of the twenty bulls meets its hour of death.[33] Ten were fought in the morning, and ten in the afternoon in a grand *fiesta.* And there was money to be made. Adrian Shubert was right to adjust Hemingway's book title for his own volume on the subject – not just *Death in the Afternoon,* but *Death and Money.*[34] The addition of detail about the economics of bullfighting may lead us into areas irrelevant to *Carmen,* but it should not be forgotten that the activity was of enormous importance to the Spanish economy until well into the twentieth century.

Debates about the ethics of bullfighting were already raging in Paris by the end of the nineteenth century, but no Spanish spectacle in Bizet's time could omit some reference to *tauromachie.* Bizet steered a course between the Spanish enthusiasms of Mérimée, from which the librettists had retained many details, and the sensibilities of the Opéra-Comique. His manipulation of the song for the bullfighter, which returns in several guises; his evocation of the *fiesta* and building up in the last act to the double killing; and the framing of the opera with what turns out to be the bullfight music in the opening Prélude are surely unparalleled as a dénouement for any opera.

33 The 1911 recording includes a good deal of extraneous noise from the crowd in the final act, suggesting that this was a feature of the opera's performances at the Opéra-Comique from the start.

34 Adrian Shubert, *Death and Money in the Afternoon: A History of the Spanish Bullfight* (Oxford, 1999).

CHAPTER EIGHT

Carmen the Gypsy

> She is of the middle stature, neither strongly nor slightly built, and yet her every movement denotes agility and vigour. As she stands erect before you, she appears like a falcon about to soar, and you are almost tempted to believe that the power of volition is hers. And were you to stretch forth your hand to seize her, she would spring above the house-tops like a bird. Her face is oval, and her features are regular but somewhat hard and coarse, for she was born among rocks in a thicket, and she has been wind-beaten and sun scorched for many a year, even like her parents before her; there is many a speck upon her cheek, and perhaps a scar, but no dimples of love; and her brow is wrinkled over, though she is yet young.
>
> George Borrow, *The Zincali*

Juxtaposing the opera with the Mérimée sources has so far compared novella and libretto and their transformation into opera. It has also identified a few possible sources of Bizet's 'inspiration', but do these really get to the heart of the characters of this spectacle? Counteracting the accusations that Bizet's opera slightens the novella, a reverse approach stemming from French nineteenth-century gypsophiles – amongst whom Mérimée was one of the most committed – reveals the seriousness with which the two librettists approached their commission, transferring the essence, spirit and locations into a text ripe with 'realism' and a visceral presentation of this troubled tale. Halévy's notebooks reveal him combing the first published collection of Mérimée's correspondence, which appeared exactly in the year he and Meilhac were transforming *Carmen* into a libretto.[1] Above all, his notes reveal a search for an understanding of Mérimée's deep attachment to Spain. Examination of both the first run and Albert Carré's 'remake' of 1898 further unveil considerable team-efforts to capture these essential Spanish qualities – Don Preciso's 'El chiste y la sal de España' – both on the stage and in the pit.

1 Halévy *cahier*, Bnf (MSS) naf 19863, p. 44 et seq.: notes on Mérimée's *Lettres à une inconnue* (Paris, 1874).

Frowned upon by some modern theatre analysts is the old-fashioned and dubious method of the 'character sketch', which was the backbone of school-level study. This has been attempted many times in relation to *Carmen*, but perhaps without much regard to Carmen's foils, Micaëla, José and Escamillo, and with little thought for the unseen character of José's Basque mother, who may be the most important figure in the show and is certainly a crucial psychological catalyst for the dénouement. Surprisingly, those inclined to Freudian analyses of both José and the 'myth' have devoted little attention to her.

Added to this is José's character – considerably weakened as compared to his real-life namesake model as well as to his portrayal in the novella. He is best viewed not as a character in himself but rather as a member of a platoon whose activities and meticulous organisation in the first staging are detailed more precisely in the *mises en scène* than in the libretto or scores. There were surely many men in the audience with military experience of one sort or another who would have been appalled at slack discipline in policing the riot in the factory and guarding the inn in Act II, and would have looked askance were the official reaction to José's misdemeanours anything less than by the book.

Semiologists' writings on theatre – although few compare operatic libretti with the literary texts on which they are based – can perhaps provide a better framework for the study of such transformations, the results of which are so often dismissed as failed distortions or simplifications of the originals. The introduction to Anne Ubersfeld's *Reading Theatre* plunges in with a statement in direct contradiction to its title: 'You can't read theatre.'[2] Certainly you can't 'read' opera either, *pace* the many who have written under the title 'Reading Opera'. True opera commentary must surely extend to the music, or more precisely to the triple presentation of drama, text and music and, most importantly, its overall effect in the opera-house. And even then, at a deeper level, individual movements, the 'grain' of the singing, and the demeanour and interpretation of the performers are central, not to mention costume and scenography, which were aspects given meticulous attention in both the 1875 and 1898 stagings. Such matters are the stuff of opera criticism at its best, only a smattering of which was produced in reaction to the early performances of *Carmen*.

Ubersfeld rehearses the view that 'characters' are not the 'basic "units" of theatre' and that 'actants' may be opposing groups providing the framework of the drama. To extend this to *Carmen*, for example, there are the bandits versus the soldiers, the soldiers and the local girls, the urchins (reminding us of the poverty of Andalusia), and also the town police and the imported military. 'Character studies' may ignore this substructure in front of which the various players act out their issues, perhaps controlled by overarching motives – aspirational, sexual, and financial, among others.

2 Anne Ubersfeld, *Reading Theatre* (Oxford, 2001).

In *Carmen* many contrarieties are explored, among them obedience to, or subversion of, the norms of the fast-emerging 'modern Spain' at first driven by the gradual rectification of financial inequalities. Other binaries are order versus disorder; freedom against subservience; crime against compliance with emerging capitalism; liberated (or loose) sexual mores against Catholic norms of marriage. Above all, these are to some extent articulated through binary oppositions between the gypsy and the *payello* or *busné*, the non-gypsy;[3] and between supporters of the age-old criminal society and the soldiers on the side of the modernising, more ordered state. Centralised control from Madrid – civilising the nation – becomes another background player in the action.

Bizet's musical response to these oppositions is a key-system and interplay of diametrically opposed genres – 'folk' versus sophisticated; quasi-Spanish versus Opéra-Comique conventional – the whole shot through with reminders of the axis of racial difference: the surge of military music and the dark undercurrent of Carmen's motive based on the gypsy scale. The characters of the opera, to various degrees developed from those in Mérimée's novella – with well-researched additions by Halévy – are inevitably more important once the story is made musical, since in the opera house their sung soliloquies, duets and ensembles can become infinitely more the centre of attention than in any 'read' text, because the audience are seduced in these moments, captivated by the power of the voices and the 'look' of the performers.

GYPSIES IN SPAIN

For years gypsies had been persecuted, often to cruel and unjustified death merely because of their race. Out of countless quotes, many by clerics, there was no shortage of Spanish writers only too ready to explain their uselessness, their threat to progress and their dirtiness and general undesirability. Examples can be found as far back as the beginning of the seventeenth century:

> Because none of them know any trade, have no rents and work no land, they must necessarily all be thieves. [...]
> How blind we Spanish have become, not to see any remedy for such pernicious damage. What good are they in the world? They are neither altar-boys, sacristans, clerics nor priests. Nor are they mayors, aldermen nor bailiffs. They are neither town criers nor gamekeepers. On the contrary, when they enter a town, its people have to watch their homes so closely that they cannot even go to their fields. They pay no taxes to the King nor tithes to the Church [...] They are as useless during wars as they are during peacetime. They are

3 These are the two words for non-*gitanos* given by Mérimée.

> totally unproductive and do great harm, and yet even though the men never work, nor the women spin wool or make cloth, they are better dressed than other peasants since they ordinarily wear clothes festooned with what they have stolen from some unfortunate newly-wed or from a vestment reserved for feast-days. Since they have no goods to confiscate – something much to be regretted – their crimes go unpunished. I find no other use for them but the galleys, may they all be of some use there.[4]

This judgement, by one Father Melchor, is just one of countless diatribes against the 'parasitic' gypsy race, to which each subsequent century added further fuel, resulting in indelible stereotypes of physiognomy, character and habit. While it is all too easy to dismiss the gypsies in the opera as a fantasy of the French Romantic imagination, their characterisation goes deeper than that. The opera takes time to explore several themes and images pertaining to the activities of Spanish gypsies in the changing context of the mid-nineteenth century as they mingle their old way of living (smuggling, wrecking, stealing, tinkering, shoeing animals, etc.) with the new tide of industrialisation – working for a wage in the tobacco factory, or 'professionally' dancing, or even giving (expensive) lessons in their art to non-gypsies and, increasingly, foreign tourists. This legacy carries on today.

Mérimée's deeply studied interest in gypsy language, customs and, in the case of women, their bodies, coupled with his eye for significant detail, ensured that Carmen was no wishy-washy watercolour sketch, but rather a strongly drawn and complex character partly based on the body of emerging literature about gypsies, which was also drawn upon by Halévy. Carmen is a 'pretty gypsy', an exception to the norm – expressed in Borrow's vignette

4 'Dejo aparte el no saber entre ellos oficio alguno ni tener rentas ni recurso a la agricultura, por lo cual necesariamente han de ser todos ladrones. [...] ¿Qué ceguedad llega a la nuestra España, pues no miramos por el remedio de un tan pernicioso daño? ¿Qué provecho tiene el mundo dellos? No son monacillos, sacristanes, clérigos ni religiosos. No son alcaldes, regidores, ni alguaciles. No son pregoneros ni guardas de los montes. Antes, cuando entran en los pueblos, tienen tanta que guardar los vecinos sus haciendas que aún no osan acudir a las del campo. No pagan tributo al Rey ni diezmos y primicias a la Iglesia. [...] No valen para la Guerra ni para paz, no son de provecho alguno y son de daño manifiesto, y con todo eso, con no trabajar ellos jamás, ni ellas hilar, ni hacer telas, andan mejor vestidos que los demás plebeyos, pues de ordinario traen las ropas guarnecidas que a la triste desposada robaron, trayendo de continuo lo que el dueño hizo para las Pascuas. Y, lo que no es poco de llorar, es que, como no tienen bienes que confiscar, quedan sus atrocísimos delitos sin castigo. Para ninguna cosa hallo yo a mi cuenta ser provechosos sino para las galerías, y ojalá aprovecharan allí todos.' From Fr. Melchor de Huélamo, *Libro primero, de la vila y milagros del glorioso confesor Sant Ginés de la Xara* (Murcia, 1607). Quoted Miguel Herrero García, *Ideas de los españoles del siglo XVII* (Madrid, 1966).

heading this chapter – who forms a continuous counterpoint to the general denigration of her race, particularly in nineteenth-century literature, in which gypsies were at the same time demonised and idealised.

Beside the assertions that gypsy women aged prematurely, were accounts of the gypsy girls as deeply attractive to northern visitors. The earliest dedicated studies of gypsies, those by Heinrich Grellmann – known to Mérimée in the French translation – were enormously influential on subsequent writers and were the first to describe them as a race apart.[5] Grellmann misses no opportunity to indulge in swathes of vitriolic prose about these 'unsocial, wandering robbers', presaging the various racist theories of the nineteenth century in branding them as 'uncivilised' and even accusing them of cannibalism – he notes 'their relish for human flesh', and one of his most extravagant claims was that they were 'accustomed to eating the bodies of those they had murdered'.[6] His lengthy testimonies on their most gruesome aspects are treated with suspicion by modern specialists, and are scarcely sweetened by his counterpoints on the powerful sexual allure of the occasional young gypsy girl, the 'fatal attraction' essential to the *Carmen* story.

The eroticisation of the female gypsy is too commonly encountered in literature to need detailing here, but one notable example is the little book by Catulle Mendès and Rodolphe Darzens, *Les Belles du monde*, illustrated by Métivet.[7] This includes sections on Egyptian, Javanese and Senegalese women, as well as a section on 'Gitanas' (see Plate XVII).[8]

5 Heinrich Grellmann, first published in German as *Die Zigeuner, ein historischer Versuch über die Lebensart und Verfassung Sitten und Schicksale dieses Volks in Europa, nebst ihrem Ursprunge* (Dessau and Leipzig, 1783). A second edition was published in Goettingen in 1787, and the same year it appeared in English as *Dissertation on the Gipsies, Being an Historical Enquiry Concerning the Manner of Life, Œconomy, Customs and Condition of this People in Europe and Their Origin*. A subsequent English edition appeared in 1807 with the author's name anglicised to Matthew Grellmann. A shortened version appeared in French in 1788 under the title *Mémoire historique sur le people nomade*, with a subtitle '*Appelé en France 'Bohémien', et en Allemagne 'Zigeuner' ; avec un Vocabulaire comparatif des langues Indienne et Bohémienne, traduit de l'Allemand de M. Grellmann par M. le B. de Bock*.' A fuller French version appeared in 1810 as *Histoire des Bohémiens ou Tableau des mœurs, usages et coutumes de ce peuple nomade*. This was translated from the second German edition by one M. J. All these remained the standard works on gypsies until Borrow's works appeared during the 1840s. For a detailed critique of his work see Sarah Houghton-Walker, *The Gypsy on the Page in the Romantic Era* (Oxford, 2014), p. 56 et seq. Mérimée's knowledge of Grellmann is documented in Auguste Dupouy, *'Carmen' de Mérimée* (Paris, 1930), pp. 82–83.

6 Grellmann, *Dissertation on the Gipseys* (1807), pp. 16–17.

7 For detailed study of the Spanish gypsy in literature see Lou Charnon-Deutsch, *The Spanish Gypsy* (University Park, PA, 2004); and Ninotchka Devorah Bennahum, *'Carmen': A Gypsy Geography* (Middletown, CT, 2013).

8 Catulle Mendès and Rodolphe Darzens, *Les Belles du monde* (Paris, n.d., probably late 1880s or 1890s).

The text plunges straight in with a distillation of the gypsy's mysterious attraction, exploiting 'our unquenchable love for the unknown, the remote and the chimerical'.[9] Both Mérimée and Bizet seem to have enjoyed the services of gypsy women – for a rendered gold coin (which young gypsy girls, as claimed by Cervantes in his *La gitanilla* [The Little Gypsy Girl], reputedly found hard to resist). Grellmann is admiring of the 'properties of their bodies' – 'neither overgrown giants nor diminutive dwarfs' – and of their agility. Carmen's fleetness at making her escape is nicely captured in the action, as is another feature commented upon in the libretto: the *gitanas*' habit of rolling their eyes seductively. In the dialogue accompanying Carmen after her knife crime, Zuniga is keen to know how she responded under interrogation. José replies that she said nothing, and 'just ground her teeth and rolled her eyes like a chameleon'.[10] Grellmann had commented on this feature:

> Their white teeth; their long black hair, on which they pride themselves very highly, and will not suffer to be cut off; their lively black rolling eyes; are, without dispute, properties which must be ranked among the list of beauties, even by the modern civilised European world.[11]

In the opera, Carmen's rolling her eyes during her interrogation is not mentioned because of their lively attraction: quite the reverse! Coupled with her annoying *balivernes* (nonsense) – a feature often mentioned in discussions of their speech, indicative of the 'rogue's tongue' or *jerigonza* – they clearly signal another stereotypical belief about gypsies in general: their total disdain for authority, order and the law, and the rank of soldiers or police.

Often stressed as the root of the *gitana*'s charms is her 'animality', a quality perceived as wanting in well-brought-up society girls. Mendès claims that, 'It is out of their animality that their strange and brutal charm arises.'[12] Quite distanced from the decadent theories of Gobineau and Michel, he hopes these wild gypsy girls:

> will strongly resist being tamed, [...] that they will continue to tell fortunes [...] to marry some handsome boy, a horse thief [...] that they will parade their nuptial linen at their windows the day after their wedding as testimony

9 'Ce qui nous attire vers ces filles sauvages, c'est notre amour toujours vivant de l'inconnu, du lointain, du chimérique'. Mendès and Darzens, *Les Belles du monde*, 'Gitanas', p. 5.

10 ZUNIGA: Et qu'est-ce qu'elle disait, mademoiselle Carmencita ? JOSÉ: Elle ne disait rien, mon lieutenant, elle serrait les dents et roulait les yeux comme un caméléon.

11 Grellmann, *Dissertation on the Gipseys*, p. 11.

12 'Et c'est de leur animalité qu'émane leur charme étrange et brutal'. Mendès and Darzens, *Les Belles du monde*, p. 30.

> to their long guarded virginity and that they – Soledad, Matilda and Vincente – will give birth to some little gypsies, simple, tough, and wild, who dance like their mothers.[13]

As a confirmed Hispanophile, Mendès had clearly let his Romantic imagination run wild.

Gypsy 'animality' worked in several directions: they were perceived as having a close affinity with animals, particularly horses, which were often depicted in images of their wanderings. In describing Carmen Mérimée recalls a Spanish saying that goes '"Gypsy eyes, wolf's eyes" ... If you have not the time to observe a wolf at the zoo, just look at your cat when it is about to attack a sparrow'.[14] In the novella Carmen walks 'swaying her hips like a filly from the Cordova stud farm' – so sexy, implies Mérimée, 'that anyone who had seen a woman dressed that way would have crossed himself'.[15] Fillies apart, she goes 'quiet as a lamb' to be interrogated. For a moment Carmen wonders whether the two 'animals' – she and José – might last. But no, not possible: 'the dog and the wolf cannot agree for long.' But, she adds, 'I am no sheep.' When she dies, the final line of Mérimée's third chapter blames gypsy culture: 'It is the gypsies who are to be blamed' – for the whole story – 'for bringing her up in this manner.'

Gypsies were considered good at metalwork: shoeing horses, picking locks, sharpening knives; in a word, 'tinkers'. Gypsy girls were reputed to carry a knife or scissors, ostensibly for grooming, but useful for self-protection if required. A nasty little manual on the art of knife crime, or defending oneself against it using *navajas*, knives or the 'gypsy scissors', ostensibly for *barateros* (men who collect gambling debts), devotes a short chapter to gypsies, whose use of the 'tijeras' is warned against: 'the wound they cause is inflicted with the two points, and is always mortal.'[16] Earlier in the book diagrams show the classic moves in a fight with *navajas*, similar to those depicted in the various drawings of the fight between Escamillo and José in Act III. In an episode described in the *mise en scène*, but in neither novella nor libretto,

13 'Qu'elles se gardent bien de s'apprivoiser, ces sauvages ! [...] Qu'elles disent la bonne aventure, [...] Qu'elles épousent quelque fier garçon, voleur de chevaux ; que le linge nuptial, à la fenêtre, le lendemain des noces, témoigne des pudeurs longtemps réservées, et que, de Soledad, de Matilda, de Vincente, il naisse de petites gitanas, simples, rudes, farouche et dansantes comme elles !' Mendès and Darzens, *Les Belles du monde*, pp. 31–32.

14 'Œil de bohémien, œil de loup, c'est un dicton espagnol qui dénote une bonne observation. Si vous n'avez pas le temps d'aller au Jardin des plantes pour étudier le regard d'un loup, considérez votre chat quand il guette un moineau.' *Carmen*, chapter II.

15 'Dans mon pays, une femme en ce costume aurait obligé le monde à se signer.'

16 Anon, *Manual del baratero; ó, Arte de manejar la navaja, el cuchillo y la tijera de los jitanos* (Madrid, 1849), p. 45.

Carmen suddenly draws a knife on José but is prevented from wounding him by Micaëla, who interposes herself between the two.[17]

Capitalising on gypsies' empathetic relations with animals, a very well-known image of Victor Hugo's Esmeralda depicts a goat seeming to be about to suckle from a very scantily clad and very pale girl with a tambourine (see Plate XVIII). This image – many times reproduced – was the work of the German painter Charles Auguste Steuben, done in 1839. Its relation to *Carmen* may at first seem rather remote, but it was certainly a well-known gypsy image and an aphrodisiac for males tempted by gypsy spectacle.

Mérimée fancied himself as an amateur philologist, later advising several correspondents about the overlaps between the gypsy vocabulary he had learnt in Spain and various words other travellers had found elsewhere. This was an important 'quasi-scientific' game which several self-appointed ethnologists played during the nineteenth century in an attempt to pin down the origins of the vagrant gypsy race. As we have seen, Mérimée was a passionate traveller – more than a mere tourist – and was especially drawn to Spain and profoundly interested in its people and its customs, but he was also a professional writer, writing a story to entertain and to make money. His own deep interest in the gypsy race and his knowledge of Calí – the gypsy language – is paraded throughout the novella, in both the body text and the purposefully erudite footnotes, the book thus gaining educational appeal to its predominantly female consumers.

Who were these *Égyptiens*? Were they migrant Indians? Or from North Africa? Mérimée sided with the Far Eastern theory, and the 'affaires d'Égypte' referred to by the smugglers are retained importantly in the opera, forming the basis of the deeply mischievous Act II Quintet. For Mérimée the terminology was clear:

> The name 'Egyptiens' was given to the first of these dark-skinned vagabonds to appear in Europe whom we now call Bohemians for no good reason. Their

17 Peters vocal score, p. 342, Act III, Finale (*livret de mise en scène* ART 1):

> José turns round and once again approaches Carmen threateningly. Carmen, exasperated, draws a dagger from her belt to attack Don José. Micaëla interposes herself between them with her arms spread out, offering herself as a victim. Carmen drops her knife and bursts out laughing. Both turn towards the wings, stage right, as they hear Escamillo's voice dying away.
>
> José se retourne et redescend vers Carmen menaçant. Carmen, exaspérée, sort un poignard de sa ceinture pour frapper Don José. Micaëla s'interpose entre eux, les bras écartés, s'offrant comme victime. Carmen jette son poignard et éclate de rire. Tous sont tournés vers la coulisse jardin écoutant Escamillo dont la voix se perd.

> bands arrived in France in the 15th century and claimed to come from Egypt to fulfil penitence by travelling across the world.[18]

Perhaps the opera's Le Dancaïre was named such because of Cairo's being the capital of Egypt. (In one of the English versions he is called El Dancaïro.)

It is against this tapestry of conflicting opinions about the origins of this vagrant and persecuted race – the people whom Mérimée's friend and correspondent Joseph Arthur Gobineau relegated to the category of 'dark-whites' – that Mérimée's creation of, and the librettists' accretions to, the character of Carmen come into focus.[19] Certainly, this contextual background is at least as important as the various literary sources that have been suggested as Mérimée's prompts. Gobineau has little to say about gypsies in his book, but he and Mérimée had many exchanges in their correspondence, much of it about details of the gypsy language and comparisons with the vocabularies of other races. Poliakov, in a chapter on French theories of racism, considers Gobineau a mouthpiece for the French nineteenth-century discourses on race, but essentially a confused and illogical writer. One of his most notable ambivalences was his view on 'mixed blood'. On the one hand he saw black Africans as the most 'primitive' of races; on the other he saw their infusion of blood into other races as of distinct benefit to music, dance and the arts. This view was perhaps a connection between his ideas and Mérimée's enthusiasm for gypsies:

> Thus, artistic genius, equally foreign to the three over-arching races [Black, White and Asian], has only emerged since the marriages of white people with negroes. [...] The world of the arts and of fine literature resulting from mixtures of blood, the improving and ennobling the inferior races, have resulted in marvels which we should applaud.[20]

Not that the gypsy 'race' was universally considered as one of 'mixed blood'. Quite the reverse: other commentators underlined its resistance to procreation with non-gypsies.

18 '... on donna le nom d'Égyptiens aux premiers de ces vagabonds au teint noir, qui parurent en Europe, et qu'on appelle aujourd'hui Bohémiens, avec aussi peu de raison. Leurs bandes arrivant en France au XV siècle, prétendaient venir d'Égypte et accomplir une pénitence en errant par le monde.' From Mérimée's edition of Agrippa d'Aubigné, *Aventures du baron de Foeneste* (Paris, 1855) p. 131, fn. 4.

19 Joseph Arthur de Gobineau, *Essai sur l'inégalité des races humaines* (Paris, 1856).

20 'C'est ainsi que la génie artistique, également étranger aux trois grands types, n'a surgi qu'à la suite de l'hymen des blancs avec les nègres. [...] Le monde des arts et de la noble littérature résultant des mélanges du sang, les races inférieures améliorées, ennoblies, sont aussi des merveilles auxquelles il faut applaudir.' Gobineau, *Essai*, pp. 256–258. See also Léon Poliakov, *The Aryan Myth*, trans. Edmund Howard (London, 1974).

There is only one reference to gypsies in Gobineau's *Essai*, where, somewhat amusingly, he claims that gypsies reach sexual maturity much earlier than the Swiss male, who sometimes does not become fully mature until the age of 20, a view corroborated elsewhere, mainly by some testosterone-fuelled French Romantics who estimated 12–15 as the ideal age of female sexual maturity.[21] In relation to *Carmen* there is one particularly revealing exchange where Mérimée suggests that in garrison towns there is less 'degeneration', and indeed some 'amelioration', of the residents.[22] There is an echo of this exchange about bloodlines early on in the novella: because she is pretty, the narrator doubts that Carmen could have a been a pure-blooded gypsy, thus buying into the stereotyping of gypsy women.[23] Seen against this, the premise of *Carmen* – available gypsies in a one such garrison town – takes on extra significance, since Seville is constantly portrayed as a town with a highly organised military presence. Bizet's underpinning of the opera with an alternation of gypsy music with military fanfares and marches underlines this juxtaposition.

Although there are many commentaries on gypsies tucked into the literature of the countless travellers to Spain, after Grellmann the next major monograph to have observed them by having lived with them was that of the English 'bible-peddler' George Borrow, whose several books appeared after 1840 and whose major work, *The Zincali; or, An Account of the Gypsies of Spain etc.*, was published in London in 1841 and translated into French in 1845.[24] Mérimée threw himself into the debates which ensued long after the publication of this key book by republishing his *Carmen* with an extra chapter that has nothing to do with the narrative of the first three, but is essentially an extended *compte-rendu* of Borrow's work.

21 '... on pourrait relever que dans plusieurs parties de la Suisse, le développement physique de la population est tellement tardif, que, pour les hommes, il n'est pas toujours achevé à la vingtième année. Une autre série d'observations, très facile à aborder, serait offerte par les bohémiens ou Zingaris. Les individus de cette race présentent exactement la même précosité physique que les Hindous.' Gobineau, *Essai*, pp. 210–211.

22 'Un certain nombre d'individus d'une espèce bien choisie à relever toute une race. Vous en verriez la preuve en visitant les villes où il y a des cuirassiers en garnison.' Mérimée to Arthur Gobineau, 20 November 1855. ('Only a certain number of a well-chosen type are necessary to revive a whole race. You can find the proof of this when visiting towns where there are *cuirassiers* in garrison.')

23 'Je doute fort que mademoiselle Carmen fût de race pure, du moins elle était infiniment plus jolie que toutes les femmes de sa nation que j'ai jamais rencontrées.' *Carmen*, p. 360.

24 George Borrow, *The Zincali; or, An Account of the Gypsies of Spain, with an Original Collection of Their Songs and Poetry, and a Copious Dictionary of Their Language* (London, 1841). Published in French as *La Bible en Espagne* (Paris, 1845), and in a heavily abridged and distorted version, *Esquisses de la vie des Gitanos d'Espagne*, trans. Mlle Léonie Dufresne in the same year.

Another important work was by Francisque Michel, who was a further highly prolific author with whom Mérimée corresponded (though, again, after he had written *Carmen*). His work on the 'cursed' races of France and Spain, and also his detailed study of Basque culture, certainly chimed with Mérimée's ideas and may have rubbed off on the two librettists.[25] Another influence – important more because it was musical than for having anything to do with Spain – was Liszt's book on Hungarian gypsies already discussed in relation to the 'Gypsy Scale'.[26]

Mérimée's interest in gypsies went back almost to his teens. Before his twenty-second birthday, in 1825, he had announced his first collection of works as a series of plays, *Le Théâtre de Clara Gazul, comédienne espagnole*, preceded by a 'Notice' and set in 1813, in the midst of the Napoleonic occupation. The fictitious Clara Gazul was a young Andalusian gypsy girl of 14 years, imagined long before Mérimée had set foot in Spain or encountered any gypsies at first hand. What he knew about them he must have read (most likely in Grellmann) or learned from other memoirs.[27] His introduction of Clara Gazul bears a striking resemblance to his first introductions of Carmen in the novella. Like the Carmen of Bizet's opera, she introduces herself with a gypsy song. Tentatively, her name might be added to the list of Carmen's forbears – certainly in Mérimée's imagination – but also as a possible contributor to the libretto.

Mérimée's 'note' on her is written in a similar voice to that of the *Carmen* novella: it is Clara herself who tells her story to the author/narrator, recounting that she 'was born under an orange tree at the side of the road, somewhere near Granada'. Her song, self-accompanied on the guitar, introduces her in much the same way as, fifty years later, Bizet's music does Carmen, it began: 'Cuando me parió mi madre la gitana' (When my mother, the gipsy, brought me into the world). The 'notice' adds that her profession was to tell fortunes. Her father, a canon, was about to be hanged by the French regime. Mérimée's formula of a double introduction – first by the narrator and then by Clara – he repeats in the *Carmen* novella.[28]

Clara Gazul's appearance presaged the *Carmen* novella in other ways, for example when we read how 'The slightly wild expression of her eyes, her long jet-black hair; her slim waist; white, even teeth; her lightly olive complexion

25 Francisque Michel, *Histoire des races maudites de la France et de l'Espagne* (Paris, 1847).

26 Franz Liszt, *Des bohémiens et de leur musique en Hongrie* (Paris, 1859).

27 Mérimée mentions a work by August Friedrich Pott, *Die Zigeuner in Europa und Asien* (Halle, 1844–1845), but this two-volume work was not translated and Mérimée was not proficient in German.

28 See Mérimée, *Théatre, Romans, Nouvelles: Le Théâtre de Clara Gazul, comédienne espagnole* [1825], Bibliothèque de la Pléiade (Paris, 1978), pp. 4–5.

do not lie about her origin.'[29] Her roots are characterised in the negative, just as the narrator in *Carmen* first asks her whether she is Andalusian, or of Moorish stock, or a Jewess. Although Clara is sent to a convent when her pious father discovers her writing a *billet-doux* at an inappropriately young age, she certainly was not, we learn, 'from old Christian stock' – 'vieux chrétien' – a phrase exactly re-used with regard to José in both novella and libretto. She declares herself Moorish before the narrator/Mérimée gloats on her physical attributes – just as he will do on Carmen. Already implanted in Mérimée's sketch of this gypsy girl are her physical features, as well as precocious sexuality and powers of divination in her bloodline.

Divination – fortune-telling or predicting *la bonne aventure* – had been recognised as a gypsy gift for centuries. In the novella the first thing Carmen offers José is to tell his fortune. But by reputation the supernatural powers of gypsies extended into the more sinister realms of the black arts and witchcraft. Typically adding a negative value-judgement in his purportedly 'scientific' book, Grellmann describes gypsy fortune-telling as if 'rules were invented to tell lies from the inspection of the hand'.[30] Gypsy potions and other accoutrements are discussed at some length and become important in the novella when Don José is wounded. Only the *bar lachi* – a magic stone which will make José immediately attractive to women – makes it into the libretto as an offer in return for freeing Carmen. This is one of Grellman's 'nostrums […] small stones, chiefly a kind of scoriae, which they say possess the quality of rendering the wearer fortunate in love'.[31] It is one of only two Calí words retained in the libretto:

CARMEN

Laisse-moi m'échapper, je te donnerai un morceau de bar lachi, une petite pierre qui te fera aimer de toutes les femmes.	Set me free and I'll give you a piece of bar lachi, a little stone which will make every woman fall in love with you.

CARMEN'S GYPSY DANCE

The other Calí word is Carmen's mention of the *romalis*, a dance she performs in front of the lieutenant and some other officers, arousing José's ingrained

29 'Je suis née […] sous un oranger sur le bord d'un chemin […] dans le royaume de Grenade. […] l'expression un peu sauvage de ses yeux, ses cheveux longs et d'un noir de jais, sa taille élancée, ses dents blanches et bien rangées, et son teint légèrement olivâtre, ne démentent pas son origine.' Mérimée, *Théatre, Romans, Nouvelles*, p. 4.

30 Grellmann, *Dissertation on the Gipseys*, p. 47.

31 Ibid., p. 48.

jealousy. Her response to this is to dance it 'just for him', a moment which becomes crucial in the opera. Bizet and his librettists made it into a turning point in the whole story, highlighting José's 'love and duty' dilemma. Should he stay in his regiment or defect to the gypsy life? The number had to be in duple time since the welling-up of the military music demanded that. But against this the dance had to be sexy. Mérimée's text describes it as a *romalis*, but – as several writers tell us – its other name was an *ole*.[32] Marina Grut tells us that this dance was really in triple time, and the dancer José Otero is precise about its steps in a long prose description. Its distinguishing feature was 'the kneel, when the dancer does the *renversé*, bending forward and doing the complete circular rotation of the upper body and arms'.[33]

Confirming Otero's affirmation that it was a very ancient dance, Grut asserts that 'this movement was, together with the rotation of the hips, much appreciated by the Romans when they came into contact with the *puellae*, girls with "honey in their hips": the dancing girls of Gadir [now Cadiz]".[34] In its several variations the shout of ¡Ole! was restricted to one in the coda, or occasionally two when another such ejaculation was permitted after the first small jump. For Mérimée (and Halévy and Bizet) it is the Roma's dance for the Rom: the gypsy wife's highly sexualised dance to excite her husband, and, as the century progressed, paying male audiences.

This is the case in the novella when Carmen – now clearly in the era when gypsies had commercialised their dances for *payello* spectators – dances for high-ranking soldiers while José, having been demoted, is humiliatingly made to stand guard at the door while the raunchy spectacle is enacted to the delight of the officers inside. He recounts the moment in chapter III of the novella: 'You know how society people take pleasure in getting gypsies to dance the *Romalis*: that's their dance and sometimes other things too, more often than not!'[35] The librettists (and Bizet) exploited this moment to the full; indeed, it is formed into one of the most important numbers in the opera. Moreover, it is melded into a gypsy scene elsewhere described by Mérimée in his *Salon de 1853*, where he links the dance – just as the *Carmen* libretto does – with gypsies feasting on *yemas* (sweets made of egg-yolks and sugar) and other delicacies.[36]

32 Various writers comment on the orthography of this word. One explanation is that the *Óle* shouted in bullfights has an accent on the O. Dance terminology places it either on the 'é' or omits it altogether (as does Otero).

33 José Otero, *Tratado de bailes de sociedad* (Seville, 1912).

34 Marina Grut, *The Bolero School* (London, 2002), p. 136.

35 'Vous savez qu'on s'amuse souvent à faire venir des bohémiennes dans les sociétés, afin de leur faire danser la *Romalis*, c'est leur danse, et souvent bien autre chose.' *Carmen*, p. 375.

36 'M. Pierre Giraud a retracé un souvenir très vif et très original des danseurs espagnols [...]. Je voudrais que M. Pierre Giraud allât à Séville et surtout à Triana, quartier general

The editors of the centenary re-edition of Otero's seminal dance-treatise confirm the licentious reputation of the *ole* in an annotation to his entry on it. It was not danced in public under the Napoleonic occupation and reappeared on the billboards in Seville only in 1836. Even under the relaxation of theatrical statutes during the *era Isabelina,* the dance could be performed only with official authorization, and contravention of this law would result in punishment, partly because the uninhibited nature of the dance would often result in civil disorder.

It is from the reminiscences of several foreign visitors that we know about this ancient dance and its extraordinary sexuality and effect of those who witnessed it. The English explorer Richard Ford devoted much space to Spanish dances in his *Handbook for Travellers in Spain,* published at much the same time as Mérimée's *Carmen.* One of the few to mention the *romalis,* he was one who confirms that it also became known as the *ole.* He claims that:

> These most ancient dances, in spite of all prohibitions, have come down unchanged from the remotest antiquity; their character is completely Oriental and analogous to the *ghowazee* of the Egyptians and the Hindoo *nautch.* [...] They are entirely different from the *bolero* or *fandango,* and are never performed except by the lowest classes of gypsies. [...] This is the *Romalis* in gypsy language and the *Ole* in Spanish; the balancing action of the hands, the beating with the feet, the tambourines and castanets, the language and excitement of the spectators tally in the minutest points with the prurient descriptions of the ancients. [...] The sight of this unchanged pastime of antiquity, which excites the Spaniards to frenzy, will rather disgust an English spectator. [...] However indecent these gypsy dances may be, yet the performers are inviolably chaste, and as far as the *Busné* guests are concerned may be compared to iced punch at a rout; young girls go through them before the applauding eyes of the parents and brothers, who would resent to the death any attempt on their sister's virtue, and were she in any weak moment to give way to a *busné,* or one not a gypsy, and forfeit *lacha ye trupos,* or her unblemished corporeal chastity, the all and everything of their moral code, her own kindred would be the first to kill her without pity.[37]

---

de la Bohème. Là il verrait danser la *Romalis* sur des bonbons et des *yemas,* c'est à dire des jaunes d'œufs sucrés. C'est un luxe que les gitanas se passent volontiers quand on leur paye.'

37 Richard Ford, *Handbook for Travellers in Spain* (London, 1845).

Ford goes on to recommend Borrow as an accurate source for his claims, particularly in relation to the gypsy concern for the chastity of their daughters and their resistance to any attempts at seduction by non-gypsies. His account of the *romalis* as an obscene dance with Eastern roots is precious, as the dance is rarely discussed in musical literature. The *ole* receives short shrift in the *Diccionario de la música Española e hispano-americana*, which merely describes it as a popular solo dance from Andalusia. Ford's rich description is more convincing.

His recollection is complemented by another account from some ten years later. After a riot in the tobacco factory (by which time mainly women would have been employed) an American judge, Severn Teackle Wallace, detailed a gypsy dance recital he witnessed despite there being a curfew in place. His description of the *ole* is of particular interest because he notes how the dancer is constantly approaching the male observer, taunting him with her sexuality through bodily gestures and facial expression and using the typical gypsy stamping we encountered in Sor's remarks about the gypsy corruption of the steps of folk-dance, and which were remarked upon by many subsequent observers of Spanish gypsy dancing:

> After gliding around the room, with the melting glances, the tossed arms, the gyrations and salutations that the case required – she lingered for an instant just in front of me, and stamping quickly twice or thrice upon the floor, went 'dolci tremore', through a dozen evolutions in a moment, of which, as I am a living man, I believe the drawing of a circle with her foot, about my head was one! A strange, topsy-turvy feeling came upon me, as if the room were upside downward, and when my bewilderment was over, the *Ole* was a shapeless dream.[38]

An unusual reaction from an American judge! Nonetheless a memoir which goes to the heart of this dance and its delirious effect, corroborating many others who fell for it.

Another particularly rich mention of the dance, which became a mid-century 'must-see' for every Romantic French traveller, is by Alexandre Dumas, who provides a further insight: the prevalence of red costume and accoutrements in its performances. He echoes Mérimée's description of Carmen as recounted by José, who remembers her 'very short red skirt [...] dainty little shoes of red Moroccan leather tied with flame-coloured ribbons'.[39] Dumas

38 Severn Teackle Wallace, *Glimpses of Spain; or, Notes of an Unfinished Tour in 1847*, p. 188. Quoted Lou Charnon-Deutsch, *The Spanish Gypsy*, Pennsylvania U. P., 2004) p. 106.

39 '... jupon rouge fort court [...] des souliers mignons de maroquin rouge attaché avec des rubans couleur de feu'. Mérimée, *Carmen*, chapter III, p. 367.

Plate 8.1 Gustave Doré, *El ole gaditano* [Ole from Cadiz], illustration for Baron Davillier's *L'Espagne* (Paris, 1874).

describes the costumes worn in a performance of the *romalis* he had witnessed early in the decade in which Mérimée penned *Carmen*, noting 'bands of vivid red ribbon' and each girl 'carrying a bunch of ruby carnations' and wearing 'scarlet sashes'.[40] This gypsy attraction to the colour red had in fact been noted by Grellmann many years before, when he remarked that 'scarlet

40 '… des tours de tête ornés de rubans d'un rose criard […] quelques œillets d'un rouge vif […] une ceinture du même rose …' Alexandre Dumas, *De Paris à Cadix* (Paris, 1874; rpt. 1984), p. 211. The full account is particularly interesting as the dance was enacted by a brother and sister, exciting several spectators to suspect an incestuous relationship, probably forgetting that, by now, gypsies dancing was a lucrative and professional activity far removed from their family relationships which, according to Borrow were conducted with strict propriety.

was held in great esteem by them', not only by women but also by men, who 'in the open street, are solicitous to purchase from him [a red habit] be it coat, *pelisse*, or breeches'.[41]

Davillier's text to the picture shown in Plate 8.2 reads as follows, and gives a rare insight into how he worked with Doré:

Dans la cour d'une maison à moitié en ruine, qu'abritait une treille gigantesque, était assise, un pandero à la main, une jeune gitana de la plus grande beauté ; sa mère, ou plutôt sa grand'mère, debout derrière elle, passait un vieux peigne édenté dans ses longs cheveux, d'un noir bleu comme l'aile d'un corbeau ; un chat et une pie, animaux chers aux sorciers, paraissaient causer en amis sur le rebord d'une fenêtre, tandis qu'un grand lévrier dont les oreilles droites se dressaient comme deux cornes regardait les deux gitanas d'un air tout à fait diabolique. 'Dépêche-toi !' dis-je à Doré, 'de crayonner cette scène, car les sorcières vont enfourcher leur balai et partir pour le sabbat.' Et discrètement abrité derrière un laurier-rose, il fit, en quelques minutes, un ravissant croquis.	In the courtyard of a half-ruined house shaded by a giant trellis, a young gypsy of a rare beauty was sitting holding a tambourine. Her mother, or rather her grand-mother ,was standing behind her, passing an old toothless comb through her long tresses, which were blue-black like a crow's wings; a cat and a magpie – animals dear to witches – seemed be talking to each other on the window sill, while a large greyhound whose ears stood up like a pair of horns was giving the gypsies a devilish look. 'Hurry up!' I said to Doré, 'and sketch this scene, as these witches will soon get astride their broomsticks and fly off to the sabbath.' Discreetly hidden behind an oleander, he did, in a few minutes, a ravishing sketch.

Looking into the history of the *ole*, a curious suggestion arises as to Mérimée's choice of 'Carmen' as the name for the principal character in his novella. Although sources suggest that this distinctly Andalusian dance originated in Jerez de la Frontera in the first decade of the nineteenth century, its heyday was just at the time of Mérimée's visit to Andalusia and his composition of *Carmen*. The dancer who first caused a furore with dancing the *ole* was a *bailerina* named *Carmen La Cigarerra*. She was primarily a singer of Spanish folk music – well before flamenco but, like the opera's Carmen, she danced simultaneously.[42] The dance's popularity could not have escaped Mérimée's notice because its heyday was in the 1840s. Another dancer, *La Curra*, caused a storm when she presented it at the same period. So famous was *La Curra*'s performance that the dance was relegated to the past and became known – and institutionalised – as the *Ole antigua* (as if it was an old historic Spanish

41 Grellmann, *Dissertation on the Gipseys*, p. 27.
42 See Grut, *The Bolero School*, p. 135.

Plate 8.2 Gustave Doré, *Toilette d'une gitana* [Gypsy Girl at her Toilette], illustration for Baron Davillier's *L'Espagne* (Paris, 1874).

dance), though it was also known as the *Ole andaluza*. According to Otero its essence was that it was always danced by a single woman.

Davillier's description beside Doré's extraordinary sketch of the dénouement of the *ole* bears out its daring qualities. He testifies that it was 'reproached for its lack of modesty'. He also claimed it as a development from the old *zarabanda*, which used to provoke excommunication by the Church and was banned by various laws. He also remarks on the *souplesse* necessary for its execution, and a special casualness (*désinvolture particulière*). He mentions – alongside many other commentators – a moment of ecstasy:

> It was a wonder to see her, after steps of a such vivacity, lean back a little; and her waist, with the flexibility of a reed, bend with such an elegant curve; her shoulders and her arms turned round smoothly and nearly touched the

> ground. For a few moments she stayed in that position, her neck stretched out, with her head on one side as if in a sort of ecstasy: then, suddenly, as if struck by an electric shock, she recovered, leaping up with her ivory castanets going, and began again the steps with which she had started.[43]

The authoritarian reaction seems to justify Dumas's and Davillier's remarks on what seems to have been an extraordinary performance. The *romalis* had become celebrated internationally.

CARMEN HERSELF

It is above all through Mérimée's correspondence with Mme de Montijo that the development of Carmen's character comes to life. He is keen to stress that she was born less of the imagination than out of considered study, in 1845 writing that 'As I have for some time very carefully studied the gypsies, I have made my heroine a gypsy.'[44] In 1874, just before Bizet's opera, Adolphe de Circourt, the historian and admiring commentator on Mérimée, wrote that 'the characteristic curiosity that [Mérimée] showed during his long literary career was nowhere more evident than in his researches into the customs, the migrations and the language of gypsies. This strange race had somehow captured his attention.'[45] His 'review' of Borrow in his added chapter to *Carmen* reveals how Borrow's view of gypsies was diametrically opposed to those put forward by Grellmann. Where Grellmann was usually derogatory, Borrow was much less so. Christian charity pervades his work, a quality which Mérimée found amusing. Mérimée was well aware of the rift between the two, siding with Grellmann on some matters – such as the sexual proclivity of the *bohémiennes* – but clearly admiring Borrow's deeper penetration into their language, origins and rituals – although, as he confesses in a letter to Mme de Montijo, he believes himself able to conduct better research into the

43 'C'était merveille de la voir, après un pas d'une vivacité entraînante, se pencher un peu en arrière ; sa taille, d'une flexibilité de roseau, se courbait avec une langueur charmante ; ses épaules et ses bras se renversaient mollement et touchaient presque la terre. Pendant quelques instants, elle restait ainsi, le col tendu, la tête électrique elle se redressait, bondissant en faisant résonner en mesure ses castagnettes d'ivoire, et achevait son pas avec autant d'entrain qu'elle l'avait commencé.' Le Baron Ch. Davillier, *L'Espagne* (Paris, 1874), p. 395.

44 Mérimée to Mme de Montijo, 16 May 1845: 'Comme j'étudie les Bohémiens depuis quelques temps avec beaucoup de soin, j'ai fait mon héroïne Bohémienne.'

45 '... le caractère de curiosité érudite qui l'accompagna dans sa longue carrière littéraire ne se montra nulle part plus marqué que dans ses recherches sur les mœurs, les migrations et la langue des Bohémiens. Cette race étrange [...] avait singulièrement fixé l'attention de Mérimée.' *Bibliothèque universelle et revue suisse,* February 1874, p. 336.

gypsies 'than a protestant and philanthropist could ever have done', driven by the idea that Calí was a very ancient, unwritten language, pre-dating Hebrew and perhaps having roots in Sanskrit.[46]

He goes on to further align himself with Grellmann rather than Borrow – a preference also discernible in many features of the libretto – suggesting that Borrow misrepresented (as a Scottish clergyman might) the sexual habits of gypsy women:

> It is a pity that [Borrow] lies through his teeth and is so excessively protestant [...] He says some strange things about gypsies, but in his capacities as both an Englishman and a Saint he has failed to see, or didn't want to describe, certain features which needed to be mentioned. He claims that the gypsy women are very chaste and that no 'Busno' (one of several words for a man who is not of their race) could ever take advantage of one. However, in Seville, Cadiz or Granada there were, when I was there, gypsy girls who could not resist one duro.[47]

Contrast this with Grellmann:

> Nothing can exceed the unrestrained depravity of manners existing among these people, I allude particularly to the other sex. Unchecked by any idea of shame, they give way to every desire. The mother endeavours, by the most scandalous art, to train her daughter for an offering to sensuality, and she is scarce grown up, before she becomes the seducer of others. Let the dance, formerly mentioned, be called to mind, it will then be unnecessary to adduce further examples, which my regard for decency oblige me to omit.[48]

Borrow countered many of Grellmann's assertions, driven by a comment in the first section of Grellmann's book on gypsy origins that 'Their degeneration is written all over their faces'.[49] This is in many aspects entirely contrary to the views expressed by Borrow himself. He claims not to have read Grell-

46 'Quand je retournerai en Espagne j'aurai des recherches à faire sur les gitanos qu'un protestant et un philanthrope n'a pu faire.' Letter to Mme de Montijo, 10 November 1844.

47 'C'est dommage qu'il mente comme un arracheur de dents et qu'il soit protestant à outrance. [...] Sur les bohémiens il dit des choses très curieuses, mais en sa qualité d'un anglais et de saint il n'a pas vu ou n'a pas voulu dire plusieurs traits qui valaient la peine qu'on parlât. Il prétend que les bohémiennes sont très chastes et qu'un Busno, c'est à dire un homme qui n'est pas de leur race, n'en peut tirer pied ni aile. Or à Séville, à Cadiz et à Grenade, il y avait de mon temps des bohémiennes dont la vertu ne résistait pas un *duro*.'

48 Grellmann, *Dissertation on the Gipseys*, p. 92.

49 'Leur dégénération est écrite sur leur visage', Grellmann, *Histoire des Bohémiens*, p. 6.

mann by the time of writing *The Bible in Spain,* but he admits in the preface to the second edition, of 1843:

> I know very little of what has been written concerning these people: even the work of Grellmann had not come beneath my perusal at the time of the publication of the first edition of *The Zincali,* which I certainly do not regret: for though I believe the learned German to be quite right in his theory with respect to the origin of the Gypsies, his acquaintance with their character, habits and peculiarities, seems to have been extremely limited.[50]

For Grellmann, the Gypsies both smoked and chewed tobacco whenever they could get hold of a leaf or two; for Borrow they never touched the stuff. Similarly with 'strong drink', Grellmann stresses their constant desire for inebriation, while Borrow claims they only drank water. The above passage from Grellmann links their depravity with song, poetry and dance in an extended chapter, but he emphasises the way in which gypsies will capitalise on their artistic skills:

> Dancing is another means they have of obtaining contributions; they generally practice this when begging, particularly of men, in the streets; or when they enter houses, to ask charity. Their dancing is the most disgusting that can be conceived, always ending with fulsome grimaces, or the most lascivious attitudes and gestures: nor is this indecency confined to the married women, but is rather more practised by young girls, travelling with their fathers, who are also musicians, and who, for a trifling acknowledgement, will exhibit their dexterity to anybody who is pleased with these unseemly dances. They are trained up to this impudence from their earliest years, never suffering a passenger to pass their parents' hut, without endeavouring to obtain something by frisking about naked before him.

Not only because gypsy singing and dancing had become an immense attraction for tourists and Spanish *payellos,* as well as profitable export, did Bizet and the librettists exploit this aspect of gypsy culture when fashioning Carmen's character. Like Clara Gazul, she introduced herself with a dance-song – even in the early Tarantella version discarded in favour of the Habanera.[51]

50 Borrow, preface to the second edition of *The Zincali,* reprinted in 1914 edition, with introduction by Edward Thomas, p. 8.

51 This earlier version has been recorded on the EMI recording with Angela Gheorghiu as Carmen, conducted by Michel Plasson. See Example 5.3.

CARMEN'S VOCAL PREDECESSORS

It could be asserted – *tout court* – that, musically, Carmen had no predecessors: gypsy spectacle was considerably more developed in dance than in opera (see Plate IV). There had been a few token gypsies in previous French operas, but although many of them had other Spanish elements – castanets, triangles and *tambours de basque* as well as Spanish forms such as *bolero* rhythms, *seguidillas* and *pasodobles* – none of them had any semblance of real Spanish music for the gypsy roles. So how could gypsy singing be represented? A glance at one or two of *Carmen*'s vocal predecessors may give us a clue.

By the end of the eighteenth century gypsy music was already seen as a particular skill, and, according to the ever-pessimistic Grellmann, essentially different from the music of non-gypsies: 'Music is the only science in which the Gipseys participate in any considerable degree: they likewise compose, but it is in the manner of the Eastern people, extempore.'[52] He had already introduced the idea of the 'gypsy fiddler', claiming that 'They scratch away on an old patched violin, or rumble on a broken base [*sic*] neither caring about better instruments, nor minding to stop in tune.'[53]

They soon learnt to polish up their dances and the accompanying music, though, for there was a burgeoning, lucrative, well-to-do audience for their displays. Plenty of *Chansons bohémiennes* appeared (under various titles) from the many publishing houses, to various degrees distinguishing their vocal style as in some way representative of a separate gypsy art, and often embellished with illustrated covers. Bizet had written a few gypsy pieces himself, but until *Carmen* none really attempted to adopt a distinct style. While there was plenty of Central and Eastern gypsy music in the classical repertoire – the *style hongrois* – the Spanish repertoire depicted gypsies in an entirely different way.[54] References to gypsies abound in the texts of the repertoire of Spanish nineteenth-century song, and the musical settings occasionally go out of their way to represent the special nature of their singing. The vocal lines of the rich anthology of songs collected by Celsa Alonso Gonzalez and published under the title *La canción andaluza* demonstrate the typical ornaments of these *canciones*, which are sometimes 'operatic', demanding elements of dramatic performance indicated in the scores. One such piece tells of a boatman bidding farewell to his gypsy girl as he sails out to sea:

52 Grellmann, *Dissertation on the Gipseys*, pp. 87–88.

53 Grellmann, *Dissertation on the Gipseys*, p. 51

54 He did have a score of Brahms's *Hungarian Dances* in his library, the only work of Brahms represented.

Olé gitanilla de mi corazón	Olé little gypsy girl of my heart
Mi barco se para al oir tu voz é	My boat no longer hears your voice
Al oir tu voz	Hears your voice
Al oir tu voz	Hears your voice

As the boatman sails away, the boatman shouts 'É!' and then each repetition is successively softened, as if heard from afar: 'fingiendo la voz de lejos' and 'como más lejos' ('feigning a voice from afar' and 'even further away').[55] Elsewhere ululation is common, though not confined to the gypsy pieces: sometimes they are quickly articulated 'Ay! Ay! Ays!'; at other times they are prolonged vowels indicated to express pain or excitement; and occasionally there are long trills.

References to both sexes of gypsy are found and there are a lot of boatmen and *toreros*. References to Triana are common, for example, in some of the purely Spanish songs of Sebastian Yradier, as opposed to the *habaneras* he brought back from Latin America.[56] 'El sol de Triana' [The Sun of Triana] – a man's song telling of a *jembra* (now 'hembra' – a woman) he has seen in Triana (the gypsy district in Seville), 'La perla de Triana' [The Pearl of Triana], and 'Aurora; o, La gitana de Sevilla' [Aurora; or, The Gypsy from Seville] all have features which might have found their way into Carmen's 'not-a-*seguidilla*.' Bizet refrains from excessive ululation, whereas another of Yradier's *canciones* extensively indulges in it: 'La soledad de los barquillos y la malagueña' [The Lonely Boatmen and the Girl from Malaga], designated a 'Canción arabe' and ending with a thank you to the gypsy who likes his song – 'mil gracias da la Gitana.' Into all these scores, occasional shouts of 'Olé' are inserted. In the 1911 recording of *Carmen*, ¡Olés! were also inserted into Bizet's gypsy spectacle in Act II.

Bizet's inventory of his own scores confirms that he possessed the anthologies of Spanish songs by Puig and Lacome, *Échos d'Espagne*, as well as some separate songs by Yradier. If there are any particular qualities that can be isolated in the gypsy songs – especially if the poem is sung by a *gitanilla* – there is a tendency to include a higher proportion of acciaccature and some downward leaps landing on the dominant in the singers' lower register. Comparison with the songs of this repertoire suggests that Bizet took more from Yradier than the well-known Habanera.

On the whole, rather than project Carmen as a *gitana* through set-pieces, Bizet bound his opera together with her motive, a better way of reminding

55 Francisco de Borja Tapia, 'El marinero,' no. 6 in *Antología (siglo XIX) la canción andaluza*, ed. Celsa Alonso González, Música Hispana 3 (Madrid, 2008).

56 Catalogued are 'La colosa', 'El jaque', 'El curro marineso', 'La calasera', 'Aí chiquita.'

us of her thorough gypsyness at every turn of the narrative. He had dabbled with gypsies before – and rather better than his minor contemporaries. The fourth of his *Chants du Rhin* [Songs of the Rhine], 'La Bohémienne', written in 1866, stands out from the others, which rather resemble the easy melodies of Mendelssohn's *Songs Without Words*. Harmonically it is a more complex piece, with sudden, somewhat twisted, modulations to distant keys. Grace-notes abound – these had become a particular signifier of gypsy song. There are also many parallel thirds and sixths in the melody line (as there are in the *Chanson bohème* in *Carmen*). In fact this was programme music, in the sense that it was a wordless evocation of a poem – by Joseph Méry – telling of a gypsy girl dancing by water to the sound of her own tambourine: a stereotypical Romantic gypsy image. The piece has dance and fantasy, but no gypsy song.

Bizet's most extended earlier portrayal of gypsies comes in the character of Mab in *La jolie Fille de Perth*, an opera very loosely based on Walter Scott, dating from the 1860s. Apart from her function as a rival to the central character, Catherine, Mab brings in the ubiquitous gypsy dance troupe who dance to a bass-less melody with eerie harmonies, often centring on the tritones within the minor scale, in a sotto voce 'Danse bohémienne' over an ostinato. It is 'different' music, but Mab never sings in anything but a conventional way.

Amongst other predecessors, Gomis's one-act piece *Le Diable à Séville* enjoyed some success, was printed (and available to consult by Bizet), and premiered at the Opéra-Comique in 1831. Its 'Chanson bohémienne' is a disappointment in musical terms: even though he must have been familiar with aspects of Spanish music, Gomis produces Rossini-like music even for his gypsies, just as the subsequent Spanish operas of Adolphe Adam – *Giralda* and *Le Toréador* – have little that suggests Spain apart from dedicated staves for triangle, *tambour de basque* and castanets in the orchestral score.

Ambroise Thomas's *Mignon*, whose eponymous heroine is captured by gypsies, has a gypsy dance in the first crowd scene, characterised by the typical stamping of feet, an ostinato bass on a pedal point, and a melody with odd chromatics. The crowd sing:

Plus vite que l'éclair même	Quicker than light itself
Filles d'Égypte et de Bohème	Daughters of Egypt and Bohemia
Frappez le sol	Stamp on the ground
D'un pied joyeux.	With joyful feet.

Another composer who dabbled in gypsies was Auber, whose gypsy music uses several features to categorise an 'other' musical language, for example in his 'Lay of the Gitana', 'Come and wander with me.' They are more in the style of Schubert, using acciaccature, parallel thirds and sudden rows of dotted notes

Example 8.1 Georges Bizet, 'La Bohémienne' (*Chants du Rhin*, No. 4), opening.

rather than any more Spanish scalic or harmonic devices. Bizet uses a similar idea in the *Chanson bohème* in Act II of *Carmen*, assigning it to the flutes.

Mérimée's conception of the female gypsy could hardly have contrasted more acutely with the sanitised gypsy leading lady of the Auber–Scribe collaboration *Les Diamants de la couronne*, which was premiered at the Salle Favart in 1841 and enjoyed worldwide success in many languages. Mérimée was not a fan of Scribe, and Gautier's opinion of *Les Diamants*, although it adopts his habitual formula of listening with his eyes rather than his ears, isolates the ridiculous portrayal of the gypsy Catarina, whom, he remarks:

> is a strange gypsy! She is blonde and fair-skinned with eyes as soft as velvet and a smile like a sketch of an English girl, wearing a charming, coquettish dress, satin and velvet skirts and a little blue bonnet.[57]

Having returned recently from a journey to Spain, Gautier could be authoritative about the real gypsies he had encountered in the Albaicín district in Granada, 'who danced the *zorongo* on the pavement while two other young gypsy girls would crouch like monkeys accompanying her with that strumming which only gypsies know how to do, and which resembles the continuous sound of crickets.' He finishes his commentary by asking whether 'this gypsy girl imagined by the librettists, is not a thousand times more preferable to a wild and haggard gypsy girl, blackened by the sun, spouting out nonsense

57 'En vérité, la Catarina est une étrange bohémienne ! elle est blonde et blanche avec des yeux veloutés, un sourire de vignette anglaise ; son costume est le plus charmant et le plus coquet du monde : jupes de satin et de velours, résille d'or et de pourpre, petite toque bleue.'

verses as would a real-life gypsy girl.'[58] For the Opéra-Comique at this time, there was no doubt that Catarina was fashioned to delight the patrons of the Salle Favart. To Mérimée, an enthusiastic opera-goer, the portrayal of a Spanish gypsy dressed up in Parisian garb would surely have been anathema, especially at this time, when, on the eve of his second trip to Spain, *Carmen* was taking shape in his mind.

Another enormously popular lyrical spectacle pre-dating *Carmen* was Balfe's *The Bohemian Girl* (*La Bohémienne*). Based on scenes from Cervantes's *La gitanilla,* in turn rendered as a ballet for the Paris Opéra in 1839, Balfe's highly successful opera reached France only in the 1860s, and Paris, at the Théâtre Lyrique, in 1869. It had been preceded by *L'Étoile de Séville,* which had fifteen performances at the Paris Opéra in 1845 but saw little success worldwide and whose music has been irretrievably lost. Critics of Balfe's work tell us that his later compositions embraced Spanish music more than the earlier operas had: no matter! His works achieved some success in London but not elsewhere. And his *Bohemian Girl* and her choruses of gypsies sing the most anodyne Victorian music, without even a whiff of Carmen's sensuality. If Bizet had looked at Balfe's scores he would have quickly turned the page. There were none in his library.

Bizet's *Chanson bohème* in Act II had some precursors. One in particular is of much interest: the 'Chanson bohémienne' from Victor Massé's *opéra-comique Fior d'Aliza,* based on Lamartine's novel of the same title. The song is sung by the character of Piccinina, adding to the dramatic tradition of gypsy children who had somehow escaped into the modern world. Her text explains:

Ma mère était bohémienne	My mother was a gypsy
Mon père que chacun maudit	My father, whom everyone
Dans les maremmes de Sienne	Cursed in the maremmes of Siena
Était bandit.	Was a bandit.

Furthermore, the first person to sing Piccinina was none other than Galli-Marié. Thus, playing the part of Carmen was her fourth gypsy role. (She had taken the part of the Gypsy Queen in Balfe's *La Bohémienne* in 1862, and sang the eponymous role in Ambroise Thomas's *Mignon* in 1866.)

58 'Une surtout que nous avons rencontrée dans l'Albaicin de Grenade et qui dansait le zorongo sur la pointe d'un pavé pendant que deux autres jeunes filles accroupies à terre, comme des singes, l'accompagnaient avec ce bourdonnement de guitare que les Espagnols seuls savent conduire et qui ressemble à s'y méprendre à la chanson enrouée des cigales.' Théophile Gautier, pamphlet of 19 March 1841, reprinted in his *Histoire de l'art dramatique en France depuis vingt-cinq ans* (Paris, 1859).

CHAPTER NINE

In the Pit, On the Stage

THE plethora of documents pertinent to the first runs of *Carmen* both inform and confuse: no single document captured what it looked or sounded like in its first creation. Yet there are many rich sources that elucidate each other in a number of ways. Only by considering them together – and in the context of the Opéra-Comique at the date of *Carmen*'s premiere in 1875 – do we begin to get a sense of the importance of Bizet's opera – particularly its role as the seed-bed of French realism.

The path to the stage had begun in June 1872, when Bizet had announced to the composer Paul Lacombe that the Opéra-Comique had commissioned a new work from him, Meilhac and Halévy. It was to be 'une chose gaie' (we might say a 'happy piece') and 'aussi serré que possible' ('as succinct as possible').[1] This may well have referred to the tendency of some *opéra-comique* plots to become too complex and convoluted. The various hurdles Bizet and his librettists encountered on the rocky road to the stage of the Opéra-Comique, especially his brushes with the directorate there, have been many times recounted and will not be revisited here.[2]

For a new *opéra-comique* the essence of the process of publication was that the text and score were always published separately. The *livret* (libretto), with both the spoken and sung text would be produced by a literary publisher, usually in a small format. The musical score would be handled by an established music publisher (in *Carmen*'s case, Choudens) accustomed to producing and distributing orchestral *matériel*. The vocal score did not include the spoken dialogue, but only *répliques* (cues) from the text to indicate when each musical number should start.

There were two different printings of the libretto published in the year of the first production:

1 Bizet, letter to Galabert, 17 June 1875.

2 For an account in French see Hervé Lacombe, *Georges Bizet* (Paris, 2000), chapters eleven and twelve; in English see Hugh Macdonald, *Bizet* (Oxford, 2014), chapter nine.

- Henri Meilhac et Ludovic Halévy: *Carmen.* Livret. Opéra-comique en 4 actes. Tiré de la nouvelle de Prosper Mérimée. 8°. 87pp. Paris, Calmann-Lévy. n.d.[3]
- Henri Meilhac et Ludovic Halévy: *Carmen.* [Livret] Opéra-comique en quatre actes. Tiré de la nouvelle de Prosper Mérimée. 12°. 68pp. Paris, Michel Lévy frères. Paris, 1875.

It was also included in Meilhac et Halévy, *Théâtre*, vol. VII, in a new printing.[4] There are only minor disparities between these three sources. Most important among the differences between the early librettos and the later printed scores is the inclusion of the 'Scène et Pantomime' (discussed in Chapter Six).

The earliest surviving source of Bizet's score is what remains of his autograph orchestral score, a heavily used document whose first thirty-four pages have been neatly recopied in an unknown hand, maybe because they had become torn and worn, but also possibly because Bizet composed the Prélude (and the entr'actes) last and someone else was employed to copy them out.[5] According to Hervé Lacombe, this score – of over 1,200 pages – was completed in two months.[6] Guiraud's *récits*, in his own hand, were bound into this score.

Of particular interest is its lack of the Act I 'Scène et Pantomime', though this may have been removed when the scene was abandoned, and deposited in a private collection, where it still, apparently, exists.[7] Composed in the last months of 1874, some commentators assume that Guiraud himself removed the episode when he added his recitatives and shortened the fight scene.[8] The renumbering of the pages is difficult to decipher: some are added with a numeration stamp, and the manuscript pagination is often altered and crossed out. Was the section written later, or was it simply taken out of the score once it disappeared from performances? The evidence is equivocal. Markings made

3 A facsimile of this version is printed in Dominique Maingueneau, *Carmen, les racines d'un mythe* (Paris, 1984).

4 Meilhac and Halévy, *Théâtre*, vol. VII (Paris, 1900).

5 This is Source A in my edition (Peters, 2020) and also in Fritz Oeser's Bärenreiter edition. It consists of four large folios and is consultable on Gallica in its entirety. The Prélude and entr'actes are written on different manuscript paper from the main score.

6 'Bizet écrit en deux mois les mille deux cents pages de la partition d'orchestre'. Lacombe, *Bizet*, p. 647.

7 See Hugh Macdonald, *The Bizet Catalogue*, http://digital.wustl.edu/bizet/.

8 For example, Robert Didion in the preface to his vocal score (Mainz: Schott, 2000), p. 13. The underlying research concerning the movement was carried out by Michel Poupet and published in an article in the *Revue de Musicologie* (1976), p. 139 et seq. Poupet suggests that because of a note in the *livre de bord*, pertaining to the thirty-first performance, on 25 May 1875 –'Mr. Duvernoy n'a pas chanté ses couplets' – that it was subsequently abandoned. This was shortly before Bizet's death on 3 June. Poupet suggests this is evidence that Bizet sanctioned the excision of the number, but this is far from conclusive.

with a numerator at the bottom of the page lead directly from a stamp of 38 on the last page of the Introduction et Chœur (originally marked by Bizet as 'Introduction No. 1' but changed in a later hand to No. 2). The 'Chœur des Gamins', which follows directly, looks as if it was originally No. 3, but this has been superimposed with a crossing out: it could have been a 2 changed to a 3. No. 3 is written above in the same, subsequent, hand used on the title page of the Introduction. A pencil numbering in the top corner of each page does not help, since each musical number begins with a fresh page number 1.

Didion, in the preface to his Schott edition, claims that the first version of the autograph score, written in Bougival (Bizet's out-of-town residence on the banks of the Seine), was submitted without either the Prélude or the entr'actes, as it was – *évidemment* – the custom at the Opéra-Comique not to finalise untexted numbers until the last minute.[9] Certainly the Prélude was done by a professional copyist, but Didion's accusation that the manuscript is shoddy is debateable. Quite the reverse! It seems better than Bizet's sketchy hand, where some passages have been done very hastily.

A tentative conclusion about the 'Scène et Pantomime' suggests that it was posthumously removed from this score, perhaps at the same time as the Guiraud *récits* were added in. This does not counter claims that the episode was written in response to complaints from Duvernoy – taking the part of Moralès – that he had not got enough to sing, but the 'Scène et Pantomime' was clearly in this score ready for the premiere.[10]

THE FULL SCORES AND PARTS

Gifted to the Bibliothèque nationale de France by Mme Geneviève Bizet-Straus – the composer's wife – the autograph orchestral score survives in four acts, now bound together. It contains some music not in the first vocal scores, in particular the Melodramas (passages where dialogue is spoken over the orchestra). The orchestral parts clearly show that these were performed, thus raising the question of the status of the vocal scores, which are perhaps best regarded as a set of parts for the singers. Certainly, unlike subsequent scores, as well as some contemporary scores by publishers from other countries, they should not be regarded as a definitive running order just because a few pages of the proofs survive, showing that Bizet went through them with a fine-tooth comb.

9 'Évidemment, il était l'usage à l'Opéra-Comique de ne pas fixer les préludes et les entractes que très peu de temps avant la création.' Bizet, *Carmen*, partition chant et piano, ed. Robert Didion (Mainz: Schott), p. 13.

10 Fritz Oeser asserts this, claiming that it was written during rehearsals late in 1874: see the *Bericht* to his Alkor edition of *Carmen*, pp. 720–722. See also Winton Dean, *Bizet*, The Master Musicians, rev. ed. (1977), p. 216.

In terms of detailed prescription of performance practice, the articulation prescribes staccatos versus slurred pairs of notes with longer legato markings over some melodies – for example the central section of the *torero*'s tune, and Micaëla's first aria, where long slurs indicate a contrasting, seamless legato, no doubt enhanced with a little portamento.[11] Subsequent layers on the score, realising that such overlong legato markings have no place in an orchestral score, add achievable bowings here and there, as do the performers' markings in their parts. Bizet clearly knew how to indicate his intentions, but more in the manner of a piano score than a performable version for strings. There are similar long legato articulations in the wind parts.

Bizet wrote out the orchestral score using a lot of abbreviations: for repeated bars and for doublings. Where there are long repeated sections (as in the opening chorus) he marks them with numbers: they indicate a professional's aim to save time and pass the detail on to the publishers. A frequent marking in the wind parts is 'col violons', and across the doubled wind, 'col flute'. No wonder he managed so many pages in such a short time! The abbreviations in the autograph give us considerable insight into how he worked so quickly, almost like an impressionist painter determined to retain 'la fraicheur de l'ébauche' ('the freshness of the first idea').

A second orchestral score, professionally copied, was used for the performances at the Opéra-Comique and possibly elsewhere.[12] A gift to the library of the Paris Opéra in 1971, its accession entry reads 'Partition ayant servi à la première représentation à l'Opéra-Comique le 3 mars 1875' ('The score used for the premiere at the Opéra-Comique on 3 March 1875'). Wear and tear and the many annotations, changes of metronome markings and various accretions suggest that this was indeed the main score used in the first run at the Opéra-Comique and many subsequent performances under various batons. It may also have been lent out before Choudens printed their orchestral score in 1877. Some of its added suggestions are extraordinary, one being a flute alternating with Carmen's part in her *romalis* for every other line – maybe that particular Carmen was short-breathed or had an 'après-midi d'aphone'. There are several markings where a singer transposes the whole movement, quite apart from alternatives to high notes for tenors, and low notes for mezzos, some of which made their way as ossias into later scores. For the reconstruction of what was done in the first run, before *Carmen*'s life after Bizet's death, this, together with the libretto, the first vocal score and the orchestral parts, must be considered a most valuable source.

11 Certainly this was the case on the very first recording of the opera, in German.

12 This is Source B in the above editions. At the time of writing it is not available to consult online.

Substantial *matériel* (orchestral parts), mostly concurring with this latter score, are still intact (Source C). Hand-copied, they are a crucial source of information of many kinds. On the serious side, they are the only source on which the various attempts to reposition the 'Scène et Pantomime' can draw, and they also give an insight into what went on in the pit. On a more amusing note, the parts are adorned with satirical drawings where the players have long gaps – brass, percussion etc.[13] Some are of the conductor, and there are a few crosswords with obscenities added. The brass parts have calculations of fees earned for performances so far. In the string parts there are a few bowings, corrections and other markings, and all parts indicate where cuts have been made, varying considerably between performances. The viola parts – predictably – have hardly any markings at all. Plus ça change!

THE VOCAL SCORES

On 6 November 1875 – some months after the premiere – the first vocal score (partition chant-piano) was listed in the *Bibliographie de France*, but several of the critics tell us that Choudens had actually put the vocal score on sale soon after the premiere.[14] The title page of this score (now a rarity) clearly designates it as an *opéra-comique*. It runs to 351 pages and is thereby distinguishable from a subsequent – much more common – score, which has 363 pages. This latter Choudens vocal score appears to be longer because it contains the recitatives composed by Bizet's friend Ernest Guiraud, thus eliminating the spoken dialogue necessary for the Opéra-Comique. In fact the opera has been shortened in this later score, as it no longer contains the Act I 'Scène et Pantomime', and the fight scene between José and Escamillo (mostly orchestral music) has been considerably reduced. In addition, there are a few other cuts and alterations. The score has been re-edited in a slapdash way, with redundant *répliques* and page-numbers retained from the former plates.

The exact date of publication of the second Choudens piano-score with the Guiraud recitatives is uncertain, but 1877 has been given as likely. Marked now as an *opéra*, rather than an *opéra-comique*, its print runs were vastly higher than that of the Opéra-Comique *piano-chant*. A now rare edition of this score with fifteen illustrations in russet ink by Hyacinthe Royet (1862–1926) can be dated to the turn of the 1880s and will be returned to in some detail. Seen alongside other images of the first production, these provide invaluable information about the scenography of the first run.

13 See the Oeser *Bericht*, for reproductions of some of these.

14 Ernest Reyer notes this in an admiring piece in the *Journal des débats politiques et littéraires* of 17 March 1875 – precisely two weeks after the premiere.

Choudens produced no printed orchestral score of the opera until 1877, once again an estimated date for an undated printing containing both the Guiraud recitatives and a lengthy ballet concocted mainly from *L'Arlésienne*. It is a useful score for preserving the original transpositions (for example of the horns and *cornets à pistons*), though there are some mistakes in these. For the purposes of reconstructing what was done in the pit of the Opéra-Comique the copied manuscript score (B) is of considerably more use, as the insertion of an Act IV ballet, to fit with traditions of Grand Opera, rather cloud the issue of what was done in the first run at the Opéra-Comique. In terms of the forward-motion of the spectacle, the ballet is totally inappropriate, but it is interesting in underlining the essentials of the different French operatic traditions operating in the late nineteenth century.

BRING BACK THE CASTANETS!

One aspect that can be gleaned is the composition of the orchestra used, at least in 1875:

> 9 1st violins, 6 violas, 7 double-basses, 3 oboes, 3 bassoons, 10 2nd violins, 3 flutes, 3 clarinets, 6 horns, 7 cellos, 3 trumpets, 4 trombones, 1 harp, 1 *tambour de basque*, 1 timpani, 1 bass drum.
>
> This makes 68 players without counting M. Adolphe Deloffre, the leader [...] he earns 5,000 francs a year, and MM Ferroud and Schulz, the deputy leaders.[15]

Certainly, there was no stinting on the cellos and basses! Perhaps most notable is the omission of castanets in this inventory, though the triangle is also omitted from the list. As for the activities of the castanets, a glance at the press reviews leaves us in no doubt that the first performances – unlike the scores – did not confine them to Carmen's *romalis*. In that old game of summarising the essence of an opera on the back of a postage stamp, one reviewer was amusingly succinct about the story of *Carmen*: 'C'est le triomphe de la castagnette sur l'honneur militaire.' (It is the triumph of the castanet over military honour.')[16]

Many of the reviews mention the use of castanets in some detail, and there can be no doubt that they were used to great effect in the gypsy scenes. But

15 From a manuscript *carnet* in the Paris Opéra library, F: *Po* (Réserve pièce 40): 'Programmes et distributions des spectacles donnés au Théâtre de l'Opéra-Comique, 1866–1889', p. 122 (beginning of 1875).

16 Oscar Commettant, *La France*, 4 March 1875. Cited Wright, *Dossier* p. 69.

more than this, they were a part of gypsy language. In the riotous dancing that begins Act II there was an orgy of them, clicking away in a celebratory way to a *bolero* rhythm. Carmen employed them as a substitute for sensible answers in the interrogation scene, thus making them a weapon in her armoury of disdain for authority, clicking against law and order. The same review implies that she clicked them as an adjunct to her insolent 'Tra-la-las' after the riot in the factory: 'On l'interroge ; elle dédaigne de répondre, et chante, pour narguer l'autorité, un gai refrain avec accompagnement obligé de castagnettes.' ('When interrogated she declines to respond, and to further irritate the authorities, sang a jolly refrain with the obligatory accompaniment of castanets.') Several writers perceived castanets as part of the gypsy language: when they 'spoke' they could communicate different meanings. Among those meanings were warning, seduction, annoyance, abandon and many more. Théophile Gautier in his reviews of Spanish dance called them 'little wooden tongues'.[17]

The same review suggests that Carmen used castanets for a more seductive purpose after the encounter with Zuniga; certainly their hypnotic ostinato in the *romalis* is a part of their sexiness. For Oscar Commetant, writing for *Le Siècle*, this dance was a clear reminder of the infamous *cachucha* danced by Fanny Elssler, and he saw Frasquita and Mercédès, as well as Carmen, using castanets as flirting-aids: 'These women moved furiously to the sounds of castanets, to achieve, in this Spanish *cabaret* of a risky character, some degree of attention from their lovers.'[18] Particularly imaginative with the pen, Comettant confirms that Galli-Marié played the castanets herself, and they survive today as an artefact in the Bibliothèque de l'Opéra. Comettant is among the most evocative in describing this crucial moment in the opera:

> The dragoon hesitates but the mad Andalusian woman is so expert with the castanets, her bosom so imposing as she undulates before him, knowing exactly how to force them on him, and with her eye burning with combustible promises, that the gentleman gives in, distraught.[19]

Léon Escudier, the reviewer in *L'Art musical*, goes even further by suggesting that the opera 'should have been called *L'Amour à la castagnette* [Love with

17 '... petites langues en bois.'

18 'Ces dames s'agitent furieusement au son des castagnettes, pour procurer, dans un cabaret espagnol d'un caractère douteux, quelques douces distractions à leurs amants ...' Oscar Comettant, *Le Siècle*. In Wright, *Dossier* p. 69.

19 'Le dragon hésite, mais la folle Andalouse manie si bien les castagnettes, son torse est si gracieux dans les mouvements ondulatoires qu'elle sait lui imprimer, et son œil est si rayonnant de combustibles promesses, que ce *caballero* cède, éperdu.' Comettant, *Le Siècle*.

Castanets] because its main events are accompanied by the sounds of this "anti-melodious" instrument which is only tolerable with limited use.' 'Oh la castagnette !', the writer continues, 'I feel that my ears, my nose, my mouth, have changed into castanets, and only function if they are clacking like those little wooden things so beloved of the Spanish. Guitars can be tolerated only on condition the players strumming them remain invisible, but castanets!'[20]

Further confirmation of the use of castanets in the *Chanson bohème* scene in the tavern is provided by Adolphe Jullien, writing in *Le Français*. He calls the movement a 'romanesca', a term increasingly used with regard to this dance:

> The opening of the second act is of a unique colour and is extremely animated thanks to the staging and the very authentic costumes and also to the music: a *romanesca* which begins muted and slow and ends in a whirlwind to peals of laughter, castanets and *tambours de basque*.[21]

There is evidence that this scene also included guitars, though these are again not mentioned in the inventory of instruments. Two 'racleurs de guitares' are prescribed in the stage directions at curtain-up in Act II, and they are mentioned by Théodore de Banville in his review in *Le National* indicating the 'patio of a *posada* resonating with songs and guitars'.[22] It is hard to imagine that these instruments, if present, would not have played. Miming would have been a poor substitute, and the number is, after all, in the guitar key of E minor. What the inclusion of these on-stage instruments achieves is a considerably increased use of the diegetic in the opera, alongside the fanfares of the changing guard and the *toques*, shouts and *pasodoble* in the bullfight.

20 'Cet opéra-comique devrait appeler *L'Amour à la Castagnette*, car les principaux incidents s'y produisent aux sons clinquants de cet instrument anti-mélodieux, qui n'est supportable qu'à la condition que l'on en use très modérément. Oh ! La castagnette ! Il semble depuis que j'ai entendu la musique de *Carmen*, que mes oreilles, mon nez, ma bouche, sont changés en castagnettes, et ne fonctionnent qu'en faisant claquer ces petits morceaux de bois si chers aux Espagnols. La guitare peut encore supporter, à la condition qu'one voie pas l'artiste qui en pince, mais la castagnette !' Léon Escudier, L'Art musical, 11 March 1874, pp. 73–74. Wright, *Dossier* p. 102

21 'Le début du second acte est d'une couleur étrange et d'une animation extrême, grâce à la mise en scène et aux costumes d'une grande exactitude, et aussi à la musique, à cette *romanesca* qui commence en sourdine et lentement, pour finir en tourbillonnant, au bruit des éclats de rire, des castagnettes, des tambours de basque.' Adolphe Jullien, *Le Français*, 15 March 1875. Wright, *Dossier* pp. 122–123. Others who mention the instrument include Jules Guillemot, *Le Soleil*, 9 March 1875 (Wright, *Dossier* p. 92).

22 '… le patio d'un posada où résonnent les chansons et les guitares'. Théodore de Banville, *Le National*, 8 March 1875. In Wright, *Dossier* p. 52.

There is one additional source confirming that the use of castanets was more extensive than the scores indicate: the aforementioned recording made in 1911 with the Orchestre de l'Opéra-Comique and some soloists with many years' experience in performing *Carmen* with this company. Read in conjunction with some of its reviews, it seems to preserve some of the performance-practice of the premiere and immediately subsequent performances. The use of castanets beyond those indicated for Carmen's *romalis* is confirmed: they are clearly to be heard in both the *Chanson bohème* and the vibrant *polo* which forms the entr'acte between Acts III and IV. On this recording no guitars are audible and nor does Carmen play the castanets in her interrogation scene, but then this was a studio recording.

The tempi of this recording are also of interest, sometimes deviating considerably from the indications in the vocal score. They are the subject of a table posted on the website for the new Peters edition.[23] It also has some interesting re-orchestrations which, although not the composer's intentions, are not unfitting. For example, in the Prélude a trumpet is added to the central section of the anticipation of Escamillo's 'tune'.[24]

STEPPING UP TO THE STAGE

So much for sounds, now to the stage. How did *Carmen* land on the boards of the Opéra-Comique? Once again we have a range of sources. There are, first of all, detailed instructions in the libretto that are summarised in the printed scores and sometimes expanded in the various manuscript scores and production materials.[25] Enriching these are the various staging manuals in the collection of the Association de la Régie théâtrale, preserved in the Bibliothèque historique de la ville de Paris. For anyone interested in how *Carmen* was first done on the stage these are gold dust, though they have to be read with care, not least because it is by no means an easy task to date some of them.

The two most important sources for the first staging are the first *mise en scène* and a *livret de mise en scène* subsequently copied but embedding – in a separate red ink – what appear to be detailed references to an 'Ancienne mise en scène'. The first of these, marked *mise en scène* and bound with an ornate cover, is a handwritten document reproduced in a system called 'autographie'

23 See the 'Links' tab at <https://www.editionpeters.com/product/carmen/ep7548a>.

24 Bar 55 in the Prélude.

25 A rudimentary comparison of these, prioritising the richest, is appended to the Peters vocal score in footnotes.

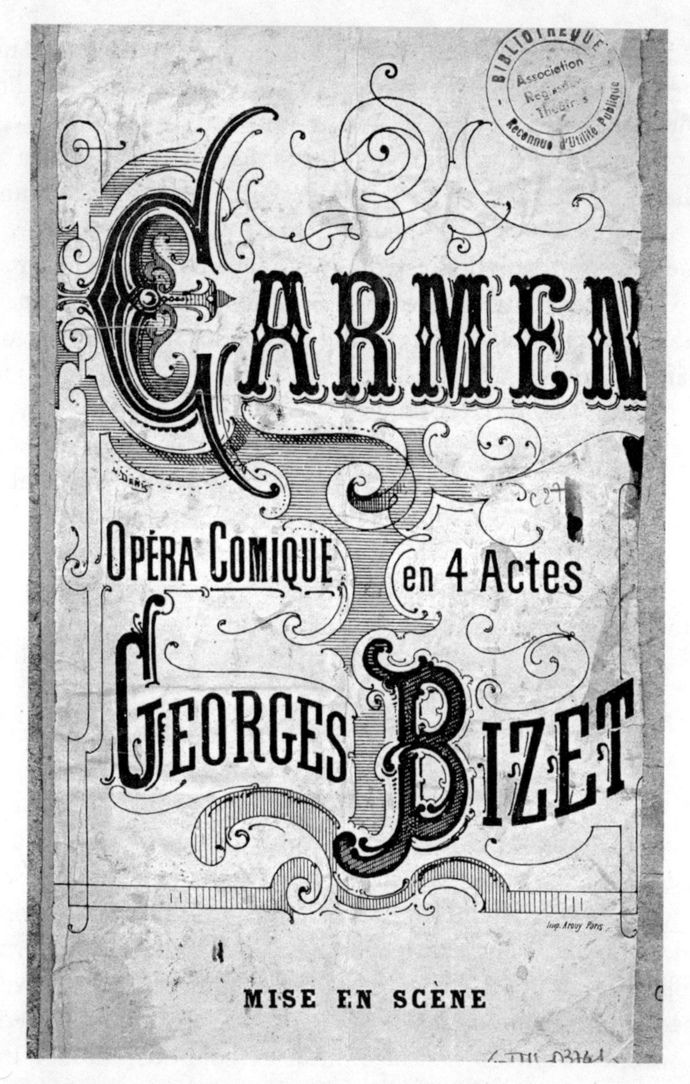

Plate 9.1 Ornate cover of Choudens's *mise en scène* for *Carmen*, which was exported to all hirers of the score and parts.

that Choudens exported to anyone who hired the performance material (Plates 9.1 and 9.2). The *livret* is an exercise book – a *cahier* – into which the pages of the printed libretto have been interleaved, with indications of stage movements, moods to be assumed, lighting and other details.[26]

The 'author' of these *mises en scène* was one Charles Ponchard, who must be credited with turning the work of the librettists and Bizet into a show.

26 The *mise en scène* was numbered C. 27 IV, and is now BIZET 06 4 TMS-03741; the *livret de mise en scène* was C. 27 I, and is now BIZET 03 4 TMS-03738.

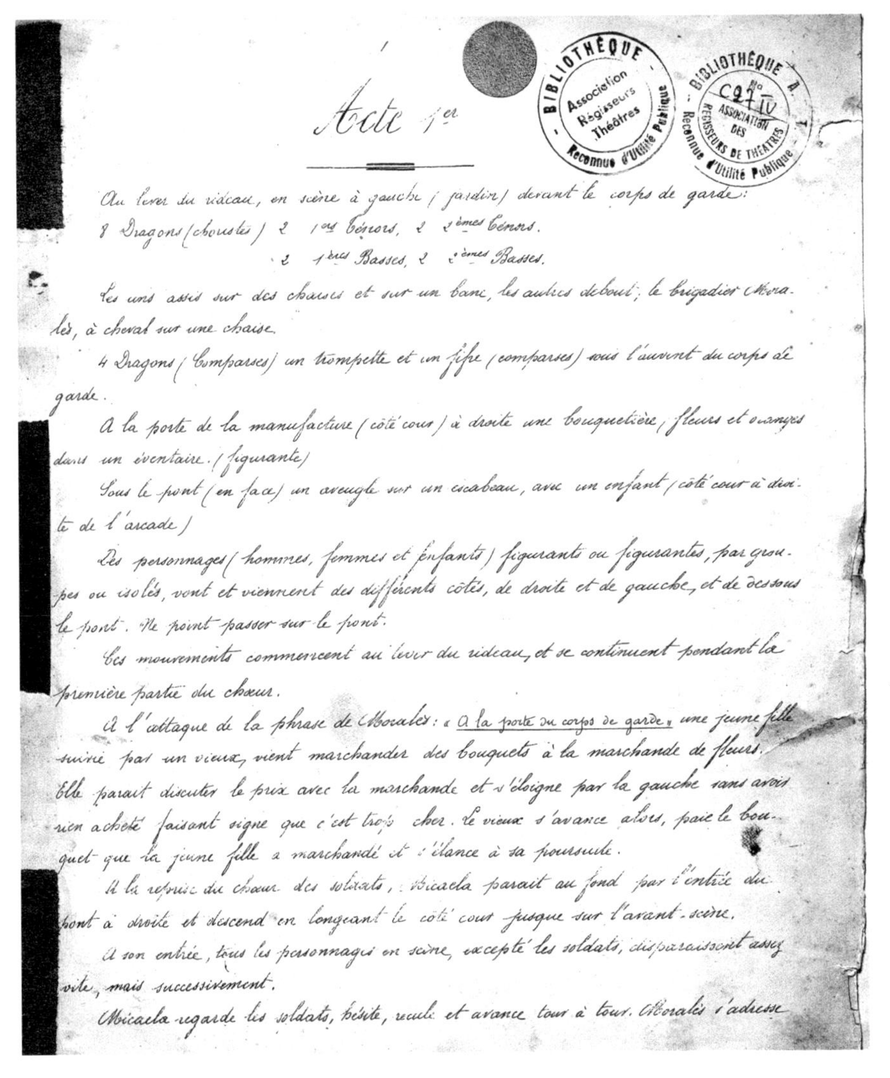

Acte 1er

Au lever du rideau, en scène à gauche (jardin) devant le corps de garde:
8 Dragons (choristes) 2 1ers Ténors, 2 2èmes Ténors.
2 1ères Basses, 2 2èmes Basses.

Les uns assis sur des chaises et sur un banc, les autres debout; le brigadier Moralès, à cheval sur une chaise.

4 Dragons (Comparses) un trompette et un fifre (comparses) sous l'auvent du corps de garde.

A la porte de la manufacture (côté cour) à droite une bouquetière, fleurs et oranges dans un éventaire. (figurante)

Sous le pont (en face) un aveugle sur un escabeau, avec un enfant (côté cour à droite de l'arcade)

Des personnages (hommes, femmes et enfants) figurants ou figurantes, par groupes ou isolés, vont et viennent des différents côtés, de droite et de gauche, et de dessous le pont. Ne point passer sur le pont.

Ces mouvements commencent au lever du rideau, et se continuent pendant la première partie du chœur.

A l'attaque de la phrase de Moralès: « A la porte du corps de garde » une jeune fille suivie par un vieux, vient marchander des bouquets à la marchande de fleurs. Elle paraît discuter le prix avec la marchande et s'éloigne par la gauche sans avoir rien acheté faisant signe que c'est trop cher. Le vieux s'avance alors, paie le bouquet que la jeune fille a marchandé et s'élance à sa poursuite.

A la reprise du chœur des soldats, Micaela paraît au fond par l'entrée du pont à droite et descend en longeant le côté cour jusque sur l'avant-scène.

A son entrée, tous les personnages en scène, excepté les soldats, disparaissent assez vite, mais successivement.

Micaela regarde les soldats, hésite, recule et avance tour à tour. Moralès s'adresse

Plate 9.2 First page of Choudens's *mise en scène* for the first staging of *Carmen*, a handwritten document reproduced by a system known as 'autographie'.

His initial conception may well have been rather a flop, but his ideas clearly survived into the period when *Carmen* became a worldwide success, filtering through into subsequent stagings. The *mise en scène* amplifies, clarifies and details many moments in the opera, especially the crucial turning points. It should be remembered, however, that this *mise en scène* was in the hands of *régisseurs* wherever it went. The idea that the staging of the opera was exported lock, stock and barrel to whichever opera company wanted it, and that its details were followed to the letter, is ridiculous: stages were different, sets were different, theatres and their audiences were different. While the idea that the 'whole opera' was exported may have been the systematic way publishers dealt with their operas, it is difficult to imagine that the *régisseurs* receiving these materials from Choudens would all have reacted to them in the same way.

The contributions of the various *régisseurs* merit an aside, as their role in managing every aspect of the staging of an opera was crucial. An article from the Grand Larousse of 1875 explains their duties in detail. A large theatre would employ three, each having different roles but covering the following aspects:

> They supervise the *mise en scène*, they choose the repertoire, they issue fines, they sign contracts, deal with indispositions, they are abused by some and given presents by others, harangue the audience if they are disorderly and usually receive a salary of four to five thousand francs for all this.

Typically there would be a *régisseur générale* who, Larousse claims, is the *alter ego* of the director of the theatre. His job includes casting, programming and organising rehearsals. He attends all performances to make sure everything is in order. Next in superiority is the *régisseur* responsible for everything that happens on the stage; often he is given the name *metteur en scène*. His authority over the stage is 'complete and absolute'. Larousse explains:

> It is he who puts the repertoire on stage, that is to say directs rehearsals, is in charge of the changes of scenery, who indicates to each actor exactly where they should be on the stage, which entrance they should use at each juncture, how the choruses and extras should be grouped. He gives advice to anyone who needs it, so in the end it is he who is responsible for a good interpretation of the all the repertoire. No mean task![27]

In the case of an opera, the *metteur en scène* would receive from the publisher the *mise en scène*, which, theoretically, he would follow in putting the work on the stage – another aspect of his role. Undoubtedly, the first *mise en scène* for *Carmen* detailed some important moments.

27 'C'est le metteur en scène qui monte les ouvrages, c'est-à-dire qui en surveille et en guide les études, qui en règle la marche scénique, qui indique à chaque acteur la place qu'il doit occuper, la porte ou le coté du théâtre par lequel il doit faire telle entrée ou telle sortie, qui groupe les masses de choristes, des figurants et des comparses, qui donne aux artistes les conseils, les indications, les avis dont ceux-ci peuvent avoir besoin ; c'est enfin à lui, à son talent, que l'on est redevable de la bonne exécution des ouvrages, de leur heureuse interprétation. On voit que tout cela ne constitue pas une mince besogne.' Entry on 'Régisseur', *Grand Larousse du XIXe siècle* (1875).

The *plantation*, that is the arrangement of the stage and the characters on it, has been carefully thought out. A separate *plantation* marked 'Ancienne mise en scène' (see Plate 6.1) shows that the original plan was to have a fountain in the middle of the plaza, with the factory behind and the guard-house at the front, stage-left; it also details still more extras and activities that eventually made their way into the final *mise en scène*. Although it was an obvious idea for a square in a Mediterranean country, the central fountain was probably abandoned – or reduced in size and moved – because it got in the way of stage movements. Its removal, however, had the distinct advantage of heightening the confrontation of the factory and its guardians by placing them opposite one another at the front of the stage.

At curtain-up, according to both the libretto and the musical scores, the plaza is busy with various activities and many more extras than was customary. This was a ground-breaking staging, focussing on the realistic, *costumbrista*, elements. To the directions in the libretto the *mise en scène* adds a blind man sitting on a stool with a child beside him, the ubiquitous orange-seller, a flower stall, etc.

In addition to this little scene within a scene, the positions of the soldiers are carefully detailed, reflecting in another way one of the recurrent underlying oppositions of the opera: order versus disorder. At the opening they are off-duty, lazing around with the brigadier Moralès, who sits astride a chair while several others are sitting on a bench and others are standing. Only in this source do we have a clever device to signal to the audience that, however relaxed these soldiers are (lounging about, probably smoking), two extras – a fifer and a trumpeter – together with four dragoons are on duty ready for action if any trouble breaks out. All this activity, the manual indicates, must continue throughout the first part of the chorus. The disorderliness of the off-duty soldiers will return later when Micaëla enters and they surround her trying (unsuccessfully) to lure her into the guard-house. She looks at the soldiers, and retreats then approaches several times in turn, the soldiers advance on her, creating a scene of female vulnerability.[28]

The set for this act has a bridge which can be crossed (in French a *praticable*, Plate 9.3) but for the moment the *mise en scène* emphasises that no-one must cross it; that higher level will be reserved for subsequent actions. One imagines that the opulence of this scene – which several reviews commented upon – excited immediate applause. Its richness in terms of both variety and activity was remarkable in the context of previous, much more static, stagings at the Opéra-Comique.

28 'Elle regarde les soldats, hésite, recule et avance tour à tour. [...] Mouvement en avant des soldats vers Micaëla.'

I. — Nous sommes en pleine Espagne, dans cette Espagne pittoresque, féerique, qui a inspiré tant de poétes et tant de romanciers. Rien qu'au début de l'histoire on prévoit des coups de stylet, des avantures andalouses.

Au lever du rideau, des soldats montent la garde; leur poste est à côté d'une fabrique de tabac.

Les cigarières arrivent, l'heure du travail ayant sonné. L'une d'elles, vous devinez déjà que c'est l'héroïne de ce récit, l'une d'elles, *Carmen*, apparaît la première.

Les jeunes ouvrières aiment les soldats. Carmen, qui a le pas sur toutes ses camarades, agace le brigadier des dragons, chef du poste, don José.

Irritation de soldats et mutinerie de grisettes ne peuvent que produire une scène charmante, avec accompagnement de chansons, de refrains et de mots joyeux, surtout sous le beau ciel d'Espagne..

Quel tableau joli, mais qu'il prend vite fin! Une cloche sonne. Que sonne cette cloche? La rentrée des ouvrières. Toutes se précipitent dans l'usine et don José voit disparaître à ses yeux Carmen qui l'a ébloui.

Plate 9.3 Drawing by Léon Sault of the opening scene from the first staging of *Carmen*, published in *La Comédie illustrée* shortly after the premiere. The bridge is clearly shown and the guard-house and factory are now opposite each other at the front of the stage.

Activity on the bridge itself is reserved for the changing of the guard, whose movements are detailed in diagrams, down to the order in which they collect their arms from the rack. No fewer than twelve extras are required for this action, in addition to the eight soldiers demanded for the chorus, as well as the fifer and trumpeter. Emphasising the friendship enjoyed by Moralès and José at this juncture – both hailing from elsewhere – they are instructed to shake hands as they chat about their backgrounds and the activities in the tobacco factory. Moralès's character is particularly deepened by the actions and *plantation* indicated in the *mise en scène*. He emerges as a soldier who, on the one hand, commands authority – the *mise en scène* places him at the front of the stage during the changing of the guard, with the fifer and drummer beside him; on the other hand he also displays his sense of humour and *camaraderie* with José.

As with the soldiers, extras are demanded for the entry of the *cigarerières* – six, to be precise – and they are all required to be smoking cigarettes. Placed equally on both sides of the stage they allow the chorus girls to sing from centre-stage. Not much is said about Carmen's movements during her singing of the Habanera, but the general laughter after she throws the flower at

José is detailed and a nice touch is that the factory workers sing the final chorus 'au nez' – 'in his face' – thus mirroring the soldiers' earlier advance on Micaëla. But now it is the Gypsies who are in control, offering their gypsy *credo* of free love.

In the scene where the factory girls pour onto the stage, the off-duty soldiers and those on duty are contrasted directly, the former rearranging the chairs outside the guard-house while leaving the latter to deal with the screaming girls. But as the tension mounts they all form an ordered line – 'une rue' – with their backs to the audience, to push the girls to the rear of the stage. Some resist and break through to attack Carmen.

The unusual moment of action in the middle of Carmen's number 'Près des remparts de Séville', when she confesses that she could love José and he is 'like a drunken man', has much more detail in the *mise en scène* at the point when he unties her hands. She realises that she must play her part, showing the audience that her hands are free, but also knows that she must keep her hands behind her back as if they were still bound. Pleading with him with her face very close, she asks him to relieve her tied hands:

> Quand José dit « Ta promesse, tu la tiendras, si je t'aime, tu m'aimeras ». Carmen en murmurant « Oui, oui » de très près de José lui indique de délier les mains, ce que fait Don José, et à la reprise de la chanson : « Près des remparts de Séville ». Carmen, les mains libres, enlève la corde qui les attachait et passe triomphalement devant José, puis va se rasseoir vivement sur l'escabeau en tenant ses mains derrière le dos, comme si elles étaient encore attachées ...

> When José says 'Your promise, you'll keep: if I love you, you'll love me' Carmen, whispering 'Yes, yes' very close to José gestures him to free her hands which he does at the reprise of the song 'Près des remparts de Séville.' Carmen, her hands free, undoes the cord which bound them and walks triumphantly in front of José, then quickly sits down again on the stool keeping her hands behind her back, as if they were still tied ...

In Act II the focus on the relations between the soldiers and the various women around – a mixture of locals and gypsies – is carefully developed. Marked as a *tableau très animé*, an even more relaxed version of the soldiers at play is presented, suggesting corrupt links between them and the criminal underworld, links strengthened by the sexual allure of the gypsy women. The *mise en scène* has a long passage detailing where everyone should be. Perhaps its essence is contained in the final line of the paragraph: 'The officers come and go offering the women drinks and drinking themselves.'[29] They are also smoking. It is an important reminder – recurring several times throughout the opera – that the soldiers who are meant to uphold the law fraternise with

29 'Les officiers vont et viennent offrant à boire aux femmes et buvant eux-mêmes.'

those they well know often contravene it. Lillas Pastia – an important mime figure – keeps trying to engage the officers in conversation, no doubt trying to impress upon them that there are local licensing rules enforced by the corregidor which have to be obeyed if his business – however corrupt – is to remain open. The stage-business of the soldiers is now further enhanced. For the entrance of Escamillo they form a two-line corridor for this 'torchlight procession'.

The bonding of the elder Moralès and the young José is now threatened as the soldiers befriend Escamillo. They 'toast' him, the word used for wishing the bullfighter luck at the beginning of a *corrida*. At moments where the action oscillates between the private and the public, the stage set has a visual signifier: the shutters. For the scene in the *baisade* where Carmen performs her dance for José the shutters are closed. The business of the money given by Carmen to José, but not spent, is described in terms of a French bistro menu rather than anything Spanish: Lillas Pastia serves them up – according to the *livret* – a 'plateau garni'!

The *romalis* itself has further detail added – in fact an element of humour, few of which can be seen in either libretto or score, but which emerge from time to time in the *mises en scène*. What has happened to Carmen's castanets? She cannot find them. In some productions she resorts to breaking a plate to sound her dance: a poor substitute. Why? The original staging book explains. For a joke José has hidden the castanets in his hat – a trick not detailed in the libretto or score. It might have been one of several masterstrokes of dramatic irony introduced into the staging, but the gag seems later to have been abandoned. He returns them again when needed, but only after Carmen has smashed some crockery. The key phrase from the *mise en scène* is uncompromising: 'Carmen danse en jouant des castagnettes' ('Carmen dances playing the castanets'). But how many Carmens – in the course of the history of the opera – could play them while singing and properly dancing the *ole*? Minnie Hauk, a celebrated Carmen, insisted that it was imperative for all aspiring Carmens to learn to play them.

There is no doubt that the indication in the first vocal score was what Bizet wanted: 'Dancing, accompanying herself on the castanets.'[30] One can imagine this to be a stunning theatrical moment if the singer could combine these skills. Another of the score's directions for playing the castanets is that 'If they are played by the singer then the rhythm should be modified at her will.'[31] This

30 'Dansant en s'accompagnant de ses castagnettes'. B. ChPC1.

31 'Cette partie sera exécutée ; soit à l'orchestre, par l'un des instrumentistes de la batterie, soit sur le théâtre, par l'artiste chargée du rôle de Carmen. Dans ce cas le rythme pourra être modifié au gré de la cantatrice'. ChPO.

must surely be one of the first calls for improvisation in French nineteenth-century opera.

In Act III a stereotypical gypsy accoutrement is introduced into the scenography, though not included in the other sources: a 'marmite', a big iron pot that itinerant gypsies traditionally carted around to cook over their wood fires in the wilds. Escamillo and José fight with their capes (*manteaux*) over their arms, reminding us of the capes used by bullfighters. In the text is Escamillo's insult against José's technique – he despises his *garde navarraise*, referring to his local knife-skills. The *livret de mise en scène* is the only source confirming the intervention of Carmen at this point, who interposes her body between the two fighters.

José's discovery of Micaëla is also detailed in the staging directions. Surprised when she turns up in the mountains, he holds her hand and hugs her: an important moment not mentioned in other sources. 'Il découvre Micaëla et la ramène en scène en la tenant par la main. José va à Micaëla qui le prend dans ses bras et s'accroche à lui. Carmen qui a continué son mouvement tournant de cour à jardin à cour.' ('He discovers Micaëla and brings her onstage holding her hand. José approaches Micaëla, who takes him in her arms and hugs him.') Carmen has continued her agitated movements, turning from right to left across the stage. A brilliant and moving moment, not least for the ladies in the audience who have perceived the future José might have enjoyed. 'Oh, why didn't he marry Micaëla?', the audience lament, with tears in their eyes. The critic of *L'Union* felt similarly: 'I was sure [Micaëla] would marry José in the end and that the *cigarrera* would go to the devil! … but no!'[32]

José, however, immediately moves to Carmen: 'Je te tiens, fille damnée !' ('I will hold you accursed woman!') 'Il la tient dans ses bras avec fureur et passion.' ('He holds her in his arms with fury and passion.') The essence of the staging here is that the torn Don José has physical contact with the two women in rapid succession: a hug from Micaëla and a passionate and furious embrace with Carmen. Another important point is that when Micaëla tells José his mother is dying – 'Ta mère se meurt' – Carmen must somehow indicate to the audience that she does not hear. Despite this moment of reconnection with Micaëla, José bars Carmen from seeing Escamillo's departure. 'She comes back down to the stage making spiteful signs', reads the *mise en scène*.[33]

32 '… j'étais persuadé qu'elle épouserait José au dénouement et que la *cigerera* s'en irait au diable … Eh bien, non !'. Daniel Bernard, 'Théâtres', *L'Union*, 8 March 1875, pp. 1–2.

33 'Puis quand Carmen veut s'élancer vers le chemin creux pour apercevoir Escamillo, José, entraînant dans son mouvement Micaëla, vient barrer passage à Carmen qui redescend la scène avec signes de dépit.'

Act IV begins with the chorus and extras divided into two: half are the tradesmen, the other half their potential customers. Among the former, the orange-sellers outnumber the rest, a detail already remarked upon in Chapter Seven. There is much detail about the order of the *cuadrilla,* and the background presence of Frasquita and Mercédès. The fact that Carmen enters on Escamillo's arm is emphasised, as is his entry at the final dénouement, after José has stabbed Carmen and is kneeling at the side of her body. The curtain of the bullring opens and the crowd, assistants and lesser members of the *cuadrilla* pour out, with Escamillo last of all. In the wake of Bizet's turbulently modulating music, his appearance at the end is a masterstroke of staging unparalleled in the majority of subsequent productions.

THE *LIVRET DE MISE EN SCÈNE*

The *livret de mise en scène* preserved in the same collection (that of the Association de la Régie théâtrale) is difficult to date precisely. Its format is totally different: a printed libretto has been cut out and interleaved into an exercise book with staging instructions, in a neat manuscript hand, numbered to concur precisely with lines from the libretto (see Plates 6.1 and 6.2). The title page of the cut-out libretto has usefully been retained and is from a much later printing: current thinking seems to be that it may be from the 1938 revival by Dignimont. On the other hand it may preserve what was done directly after the first run – before Carré's new staging, but after what it calls the 'Ancienne mise en scène' was abandoned. Embedded in it are sections in red ink that preserve this original version. According to Odile Gigou, a former curator of the collection at the Association de la Régie théâtrale, it was recopied from a decaying document which no longer exists as an act of preservation. It is close to the *mise en scène* itself, suggesting that its black-ink stage directions were inherited from – or perhaps developed from – the original staging.[34] Separate from this is a typed, detailed itinerary of the Act IV *cuadrilla* numbered to coincide with the vocal score. These numberings confirm that it tallied with the second Choudens vocal score (1877). Although this second 'opéra' version incorporated Guiraud's recitatives, only one of these was used at the Opéra-Comique, as the surviving parts clearly show – this was the *récit* before Micaëla's Act III aria.

34 The dating of the document as c.1938 was made by Michela Niccolai, who worked on these documents. The idea that it was professionally retyped because of the decay of original documents was suggested to me by Marie-Odile Gigou.

The red-ink sections detailing the 'Ancienne mise en scène' indicate the way in which the 'Scène et Pantomime' was incorporated into the action and, despite the late copying of the document, bear out the view that it was an accurate copy of a former *livret de mise en scène*. To my knowledge the 'Scène et Pantomime' was never revived between its abandonment shortly after Bizet's death and the later twentieth century. This *livret* thus may be a historical document of some importance to those interested in how *Carmen* was done in its first run, preserving details of the original staging with diagrams of stage movements amplifying the prose description in the *mise en scène* itself.

The list of extras (*figurants* or *comparses*) is particularly rich in this document, specifying two florists, a young man wooing a young girl under the arcades, two vendors selling soup (*gazpacho*, one imagines), others selling water, a beggar and eight dancers, one of whom sells pitchers; there is also a vendor who sells figs, as well as the ubiquitous sellers of oranges and fans. A new couple come in during the scene: a mother with a little girl. It is also detailed that the water-seller sits down under a street lamp. The comings and goings are detailed throughout Act I; there is constant activity in the plaza, continuing right through the riot and Carmen's arrest. The stage was never bare, and there was always some secondary action taking place.

To preserve the essential moment in the opera when Carmen first enters, she is the first to appear on the bridge, at a higher level than anyone else. Meanwhile, all the activity in the square continues, including the Englishman now coming out of the factory. While José is sent into the factory to investigate, Zuniga sits back in a chair and laughs; riots must have been a common occurrence. In the scene where José reads the letter from his mother – deeply moved – one might imagine an empty stage and a spotlight. But this was not how it was done. The urchins returned to the scene – if I am right about the dating of this staging plan – playing games in the background. There are several indications to suggest that Zuniga has an eye for Carmen, perking up whenever she comes on stage. A particularly clever moment where music and libretto are united is where the Habanera is recapitulated. José pricks up his ears: he has heard that tune before … Penultimate numbers to an act are often climactic in the sense that issues from previous events come to a head. The end of Act I of *Carmen* is no exception. Carmen fancies José and he has fallen madly in love with her; this is the enactment of that moment.

The 'Ancienne mise en scène' indicates that Carmen originally danced her song 'Près de la porte de Séville'.[35] Just as in her interrogation scene, the printed libretto indicates that she must 'hardly sing, but murmur' ('à peine

35 This was the original first line in the printed libretto, altered to 'Près des remparts de Séville' in the musical sources.

chanté, murmuré'), but whereas her murmuring during the interrogation signalled insolence, her singing under the breath and suggestive dancing as she approaches José must have made one of the most intimate moments of their encounter – one which, no doubt, Galli-Marié acted rather well. The *livret* indicates the movements between the two of them very precisely at this point: José paces up and down nervously but, as he hears the *Séguedille* begin, he turns round to approach Carmen. Maybe she used her castanets here, too. Precisely at the line 'Real pleasure can only be had by two' ('Et les vraies plaisirs sont à deux') she secretly looks at him – 'Carmen regarde José à la dérobée'. At the line 'Mon amoureux, il est au diable' ('I have sent my lover packing' – referring to a previous lover), two 'little cigar girls' buy some figs; a woman with a small child passes across the stage, and the water-seller establishes himself under the street light. How on earth it was realised is hard to imagine, but at the line where Carmen confesses that she 'might love a certain officer one of these days', José is instructed to 'tremble'.[36]

Then he begins to untie her: the *livret* indicates they are 'tête à tête' ('brow to brow'). As soon as she is freed she begins to dance to the last stanza of the *Séguedille*, but Zuniga comes in ... The chorus are instructed to crowd onto the stage at the end of the number, though they do not sing. Then comes the other crucial moment: Carmen pushes José over and niftily escapes – in the fleet way gypsies were renowned for. The scene ends with another clever staging detail: Zuniga has seen what had happened and with 'an imperious gesture orders José to get back into the guard-house and await a serious punishment'.[37]

Directions for staging the set-piece – the *Chanson bohème* – at the beginning of Act II take into account various possibilities including that of employing dancers alongside Carmen. From the reviews of the premiere and also from the 1911 recording, which includes a chorus of castanets, it is clear that this was a particularly spectacular tableau. The *livret* has a clear strategy at curtain-up, emphasising that the soldiers misbehave (or hope to) with the gypsy girls: Mercédès, for example, is sitting on Moralès's lap. 'Everybody claps to the music.'[38]

Carmen's constant attraction to new men is re-introduced at Escamillo's entry. She eyes him up, and, according to the *livret*, is 'allowed to smoke a

36 Carmen sings, 'Mon officier n'est pas un capitaine, Pas même un lieutenant, il n'est que brigadier.' The *livret* reads 'José tressaille'.

37 'Zuniga qui allait entrer dans le poste se retourne et comprenant tout, d'un geste impérieux ordonne à José de rentrer au Poste et qu'une punition sévère l'attend.'

38 'Tout le monde frappe dans les mains.'

cigarette while doing this.'[39] The sexual chemistry is woven in as, a few lines later, Escamillo blows Carmen a kiss. They have noticed each other.

The business of José hiding Carmen's castanets in his hat has been abandoned in this staging: perhaps it was too detailed – or too frivolous – to make the joke work. Whoever captured this libretto knew about the dances where gypsies threw themselves at their observers – as in the *ole* described in Chapter Eight. José leans forward during this dance, and Carmen's game is to come within reach of him: he tries to grab her, but she always escapes, laughing.[40]

One of the remarkable aspects of how the libretto was interpreted is the way in which arias became dramaticised. For example, when Carmen and José have argued about his wanting to leave to rejoin the military escapade, and he sings his flower song – 'La fleur que tu m'avais jetée' – with the music of the band welling up in the background, she at first pouts as she listens. But as the aria goes on she softens, eventually cradling his shoulders in her arms while he kneels before her.[41]

It would appear that this *metteur en scène* had some knowledge of Spanish customs, as when Zuniga embarrassingly encounters José when he comes to meet Carmen – with a clear purpose in mind – he raises his glove to his inferior in a traditional Spanish insult: to deliver a slap to the face between two males ('Zuniga lève son gant ...'). Considerable violence follows, with Le Dancaïre and Remendado chipping in, pistols drawn. Once again this crucial penultimate scene, with its accelerated action, is resolved by an *entrée générale*.

In the card scene Carmen stood up, dealing herself one card at each stanza. In the *navaja* fight between José and Escamillo – pictured with varying degrees of success in the various illustrations – musical examples are inserted into the *livret* to clarify where each movement is to take place. Most important are the two interpositions, first of Le Dancaïre and subsequently of Micaëla, who offers herself as a sacrifice – a rather forgotten detail but one that gives an important psychological insight into Micaëla's character.

As anyone who has sat in the gods will know, the cheaper seats at the Opéra-Comique are not that salubrious. Thus the entry of some 'cushion-vendors' might have provoked some amusement: more extras not detailed in any other sources. The grand spectacle of the last act is the procession, the

39 '... elle peut fumer une cigarette en regardant José.'

40 'Pendant la danse, José assis, le corps penché en avant, essaie de saisir Carmen, quand elle passe près de lui, elle lui échappe en riant.'

41 'Pendant l'air : Carmen au début, boudeuse tournant le dos à Don José puis peu à peu elle s'attendrit. José s'agenouille aux pieds de Carmen toujours assise. Carmen entoure de ses bras les épaules de José toujours à genoux.'

cuadrilla, where the adjuncts to the *corrida* and the town officials process into the arena. This is detailed precisely over several pages, and was clearly a major tableau in the overall show.

There is one addition to the *plantation* of this scene: a 'vierge' (virgin) is specified on stage left, just outside the main entrance to the ring, 'watching' – as it were – over the final dénouement of the opera. It is the third hint of religious belief in the opera, the others being Micaëla's attendance at church with José's mother, and her prayers before she goes to the mountains to tell José of his mother's terminal illness. It is realistic in one way: bullrings had (and have) elaborate chapels. In another it is a call to order from the status quo of whatever time the opera is set in: why is this murder taking place? Whenever this *mise en scène* dates from, the *livret* has a fine description of the dénouement: 'Escamillo, carried in triumph by his friends appears at the bullring gate, he falls to the earth, takes off his cape and kneels beside Carmen's corpse.'[42] An end more moving than many one has seen since, however much the music of this moment catches in the throat.

PICTURES OF THE SET

Before progressing to some interesting clues in this *livret*, it will be useful to glance at a few visual sources depicting the set. In some ways these are of interest in relation to the *mises en scène*; in others they are fraught with problems of accuracy and, in particular, of dating.

Here is a preliminary inventory:

1 *Album rose. Carmen*, by Léon Sault, 1875. From a series *La Comédie illustrée* presenting an illustrated synopsis with plates and a text relating to each illustration. An advert on the last page details seven items published to date: there is one other *opéra-comique* (*La Belle Bourbonnaise*, by Cœdès), and Strauss's operetta *La Reine indigo*. The others are plays. This album consists of an ornate cover page; a full-page portrait of Carmen and Don José, bearing little resemblance to the singers; and seven plates which are black-and-white sketches with hand-coloured sections. Sault ran a press under his own name which operated from the rue 4 Septembre (very close to the Opéra-Comique). Each volume sold for 40 *centimes*. The same illustrations had been published without colour in smaller format in *La Comédie illustrée* on 28 March 1875.[43]

42 'Escamillo, porté en triomphe par ses amis, apparait à la porte des Arènes, côté cour, il saute à terre, étale sa cape, met un genou à terre devant le cadavre de Carmen.'

43 The coloured source for this is accessible via Gallica.

2 A set of illustrations by Hyacinthe Royet (1862–1926), who originated from Avignon and studied with Horace Vernet. His plates probably date from about 1889–1891, a period when he was working for various music publishers as an illustrator (for covers, etc.). These were appended to the second edition of the Choudens vocal score and consist of fifteen russet-coloured line-drawings of 'moments' in the opera. The edition is rare: the National Library of Australia is the only public source I have been able to find. Several commentators mistakenly assert that these images were published in the first vocal score, at which time Royet would have only been 13 years old.
3 A set of illustrations of each act by Auguste Lamy, commissioned by Choudens at the time of the first staging. A celebrated illustration for the Act II 'tavern' scene, published in *L'Illustration* of 13 March 1875 (p. 174), was surrounded with vignettes of other moments in the opera (see Plate 9.7).[44]
4 Poster by Prudent Louis Leray for the Opéra-Comique, depicting the final moment when Escamillo comes out of the bullring to see that José has murdered Carmen. Leray (1820–1879) was a celebrated painter of religious and genre scenes and had some experience as a designer of opera posters. His previous posters included Berlioz, *Les Troyens*; Gounod, *Roméo et Juliette*, and Offenbach, *Madame Favart*. The poster was commissioned by Choudens. One format measured 7,264 mm × 9,774 mm, confirming that the image was used as a poster as well as reduced for incorporation as a frontispiece in scores.[45]
5 'Reconstitution par Émile Bertin des décors de la creation' ('Revival by Émile Bertin (1878–1954) of the scenes for the premiere'). There is one of these for each of the four acts. His depiction of Act IV shows that these were based on the 1898 revival by Albert Carré.[46]
6 Bizet, *Carmen*, 'morceaux détachés', Choudens, n.d. Sheet music of individual numbers from the opera, illustrated covers of Galli-Marié as Carmen and Bouhy as Escamillo.

Although its illustrations are really rather poor, the *Album rose* (1) is perhaps the most reliable source in this inventory of sketches as its date confirms that the intention was to represent the scenography of the first run. The layout, now with the factory moved to front stage left, and the guard-house opposite, is that used in the first run: a layout retained by Carré. Among its weaknesses

44 See Evan Baker, 'The Scene Designs for the First Performance of Bizet's *Carmen*', *19th Century Music*, 13/3 (1990): pp. 230–242; and H. R. Cohen, *Les Graveurs musicales dans 'L'Illustration'* (Québec, 1983), vol. II, no. 1672.
45 The indication of their name on copies gives their name as 'Choudens Père et Fils' and their address as rue St-Honoré 265. The poster is signed in the lower right-hand corner.
46 *F-PO* [Esq. O. C. 1875]. Note that Bertin was not born until three years after the premiere of *Carmen*.

Plate 9.4 Cover for the sheet music of the Habanera (Choudens), with a portrait of the first Carmen: Célestine Galli-Marié.

are the undistinguished faces, which have little Spanish, let alone gypsy, character. It is difficult to confirm whether the colourings, added by hand, are faithful to the original. The set of landscape-format plates with texts below is preceded by a romanticised, larger, rather sugary portrait-format drawing of Carmen and José separated by a trellis. In this, the hand-coloured version Carmen's skirt for Act I is striped in red and green and, for the time, very short (as Mérimée's novella clearly indicates), but nothing like the ruffed skirts depicted by the *costumbristas*. A more exuberant costume was reserved

Plate 9.5 Cover for the sheet music of the Toréador song (Choudens), with a portrait of the first Escamillo: Jacques Bouhy.

for the Act II scene in the tavern, while for Act III she wore a heavy selection of capes and *manteaux*; she is rarely depicted in such garb, though it is certainly more functional for the Sierra. In Act IV, where she is described as 'très bien nippée' for her entry with Escamillo, she wore an embroidered skirt which was more conventionally Spanish but less gypsy.

Similarity to the Sault illustrations confirms that Royet (2) attempted to capture the same basic scenography, and certainly not the later Carré staging of 1898. In both sets of drawings there is a wooden table and chairs casually placed in front of the guard-house, which is an edifice with pillars. This reinforces the fundamental opposition between transgression and order that is the major theme of the first act. The soldiers enact their symmetrical rituals while on duty, yet while they relax – smoking, drinking and flirting with the girls they are meant to control – they slouch around.

In Royet's drawing of Carmen and her *cigarerra* companions Carmen has a cigarette in her mouth as well as the typical 'gypsy elbow', with her hand on her hip. She has a fuller skirt with more ruffs than Sault shows, a *mantilla*, and a haughtier look. Whereas Sault's gypsies have similar, plainer skirts though of different colours, Royet's Act I image singles Carmen out in several ways: she is more up-front and therefore larger than the other gypsies, and her clothes are far more ornamental than those of the other factory girls, who wear unpleated, plainer dresses. Carmen's costume stresses her authority, no doubt; she is the Queen Bee in the factory. The drawings in this illustrated appendix are far closer to moments in the libretto: José, for example, is depicted working on his priming pin, which is secured to the back of his chair. The soldiers' costumes, with their parallel braids, designed by the celebrated military painter Édouard Detaille, are very similar in both this and Sault's illustrations.

The arched crossable bridge is balustraded in these Royet illustrations, whereas it was not in Sault. Royet's perspective also includes the sky with the ever-present tower of the Giralda. (Many *costumbristas* used this device, sketching in the tower to leave no doubt as to the Seville setting.) There are also ominous – perhaps symbolic – storm clouds recurrent in many of his drawings. As might be expected in an appendix to a score, Royet's drawings are closer to the musical numbers, though he was not proficient enough to capture the passion of the dances. Royet's José, watching Carmen dance the *romalis*, hardly reflects the descriptions we have encountered. In fact he looks rather boyish, even somewhat silly, and there is none of the rising testosterone suggested by the texts. The plate before this is perhaps more successful, as José enters what in the novella was Dorothée's *baisade*, Carmen is at her toilette in front of a mirror. Still in the same scene in another corner of the *posada*, in an image entitled 'Il va pleuvoir des coups', Carmen is seen interposing herself between Zuniga and José, who both have swords drawn threateningly, an action rather forgotten but shared between this image and directions in the *mise en scène*.

Similarly, the illustration for the Act II *Chanson bohème* lacks both movement and fire. As with Sault's rather sparsely populated image, so Royet's static picture confirms the balcony in the set but also the playing of the castanets: Carmen, Frasquita and Mercédès are playing them, indicated by their dropped-hand position. Only Sault gives Carmen a tambourine, held high

N° 6 ACTE II —— CARMEN, DON JOSÉ *« Mais qui donc attends-tu? »*

Plate 9.6 Plate by Hyacinthe Royet for the illustrated edition of the *Carmen* vocal score (Paris: Choudens, c.1890), showing Carmen at her toilette and José entering.

above her head: a viable substitute since you cannot play both the tambourine and the castanets at once. Perhaps she alternated. The best image of this scene was perhaps Lamy's engraving in *L'Illustration* (Plate 9.7). All three confirm the all-important balustraded balcony with a *praticable* giving access from stage right.

Sault's Act III set in the mountains is rather different from Royet's in that it indicates background trees. The essence of the written *mise en scène*, confirmed in the libretto by Micaëla and her guide, was the sinister nature of the

Plate 9.7 Auguste Lamy, the scene for Act II of *Carmen* as printed in *L'Illustration*, surrounded by vignettes of other moments in the opera (1875).

place, accessed by a 'chantier creux' – which Royet's image suggests is a path between high rocks and is the only entry to the gypsy camp. Royet has an interesting layout for the card scene. José and another soldier guard the path leading to their hide-out while the gypsies consult the tarot cards with cloths laid out on separate *ballots*. Frasquita and Mercédès deal the cards on one, while Carmen is separated and dressed more darkly than her companions on the other, in a distressed posture. The fight with the *navajas* occurs only in Royet's depictions and captures the detail in the libretto as well as the concentration of the male combat: for example, they both have their capes over their arms as they fight. Royet would have had plenty of illustrations – Doré's, for example – on which to model his depiction of this scene.

The various images for the final act all depict a keyhole arch as the entry to the bullring, which bears no resemblance to the actual *Plaza de toros* in Seville but was transferred from the massive arch that looks on to the Giralda. A curtain was drawn over the bullring entrance, and opened as Escamillo makes his triumphant exit revealing the Giralda towering behind. Carmen's corpse lies more or less centre-stage with José contemplating what he has done.

Such are the visual sources giving some impression of how the opera was first staged. Looking again at these, the over-arching principle of the first staging seems to have been its emphasis on pace and movement, certainly in Acts I and II: the square is a hive of activity and the bar is buzzing. For example, the *sonnerie de trompettes* announcing the changing of the guard is dovetailed with the end of the 'Scène et Pantomime', and at this point the Englishman goes into the factory. Although it is detailed in the *Ancienne plantation*, but nowhere to be seen in the illustrations, there is also activity around the rim of a fountain, unfortunately not clearly visible in any of the pictorial sources of Act I: its first visitor is a monk, and later two lovers appear, although these are red-ink references to the *ancienne mise en scène*.

In addition to the various illustrative and literary testimonies there is some evidence in Ludovic Halévy's recollections of the early stages of the opera, written to celebrate its 1,000th performance. He does not mention the original *metteur en scène*, Ponchard, but other sources suggest he was too set in his ways to stage the innovative, vibrant movements envisaged by Bizet and his librettists, particularly in regard to the chorus. Halévy's recollection was that 'The chorus was used to singing ensembles standing up and not moving, in straight lines, arms at their sides, their eyes fixed on the conductor and their thoughts elsewhere.'[47]

As we have seen, the final moment of the opera – visually – is Escamillo's triumphant exit through the doors of the bullring, but what about José? Might his fate be in the back of some of the audience's minds? One scenographic possibility suggested by the illustrations added to the Choudens score can be seen from the corner of a small gothic arch situated at the foot of the staircase. Maybe this was the fountain, but it may have become an image of the Virgin, which would be appropriate as a background for José's journey from his younger devotion (his training for the priesthood) to serious transgres-

47 'Les choristes avaient l'habitude de chanter les ensembles, bien alignés, immobiles, les bras ballants. Les yeux fixes sur le bâton du chef d'orchestre et la pensée ailleurs.' Ludovic Halévy, 'La Millième représentation de *Carmen*', *Le Théâtre*, January 1905, p. 5.

sion. This may have been a way of mirroring José's return to religion, which is detailed in the novella but absent from the opera. The *mise en scène* could restore themes just as powerfully as could libretto and score. As he kills, or has just killed, Carmen, an image of the Virgin Mary watches over José from a shrine, reminding him of his past ambition to join the priesthood, of his mother's enduring faith, and – in the novella – of his confession to a hermit, before facing execution, with a white veil over his head and attended by priests in full regalia, by garrotting machine in the unwritten, uncomposed, and unthought-of, Act V.

Select Bibliography

MANUSCRIPT SCORES

Bizet, Georges. *Carmen*. Opéra[-Comique] en 4 Actes, Paroles de M. M. Meillac [*sic*] et Lud. Halévy (manuscrit autographe), [4 vols]. 1875. F-*Po*. Gallica. (Oeser and Langham Smith Source A.)

———. *Carmen*. Opéra-Comique en 4 Actes. Partition ayant servi à la première representation. 3 vols. 1875. F-*Po*. (Oeser and Langham Smith Source B.)

———. *Carmen*. Orchestral parts (Matériel – Fonds de l'Opéra-Comique). F-*Po*. (Oeser and Langham Smith Source C.)

PROOFS

Bizet, Georges. *Carmen*. Partition piano et chant. Fragments d'épreuves corrigées par l'auteur. (20pp.) F-*Pn*.

PRINTED SCORES

Bizet, Georges. *Carmen*. Opéra-Comique en 4 Actes tirée de la nouvelle de Prosper Mérimée. Partition piano et chant. Choudens père et fils, Paris, n.d. [1875].

———. *Carmen*. Opéra en 4 Actes. Partition d'orchestre. Choudens, Paris, n.d. [1877]. (Contains ballet music drawn from other works by Bizet as well as the recitatives by Guiraud.)

———. *Carmen*. Opéra en 4 Actes. Partition piano et chant. Choudens, Paris, n.d. [1877]. (Contains the recitatives by Guiraud.)

———. *Carmen*. Morceaux détachés, chant et piano. Choudens, Paris, 1883–1885.

———. *Carmen*. Opéra en 4 Actes. Partition piano et chant: Édition illustrée. Choudens, Paris, n.d. [1889–1891?]. (Appended are a set of 15 illustrations printed in a russet colour by Hyacinthe Royet.)

———. *Carmen*. Kritische Neuausgabe nach den Quellen. Partitur. Klavierauszug und Bericht. Alkor-Edition. Kassel, 1964–1965. (Edition by Fritz Oeser, first language German with French appended. Includes many variants and both the Opéra-Comique texts and the Guiraud recitatives.)

———. *Carmen*. Klavierauszug by Robert Didion. Schott, Mainz, 2000. Orchestral score, Eulenberg, Mainz, 2003.

———. *Carmen*. Vocal score by Richard Langham Smith. Peters Edition, 2013. (Orchestral score on hire and revised edition forthcoming.)

———. *Carmen*. 'Comprehensive edition' by Michael Rot. Hermann, Vienna, 2015.

WEBSITE

The most comprehensive catalogue of scores of *Carmen* will be found on Hugh Macdonald's Bizet Catalogue, http://digital.wustl.edu/bizet/

LIBRETTO

Meilhac, Henri, and Ludovic Halévy, *Carmen*. Livret. Opéra-comique en 4 actes. Tiré de la nouvelle de Prosper Mérimée. 8° (87pp). Calmann-Lévy, Paris, n.d. [1875].

Théâtre de Meilhac et Halévy. Paris, 1900–1902.

OTHER MANUSCRIPT SOURCES

Bizet, Georges. *Répertoire des œuvres de 241 compositeurs de musique (1686 à 1875)*. (Catalogue of Bizet's own collection of scores). F-*Pn* (Musique).

Halévy, Ludovic. Fonds Halévy: *Œuvres et cahiers ; Journal intime ; Dossier de presse ; papiers ; Notes et souvenirs*. F-*Pn* (Manuscripts). 1872–1876.

MÉRIMÉE SOURCES

Editions of Mérimée's *Carmen*

Mérimée, Prosper. *Carmen*, *Revue des deux mondes*, 1 October 1845.

———. *Columba* and *Carmen*. Ed. Edmund Gosse, with a preface by Arthur Symons. London, 1907.

———. *Carmen* etc. Introduction by Auguste Dupouy. Paris, 1927.

———. *Carmen: A Romance*. Trans. Lady Mary Loyd, with a study of the opera by Winton Dean. London, 1949.
———. *Œuvres*. Preface by Georges Amex. Lausanne, 1959.
———. *Romans et nouvelles*. Ed. Maurice Parturier. 2 vols. Paris, 1967. (Includes *Lettres d'Espagne*.)
———. *Carmen*. Ed. Jean Balsamo. Paris, 1996.
———. *Carmen*. Ed. Adrian Goetz. Paris, 2000.

Other Works of Mérimée

Mérimée, Prosper. *Théâtre de Clara Gazul, comedienne espagnole*. Paris, 1825.
———. *Lettres à une inconnue*. Paris, 1874.
———. *Correspondance générale*. Ed. Maurice Parturier with Pierre Josserand and Jean Mallion. 17 vols. Paris and Toulouse, 1941–1961.

Mérimée Studies

Bataillon, Marcel. 'L'Espagne de Mérimée d'après sa correspondance'. *Revue de Littérature Comparée*, XXII (1948): pp. 35–66.
Cogman, Peter. *Columba and Carmen*. London, 1992.
Darcos, Xavier. *Prosper Mérimée*. Paris 1998.
Dupouy, Auguste. *'Carmen' de Mérimée*. Paris, 1930.
Freustié, Jean. *Prosper Mérimée*. Paris 1982.
Géal, François. *Relire les 'Lettres d'Espagne' de Mérimée*. Paris, 2010.
Ozwald, Thierry. 'Une figure propitiatoire : Le touriste anglais, dans trois nouvelles de Mérimée'. *French Studies Bulletin*, 95 (Summer 2005): pp. 8–12.
Pommier, Jean. 'Notes sur *Carmen*'. *Bulletin de la Faculté des Lettres de Strasbourg*, Nov. 1929–Apr. 1930.
Raitt, Alan. *Prosper Mérimée*. New York, 1970.
Requena, Clarisse. *Unité et dualité dans l'œuvre de Prosper Mérimée : Mythe et récit*. Paris, 2000.
Trahard, Pierre, and Pierre Josserand. *La Jeunesse de Prosper Mérimée*. Paris, 1925.
———. *Prosper Mérimée de 1834 à 1853*. Paris, 1928.
———. *Bibliographie des œuvres de Prosper Mérimée*. Paris, 1929; rpt. 1971.

WORKS ON BIZET

Bellaigue, Camille. *Georges Bizet*. Paris, 1890.
Bizet, Georges. *Lettres, 1850–1875*. Ed. Cl. Glayman. Paris, 1989.

Blaze de Bury, Henri. *Musiciens du passé du présent et de l'avenir*. Paris, 1880: pp. 317–330.

Bois, Mario. *Comment Carmen tua Bizet*. Paris, 2013.

Cardoze, Michel. *Georges Bizet*. Paris, 1982.

Curtiss, Mina. *Bizet and his World*. London, 1959. French edition: *Bizet et son temps*. Paris, 1961.

Dean, Winton. '*Carmen*: An Attempt at a True Evaluation'. *The Music Review* (1946): pp. 209–220.

———. *Bizet*. Master Musicians. London, 1948; rev. ed. 1975.

———. *Georges Bizet: His Life and Work*. Rev. ed. London, 1965.

———. 'The True *Carmen*?' *The Musical Times* (Nov. 1965): pp. 846–855. Rpt. in *Essays on Opera*. Oxford, 1990.

———. 'The Corruption of *Carmen*: The Peril of Pseudo-musicology'. *Musical Newsletters* (October 1973): pp. 7–12.

Galabert, Edmond. *Georges Bizet : Souvenirs et correspondance*. Paris, 1877.

Gauthier-Villars, Henri [Willy]. *Bizet*. Les Musiciens Célèbres. Paris, 1928.

Lacombe, Hervé. *Georges Bizet*. Paris, 2000.

Landormy, Paul. *Bizet*. Paris, 1950.

Macdonald, Hugh. *Bizet*. Master Musicians. Oxford, 2014.

Musica. Bizet issue. June 1912.

Robert, Frédéric. *Georges Bizet*. Paris, 1965; rev. ed. 1981.

STUDIES OF *CARMEN*

Beardsley, Théodore. 'The Spanish Musical Sources of Bizet's Carmen'. *Inter-American Music Review* (1989): pp. 143–146.

Cooper, Martin. *Bizet, 'Carmen'*. ENO Opera Guide. London, 1947.

Gaudier, Ch. *Carmen de Bizet : Étude historique et critique, analyse musicale*. Paris, 1922.

Gribenski, Jean. 'Autour d'un fragment de la partition de *Carmen*'. *Revue de Musicologie* (1978): pp. 109–111.

Heim, Matthieu. '*Carmen* : L'identité espagnole en question'. *Revue Musicale de Suisse Romande* (June 2014): pp. 4–24.

Istel, Edgar. '*Carmen:* Novel and Libretto'. *Musical Quarterly* (1921): pp. 493–510.

———. Bizet und *Carmen*. Stuttgart, 1927.

Klein, J. W. 'The Two Versions of *Carmen*'. *Musical Opinion*, 3 (1949): pp. 291–293.

———. 'The Spoken Dialogue in *Carmen*'. *The Chesterian*, 33 (1959): pp. 109–113.

Lacombe, Hervé. 'La Version primitive de l'air d'entrée de Carmen : Réflexion sur la dramaturgie et "l'autorialité" d'un opéra'. In *Aspects de l'opéra français de Meyerbeer à Honegger*, ed. J. C. Branger and Vincent Giroud. Lyon, 2009.

———, and Christine Rodriguez. *La Habanera de Carmen : Naissance d'un tube.* Paris, 2014.
Landormy, Paul. *Bizet.* Paris, 1950.
Laparra, Raoul. *Bizet et l'Espagne.* Paris 1935.
Lowe, David A. 'Pushkin and *Carmen*'. *19th Century Music,* 20/1 (1996): pp. 72–76.
Macías, Rafael Utrera, and Virginia Guarinos. *Carmen global: El mito en las artes y los medios audiovisuales.* Seville, 2010.
Maingueneau, Dominique. *'Carmen' : Les Racines d'un myth.* Paris, 1985.
Malherbe, Henry. *Carmen,* Paris, 1951.
Poupet, Michel. 'A propos de deux fragments de la partition originale de *Carmen*'. *Revue de Musicologie* (1976): pp. 139–143.
Ravoux-Rallo, E. *Carmen.* Paris, 1997.
Tiersot, Julien. 'Bizet and Spanish Music'. *Musical Quarterly,* 13 (1927): pp. 566–581.
Wright, Lesley A. 'A New Source for *Carmen*'. *19th Century Music,* 2/1 (1978): pp. 61–71.
———. *Dossier de presse Parisienne.* Weinsberg, 2001.

GENERAL BIBLIOGRAPHY

Aguilera. Emiliano M. *Los trajes populares de España vistos por los pintores españoles.* Barcelona, 1948.
Alonso, Celsa. 'La Réception de la chanson espagnole dans la musique française du XIX siècle'. In *Échanges musicaux franco-espagnols XVIIe–XIXe siècles,* ed. François Lesure. Villecroze, 2000: pp. 123–160.
———. 'En el espejo de "los otros": Andalucismo, exotismo e hispanismo'. *Creación musical, cultura popular y construcción nacional en la España contemporánea.* Madrid, 2010.
Álvarez Junco, José. *Mater dolorosa: La idea de España en el siglo XIX.* Madrid, 2001.
Álvaro Ocáriz, José Andrés. *Sebastián Iradier.* Álava, 2016.
Arkin, Lisa C. 'Spanish Seductress or Sublime Stylist: Authenticity or Exoticism in Fanny Elssler's *La cachucha*'. *Dance Reconstructed* (Oct. 1992): pp. 65–72.
Artola, Miguel de. *Los Afrancesados.* Madrid, 1953.
Auraix-Jonchière, Pascale, and Gérard Loubinoux (eds). *La Bohémienne : Figure poétique de l'errance aux XVIIIième et XIXe siècles.* Clermont-Ferrand, 2003.
L'Avant-scène. 'Carmen'. Nos. 26 and 251 (1980/2009).
Aymes, Jean-René. *Séville sous le regard des voyageurs français.* Paris, 2003.
———. *Españoles en Paris en la época romántica, 1808–1848.* Madrid, 2008.
Baker, Evan. 'The Scene Designs for the first Performance of Bizet's *Carmen*'. *19th Century Music,* 13/3 (1990): pp. 230–242.
———. *From the Score to the Stage.* Chicago, 2013.
Balard, Françoise. *Geneviève Straus: Biographie et correspondance avec Ludovic Halévy, 1855–1908.* Paris, 2002.

Bara, Olivier. 'Les Bohémiens à l'opéra au XIXe siècle : Du spectacle de l'autre au drame de l'altérité'. In *Le Mythe des Bohémiens dans la littérature et les arts en Europe*, ed. Sarge Moussa. Paris, 2008.

Barthélemy. *L'Art de fumer ; ou, La Pipe et la cigare*. Poème en trois chants. Paris, 1844.

Bartoli, J.-P. 'L'Orientalisme dans la musique française du XIX siècle: La *ponctuation*, la seconde augmentée et l'apparition de la modalité dans les procédures exotiques'. *Revue Belge de Musicologie*, 51 (1997): pp. 137–170.

Bates, Katherine. *Spanish Highways and Byways*. New York, 1900.

Bégin, Émile. *Voyage pittoresque en Espagne et en Portugal*. Illustrations by Rouargue Frères. Paris, 1852.

Bellman, Jonathan. *The Style Hongrois in the Music of Western Europe*. Boston, 1998.

Bennahum, Ninotchka Devorah. *Carmen: A Gypsy Geography*. Middletown, CT, 2013.

Bergadà, Montserrat. 'Musiciens espagnols à Paris entre 1820 et 1868 : état de la question et perspectives d'études'. In *La Musique entre France et Espagne: Interactions stylistiques, 1870–1939*, ed. Louis Jambou. Paris, 2001: pp. 17–38.

Blasis, Carlo. *Code complet de la danse*. Paris, 1830.

Blondel, Spire. *Le Tabac : le livre des fumeurs et des priseurs*. Paris, 1891.

Bois, Mario. *Manet: Tauromachie et autres thèmes espagnols*. Paris, 1994.

———. *La Trilogie de Séville: Don Juan, Figaro, Carmen*. Paris, 1999.

Borrow, George. *La Bible en Espagne*. Paris, 1845.

———. *Esquisses de la vie des Gitanos d'Espagne*. Paris, 1845.

Briggs, A. D. P. 'Did *Carmen* Really Come from Russia (with a Little Help from Turgenev)?' In *Turgenev and Russian Culture: Essays to Honour Richard Peace*, comp. Derek Offord. Amsterdam, 2008.

Bueno Carrera, José Maria. *La Guardia Civil*. Madrid, 1977.

Calderón, Serafín Estébanez. *Escenas Andaluzas*. Illustrations by Lemeyer. Madrid, 1847.

Cars, Jean de. *Eugénie, la dernière impératrice*. Paris, 2003.

Casares Rodicio, Emilio. *Diccionario de la Zarzuela española y hispanoamericana*. Madrid, 2002.

Cham. *Douze années comiques: 1,000 dessins par Cham*. Introduction by Ludovic Halévy. Paris, 1880.

Champfleury. *Le Réalisme*. Paris, 1857.

Chantavoine, Jean. 'Quelques inédits de Georges Bizet'. *Le Ménestrel* (4 Aug. and 22 Sept. 1933).

Charnon-Deutsch, Lou. *The Spanish Gypsy: The History of a European Obsession*. University Park, PA, 2004.

Christoforidis, Michael, and Elizabeth Kertesz. *Carmen and the Staging of Spain: Recasting Bizet's Opera in the Belle Epoque*. Oxford, 2019.

Clément and Larousse. *Dictionnaire lyrique, troisième supplément*. Paris, 1977. (Entry on *Carmen*.)

Cobaleda, Mariate. *El simbolismo del toro*. Madrid, 2002.
Cohen, H. Robert. 'La Conservation de la tradition scènique sur la scène lyrique en France au XIX siècle : Les livrets de mise en scène et la Bibliothèque de l'Association de la Régie Théâtrale'. *Revue de Musicologie* (1978): pp. 253–257.
———. *Les Gravures musicales dans 'L'Illustration', 1843–1899*. Québec, 1983.
———, and M. O. Gigou. *Cent ans de mise en scène lyrique en France*. New York, 1986.
Collie, Michael. *George Borrow: Eccentric*. Cambridge, 1982.
Contreras Iñiguez, Montserrat. *Pliegos de cordel y romances de ciego durante el romanticismo: Bandoleros y delincuentes en Andalucía*. Granada, 2011.
Coons, Lorraine. 'Artiste or Coquette? "Les petits rats" of the Paris Opera Ballet'. *French Cultural Studies*, 25/2 (2014): pp. 140–164.
Courthion, P., and P. Cailler. *Manet raconté par lui-même et par ses amis*. Geneva, 1945.
Davillier, Le Baron Ch. *L'Espagne*. Illustrated with 309 engravings by Gustave Doré. Paris, 1874.
De Carmen à Bizet. Exh. cat. Bougival, 2001.
De Pauli, Domenico. 'Bizet and his Spanish sources'. *The Chesterian*, XXII (January 1948).
Descola, Jean. *La Vie quotidienne en Espagne au temps de Carmen*. Paris, 1971.
Diccionario de la música española e latina-americana. Ed. Emilio Casares Rodicio. Madrid, 1999–2004.
Don Preciso [pseud. Juan Antonio de Iza Zamácola]. *Colección de las mejores coplas de seguidillas, tiranas y polos que se han compuesto para cantar a la guitarra, con un discurso sobre las causas de la corrupción y abatimiento de la música española*. Madrid, 1799; rpt. 1805, 1816.
Douglass, Carrie B. *Bulls, Bullfighting and Spanish Identities*. Tucson, AZ, 1999.
Driessen, Henk. 'The Noble Bandit and the Bandit of the Nobles'. *European Journal of Sociology*, 24 (1983): pp. 96–114.
Dumas, Alexandre. *Impressions de voyage : De Paris à Cadix*. Paris, 1846.
Duret, Théodore. *Manet y España*. Paris, n.d.
Échos d'Espagne. Ed. P. Lacome and J. Puig y Alsubide. Paris, [1872].
Elssler, Fanny. *Materialen*. Vienna, 1984.
Etzion, J. 'The Spanish Fandango, from Eighteenth-Century Lasciviousness to Nineteenth-Century Exoticism'. *Anuario Musical* (1993): pp. 229–250.
Exil politique et migration économique : Espagnols et Français aux XIXe–XXe siècles. Paris, 1991.
Exposition Georges Bizet. Exh. cat. Paris, 1938.
Fauquet, Joël-Marie. *Lalo*. Madrid, 1980.
Fitzlyon, April. *The Price of Genius: A Life of Pauline Viardot*. London, 1964.
Gallet, Louis. *Notes d'un librettiste*. Paris, 1891.
Gasser, Luis (ed.). *Estudios sobre Fernando Sor*. Madrid, 2003.
Gautier, Théophile. *Voyage en Espagne*. Paris, 1843.

———. *Histoire de l'art dramatique en France depuis vingt ans*. Paris, 1858–1859.

———. *Histoire du romantisme*. Paris, 1874.

———. *Écrits sur la danse*. Ed. Martine Kahane. Lyon, 1995.

Girard, Pauline. *Léo Delibes : Itinéraire d'un musicien des Bouffes-Parisiens à l'Institut*. Paris, 2018.

Gisbert, Rafael. *José Melchior Gomis : Un músico romántico y su tiempo*. Ointinyent, 1988.

———. 'Luis Viardot et le compositeur José Melchior Gomis : Une amitié de jeunesse'. *Cahiers Ivan Tourgueniev*, 12 (1988).

Gistau Ferrando, Miguel. *La Guardia Civil: Historia de este instituto.*

Gobineau, Arthur-Joseph. *Essai sur l'inégalité des races humaines*. Paris, 1853–1855.

Goetschy, Gustave. *Les Jeunes peintres militaires*. Paris, 1878.

Gómez Amat, Carlos. *Historia de la música española, siglo XIX*. Madrid, 1984.

González Lopez, Carlos, and Axelá, Martí. *Pintores españoles en París, 1850–1900*. Barcelona, 1989.

Gonzalez-Troyano, Alberto. *La desventura de Carmen: Una divagación sobre Andalucía*. Madrid, 1991.

———, et al. *La imagen de Andalucía en los viajeros románticos*. 1984 conference proceedings. Málaga, 1987.

Goya, Francisco. *Los desastres de la guerra*. Madrid, 1863.

Grut, T. Marina. *The Bolero School*. London, 2002.

Grellmann, Heinrich. *Histoire des Bohémiens ; ou, Tableau des mœurs, usages et coutumes de ce people nomade, suivie de recherches historiques sur leur origine*. Paris, 1810. (Translated from the 12th German edition.)

Guest, Ivor. *The Romantic Ballet in Paris*. London, 1966.

———. *The Ballet of the Second Empire*. London, 1974.

Hansen, Eric C. *Ludovic Halévy: A Study of Frivolity and Fatalism in Nineteenth-Century France*. Lanham, MD, 1987.

Hauk, Minnie. *Memories of a Singer*. New York, 1925; rpt. 1977.

Hemingway, Ernest. *Death in the Afternoon*. London and New York, 1932.

Hewitt, R. M. 'Pushkin, Mérimée and Borrow'. *Journal of the Gypsy Lore Society*, 23 (1944).

Hoffmann, Léon-François. *Romantique Espagne : L'Image de l'Espagne en France, 1800–1850*. Paris, 1961.

Houghton-Walker, Sarah. *Representations of the Gypsy in the Romantic Era*. Oxford, 2014.

Huebner, Steven. '*Carmen*' de Georges Bizet: Une corrida de toros'. In *Le Théâtre lyrique en France au XIXe siècle*, ed. Paul Prévost. Metz, 1995: pp. 181–218.

Hutchinson Guest, Ann. *Fanny Elssler's Cachucha*. London, 2008.

J. de O. [Anon.]. *La Petra Camara, biographie*. Paris, 1853.

Jacobshagen, Arnold. 'Staging at the Opéra Comique in Nineteenth-Century Paris: Auber's *Fra Diaolo* and the *Livrets de mise en scène*'. *Cambridge Opera Journal*, 13/3 (2001): pp. 239–260.

Jeffrey, Brian. *Fernando Sor, composer and guitarist*. London, 1977.

———. *España de la guerra: The Spanish political and military songs of the war in Spain, 1808–1814*. London, 2017.

Jordan, Ruth. *Fromenthal Halévy: His Life and Music*. London, 1994.

Lacombe, Hervé. 'Destins mêlés, Bizet et les Halévy.' In *Entre le théâtre et l'histoire : La Famille Halévy, 1760–1960*. Exh. cat. Paris, 1996: pp. 100–105.

———. *Les Voies de l'opéra français au XIXe siècle*. Paris, 1997.

———. 'L'Espagne à l'Opéra-Comique avant *Carmen* : Du *Guitarrero* de Halévy (1841) à *Don César de Bazan* de Massenet (1872). In *Échanges musicaux franco-espagnols, XVIIe–XIXe siècles*, ed. François Lesure. Villecroze, 2000: pp. 123–160.

———. 'L'Espagne à Paris au milieu du XIXe siècle (1847–57)'. *Revue de Musicologie* (2002): pp. 389–431.

Lacouture, Jean. *Carmen : La Révoltée*. Paris, 2011.

Lainsa de Tomás, Eva. 'Canto y muerte de Escamillo'. *Revista de Estudios Taurinos* (1994): pp. 69–92.

Lalo, Edouard. *Correspondance*. Ed. Joël-Marie Fauquet. Paris, 1989.

Lanzagorta, J. Luis O de. *Las cigarreras*. Seville, 1981.

Laplace-Claverie, Hélène. 'Bohémiennes de ballet aux XIXe siècle'. In *La Bohémienne : Figure poétique de l'errance aux XVIIIième et XIXe siècles*, ed. Pascale Auraix-Jonchière and Gérard Loubinoux. Clermont-Ferrand, 2003.

Le Dhuy, Adolphe, and Henri Bertini. *Encyclopédie pittoresque de la musique*. Paris, 1853. (Entries on Bolero and Sor.)

Leblon, Bernard. *Les Gitans d'Espagne*. Paris, 1985.

———. *Gypsies and Flamenco*. Hatfield, 2000.

Les Bals de l'Opéra. Exh. cat. Paris, 1994.

'Les Espagnols à Paris'. *Revue Internationale de Musique Française*, 26 (June 1988).

Liszt, Franz. *Des Bohémiens et de leur musique en Hongrie*. Paris, 1859.

Locke, Ralph P. 'Nineteenth-Century Music: Quantity, Quality, Qualities'. *Nineteenth-Century Music Review*, 1/1 (2004): pp. 3–41.

———. *Musical Exoticism*. Cambridge, 2009.

———. 'Spanish Local Color in Bizet's *Carmen*: Unexplored Borrowings and Transformations'. In *Music, Theater and Cultural Transfer: Paris, 1830–1914*, ed. Annegret Fauser and Mark Everist. Chicago, 2009: pp. 316–360.

López Ontiveros, Antonio. *La imagen de Andalucía según los viajeros ilustrados y románticos*. Granada, 2008.

López Tabar, Juan. *Los famosos traidores: Los afrancesados durante la crisis de Antiguo Régimen (1808–1833)*. Madrid, 2001.

Loya, Shay. *Liszt's Transcultural Modernism and the Hungarian-Gypsy Tradition*. Rochester, 2011.

Luxenberg, Alisa. *Baron Taylor and his 'Voyage Pittoresque en Espagne'*. Madrid, 2013.

M. de R. [Anon.]. *Manuel del baratero; o, Arte de manejar la navaja, el cuchillo, la tigera de los gitanos*. Madrid, 1849.

Maingueneau, Dominique. *Féminin fatal*. Paris, 1999.

Manet, Edouard. *Voyage en Espagne*. Ed. Juliet Wilson-Bareau. Paris, 1988.

Manet and Spain. Exh. cat. Ann Arbor, MI, 1969.

Manet–Velásquez: La Manière espagnole au XIXe siècle. Exh. cat. Paris, 2002.

Manuel, Peter. 'From Scarlatti to "Guantanamera": Dual Tonicity in Spanish and Latin-American Musics'. *Journal of the American Musicological Society*, 55 (2002): pp. 311–336.

Martinez Ruiz, E. *Creación de la Guardia Civil*. Madrid, 1976.

McClary, Susan. *Carmen*. Cambridge Opera Handbook. Cambridge, 1992.

Meglin, Joellen A. 'Fanny Elssler's Cachucha and Women's Lives: Domesticity and Sexuality in France in the 1830s'. *Dance Reconstructed* (1993).

Mendès, Catulle. *Les Belles du monde*. Paris, 1898.

Méndez Rodriguez, Luis. *La imagen de Andalucía en el arte del siglo XIX*. Seville, 2008.

Mercado, José. *La Seguidilla gitana*. Madrid, 1982.

Michel, Francisque. *Histoire des races maudites de la France et de l'Espagne*. 2 vols. Paris, 1847.

———. *Le Pays basque : Sa population, sa langue, ses mœurs, sa littérature et sa musique*. Paris, 1857.

Mitjana, Rafael. 'XIXe siècle, Espagne', in *Encyclopédie de la musique et dictionnaire du Conservatoire*, 1ère partie. (Paris 1920) p. 2296 et seq.

Montes, Francisco. *Tauromaquia completa*. Madrid, 1836.

Murphy, Kerry. '*Carmen*: "Couleur locale" or The Real Thing?' In *Music, Theater and Cultural Transfer: Paris, 1830–1914*, ed. Annegret Fauser and Mark Everist. Chicago, 2009: pp. 293–315.

Museo Carmen-Thyssen, Málaga. *The Collection Guide*. Málaga, 2011.

Musset, Alfred de. *Contes d'Espagne et d'Italie* [1830]. Rpt. ed. with preface by Eileen le Breton. Paris, 1973.

Otero, J. *Tratado de bailes de Sociedad, regionales españoles, especialmente andaluces, con su historia de ejecutarlos*. Seville, 1912; rpt. 2012.

Peña y Goñi, Antonio. *La ópera española y la música dramática en España en el siglo XIX*. Madrid, 1881.

———. *La Pelota y los Pelotins*. Madrid, 1892.

Pigot, Charles. *Georges Bizet et son œuvre*. Paris, 1886; rev. ed. with preface by A. Boschot, 1912.

Pintura Andaluza en la collección Carmen Thyssen-Bornemisza. Exh. cat. Madrid, 2004.

Plaza Orellana, Rocio. *El Flamenco y los románticos: Un viaje entre el mito y la realidad*. Seville, 1999.

———. *Bailes de Andalucía en Londres y Paris*. Madrid, 2005.

———. *Los bailes españoles en Europa: El espectáculo de los bailes de España en el siglo XIX*. Cordoba, 2013.

Poliakov, Léon. *The Aryan Myth*. London, 1974.

Pougin, Arthur. *Marie Malibran : Histoire d'une cantatrice*. Paris, 1911.
Quinet, Edgar. *Mes vacances en Espagne*. Paris, 1846.
Quiros, C. Bernaldo de, and Luis Ardilla. *El Bandolerismo Andaluz*. Madrid, 1931; rpt. Valladoldid, 2005.
Radomski, James. *Manuel García (1775–1832): Chronicle of the Life of a Bel Canto Tenor at the Dawn of Romanticism*. Oxford, 2000.
Rees, Margaret. *French Authors on Spain, 1800–1850*. London, 1977.
Reina Palazón, Antonio. *La pintura costumbrista de Sevilla (1830–1870)*. Seville, 1979.
Reparaz, Carmen de. *Tauromaquia romántica*. Madrid, 2000.
Richardson, Joanna. *Théophile Gautier*. London, 1958.
Rodriguez, Christine. *Les Passions du récit à l'opéra : Rhétorique de la transposition dans Carmen, Mireille, Manon*. Paris, 2009.
Rodriguez Gordillo, José Mañuel. 'El personal obrero en la Real Fábrica de Tabacos'. *Sevilla y el tabaco*. Exh. cat. Seville, 1984.
———. *Historia de la Real Fábrica de Tabacos de Sevilla*. Seville, 2005.
Rutherford, Susan. 'Pretending To Be Wicked: Divas, Technology and the Consumption of Bizet's *Carmen*'. In *Technology and the Diva*, ed. Karen Henson. Cambridge, 2016: pp. 74–88.
Sala, C. *Méthode de castagnettes : Rédigée par M. J. L. Heugel d'après le système de C. Sala*. Paris, [1845].
Sánchez Mantero, R. *Liberales en el exilio*. Madrid, 1975.
———. *Estudios sobre Gibraltar política, diplomacia y cóntrabando en el siglo XIX*. Jerez, 1989.
Sanz de Pedre, Mariano. *El pasodoble español*. Madrid, 1961.
———. *La música en los toros y la música de los toros*. Madrid, 1981.
Séailles, Gabriel. *Alfred Dehodencq*. Paris, 1885; rpt. 1910.
Seymour, Bruce. *Lola Montez: A Life*. New Haven, CT, 1995.
Shubert, Adrian. *Death and Money in the Afternoon: A History of the Spanish Bullfight*. Oxford, 1999.
Smith, Richard Langham. '*Carmen*: From Mérimée to Bizet' and '*Carmen*: Libretto [translation]'. In *Carmen, Bizet*. Overture Opera Guides. London, 2013.
Smith, Richard Langham and Rowden, Clair. (eds.) Carmen *Abroad: Bizet's opera on the Global Stage*. Cambridge, 2020.
Solis Sanchez, Antonio de. *Anales de la Real Plaza de Toros de Sevilla*. 2 vols. Seville, 1992.
Soubies, A., and C. Malherbe. *Histoire de l'Opéra-Comique*. 2 vols. Paris, 1893.
Steen, Michael. *Enchantress of Nations: Pauline Viardot, Soprano, Muse and Lover*. Cambridge, 2007.
Steingress, Gerhard. *... y Carmen se fue a París*. Cordoba, 2006.
Taylor, Baron Justin. *Voyage pittoresque en Espagne, en Portugal et sur la côte d'Afrique, de Tanger à Tétouan*. Paris, 1826–1832.
Tinterow, Gary, et al. *The French Taste for Spanish Painting*. New Haven, CT, 2003.

Toro Buiza, Luis. *Sevilla en la historia del toreo*. Seville, 1947.

Ubersfeld, Anne. *Reading Theatre*. Toronto, 1999.

Una Puerta abierta al mundo: España en la litografía romántica. Exh. cat. Madrid, 1994.

Val, Venancio del. *Sebastián Iradier*. Álava, 1994.

Viardot, Louis. 'José Melchior Gomis'. *Le Siècle*, 30–31 July 1836.

———. Entry on 'Bohémien'. *Grand Larousse Universel*.

Vidal, José Perez. *España en la historia del tabaco*. Madrid, 1959.

Waddington, Patrick. *The Musical Works of Pauline Viardot-Garcia (1821–1910)*. Upper Hutt, New Zealand, 2004.

Wright, Lesley. 'The Directors of the Opéra-Comique (1870–1900): Responsibility and Opportunity'. In *The Opéra-Comique in the Eighteenth and Nineteenth Centuries*, ed. Lorenzo Frassà. Turnhout, 2001.

Zugasti, Julián. *El bandolerismo*. Ed. E. Inman Fox. Madrid, 1982.

SCORES AND LIBRETTI

Adam, Adolphe. *Le Toréador*. 1849.

Album de la Señores Viardot-García, Castellan y Alboni: Arias y canciones nacionales a una y a dos voces. Paris, [1860].

Asenjo Barbieri, Francisco. *Pan y toros*. Zarzuela, 1864. (Música Hispana 33, 2001.)

———. *El bandido José Maria*, 1865. (Théâtre des Variétés, Paris.)

Auber, Daniel. *Fra Diavolo*. 1855.

Los bailes nacionales: Seis canciones españolas. Madrid, 1850.

Balfe, Michael William. *La Zingara*.

———. *L'Étoile de Séville*. (Opéra IV). 1845. Ms. *Po*.

Bizet, Georges. *Vasco da Gama*. Ode Symphonique. 1860, 1863.

———. *Chants du Rhin*. Paris, 1866.

Castro de Gistau, Salvador. *Six séguidilles, ou chansons nationales espagnoles*. Paris [1830s?].

La canción andaluza. Música Hispana 3. Oviedo, 1996; 2nd ed. 2008.

La canción con acompañamiento de guitarra, siglo XIX. Música Hispana 2. Madrid, 1995.

Cien años de canción lírica española. Música Hispana 8, 12. Madrid, 2001, 2005.

Cohen, Jules. *José Maria*. (Opéra-Comique III). 1866.

Croisez, Alexandre. *Airs havanais variés*. Paris, 1861.

El eco de ambos mundos: Álbum filarmónico español bajo la dirección de los Profesores D. Santiago Figueras y D. Francisco Alonso. Madrid, 1852.

García, Mañuel. *Six chansons espagnoles à duo avec accompagnement de guitare*. n.d.

———. *Caprichos líricos españoles*. Paris, 1830.

———. *El Contrbandista: Air célèbre espagnol, comme chanté par Madame Malibran.* London, 1830.
———. *El Contrabandista: Tirana chanté dans tous les concerts par Mme. Malibran.* Berlin, 1838.
———. *Canciones y caprichos líricos.* Ed. Celsa Alonso. Musica Hispana 1. Madrid, 2003.
———. *La maja y el majo.* Ed. Juan de Udaeta. Musica Hispana 78. Madrid, 2008.
Gide, Casimir. *Le Diable boiteux.* 1836. Ms. F-*Po.*
Gomis, J. M. *Le Diable à Séville.* (Opéra-Comique I). 1831.
Liszt, Franz. *Rondeau fantastique sur un thème espagnol: El Contrabandista.* 1836.
———. *Feuille morte : Élegie pour piano d'après Soriano.*
Massenet, Jules. *Don César de Bazun.* (Opéra-Comique IV).
Paz, Narcisse. *Collection des meilleurs airs nationaux espagnoles, boleras et tiranas.* Paris, 1812–1813. *Deuxième collection,* 1815–1817.
———. *Collection(s) d'airs espagnols avec accompagnement de piano ou guitare.* Paris, 1818.
———. *Les beaux jours de Séville : Collection des plus jolis airs.* Paris, 1845.
Regalo lírico: Colección de boleras, seguidillas, tiranas y demás canciones españolas por los mejores autores de esta nación. Paris, 1831.
Sor, Fernando. *Seguidillas: 12 Songs for Voice and Guitar.* London, 1976.
Soriano Fuertes. *Ecos del Guadalquivir: Seis canciones españolas compuestas y dedicados a la Emperatriz de los Franceses, Eugenia de Guzmán.* Barcelona, 1853.
Yradier, Sebastien [Iradier]. *El Arreglito: Chanson havanaise chantée par Mlle Trebelli du Théâtre Italien.* Paris, n.d.
———. *Échos d'Espagne : Collection de chansons espagnoles chantées par Mmes Bosio, Pauline Viardot, Didier et Tedesco.* Paris, 1864.
———. *Chansons espagnoles del maestro Yradier : Paroles françaises de Paul Bernard et D. Tagliafico.* Paris 1865/1870.
———. *Fleurs d'Espagne : Chansons espagnoles par le Chevalier de Yradier.* Mayence, 1874.

Index

Adam, Adolphe
Le Toréador 242
afrancesados 6–9, 15, 19, 24–5, 33–4, 67
Aguado, Dionisio 17, 22–3
Alberti bass 4, 19, 29
Ambre, Émilie 62–3
the Americas 7–8, 11, 38, 45, 47, 67, 75, 77, 87–8, 98, 134, 141, 168, 233
see also Latin America
alhambrismo 96
andalucismo 14, 35, 41, 46, 96, 127–8, 134, 143
in dance 65, 83, 235
in illustration and painting 33, 41, 85, 208
as a marketable commodity 29, 33
Astruc, Zacharie 59, 85
Sérénade 86–7
Auber, Daniel
Les Diamants de la couronne 243
Le Domino noir 187
'Come, wander with me,' 242
Fra Diavolo 116, 172–3
La Muette de portici 164

Balfe, Michael
La Bohémienne (*The Bohemian Girl*) 244
L'Étoile de Séville 67, 244
Ballet 64–6, 68–70, 72–5, 78–86, 250
bandoleros/bandolerismo (bandits/banditry) 38–9, 49, 52–9, 61, 94, 97–8, 115, 160, 179, 193, 195, 198, 201–2, 204, 209–10, 212, 214–16, 244
Barbieri, Francisco Asenjo
Pan y toros 127, 158
Barthélemy, Auguste Marseille 203, 204
Baudelaire, Charles 59, 63, 85–6
Beethoven, Ludwig van
Wellingtons Sieg 4–5
Bejarano, Manuel Cabral 46
Bizet, Geneviève (see under Halévy) 106, 247
Bizet, Georges 60–62, 134 + n20, 135–8, 224, 247–8
L'Arlésienne 250
Carmen
Libretto (See also Halévy, Ludovic and Meilhac, Henri) 48, 50, 91–160, 164, 171, 173–5, 179, 188, 193, 196–203, 206, 210, 212, 214–15, 217, 219–20, 224–5, 229–31, 245, 248, 253–4, 257, 260, 262–5, 274
ACT I
Prelude 113, 125–30, 132–3, 158–9, 218, 246 + n5, 247, 253
Carmen's entrance 35, 67, 75, 122, 132–5, 138, 143, 229, 263
Childrens' chorus 114, 131–2, 169, 206–7, 247
Cigarières' chorus 95, 101, 132, 171, 204, 258–9
Conclusion 145–6, 263–4
Illustrations of early stagings 167, 204, 212, 257–8, 262–5, 273–4
Habanera 26, 33, 35, 75, 124, 132–8, 241, 258, 263, 268
Interrogation scene 102–4, 113, 140–3, 224, 251, 253, 263–4
José/Micaëla duet 120–21, 138–9, 155, 216, 248
Scène et Pantomime/Scène de l'Anglais 80, 161–89, 246–7, 249, 263, 273
Soldiers' chorus 50, 130
ACT II
Chanson bohème 22, 29, 62, 146, 242–4, 252–3, 264, 270

Entry of Escamillo 147–8, 213, 260
Flower song 125, 139, 150, 152, 265
Quintet 57n29, 121, 149, 226
'La Flamenca' (interpolated ballet) 65
Romalis/Ole (Carmen's dance for José) 75, 102, 130, 146, 150–1, 210–11, 214–15, 230–4, 237, 248, 251, 253, 260–6, 271
Toreador song 125, 127–8, 148, 154, 159, 269
ACT III
Card scene 114, 125, 145, 154, 157, 179–80, 199, 265, 272
Entr'acte 57, 152–3
José and Escamillo's fight 52–3, 122, 154–5, 180, 199, 225, 249, 261, 265, 272–3
Micaëla's aria 154, 216
Smugglers' chorus 57–9, 95, 121, 152
ACT IV
cuadrilla (procession) 94, 159, 215, 217–18, 262, 265–6
Entr'acte 16+n21, 29, 155–7, 246–7, 253
Finale 122, 125+n2, 155, 262, 266–7, 272–4
GENERAL
Carmen's motive 109, 114, 126–30, 133, 137–40, 152, 154, 156–9, 221, 241–2
Cigarreras/cigarières 50, 52, 95, 132, 138–40, 170–1, 204–9, 258–9, 270
Contrabandistas/smugglers (Le Dancaïre and Le Remondado) 38, 49, 55–9, 116, 118, 120, 149–50, 152, 154, 175–9, 195, 199, 202, 213, 226–7, 265
Costume 36–7, 48–9, 81, 84–7, 94, 101, 113, 122, 268–72
Curtain-up 36, 98, 122, 130, 132, 146, 152, 167, 212, 251–2, 257–8, 264
Dance 75, 78–88, 105, 113, 122, 143, 146–7, 211, 214–15, 250–3, 260–1, 264–5, 270–1
Don José 50–2, 55, 72, 75, 79, 92, 94, 96, 98, 101, 103–4, 107–22, 113–15, 117–21, 125, 130–2, 137–9, 142–3, 145–6, 150–2, 154–5, 158–60, 171, 173n13, 176–80, 196, 203, 206, 210–12, 214–16, 220, 224–6, 230–3, 249, 258, 260–5, 273–4
Don José's mother 110, 114, 116–18, 120–1, 138–9, 196, 220, 261–6, 274
Escamillo 52, 104, 112–13, 115, 122, 127, 147–9, 154–5, 159, 180, 199, 213, 217, 220, 225, 226n17, 249, 262, 264–7, 269, 273
Frasquita and Mercédès 112, 117, 175, 179–80, 251, 262, 264, 270, 272
Gamins (urchins, children: see also Act I childrens' chorus) 58, 130–2, 152, 169–70, 206–7, 220, 247, 263
Harmonic/Key-structure 125, 131–2, 138–9, 142–5, 149, 159, 221
Illustrations 46–7, 120, 151, 249, 266–73
Libretto 39, 41, 48, 50, 56, 91–160, 162, 164, 166, 171, 173–4, 179, 187, 193, 196–201, 203, 206, 210–12, 214–15, 217, 219–20, 224–6, 229–31, 245–6, 248, 253–4, 257, 260, 262–5, 270–4
Lillas Pastia 62, 111, 113, 144, 150, 212–15, 260
Manuscripts (See also Bibliography) 129, 141, 247–9
Micaëla 50, 77–8, 109–10, 112, 114–18, 120–1, 129, 131, 138–9, 154–5, 162, 187, 196, 199, 204, 211, 213, 216, 220, 226+n17, 248, 257, 259, 261–2, 265–6, 271–2
Mise en scène 45n14, 98n12, 110, 167–71, 212–14, 220, 225–6, 253–63, 266, 271–4
Moralès 131, 161–6, 185, 187–8, 213, 247, 257–8, 264
Reception 104–6, 115–16, 121–3, 126, 185–9, 250, 257, 261, 264
Revivals/later stagings 44–8, 104, 149, 154, 162, 219–20, 248, 255–6, 260, 262, 267
Scenography 36–7, 44–7, 113, 120, 122, 130, 161–89, 249, 252–74
Scores 47, 106, 125n2, 129, 134, 141–2, 144–6, 150–1, 154–5, 159–63, 166, 245–50, 262, 266–71, 273–4
Séguedille (*Seguidilla*) 9–10, 15–16, 18–19, 22–3, 67, 73–5, 81, 142–6, 213, 240–1, 259, 263–4
Soldiers 39, 95, 110, 113–14, 120, 130–1, 140, 162–4, 172–3, 210–11, 213, 215, 220–1, 224, 232, 257–9, 264, 270–1
Recordings (Audio)
1908 (in German) 248n11
1911 (in French) 121, 129n12, 146, 149, 175+n16, 241, 253, 264
2003 (includes 'Scène de l'Anglais') 162n5
(Video) 162n5

Zuniga 50, 101–2, 111, 114, 120, 130, 140, 145, 148, 152, 171, 199, 202 + n12, 213–14, 224+n10, 251, 263–5, 270
Chants du Rhin : 'La Bohémienne' 242–3
Don Rodrigue 60
Grisélidis 152
La jolie Fille de Perth 242
Les Pêcheurs de perles 106
Blasis, Carlo 66–7, 73, 75, 164–5
Boieldieu, François-Adrien,
La Dame blanche 130
Boigne, Charles de 80
Bois, Mario 85
Borrow, George 219, 222–3, 228, 233, 234n40, 237–9
The Zincali 228, 239
Bournonville, August,
La Sylphide 65
Brahms, Johannes,
Hungarian Dances 240n54
Bullfighting 38–9, 48, 58–61, 96–7, 112–13, 125–8, 132, 148–9, 158–9, 200–1, 217–18, 252
banderillos 42, 93, 197
cuadrilla (procession) 94, 127, 158, 200, 215, 217, 262, 266
matador (torero, toréador) 39, 42, 48, 58–60, 93–4, 113, 117, 127, 147–9, 158, 194, 197, 201, 217–18, 241, 248
picadors/chulos 44, 94, 148–9, 159, 217

Calderón, Estébanez, (El Solitario) 41–2, 51, 96–7, 99, 194, 195, 200, 206
Escenas andaluzas 41–3, 48, 52, 96–7
Cámara, Petra 83–6
Camprubí, Juan 76, 77
Les Contrebandiers de la Sierra Nevada 67
Camprubí, Mariano 85
Can-Can 68, 71
Canteloube, Joseph 30
Carmen La Cigarrera 235
Carré, Albert 44–8, 104, 219, 267, 269
Carvalho, Léon 188
cassia flower/fleur de cassie/senna pod 45–6, 118–20, 137–9, 258
castanets, 22, 29, 49, 65–6, 76, 78, 80, 84–5, 101–2, 111–12, 146, 154, 214–15, 232, 237, 240, 242, 250–3, 260, 264–5, 270–1
casticismo 96, 194–5
Cererols, Joan 18
Cervantes, Miguel de 12
Don Quixote 101n18
La gitanilla 224, 244
Chabrier, Emmanuel 29n33, 32, 61–2
España 32
'Cham' (Charles Amédée de Noé) 184–5
Chassériau, Théodore 86
Cherubini, Luigi 25, 126
Chopin, Frédéric, 14, 32
Choudens père et fils (see also under Carmen: scores 275–6) 134, 141, 146, 150, 154, 155n37, 162n6, 166, 245, 256, 248–50, 267
cigarreras (factory girls) See under Spain/Andalusia/cigarreras.
Circourt, Adolphe de 237
Colbran, Isabella 16
Commetant, Oscar: quoted 251
contrabandistas (smugglers) 14, 38, 49, 54–7, 59, 118, 120–2, 149–50, 152, 154, 175, 193, 201–3, 213–14
Coralli, Jean, (choreographer)
Giselle 77
Le Diable boiteux 77–8
costumbristas 41–2, 45–62, 84–5, 96, 146–7, 194n5, 196–7, 212, 257, 269–70
in painting/illustration, 41–2, 45–8, 49, 52–3, 55, 58, 59, 60, 62, 85, 147, 269–70
Courbet, Gustave 86
Cuendias, Manuel de, and V. de Féréal 39, 44
Custine, Marquis de 39–42, 49–51, 194n5, 196–7

Dance (Spanish and gitano) 9, 13, 15–16, 64–88, 212–14, 222, 232–7
bolero and seguidilla-bolero 9, 16, 19, 21–3, 64–7, 73–6, 82, 142, 146–7, 157–8, 213, 232, 240
cachucha 67, 72, 74–81, 147, 251
escuela bolera 64–6, 76, 82, 85, 125, 143
fandango 9, 23, 65, 67, 76, 232
flamenco 46, 65, 73, 85, 86, 142, 235
habanera 33, 35, 200, 241 see also under Carmen: Act I
pasodoble 126–7, 131, 159, 240, 252
pasodoble taurino 126–8, 148, 158, 252
pas redoublé 126

polo 9, 15–16, 29–30, 65, 67, 155, 156, 253
romalis/ole 102, 130–1, 151, 211, 214–15, 230–7, 239, 248–50, 253, 260, 270
sevillanas 34, 134
tirana 9–10, 15 + ex1.2, 16, 32
vals (waltz) 15, 142, 143
zarabanda 236
zorongo 243–4
zortzico 113, 139
Darzens, Rodolphe (and Catulle Mendès)
Les Belles du monde 223–5
Davillier, Baron 38+n4, 39, 53–4, 180–3, 207, 234–7
Dean, Winton 26n30, 122–3, 137, 161, 247
Debussy, Claude 60, 63
Dehodencq, Alfred 46
Detaille, Édouard 132, 270
'Don Preciso' (Juan Antonio de Iza Zamácola) 9+n7, 10, 13, 64, 66, 219
Doré, Gustave 38–9, 46, 53–4, 58–9, 99, 131, 180–4, 207, 234–6, 273
Driessen, Henk 209–10
Dumas *père*, Alexandre 39, 196, 233–4, 237
Duret, Théodore 61, 85
Duvernoy, Edmond 165–6, 173, 187, 246n8, 247

Elssler, Fanny 34, 71–2, 74–81, 86–8, 146, 164, 251
Empress Eugénie *see* Montijo family: Eugenia
England/English (also British) 38, 51, 69, 80, 161–89, 243
Bristol 56, 168
London 10, 24–5, 36, 38, 51, 56n27, 66–7, 72, 82–3, 169, 184
as centre of music publishing 4, 7, 19–20, 134, 156n40
Hyde Park 'Great Exhibition,' 83
Illustrated London Life 72
Spanish emigrés 7, 25, 67, 169
Her Majesty's Theatre 82
King's Theatre 66
Somerstown 25
military in Spain 3–4, 8, 173, 179
Spanish emigrés 7, 25
trade with Spain 56, 168–9, 174
travellers to Spain (see also Gibraltar) 36–7, 56+n27, 173–4, 180–1, 201, 213, 216, 232–3
see also Gibraltar
épinglette (priming pin) 72, 96, 119–20, 137, 270
era Josefina 4, 5, 9, 12–13, 18+n22, 19, 40, 65, 194, 198, 232
Escalonia de Montserrat 17

Faure, Jean-Baptiste 62, 85
Fernando VII, King of Spain 3, 9, 24, 39–40, 56
Fétis, François-Joseph 14
Flores, Antonio 207
Fontana, Uranio 69, 70n9
Ford, Richard 54, 56–7, 232–3
France/French 35, 66, 85, 211, 227
Bayonne 12, 64
Bougival 247
Marseillaise, La 4
Montretout, Saint-Cloud 182–3
Paris/Parisians 64, 66–88, 124, 184–5, 218
Ambigu-Comique 68
Bibliothèque nationale de France 25–6, 33–4, 247
Commune 181, 185
Conservatoire 106
Expositions universelles 59
Folies dramatiques 68
Gymnase-Dramatique 83, 84+n34
Hippodrome 68, 85
Hôtel Favart 24
Jockey Club 82
Music publishers 7, 14, 19–20, 25–7, 35, 88, 134, 156n40
Odéon 85
Opéra-Comique (See also Salle Favart) 60, 62, 68, 105–8, 107n32, 115–16, 124–5, 129, 131, 135–6, 139, 142–3, 154, 158, 161, 166, 172–3, 175–6, 187, 189, 212, 216, 218, 221, 242–5, 247–9, 253, 257, 262, 265–7
Chorus 152
Palais Royale 81
Théâtre Italien 12, 24
Salle Favart 11, 158
Salle Ventadour 16, 67
Théâtre de la Renaissance 68
Théâtre lyrique 244
Théâtre Molière 68
Théâtre National de l'Opéra 67–8, 70, 72–3, 77, 82, 146, 244, 248
Variétés 68
Vaudeville 68

Tarbes 75
Versailles 83, 181

Gallet, Louis 116, 172–3, 189
Galli-Marié, Célestine 104, 132–5, 244, 251, 264, 267
Garcia family 10–12
Joaquina (*née* Briones) 11
Manuel *père* 11+n8–17, 22, 25, 30, 156
Caprichos líricos españoles, 14–16
El contrabandista, 16, 32, 134, 156+n40
'Cuerpo bueno, alma divina', 16–17, 29, 31, 155
'Yo que soy contrabandista' 14, 34, 57
Manuel (Palacio-*fils*) 11, 32
Maria ('La Malibran') 11+n10, 13–14, 16, 32, 156n40
Pauline (Viardot) 12+n11 16, 25, 32–3, 156
Garrotte (garrotting) 55, 94, 160, 195–6, 200, 274
Gautier, Théophile 39, 42–4, 49, 52, 60, 68–73, 75–7, 79, 80–2, 84–5, 100, 186–7, 243–4, 251
Mademoiselle de Maupin 69
Voyage en Espagne 39, 51–2, 69, 75, 76, 99–101, 195–6, 208
Gaztambide, Joaquin
En las astas del toro 158
Germany/Germans 32, 79+n25, 81, 82, 134, 156n40
Gibraltar 44, 55–8, 113, 122, 149, 172, 175, 177, 189, 213
Gide, Casimir 78, 146–7, 156–7
Gobineau, Joseph Arthur de 224, 227–8
Godillot, Alexis 49
Gomis, José Melchior 16, 24–5
'El Corazon en venta' 25
Le Diable à Séville 67, 242
La favori, 25
Gottschalk, Louis Moreau 134
Gounod, Charles 125, 138–9, 216
Roméo et Juliette 107, 267
Goya, Francisco, 24–5, 60, 85, 127
The Disasters of War, 160
Grellmann, Heinrich 223+n5–24, 228–30+n27, 234–5, 237–40
Grisi, Carlotta 34, 70
Grut, Marina 74, 231, 235
Guardia Civil 38–9, 58, 114, 179, 197, 199, 201–2, 209–11
Guiraud, Ernest 133n17, 246 *see also under Carmen:* scores
guitar-playing 13, 17–22, 29, 33, 83, 158
Gypsies
anti-Romanist prejudice (see also Grellmann) 66–7, 74–5, 100
busné (non-gypsies) 221+n3, 232, 238
caló (Romany language) 75, 176, 222, 226–7, 230–1, 238
divination 230
Égyptien(ne)s 119n41, 226–7, 232
gitanismo 73–83, 85, 86, 88, 96, 141–3
gypsy elements in *Carmen* (novella) 38, 50, 113, 119+n41, 176–7
gypsy elements in *Carmen* (opera) 29, 107, 120–2, 132, 141–50, 212, 221–45, 261, 268–9
gypsy elements in Mérimée's *Lettres* 97
gypsy scale 128–9, 221, 229
jerigonza ('rogue's tongue'), 224
Romalis/Ole (See under Dance)

Halévy family 61, 62n35, 106
Élie 62n35
Fromental 106
Geneviève (wife of Bizet, later of Émile Straus) 106, 247
Ludovic 48, 70, 102, 105–7, 124n1, 133–5, 172, 181, 184, 197–8, 218–9, 221, 222, 231, 245–6, 273
Haydn, Joseph 17, 18
Hemingway, Ernest 97, 218
Huerta, Trinidad 23, 24n27
Hugo, Victor 226

Impressionism/Impressionists 58, 61, 248
Irving, Washington 45
Isabella II, Queen of Spain 9, 37, 232

José María 94–5, 113, 120, 202, 215–16, 220
Joseph Napoleon Bonaparte 3, 7–8, 19 (*see also* Spain: *era Josefina*)
Jullien, Adolphe 252
Jusseaume, Lucien 36, 46, 48

Lacombe, Hervé 130–2, 134–5, 137, 161, 165n8, 245n2
Lacombe, Paul 107, 245
Lacome, Paul, and J. Puig y Alsubide 26n30
Échos d'Espagne 29+n33, 30–2, 156, 241

Fleurs d'Espagne 30, 34
Lalo, Édouard 136
Symphonie espagnol 136–7
Lameyer y Berenguer, Francisco 42–3, 52
Laparra, Raoul 126+n3–4, 128, 138–9, 150–2, 154, 155+n37, 156, 216
Latin America 67, 77, 204
Havana, Cuba 134, 204, 204–5
musical influences 26, 35, 122, 134, 241
tango 136–7
Ledhuy, Adolphe & Henri Bertini
Encyclopédie pittoresque de la musique 17–18, 18n22, 22–4, 73–4
Lesage, Alain-René 94, 101+n18
Histoire de Gil Blas de Santillane 101+n18
Le Diable boiteux (libretto) 77, 78, 101n18, 146
Liszt, Franz 25, 82, 128–9
Des Bohémiens et leur musique en Hongrie 229
Piano Sonata in B minor 128–9
Lorca, Federico García 217
Louis Philippe I, King of France 41, 203

Majos and majas 29, 36–7, 45, 48–9, 59–60, 84, 94, 164, 168, 174, 195, 212
Mallarmé, Stéphane 63
Manet, Édouard 41, 46, 49, 59–63, 85–7, 99
Ballet espagnol 85–6
Concert in the Tuileries Gardens 60
lithograph of Lola de Valence 86–7
Olympia 86
Spanish Guitar Player 60
visit to Spain 59–61
mantillas 49, 84–6, 98, 270
manzanilla 143–4, 150
Mapleson, Colonel J. H. 62
maquila 51, 178–9, 197, 216
Maria Cristina, regent of Spain 40
Marsanau, Santiago de 24+n28
Massenet, Jules 60
Massé, Victor
Fior d'Aliza 244
Mazilier, Joseph, and Paul Foucher (music by Édouard Deldevez)
Paquita 67
Meilhac, Henri (see also under Bizet: *Carmen*: libretto) 93, 102, 105–7, 172, 197, 219, 245–6
Mendelssohn, Felix, *Songs without Words* 242
Mendès, Catulle (and Rodolphe Darzens)
Les Belles du monde 223–5
Mendizábal, Juan Álvarez 40
Mérimée, Prosper 11n10, 34, 37–9, 42, 44–5, 47, 50–1, 53–5, 58–9, 69, 83, 91–107, 109, 113, 115, 117–19, 122–4, 131, 134, 138–9, 149, 160, 166, 169, 176, 178n21, 180, 186, 189, 193–8, 200–8, 206, 210–12, 214, 216, 218–19, 221+n3, 222–31, 237–8, 243–4, 246, 268
La Chambre bleue 176
Columba 176
Lettres d'Espagne 39, 54+n25, 92–8, 100, 103, 109, 115, 111, 149, 193+n1, 195, 201n11, 208n20, 212, 215n32–16, 218
Salon de 1853 231
Le Théâtre de Clara Gazul 229–30, 239
translation of Pushkin 102–4, 140, 142n28
visits Andalusia 48, 91, 94, 96–8, 101, 193, 215, 218, 235, 238
visits Madrid 54, 92, 93
visits Spain 39, 42, 53, 54, 91–9, 193, 196, 200, 202, 205, 226, 244
Meyerbeer, Giacomo,
Robert le diable 116
Michel, Francisque 224, 229
Mitjana, Rafael 14+n18, 16n21, 24
Montes, Francisco Montes Reina, (Paquiro) 48, 127, 148, 201, 218
Montez, Lola 82–3, 143
Montijo family 34, 92
Eugenia (later Eugénie, Condesa de Teba; subsequently Empress of France) 34–5, 92–3, 127, 134
Maria Francisca 34
Maria Manuela, (later Condesa Montijo) 34, 51+n21, 92, 96, 99+n13, 237
Musset, Alfred de 12n11, 14, 97, 101–2
Contes d'Espagne et d'Italie 39
Mimi Pinson 101

Napoleon Bonaparte/Napoleonic regime 3, 5, 7–8, 12, 18–19, 33, 35, 37, 41, 126–7, 180, 198, 229, 232
Napoleon, Joseph/*era josefina* 3–4, 6–9, 127, 194, 198, 229, 232
Napoleon III 34–5, 92

navajas 52+n23, 53–4, 112, 180, 197, 225, 265

Offenbach, Jacques 60, 106, 121, 125, 149, 154, 267
opéra-bouffe 121, 161, 164
Opéra-comique (see under France/Paris)
Otero, José 231nn32–3, 232, 236

Pacini, Antonio-Francesco-Saverio 16, 32
Paër, Ferdinando 13–14, 25
Paganini, Niccolò 73
Palestrina, Giovanni Pierluigi da 120–1
Paz, Narciso 3, 75
Pedrell, Felipe 152–3
Pepe Illo (José Delgado Guerra) 127, 148
Perrot, Jules 69–70
  La Esmeralda 67
Petipa, Marius 70+n10, 76
Picasso, Pablo 86
Pigot, Charles 132–3n13, 161, 166, 187–8
Poliakov, Léon 227
Ponchard, Charles 254–5, 273
Portugal 3, 8
Pougin, Arthur 13–14, 105–6
Pushkin, Alexander (see under Mérimée, translation of Pushkin)

Racism 67, 223, 227
Raitt, Alan 104–6, 108
rasgueadas (strumming), 24, 146, 158, 243, 252
Ravel, Maurice 63
régisseurs 131, 255–6
Rodriguez, Christina 108
Roldán y Martinez, José 58
Romanticism 13, 25, 36, 37, 38, 40, 42, 46, 58, 96
  in dance 65, 79, 82, 156
  in illustration/painting 39, 46, 268
  in music/opera 24, 26, 125, 222, 242
  in popular song 14, 25, 29
  in writing 44, 52, 55, 71, 83, 196, 225, 228, 233
Rosi, Francesco 57, 152
Rossini, Gioachino 12, 16–17, 25, 138–9, 242
  The Barber of Seville 32, 94
  Guillaume Tell 126
Russia/Russian 11, 32, 102, 152

Saint-Léon, Arthur 84
Sand, George 14
Sanz de Pedre, Mariano 127, 128
Sarasate, Pablo de 136
Schubert, Franz 129, 242
Scribe, Eugène 105, 116, 173–4
  Robert le diable 116
  Les Diamants de la couronne 243
  Fra Diavolo 116, 173, 177
Serral, Dolores 76, 77
Sevilla, Francisco 44, 94, 194
Sor, Fernando 8, 11n8, 16, 17–23, 25, 66–7, 73–4, 82, 142, 233
  Méthode pour la guitare 22
  Three Favorite Spanish Boleros 19–21
Soriano Fuertes, Mariano 26, 142
  'L'Éventail'/'El Abanico' (The Fan), 26–9
sostenidos (stamping) 74, 128–9, 137, 232–3, 242
Spain/Spaniards 30–7, 40, 51, 64, 193–218, 267–8
  canciones/songs/poems/collections 16, 18, 25, 33, 142, 143, 240–1
    Regalo lírico 16, 20, 155, 156
    zarzuelas 25, 26, 34, 94, 127, 148–9, 155, 158, 217
  Andalusia 14, 18, 29, 36–63, 83–4, 91, 101, 113, 118, 126–7, 139, 142, 172n12, 193, 195–7, 203, 207, 209–11, 214–15, 220, 234, 251
    Algeciras 55
    Cádiz 4, 13, 18, 24, 44, 55–6, 58, 82, 204, 231, 238
    Córdoba 32, 44, 46, 215, 225
    Granada 32, 44–6, 177, 180–1, 229, 238, 243
    Guadalquivir river 56, 168n9
    Huelva 56+n27, 168n9
    Jaén 44
    Jerez de la Frontera 8, 18, 56, 235
    Málaga 41–2, 44, 55, 58, 99, 241
    Ronda 52n23, 160, 217
    Seville 13, 32, 36–7, 41, 44, 46–9, 51, 53, 56, 58, 67, 82–4, 100, 115, 140, 148, 158, 166, 168–9, 174, 183, 201–8, 213, 215, 217–18, 228, 232, 238, 242, 259, 263–4, 273
      Barrio de Santa Cruz 47, 203
      Calle Candelejo 177+n20, 178n21, 203, 214
      Calle Sierpes 49, 112
      '*Carmen* trail' 213–14

cigarreras (factory girls) 38, 95, 131–2, 140, 170–1, 200–1, 204, 206–9, 258–9
Fábrica de Tabaco/tobacco factory 38–9, 47, 53n24, 95, 100, 130–1, 138, 168, 201–9, 214, 217, 222, 258
género andaluz 65
Giralda 30, 36, 46–7, 270, 273
musical style 142–6
Plaza de San Salvador 13, 49
Plaza de Toros/Maestranza (bullring) 39, 46–8, 93, 112–13, 201, 211, 213, 215–18, 262, 266, 273
Puerta de la carne 214
Teatro Real 82, 84
Torre del Oro (Golden Tower) 46
trading centre 56, 174
Triana 83–4, 86, 113, 231n36, 241
Aranjuez 18
Basque Country and language 51, 107, 113, 115–17, 119, 138–9, 142, 150, 152, 173n13, 177, 196–7, 176, 216, 229
Elizondo 142
Etchalar 142, 196
Irun 64
Lanciego 33
Vitoria (and battle) 3–4, 7–8, 19, 33, 76
Castilla-La Mancha 18
Albacete 52–3
Catalonia 17
Barcelona 18, 64
Teatro del Liceu 64
French enthusiasm for 7, 12, 25–7, 48, 60–3, 67–8, 88, 156, 225
Galicia 211
Madrid 9, 16, 18, 33–4, 204, 206, 208, 217, 221
Teatro de la Zarzuela 158
Teatro Real 64, 77, 8
Navarre 113
Pamplona 117, 194
Ontinyent 24
Valencia 18–19, 92

Stendhal (Marie-Henri Beyle) 11n10, 91, 93, 131, 196
Symbolists 63

Taglioni, Maria 34, 70, 79, 80, 81
tambourine/*tambour de basque/pandereta* 49, 78–9, 84, 93–4, 113, 146, 212, 226, 232, 235, 240 242, 250, 252, 270–1
tarantella 67, 133–5, 239
tarot cards, 125, 145, 154, 176–7, 179–80, 265, 272
Taylor, Baron 38 +n3, 39, 41, 49, 55–6, 58, 60
Thomas, Ambroise
Mignon 242, 224
Tobacco trade 168–9
Turgenev, Ivan 32

Ubersfeld, Anne 220

Valence, Lola de (Lola Menea) 60, 85–7
Velázquez, Diego 41, 60
Velázquez, Eugenio Lucas 49, 59, 62
ventas/posadas 45, 62, 65, 93, 144, 146, 212, 270
Verdi, Giuseppe 62
Verlaine, Paul 63
Viardot, Louis 12+n11, 25, 32, 34
La favori (libretto), 25
Vidal, José Pérez 206, 211

Wagner, Richard 121, 137
Wallis, Severn Teackle 233
Wellesley, Arthur, Duke of Wellington 3–4, 8, 18, 19, 169

Yradier, Sebastián 22, 26n30, 33–5, 134, 142, 241
Album filarmónico 33–4
'El arreglito' 33, 35, 134–6
'Aurora' 241
'El Charrán' 34
'La negrita' 136–7
'La perla de Triana' 241
'El sol de Triana' 241
'La soledad de los barquillos' 241